2601

bo
w.
ti

Complete Northumbria

Complete Reference

Complete Northumbria

Edited by Leslie Godfrey

Sections on County Durham and Cleveland
by Hilda and Noel Turnbull

Ward Lock Limited · London

© Ward Lock Limited 1979

First published in Great Britain 1979
by Ward Lock Limited, 116 Baker Street,
London, W1M 2BB, a Pentos Company.

Layout and maps by Design Practitioners Limited

Text set in 9/11 pt VIP Plantin, printed and
bound in Great Britain at The Pitman Press, Bath

Complete Northumbria. – (Red guides).
    1. Northumberland – Description and travel
    – Guide-books   2. Durham (County) –
    Description and travel – Guide-books
    3. Tyne and Wear (Metropolitan County) –
    Description and travel – Guide-books
    I. Godfrey, Leslie   II. Series
    914.28'04'857   DA670.N8

    ISBN 0-7063-5353-6   ✓ B
        0-7063-5354-4 Pbk

Contents

The Country Code (issued by the Countryside Commission)

Guard against all risk of fire.
Fasten all gates.
Keep dogs under proper control.
Keep to the paths across farm land.
Avoid damaging fences, hedges and walls.
Leave no litter.
Safeguard water-supplies.
Protect wildlife, wild plants and trees.
Go carefully on country roads.
Respect the life of the countryside.

List of Maps and Plans

List of Illustrations

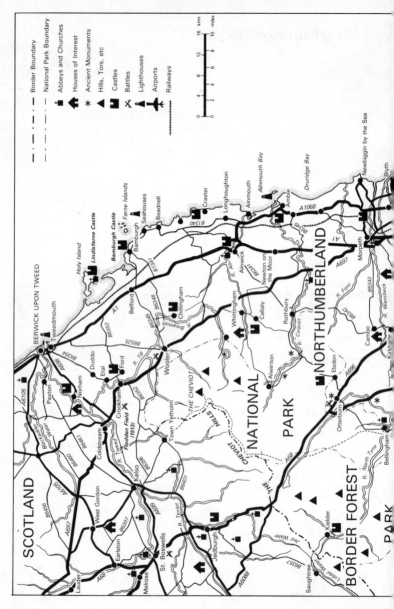

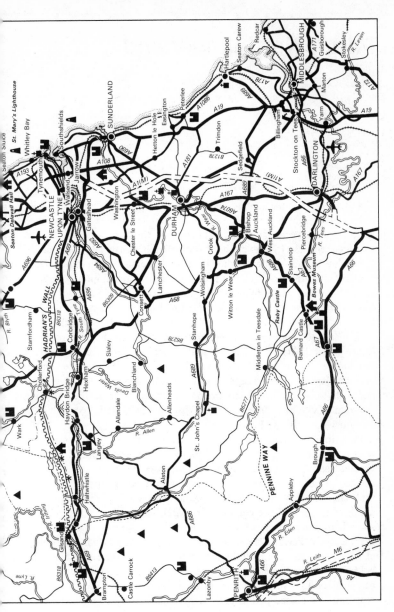

Part I: Northumberland

Northumbria began as a no-man's land, a region of fierce and wild independence north of the Humber. The early Saxon invasions respected this, inspired perhaps by the remnants of the vast wall left by the Romans, who had tried to cut it off altogether and designate it barbarian. It was left to the Anglians, when land for settlement was already short, to alight on Bamburgh rock in 547 and attempt to turn it into a kingdom. In the centuries which followed the warring factions of Celt and Saxon, Viking and Dane crossed and recrossed its isolated landscape, building, but more often destroying, those remote pockets of early Christianity in such places as Lindisfarne, Tynemouth and Hexham. Even as remote a figure as King Arthur – that legendary leader of post-Roman Britain – fought some of his famous battles on Hadrian's Wall and, according to one local legend, is still sleeping in a cave near Sewingshields, awaiting a new call to action. Fact and fiction intermingle across the brooding moorlands with Sir Lancelot's castle, Joyous Gard, identified with both Bamburgh and Alnwick.

Described frequently in early documents as a wasteland, a no-man's land it has remained for much of its history, a useful buffer between England and Scotland, sometimes taking sides but owing allegiance to neither. A curious mixture of race and interbreeding, the early Northumbrians revealed elements of civilization and religious zeal long before much of the rest of the country. The Archbishop of York, technically second to Canterbury, still ranks as *primus inter pares* in many people's eyes, while St Peter's School in York, founded by the Danes for the sons of Eldermen, still claims to be one of the oldest in the land. They also held on to their independence as long as they could, and it was not until 920 that the first submission to an English king took place, and in 954 Northumbria passed permanently under the English Crown.

In the struggle of the 16th century back and forth across the border and the eventual Union of Crowns Northumbria could have been so easily overlooked. By the time of the Norman Conquest Scotland had pushed her frontier back to the line of the Tweed and claimed Northumbria as well, while every English king looked longingly at Scotland, and nine of them – between the 12th and 15th centuries – came to take a look. Northumbrian culture grew from its acquisitive neighbours, adopting the best and worst of each: their legends, their songs and such bad habits as the art of 'reiving' – the rustling of cattle which grew into a local sport.

To dub this Border area romantic, as Scott has done, is to see but one side of the coin, for the whole of Northumbria remembers the battles which have been fought on its isolated fastness, and the many pele towers and strengthened churches that gave shelter to cattle and families remain as evidence of its past. There is no sadder story in Northumbrian legends than that of the Earl of Derwentwater and the abortive rising of 1715, when the grandson of Charles II led his small band out from Haydon Bridge to end up on the block; and there was Ridley, the Bishop of London and companion of Latimer, who fuelled the fires as one of the Oxford martyrs and 'lit the candle in England, as by God's grace shall never be put out'. Heroes there have been in plenty who have acted out their parts in the rivalry between England and Scotland: the Percies and the Douglases – those traditional opponents of the Border – and none better revered perhaps than Harry Hotspur, immortalized by Shakespeare. In spite of the breaks in line both families exist today, and a Percy, now the Duke of Northumberland, rules in Alnwick Castle. The Greys, the Fenwicks and the Swinburnes have all contributed to its saga of integrity, so much so that even today a Northumbrian still considers his nationality as distinct from English or Scottish.

At the height of its power Northumbria stretched from the Humber to the Firth of Forth and crossed The Pennines to reach the coast of Cumbria. In time the consequences of history, and perhaps defence, forced it back on its natural fastness – The Pennines to the west, The Cheviot Hills to the north and the line of the river Tees to the south. Today it has resolved itself into the four counties of Northumberland, Durham, Tyne and Wear and Cleveland, which together make up the modern Northumbria. Three great rivers flow across it – the Tees, Wear and Tyne – each characteristic of a different breed of man and environment, yet sharing a similarity and range of scene common to all. Language too has its variety – from the traditional 'Geordie' of Newcastle to the 'Tweedside' intonations of Berwick. Northumbria is a land of contrast, ranging from the heaviest industry to the more gentle touch of a water-mill, from the teeming capacity of its industrial areas to the loneliness of the moorlands, but to the average inhabitant both are well within his grasp, and a change of air or scene is readily within striking distance.

Some of our finest coastline lies along the north-east, and to add to the vastness of its beaches and the bracing air are the charm of such islands as Lindisfarne, where shot-guns still herald a wedding and the brides jump over the 'petting stool'. Here too you can taste mead, made in the shadow of the great priory founded by St Aidan, or walk the causeway to the mainland, as the monks once did, watching the rising tide. Nearby are the Farne Islands, famous for their seals and wild bird life. Tales of salvage and ships abound and the sad story of Grace Darling, who died of consumption four years after her famous lifeboat rescue. Like that other Northumbrian heroine Dorothy Foster, who rescued her brother from Newgate Prison in London, Grace Darling is buried in Bamburgh churchyard. A little further south lies Coquet Island, which also had a monastic foundation dating from Saxon times.

For the mountaineer and the hill-walker the line of The Cheviot Hills, rising up to almost 900m (3,000ft), produces a challenge as it did to the Romans. You can still trace their road in the dead straight switchback experience of the A68 between Corbridge and Otterburn or follow the zigzags across a river valley that would not allow the might of Rome to pass without some detour. Dere Street, so often referred to by Northumbrians as Watling Street, is one of their finest roads prospecting the way into Caledonia of old. Some of the finest Roman remains in the country exist along the line of Hadrian's Wall, but that is worth another holiday by itself. Northumbria offers something for everyone, from fly-fishing in such delightful streams as the Coquet to the first taste of Tweed salmon and from early locomotives to the colour and pageant of the Alnwick Fair. Possibly more than anything else it offers space in the charm and gentleness of its vast National Park, which together with the Border Forest attached provides some 575 square miles of really unspoilt natural countryside, where the overcrowded conditions of life today can be forgotten.

1 Berwick-upon-Tweed

(Including excursions along the Tweed Valley, the Berwickshire coastline, the Lammermuir Hills, Flodden Field and Ford Castle)

Bowls Visitors are welcome to use the greens at Magdalen Fields, Tweedmouth (Riverside Road) and Spittal (Sea Road).

Camping and caravanning Nearest site 1 mile from Berwick on the A698, then at Beal (7½ miles south), Bamburgh and Beadnell.

Distances Alnwick, 29 miles; Bamburgh, 20 miles; Edinburgh, 57 miles; Hawick, 43 miles; London, 337 miles; Newcastle, 63 miles; Seahouses, 23 miles.

Early closing Thursday.

Freshwater fishing Good fishing for brown trout, sea trout and salmon in the Tweed, Whiteadder and Till. Information from fishing-tackle shops in Marygate and Castlegate.

Football Berwick Rangers play Scottish League Association football at Shielfield Park.

Golf Municipal course at Magdalen Fields. *Berwick-upon-Tweed Golf-Club* is at Goswick, 4½ miles to the south, off the A1.

Guided tours These are available along the Elizabethan ramparts from the guide's office next to Cowport Arch. Also in the Town Hall on prior application.

Hotels *Castle, Hen and Chickens, King's Arms, Ness Gate, Queen's Head, Ravensholme, Turret, Tweed View* and *Joil Guest-House*.

Information centre Northumbria Tourist Board in Castlegate Car Park (*open summer only*).

Library, Art Gallery and Museum In Marygate.

Population 11,610.

Post Office The GPO is in the Woolmarket.

Rowing *Berwick Amateur Rowing Club* in the boat-house under Royal Tweed Bridge.

Sailing (and water-skiing) *Berwick Sailing Club*, Spittal, and at Beadnell.

Sea-fishing trips From Spittal, Tweedmouth, Eyemouth and Seahouses.

Skin-diving At Bamburgh, Seahouses, Beadnell and the Berwickshire coastline.

Speedway Meetings are held in the summer at Shielfield Park.

Swimming-pools Heated indoor pool in Sandgate and an open-air pool at Magdalen Fields.

Tennis Public courts at Pier Field and at Spittal.

Tourism Officer Council Offices, Wallace Green.

Berwick, a relatively small community at the mouth of the river Tweed, is unique both historically and aesthetically. No other town (the northernmost in England) has such a chequered background of war and strife, and yet, conversely, few lie in such charming surroundings. On the opposite bank of the river the suburbs of Tweedmouth and Spittal lead through to some fine stretches of sand on the North Sea coastline, and there are facilities for all kinds of sport and entertainment.

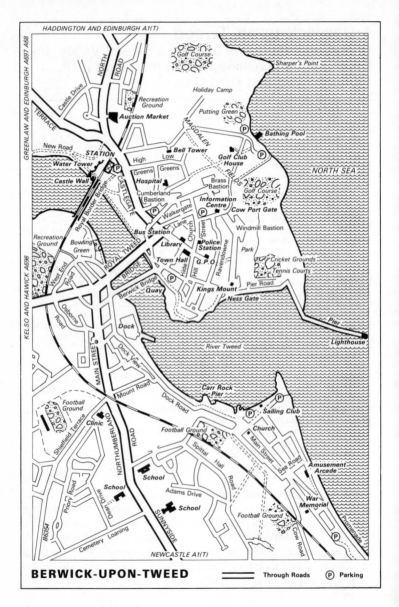

BERWICK-UPON-TWEED ━━━━ Through Roads Ⓟ Parking

Berwick's history goes back to the Kingdom of Bernicia, founded by Ida at Bamburgh in 547, and its chronicled records stem from the 9th century. Claimed as a Scottish town along with the river Tweed by King Malcolm II after the Battle of Carham in 1018, it quickly developed as a port. By the time David I (1124–53) came to the throne of Scotland four royal burghs were created: Berwick, Roxburgh, Edinburgh and Stirling and of these Berwick was the most important. Thus it remained until 1174 when William the Lion, retreating from a raid into Northumbria, was forced to yield the town to his English captors as part of his ransom, and for the next fifteen years Scotland was forced to acknowledge England as her master.

It was the start of a period, lasting 300 years, when Berwick became the bone of contention between the two sides. To raise money for his crusade Richard the Lionheart sold the Scots their independence back again, but by 1216 more trouble loomed when King John entered the town and committed barbarous atrocities. In spite of the mayhem, however, Berwick continued to prosper and by the middle of the 13th century so extensive had its commerce become that it was compared to Alexandria, a city of merchant princes trading extensively with the continent and the major port of Scotland.

The ambitions of Edward I brought the next step in the city's destiny. Fresh from his conquests in Wales, he declared a right to arbitrate over the vacant Scottish throne and by promoting John Baliol against Robert the Bruce, then treating the former with arrogant contempt, he provoked the series of revolts that followed. Berwick was the first to sign the Treaty of Revolt, and Edward exacted a terrible revenge. The glorious seaport of the north was reduced to a pile of ashes and its trading importance was gone. New walls were ordered to defend the town and a parliament summoned to govern his new holding, but Edward could not stop the revolts. First Wallace, then Bruce the Younger, grandson of the original alternative claimant to the throne, took up the challenge. In 1312 Bruce tried to take the town, but a barking dog gave his attempt away, and he had to wait another six years for the privilege.

Berwick has probably seen more history than any other equivalent town of its size in the country, as procession after procession of kings and queens rolled through this Border fortress, in victory, defeat or sheer retribution. Edward II fled to Berwick in 1314 after his defeat at Bannockburn, and nineteen years later his son's longbowmen devastatingly revenged the father's name at the Battle of Halidon Hill. In the War of the Roses Henry VI gave the town back to the Scots who held it for twenty-one years, but backwards and forwards the marauding armies came, until finally in 1482 the town was regained for England by Richard 'Crookback' (later Richard III) who won it for his brother Edward IV.

From this time on Berwick has remained an English town but the process of integration was prolonged by a passionate wish to belong to neither side. Under a treaty between Mary, Queen of Scots, and Edward IV Berwick was created a free burgh, maintaining this delicate status until the Reform Act of 1885 which was introduced, curiously enough, by a Northumbrian prime minister. But even though for a while the inhabitants managed to be conveniently forgotten, they continued to bear witness to the sad and shocking events of the Border, and the town became a Border fortress against the intrigues from the north. Less than forty years later James V of Scotland walked across the old wooden bridge over the Tweed to unite the two countries in the Union of Crowns of 1603. His mother Mary, Queen of Scots' dying wish had at last been granted and he became James I of England as well, and King of Great Britain, France and Ireland.

And there it might have ended but for the Jacobite risings and the surprising victory for Bonnie Prince Charlie at Prestonpans which brought General Johnnie Cope galloping into the town to announce his own defeat and the arrival of the 'forty-five'. But Berwick, in spite of being a base for the Hanovarian forces, preferred its independence and its special isolation. In 1746 an attempt was made to bring it back into line: the Wales and Berwick Act stated quite simply that 'in all cases where the Kingdom of England or that part of Britain called England hath been or shall be mentioned in any Act of Parliament, the same has been and shall henceforth be declared and taken to comprehend and include the Dominion of Wales and the Town of Berwick-upon-Tweed'. But in spite of this Berwick failed to sign the Peace Treaty after the Crimean War and is still technically at war with Russia!

Berwick today accepts the best of both worlds, still standing as the key to the romantic and tragic Tweed – a Scottish river – but the town itself is English. The incongruity goes further: Berwick, which lost its Scottish burgh status in 1368, regained it with the restoration of its ancient rights by the Lord Lyon of Scotland in 1958 and instead of belonging to neither side it belongs at last to both. Its county boundary extends 3 miles beyond the river line that separates England from Scotland. Its police- men are English, its banks mainly Scottish, while its local dialect is a

Berwick-upon-Tweed, Jacobean Bridge

modern blend of both, known locally as 'Tweedside'. The 'Final Act of Union' predicted by Robert Stephenson when he built the Royal Border Bridge has at last become a reality.

Berwick life has always centred about its river and its salmon, a fact that has led it in the past to reject ideas of becoming more industrialized. It is the gateway to that long valley, stretching inland for over 100 miles, where the quiet Tweed flows past some of the richest grazing land in the country, and where English barley now grows for Scottish distilleries.

Some of the finest fishing water in Great Britain lies along its banks, past ancient castles and pele towers immortalized in verse by Sir Walter Scott.

Around the town

The most significant features of the city are its three river bridges, the Elizabethan walls and gateways and some very fine Georgian houses. Although we describe the interior of the city first, it is strongly recommended that a tour of the Elizabethan walls gives the best orientation of the whole area.

The Great North Road (A1) enters Berwick from the north by **Castlegate**, where the stocks, in use until 1857, were removed to from the Town Hall. This descends to **Scotsgate**, one of the gateways in the Elizabethan wall structure. The original was removed in 1816 as being too narrow, and the present, much restored, gateway erected. Beyond Scotsgate the main street is known as **Marygate** (High Street). Along this broad thoroughfare, which is also used as a market-place, and less than half-way down the through road turns into **Golden Square** (so named after a former mint), leading to the **Royal Tweed Bridge**, completed in 1928, which takes the Great North Road southwards across the river.

At the foot of Marygate in the centre of the road lies the **Town Hall** or Guild Hall, built between 1750 and 1761, surmounted by tower and spire and with an impressive portico. Visits may be made inside the building on prior application. Just before reaching the Town Hall on the north side of Marygate are the **Museum, Art Gallery and Library**. Beyond the Town Hall Church Street turns left towards the Parade and **Wallace Green**, where the Council offices lie. Wallace Green is a reminder of Sir William Wallace's seizure of Berwick in 1297. After his capture and execution as a traitor (although he had never offered allegiance), his quartered left arm was ordered to be exhibited in the town in 1305.

Behind the Presbyterian church at the junction of Wallace Green with the Parade, lies **Holy Trinity Parish Church**, one of the only two churches built and completed during the Commonwealth from 1649 to 1653. The church is classical in style, somewhat puritanical in its lack of adornment, and has two curious 'lantern' towers. Opposite the parish church on the other side of the Parade lie **Ravensdowne Barracks**, designed by Vanbrugh, built between 1717 and 1721, and reputed to be the first barracks ever built. It now houses the Regimental Museum of the King's Own Scottish Borderers and is open to the public.

From the Parade a way lies through **Cow Port Gate** (the only original main gateway left in the Elizabethan walls) to **Magdalen Fields**, where there are golf-links and putting- and bowling-greens. A short walk across these fields leads to the swimming-pool and the beach at **Fisherman's Haven**.

Returning to the foot of Marygate by the Town Hall, a left turn takes us into the **Woolmarket**, where the main post office lies, and into the area formerly occupied by Flemish weavers introduced in the 13th century. Straight on leads down Hide Hill, descending towards the quay and the streets leading to the pier. At the foot of Hide Hill Sandgate leads to the old **Shore Gate** with its massive ancient doors. There is a heated swimming-pool also in Sandgate.

Along Bridge Street (from the foot of Hide Hill) we reach **Quay Walls** and the fine 18th-century **Custom House**, still in use, by way of the **Sally Port** through the city walls. A recent acquisition by the National Trust has preserved **Nos. 12, 13 and 20 Quay Walls** as similar examples from the Georgian period.

In the other direction from the foot of Hide Hill Silver Street (again a reminder of earlier minting activities) leads out along Ness Street and the Ness Gate to the Pier Road. Just south of Silver Street, through Fulford and Palace Streets, the way leads through to **Palace Green**, where the fine residence formerly occupied by the Governors of Berwick-upon-Tweed should be noted.

The way out through the Ness Gate also reveals the port and harbour of Berwick-upon-Tweed, with its fine pier and a lighthouse. The forerunner of the present pier was built as early as 1576, and the present one, erected between 1810 and 1821 is 864m (960 yards) long. The limits of the port run from St Abb's Head to Seton Point.

Around the walls

There are two sets of these – the earlier Edwardian ones, and the later Elizabethan fortifications.

The Edwardian walls

In 1296 Edward 1 took and sacked Berwick after a stubborn resistance emanating from a Scottish revolt and ordered new walls to be erected to defend the town. The remains of these are best seen west of the station by the Royal Border Bridge, where Berwick Castle also once stood. **Castle Wall, Breakneck Stairs, White Wall** and the fine river view from the ruined **water-tower** are especially worth noting. Across Castle Terrace in

Northumberland Avenue there is the **Elizabethan Bell-Tower**, the octagonal former watch-tower which stands on a circular base from the earlier wall. At the wall angle between here and Magdalen Fields lies **Lord's Mount**, added in 1555 just before Queen Elizabeth ordered a completely new wall. Only the lower part remains, and from here onwards the Edwardian walls continue outside the later defences.

The Elizabethan walls

By far the most important antiquity in the city and amongst the finest and most important examples anywhere in Europe, these walls are in an excellent state of preservation. Since 1847 the ramparts have been open to the public, and the 2-mile walk around is strongly recommended, starting at Meg's Mount which is reached by way of Marygate and Scotsgate.

This complete new system of fortification was modelled on an Italian plan, turning the medieval flanking tower into a bastion from which gunfire could be directed to cover the intervening space. Begun in 1558, they took eight years to build, with walls up to 3m (10ft) thick in places. Designed purely as a defence against gunpowder they were modelled on earlier versions at Antwerp, Lucca and Verona.

There are three main bastions: **Cumberland's**, or Middle Mount Bastion, **Brass Mount** and **Windmill**, plus two half-bastions – **Meg's Mount** and **King's Mount**. Originally they were surrounded by a ditch 60m (200ft) wide in the centre of which was a moat 3·6m (12ft) wide and 2·4m (8ft) deep. Charles I added a number of additional guns taken from Wark Castle against a threatened invasion from France or Spain. In 1688 a request was made by the Governor to raise a new regiment to oppose the landing of the Dutch King William, and as late as 1770 the walls were still being strengthened, especially on the river side.

From Meg's Mount there are good views along Marygate and beyond as one crosses the top of Scotsgate itself. Beyond this lies the Cumberland or Middle Mount Bastion, followed by the Brass Mount Bastion, so named from its brass cannon. The wall now turns southwards, and from the Brass Mount Bastion a curious ditch can be seen running out to the cliff edge, ending in a prominent outwork. Here also is the **Batardeau**, a wall for regulating the water in the moat.

We now cross the Cow Port Gate, with the prominent barracks inside the wall. Continuing clockwise, we pass the Windmill Bastion, in the centre of the eastern section, with steps leading down to the cricket field

Royal Border Bridge, Berwick-upon-Tweed

and tennis-courts outside. The Elizabethan walls end at King's Mount, just below which is the **Black Watch-Tower**, the only remaining example of an Edwardian bastion.

Crossing the Ness Gate, our walk continues along and above the Quay, past Wellington Terrace and Palace Green as far as the **Old** or **Berwick Bridge**, a quaint stone structure of fifteen stoutly buttressed irregular arches, which crosses the river to Tweedmouth. The present structure was started in 1611, taking just over twenty-four years to build. From the north side of the Old Bridge West Street leads back again into the centre of the town and Marygate, while Bridge Street leads eastwards to the foot of Hide Hill.

Continuing our riverside walk, Bankhill leads up to Meg's Mount again to complete the circuit of the walls. The lower path (Lover's Walk) develops into a pleasant river bank stroll, passing under the Royal Tweed Bridge (see page 20) and past a well-preserved fragment of the Edwardian walls to approach the **Royal Border Bridge**. Designed by Robert Stephenson to carry the main London–Edinburgh railway across the

Tweed, this great curving viaduct with its twenty-eight tall, semicircular arches stands 47·8m (126ft) above the river and was completed between 1847 and 1850. It was opened by Queen Victoria on 29 August 1850.

Passing under the bridge, the riverside path leads us back to the low arches of the Water-Tower, which with the wall climbing the hill above it and the two connected flanking towers at the top form the sole surviving part of the castle. The other remaining part was acquired by the North British Railway Company in 1843 and blown up with gunpowder to make way for the station.

Berwick Castle was probably begun between 1150 and 1167 and rebuilt in Henry II's reign prior to 1189. It was here, in 1292, that Edward I convened the memorable gathering to decide the future ruler of Scotland. The **Great Hall** is now the station waiting-room, and a plaque may be seen commemorating the occasion. It reads: 'This station stands on the Great Hall of Berwick Castle. Here on Nov. 17th 1292 the claim of Robert Bruce to the throne of Scotland was declined and the decision in favour of John Baliol was given by Edward I before the full Parliament of England and Scotland, a large gathering of the nobility and populace of both England and Scotland.'

Tweedmouth and Spittal

These suburbs of Berwick across the Tweed estuary are best reached by way of the Old Bridge.

Tweedmouth, on the south bank, is a purely industrial and dormitory town, but serves to give an excellent viewpoint of Berwick itself. Near the war memorial is the **Louping Stone**, over which newly-weds jump for luck, a custom that survives also in Bamburgh and Lindisfarne. In the house next to the *Royal Hotel* the novelist Smollett wrote part of *Humphrey Clinker*. Along the riverside close to the Royal Border Bridge is a spot known as **Hang-a-Dyke Neuk**, where, just before the Battle of Halidon Hill in 1333, the two sons of Sir Alexander Seton were hanged within sight of their parents. Seton was the Deputy Governor of Berwick at that time, who, having been called upon to surrender to Edward III, refused to do so until a certain date and gave his sons as hostages. A few Scottish troops relieved the city, and Seton refused to give it up. Edward therefore claimed the agreement had been broken. In Tweedmouth, as in Berwick, the ancient custom of selecting a salmon queen, revived in 1945, takes place in the third week in July.

From Main Street in Tweedmouth Dock Road leads past the Tweed

Dock along to **Spittal**, where the Lifeboat House and the Sailing and Canoeing Club are situated. Spittal has a long stretch of fine sands and serves as Berwick's seaside resort. There is a promenade with beach chalets, an amusement arcade and various sports facilities.

Excursions from Berwick

1) The Tweed Valley: Berwick – Horncliffe – Norham – Twizell Bridge – Cornhill-on-Tweed – Wark – Carham – Roxburgh – Kelso – Coldstream – Ladykirk – Paxton – Berwick (approx. 44 miles)

Joining the A698 off the south end of the Royal Tweed Bridge, we follow the road along the south bank of the river Tweed. For the first few miles as far as Horncliffe one cannot see the river. Follow the road through East Ord, then Middle Ord (3 miles) and take the right-hand turn opposite **Longridge Towers**, now a hotel, signposted Horncliffe. In another mile the road swings left after passing a disused railway line. One mile further on there is a right-hand turn leading into Scotland over the **Union Bridge**, better known as the Chain Bridge, built in 1820, and the earliest vehicular suspension bridge in Britain.

The road continues into **Horncliffe** itself, a pleasant village on a high bank overlooking a wide sweep of the Tweed. Just above the village is Horncliffe glen, which can be ascended as far as the mill. A footpath from the foot of the glen goes to Norham Castle. From Horncliffe the road to Norham swings sharply inland and then, just before the railway line and rejoining the A698, swings sharply to the right. It skirts the knoll on which Norham Castle stands before reaching **Norham** itself. This ancient village, one of the most attractive in Northumberland, was at one time the capital of a district known as Norhamshire, part of the County Palatine of Durham, which existed until 1836.

The village cross on the green stands on a medieval base, but the upper part was erected in the 19th century. From the north-west corner of the green a lane leads to the churchyard. The church was reputedly built by Bishop Flambard (1099–1128), but an earlier church existed on the site from about 830. The chancel, with the chancel arch (excluding the east end) and the south arcade, are the only parts surviving of the original Norman building, generally accepted as the finest parts of the church.

25

The windows on the south side of the chancel are particularly interesting: their exterior exhibits a type of 'beak-head' ornament and a moulding of chevron and pellets. On the south side of the chancel is a very fine 14th-century tomb containing a male effigy with a mutilated face. The pulpit and three desks are from Durham Cathedral, dating from the 17th century.

Norham Castle (*open daily, charge*) was originally built (in Norman style) as part of the defences of the Palatinate of Durham in 1121 and played an important part in Border affairs from the time of Edward I (1272–1307) to Henry VIII (1509–47). It was attacked, demolished, restored, besieged both by the Scots and the English over a period of 400 years. In 1513 it was captured by James IV of Scotland, but after the battle it was returned finally to the English and roughly repaired. The last attack was in 1530, and it fell into decay in the time of Queen Elizabeth I. It is now in the care of the Department of the Environment.

Norham was the first place where Edward I asserted his claim to be Lord Paramount of Scotland. Eight competitors for the throne of Scot-

Norham Castle

land met him there and two – Bruce and Baliol – were selected. Norham was always at the centre of the strife that went on along this delightful valley, and in the 14th century even the church was fortified and made into a strong point, and one of many peace treaties was concluded within its walls.

From Norham we rejoin the main road (A698) and in 3 miles reach **Twizell Bridge**, a bold, single arch high over the river Till, the only English tributary to the Tweed, which joins it a mile or so north at Tillmouth. It was at this bridge, built about 1450, that the Battle of Flodden (1513) was really lost, for within sight of James IV's army the Earl of Surrey's vanguard were allowed to bring their artillery across to dominate the battlefield some 3 miles south of here. High on the bank to the right can be seen *Tillmouth Park*, built in 1822 and now one of the Tweed's leading fishing hotels. In the angle between the two rivers lie the ruins of **Twizell Castle**, built in the late 18th century in Norman style and occupying the site of an earlier castle, destroyed in 1496 by James IV of Scotland when he pillaged Northumberland in support of the cause of Perkin Warbeck. Nearby are the ruins of a small chapel where it is said the remains of St Cuthbert once rested.

Four miles from Twizell Bridge, **Cornhill-on-Tweed** appears quiet and empty compared to its busy neighbour on the opposite bank at Coldstream. It is a pleasant, well-spaced-out residential town through which the main road from Newcastle to Edinburgh (A697) crosses the Border. Three miles to the south (off the A697) lie Branxton and Flodden Field (see page 38). From Cornhill-on-Tweed a secondary road (B6350) continues along the south bank of the Tweed to Wark Castle.

Less than 3 miles from Cornhill-on-Tweed, **Wark Castle** was the English watch-dog on the Tweed, blocking the best Scottish invasion point. From the 12th to 16th centuries it saw more attacks and sieges than any other castle on the Border defence line. The low mound of the ruined keep is all that remains and at first glance almost passes unnoticed, yet Wark Castle in its heyday was visited by every English king from Henry I (1100–35) to Henry IV (1399–1413) except for the two Richards. Built in 1130, it originally consisted of a high tower placed within an inner court and surrounded by a double wall. Inside the outer wall the space provided shelter for the local populace, while the inner was defended by a fosse and flanking towers.

The most famous incident at Wark was when Edward III hurried north to relieve a Scottish siege of the castle and celebrated his victory with a ball, where tradition has it that he danced with the Countess of Salisbury, who dropped a garter. Edward picked it up (some say with his sword point, but this seems hardly likely when dancing), fastened it to his own leg and rebuked the tittering bystanders with the remark *'Honi soit qui mal y pense'*. This was the origin of the Order of the Garter.

Wark was captured by the Scots a number of times, but the English returned again. In 1513 James IV took the castle, as well as Etal, Duddo and Ford, on his way to Flodden, and after his death and defeat Lord Dacre heightened the keep to four storeys and enlarged the outer ward. In the reign of Elizabeth Wark became a refuge for the Earls of Mar and Angus and other Protestant nobles who had conspired against James VI of Scotland.

Less than 2 miles from Wark lies **Carham**, very close to the point where the Scottish border leaves the Tweed. On the hilltops to the south are extensive numbers of early British camps, and this area has from time immemorial formed a focal area between the barrier of The Cheviot Hills and the Tweed. On our right is **Carham Hall**, lying close to the river, and in 1 mile from Carham the Border is crossed where the road and river come together at a bend. In 3 miles we reach Sprouston, and in a further 3 miles the B6350 joins the A698 at the southern end of the bridge leading into Kelso. Instead of heading directly into Kelso, turn left just before the bridge onto the A699 (the Selkirk road). About 1¼ miles to the west of Kelso, just after crossing the river Teviot (which joins the Tweed at this point), the road curves left into the narrow neck of land between the two streams where **Roxburgh Castle** ruins lie on a precipitous bank. All that remains of the buildings are a few lengths of wall with some suggestion of very solid corner towers.

The early town of **Roxburgh** (not to be confused with the present-day one) lay over 2 miles to the west of the castle and was one of the earliest Scottish burghs. Roxburgh Castle existed in Saxon times and it became a royal castle for a procession of Scottish kings from David I (1124–53) to James II (1437–60). In 1207 the greater part of the town was burned, and a few years later King John (1199–1216) approached the Border with a threatening army, but the Scots burned Roxburgh to prevent him having it. Roxburgh was again burned down in 1244, but eleven years later Henry III of England was royally entertained here by King Alexander III who had married his daughter, Margaret.

Very much a Border outpost, Roxburgh was divided in itself for on occasions the town was occupied by the Scots and the castle by the

English. William the Lion had been forced to surrender it as part of his ransom, along with Berwick in 1174. In 1342 Sir Alexander Ramsay surprised and killed the garrison of forty and was made Governor for his exploits. The English retook it, however, and towards the end of the 14th century at the annual Roxburgh Fair a Scottish servant of the Earl of March was killed by some English soldiers from the castle in a brawl. Next year at the same Fair the Earl surrounded the town, slew all the English and set fire to the houses where they had taken refuge. Such was Border vengeance.

In 1460 James II of Scotland took the town and demolished it, then besieged the castle. Both the town and the castle were demolished at this time; the town ceased to exist, but the castle was partly rebuilt later.

In 1547 the English Protector, Somerset, repaired the fortifications and left a garrison there of 500 men, but in a treaty between England and France signed three years later Edward VI agreed to demolish the castle as a sop to the 'Auld Alliance' between Scotland and France. In 1574 the remains were granted to Robert Ker, son of Ker of Cessford, a famous Border family, by James VI, who in 1616 became the Earl of Roxburgh.

Returning from Roxburgh by the A699, we cross the Tweed bridge built by Rennie in 1803. Finely placed in a bend of the river where the Teviot joins the main stream, **Kelso** is an attractive town. It is a favourite resort with plenty of hotels and guest-houses, camping and caravan sites. The fishing is exceptionally good, and for the visitor there is golf, swimming, pony-trekking, a race-course and an ice-rink. Although not as important in its early days as Roxburgh, Kelso has survived and flourished into one of the most pleasant towns along the Tweed. Sir Walter Scott was educated at the local grammar school and once described it as the most beautiful, if not the most romantic village in Scotland.

The remains of **Kelso Abbey**, founded in 1128, are one of the chief points of interest. Little now remains of what was once the oldest and most powerful of all the Border abbeys, and the stones have been taken away for centuries for other buildings. All that remains is but a part of the west end of the original church. The four great piers that support the surviving western tower are typically Norman, but the windows and arcading are Romanesque. Like many abbeys of its time, Kelso was built more like a fortress than a church and it survived a number of attacks. In 1523 English forces set fire to the woodwork and stripped off the roof, and in 1545 troops led by the Earl of Hertford breached the walls with

29

The Abbey, Kelso

guns. The Reformers ousted the last monks in 1560 and smashed up everything that was left. In later days the abbey served as a patched-up parish church until a new one was built in 1771.

At the western end of the town is **Floors Castle** (*gardens usually open on Wednesdays*), seat of the Duke of Roxburgh. Designed by Vanbrugh in 1718, it was altered in the early 19th century. A holly tree in the grounds marks the spot where James II was killed by a bursting cannon at the siege of Roxburgh in 1460.

From Kelso we leave by the A698 along the north bank of the Tweed through the village of Birgham and on in 9 miles to reach **Coldstream**. The A697 (Edinburgh–Newcastle road) crosses the Border at this point to Cornhill-on-Tweed, the original ford having been replaced by a fine bridge built by Smeaton in 1766. Coldstream is very busy during the summer season, with hotels, camping and caravan sites, fishing and golf. Its name has become known world-wide with the founding by General Monck in 1650 of the Coldstream Guards as part of Cromwell's New Model Army. After the Restoration of Charles II the Republican army was disbanded, but the Coldstream Guards remained to form the nucleus of a regular army. A plaque near the market shows the position of Monck's house, now the town museum. Coldstream became one of the many Border crossings for runaway English couples, who up to 1856 could marry in Scotland by a plain declaration before witnesses without the present-day residential qualifications. Close to the town itself the grounds of the **Hirsel** estate, home of Lord Home, are open to visitors at all reasonable times. There is a wildlife preserve and woodland around a small lake.

From Coldstream we follow the A6112 towards Swinton, but just after passing Lennel turn right on to the B6347, which follows the river line for a while before turning inland. After 5 miles or so we turn right at the junction of the B6470 to the small hamlet of **Ladykirk**, which lies on the north bank of the Tweed opposite Norham. At the crossroads ¼ mile before the river we turn left into the village. King James IV of Scotland, returning from a raid into England, found the river in flood and dangerous to cross. He made a vow that if he and his men could cross the stream safely he would build a church to the Virgin that neither fire nor flood could destroy. In the Gothic style, shaped like a Latin cross with belfry added later, the **Church of Our Lady** was one of the last pre-Reformation churches built in Scotland. On the opposite side of the crossroads lie the grounds of **Ladykirk House** and **Upsettlington**, where Edward I first met the Scottish nobles and extracted a promise of vassalship from them.

Continuing through the village of Ladykirk we follow the unclassified road to New Ladykirk and on to Horndean, where in less than 2 miles it joins the B6461 (A699) towards Berwick. At Fishwick, a mile further on, there is a right-hand turning down to the Union Bridge. Just after **Paxton** and the grounds of Paxton House we re-enter the liberties of the borough and town of Berwick-upon-Tweed.

2) The Berwickshire Coastline and the Lammermuir Hills: Berwick – Burnmouth – (Ayton) – Eyemouth – Coldingham – St Abb's Head – Cockburnspath – Abbey St Bathans – (Cranshaws) – (Longformacus) – Duns – (Polwarth) – Edrom – Chirnside – Halidon Hill – Berwick (approx. 46–64 miles)

Taking the A1 road north out of Berwick, we climb steadily to **Lamberton Toll**, the northern boundary of the liberties of Berwick-upon-Tweed, and cross the Border into Scotland. Like Gretna Green and Coldstream the Toll House here also had a reputation for runaway marriages, and in July 1502 it was the point where Henry VII's daughter Margaret was handed over to the Scottish Commissioners on her way to marriage with James IV of Scotland. On our left to the south-west is **Halidon Hill**, where Edward III gained his victory over the Scots in 1333.

Our road follows the hillsides above the sea with fine views to Eyemouth Point. Three miles further on we turn right on to the A1107 and almost immediately right again into the unclassified road leading down to **Burnmouth**. The road winds down to the rocky cove, where a pier and jetty enclose a small harbour. The village lies at the foot of the cliffs. In the next cove to the south is the tiny hamlet of Ross. Returning to the junction at Burnmouth station, we continue on the A1107 north towards Eyemouth less than 2 miles away. There are fine views of the Lammermuir Hills, Ayton Castle and along the coastline to St Abb's Head with its white lighthouse. The road descends and crosses the river Eye, before following it down to the coastline.

Eyemouth is the largest coastal resort in the area with bathing, boating and golf. The picturesque harbour, formed by building a quay wall in the river mouth, is a busy fishing port, noted for its shellfish. The bay is locked in by red sandstone cliffs, and there are good caves to the north and south of the town. At one time smuggling was rife here, and it is said that most of the town lies underground in secret passages and cellars. The gardens of **Gunsgreen House**, itself an old smuggler's haunt, overlook the harbour.

From Eyemouth the A1107 leads on to Coldingham less than 3 miles away, but a secondary road (B6355) follows the wooded valley of the river Eye to **Ayton**, which is a small village 2½ miles away, on the A1. A return to Berwick can be made this way, passing the modern **Ayton Castle**, a red sandstone mansion built in the Scottish baronial style.

Coldingham is a quiet holiday resort, famed for the remains of its

Norman priory, lying just inland from a fine, sandy bay. There are hotels, a youth hostel and caravan and camping sites in the area. Sea angling, boating and skin-diving are also possible, and there is a diving centre. At nearby West loch there is pony-trekking, riding and fishing.

Coldingham Priory, just to the east of the village cross, was founded in 1098 as a Benedictine settlement. It was built on the site of an earlier nunnery founded by St Ebba, who gave his name to St Abb's Head. Partly preserved, it is now used as the parish church, but excavations continue.

From Coldingham the B6438 leads off to **St Abbs** and **Coldingham Bay**, where there is a picturesque little fishing harbour where sea angling and subaqua activities take place. **St Abb's Head**, with its lighthouse high above the waves, is the most striking promontory along this coastline and forms the highest cliff-line in southern Scotland. Four miles along the coast north-westwards lies **Fast Castle**. Little remains of this imposing and wellnigh impregnable fortress, built on a precipitous crag and linked to the mainland by a narrow ridge.

St Abb's Head

Fast Castle

Returning to the A1107 at Coldingham, the road leads northwards across Coldingham Moor for 6 miles to Cockburnspath. Passing Brown Rigg (190m, 634ft) on our right and then Meikle Black Law (241m, 803ft) on the left, the road descends towards Pease Bay, rejoining the A1 after crossing the main railway line from London to Edinburgh, and thence into the village of Cockburnspath.

Pronounced 'Co'spath' locally, **Cockburnspath** lies between the foothills of the Lammermuirs and the North Sea, with pleasant sands at nearby **Pease Bay**. A farm track leads off from this point to Fast Castle, along the coastline to the south, some 4 miles away. Also in this direction lies **Siccar Point**, where geologists will be interested in the Old Red Sandstone beds lying on the upturned edges of the earlier Silurian. To the north lies the cove of **Reed Point**. Rumours of a Spanish Armada treasure ship in the bay provide skin-divers with interesting speculation from time to time. From Cockburnspath we turn inland, following the A1 south from the village for $\frac{1}{2}$ mile, where an unclassified road goes straight on as the A1 bends to the left and leads towards Abbey St Bathans. The road crosses the Heriot Water below **Ewieside Hill**, on the top of which an ancient fort lies, then into Eclaw, where after ½ mile the road swings left along the north-eastern flank of Eclaw Hill (273m, 910ft). In 2 miles from this junction we cross the Eye Water, and in just over another mile a right-hand turning leads in 2 miles to the valley of the Monynut Water.

Abbey St Bathans, reached in less than 1 mile by turning left, is a pleasant little village deep in the Lammermuir Hills at the junction of the Monynut Water and the Whiteadder Water, the latter a main tributary of the Tweed. The church incorporates part of the important 12th-century abbey. The road continues towards Duns, turning to the right along the Eller Burn at the foot of Cockburn Law (320m, 1,065ft). On the top of this hill is **Edinshall Broch**, one of the very few Iron Age brochs (stone towers) in lowland Scotland.

The road soon joins the B6355, turning left to reach Duns in 3 miles. However, a diversionary excursion can be made at this point by turning right and climbing into the heart of the Lammermuir Hills. This road is impressive with wildly beautiful scenery, passing Ellemford and Cranshaws to the Whiteadder Reservoir. Past Sparelton Edge we reach the junction by Newlands Hill at a height of 404m (1,346ft) above sea-level. The return to Duns is made by turning left here past Penshiel Hill and Wether Law to **Longformacus**. This diversion adds some 18 miles to the excursion.

Duns is little more than a village but it is the administrative centre of Berwickshire District, with hotels, golf, fishing and swimming. At one time the former county of Berwickshire formed part of England. The word Duns, or Dunse as it originally was, comes from the Celtic word for a fortified hill and obviously refers to **Duns Law** (214m, 713ft), a rounded hill to the north, where there is a wide view along lower Tweeddale. A stone monument on the top commemorates a camp made here in 1639 by General Leslie and his Covenanters (supporters of the Scottish Reformed Church) before they marched on Newcastle.

Duns church is relatively modern, having been built in 1880. Two famous natives of Duns are commemorated locally: in the park is a statue to John Duns Scotus (1265–1308), one of the most notable thinkers of his age, who taught at Oxford and Paris and died in Cologne. In the Burgh chambers in Newton Street a museum has been created with all the trophies of the racing driver James Clark, who was killed in 1968. Clark was an Honorary Burgess of the town. **Duns Castle** to the north-west of the town is modern but retains an ancient tower and has a castellated gatehouse. In the grounds there is a nature reserve.

Polwarth lies 3 miles to the south-west of Duns on the Greenlaw road (A6105). The church there has several interesting features. Rebuilt in 1703, it lies in the grounds of **Marchmont House**. Our return to Berwick takes the eastern direction along the A6105 to **Edron** and Chirnside. Four miles along this road lies Edron church, now ruined but with a beautiful Norman doorway.

Chirnside, reached in 7 miles, is noted as a pleasant angling resort, with good views of the Lammermuirs. The parish church has a Norman doorway incorporated in the tower, and there is also a two-storeyed tithe barn. In the churchyard is the grave of James Clark, the world-champion racing driver who was killed while racing in Germany.

Following the valley of the Whiteadder, the A6105 reaches **Halidon Hill** in 6 miles, where the memorable battle against a Scottish relieving force took place in 1333. Just before reaching the hill we re-enter the liberties of Berwick-upon-Tweed, and a further 3 miles brings us back to the centre of the city.

---

3) Flodden Field and Ford Castle: Berwick – Duddo – Etal – Crookham – Branxton – Flodden Field – Ford – Barmoor – Ancroft – Berwick (approx. 28 miles)

Leaving Berwick by the A1 south over the Royal Tweed Bridge, we turn right on to the B6354, signposted to Duddo. The road climbs up to **Ordhill** from where there is an impressive view to Berwick and across the mouth of the Tweed and reaches **Duddo** in 7 miles. To the left of the village as we enter are the remains of **Duddo Tower**, built at the end of the 16th century but probably occupying the site of an earlier look-out tower. About 1 mile to the north-west of Duddo a very fine Bronze Age stone circle lies on the escarpment overlooking the Till Valley.

The road descends into the valley of the river Till and in 2 miles meets it at the village of **Etal**. On a green overlooking the river lie the ruins of **Etal Castle**, a 14th-century quadrangular structure. The subject of many earlier attacks, the castle was one of the many laid waste by James IV on his way to Flodden in 1513. Below the castle there is a salmon leap. The parish church, built in 1858, lies just in the grounds of **Etal Manor** on the other side of the road.

Etal Church

One and a half miles along the B6354 from Etal and just before reaching Ford there is a junction to the right (where the B6353 links with our road). Turn right here, immediately crossing the Till, and in less than ½ mile take the right fork into **Crookham**, reached in 1½ miles. After passing through the village, we join the A697 Coldstream road. Almost immediately again, by the Black Bull Inn, a left-hand unclassified turning leads us past pleasant cornfields to **Branxton**. The site of the **Battle of Flodden Field** (1513) is at the far end of the village, past the church and ½ mile on to a lane on our left.

In the early summer of 1513 James IV of Scotland, using the official pretext that his warden of the Eastern March (as this part of the Borders was known) had been killed in a brawl, decided to invade England. He gathered an army estimated at between 60,000 and 100,000 men and marched south, crossing the Tweed at Coldstream and destroying the fortresses of Wark, Norham and Etal as he came. He made his headquarters at Ford Castle. The English forces needed time to rally, and in the eighteen days which elapsed between his crossing the Border and the battle itself they had time to do so. Some historians say that as a result of this James's army dwindled away down to a mere 30,000 men. Meanwhile the Earl of Surrey, as Henry's representative, had landed English archers at the port of Tynemouth, joined them with the forces of Northumberland under the Percies and those of the Bishop of Durham and assembled 30,000 men at Bolton, just west of Alnwick, before marching to Wooler Haugh where he made his headquarters. His plan was simple: James, on a day to be always known thereafter as 'Black Friday' (9 September 1513), had taken his stand on Flodden Hill. The Earl of Surrey divided his forces, sending the vanguard together with his artillery circling round the Scots and crossing the Till at Twizell Bridge, while the rearguard forded the stream near Crookham, aiming to link up again near Branxton (where Surrey made his eventual stand) and thus keeping James from his base. As a result of this James unwisely relinquished his position and took up a new one on the Branxton slopes. After this initial manoeuvring the battle began at four o'clock in the afternoon, and rushing downhill to meet the English archers, the Scots gained some early successes.

By nightfall it was all over; James himself is reported to have died bravely, cut off and surrounded by only a few of his nobles, and his natural son, the Archbishop of St Andrews, was also killed. Scotland lost at least 9,000 men. The body of James IV was brought to Branxton's

12th-century church and taken from there to Berwick. The English too lost almost 5,000 men.

Each year in August, as part of the Coldstream Civic Week, a procession makes its way to Flodden Field to lay a wreath on the simple granite memorial erected there in 1910, and a piper plays the famous Scottish lament 'The Flowers of the Forest', written after the event.

Returning to Branxton itself, there is a famous garden here known as the **Stone Jungle**, which is open to the public. We retrace our road back to the A697 just before Crookham, then left by the B6353 to cross the river Till once more. At the junction a right-hand turn takes us almost immediately into Ford.

The village of **Ford** is set on a spur facing Flodden Hill and The Cheviot Hills. On the left, as we turn into the village, is the entrance to Ford Castle and also the way into the churchyard. The church dates from the 13th century and was restored in 1853, when the north arcade was constructed. The bell turret is mounted on a huge pillar forming a buttress for the west gable.

Ford Castle (*not open*) lies on the banks of the river Till, which runs some 9 miles north from this point to join the river Tweed. Built in 1287, it is one of the earliest examples in Northumberland of a crenellated quadrangular building with four massive corner towers. The castle was taken by the Scots in 1385 and demolished but later rebuilt. At the time of Flodden it suddenly came into prominence. The owner, another Sir William Heron, was in prison in Scotland, and his young wife, aware that she could not hold out against the massive army of James IV, is reported to have approached the Earl of Surrey asking for his assistance in having Ford spared. Surrey wrote to James IV offering to exchange two Scottish noblemen if the king would spare the castle, but James refused, advanced and took Ford, where he made his headquarters. There are stories that Lady Heron became his mistress, but however ardent the passion between them, it did not prevent James burning the castle down as he left for Flodden.

Sir William Heron was liberated after the battle, and the castle was partially restored in 1542. It then subsequently passed into the hands of the Blake and Delaval families, one of whom, the Marchioness of Waterford, made it into the imposing mansion it is today, with two of the original towers remaining intact.

Close by, in what was once the village school, is the **Lady Waterford Hall**, open to the public, which contains a collection of late 19th-century

39

paintings made by Lady Waterford of local villagers in various biblical scenes.

Recently restored, **Heatherslaw Mill** is one of the oldest water-driven flour mills in existence, dating from the 13th century but largely rebuilt in the 18th. It lies close to the river Till between Ford and Etal and is open to the public in the summer months.

From Ford we continue eastwards on the B6353 towards **Barmoor** and Lowick, climbing steadily. At Barmoor crossroads, reached in 4 miles, the B6525 (A6111) turns left for Berwick. Lowick (1 mile straight ahead) is hardly worth a diversion, except as a viewpoint towards the Northumberland coastline and Holy Island. It also lies on the line of the Devil's Causeway, the Roman road that linked Corbridge with Berwick-upon-Tweed. If a diversion is made, a left-hand turn at Lowick crossroads for $1\frac{1}{2}$ miles, turning left again for 1 mile, brings us back to the B6525. Alternatively, you can continue to Fenwick and turn left on the A1 for Berwick.

Ancroft is reached in just over 3 miles. The church on the left has a 14th-century tower, probably built for defence, and a striking Norman south door. Just past the village, where the road crosses the Allerdeanmill Burn, the Devil's Causeway again crosses our path. In another mile we join the A1 and turn left towards Berwick-upon-Tweed, passing through Scremerston and reaching the city in a further 2 miles.

Other excursions from Berwick-upon-Tweed

1) North of the Border

Abbotsford House, Melrose (Sir Walter Scott's home); Bowhill House, Selkirk; The Border Abbeys of Melrose, Jedburgh and Dryburgh; Mellerstain House, near Gordon; Traquair House, near Innerleithen.

For the enthusiast there are also historic buildings, Border castles, pele towers or fortified mansions at Branxholm, Cessford, Ferniehurst, Smailholm Tower, Hume Castle, Niedpath, Harden, Newark, Hermitage Castle, Gilnockie Tower, Drumelzier Castle, Eilbank, Oakwood and Bemersyde.

South of the Border

Alnwick Castle (see page 76); Bamburgh Castle (see page 60); Brinkburn

Priory (see page 99); Callaly Castle (see page 83); Chillingham Castle (see page 49); Craster Nature Reserve (see page 69); Dunstanburgh Castle (see page 69); Farne Islands (see page 65); Holy Island (Lindisfarne) (see page 52); Wallington Hall, Cambo (see page 103); Warkworth Castle (see page 89).

2 Wooler and Glendale
(Including local excursions)

Buses From the market-place to Alnwick, Berwick, Chillingham, Edinburgh, Morpeth, Newcastle, Whittingham and Yetholm.

Caravanning Nearest site 4 miles east on the A697 (March to October).

Distances Alnwick, 18 miles; Bamburgh, 15 miles; Berwick, 16 miles; Coldstream, 14 miles; Edinburgh, 63 miles; London, 320 miles; Morpeth, 31 miles; Newcastle upon Tyne, 46 miles.

Early closing Thursday.

Golf *Wooler Golf-Club* (9 holes) south-west of the town.

Hotels *Tankerville Arms, Black Bull Hotel, Ryecroft Hotel*.

Information centre Padgepool Place Car Park.

Population 1,833.

Set on the extreme north-eastern slopes of The Cheviot Hills, Wooler overlooks the wide valley of the river Till known as Millfield Plain. Lying at the edge of the Northumberland National Park (see page 00), there are some 398 square miles of open country (or 575 if we include the Border Forest area) shielding it on the west, which makes it an attractive centre for fishing and hill-walking. It is a small but very active market town, noted for the bracing air of The Cheviot Hills and as a health resort. The town is skirted by the main A697 Newcastle–Edinburgh road.

Capital of the district of Glendale, many cattle fairs were once held at Wooler. On the hills roam Blackfaced sheep and the Cheviots which have given this little town its industry. Herds of wild goats abound, and in the sheltered pastures of the Cheviot valleys high-grade beef and barley are also produced.

Wooler's peaceful setting says little of its past, set on one of the main routes from England into Scotland and guarding the outcrop of the virtually impassable hills behind. It is a focal point of routes which, like the many streams, meander to this point. At the foot of its hill the Wooler Water joins the river Till, which again is joined just north of the town by the river Glen. Confusions of local names abound – the Wooler Water higher up its source is known as the Harthope Burn and leads the way up the long valley between Hedgehope Hill (704m, 2,348ft) and The Cheviot itself, which at 803m (2,676ft) is the highest peak in the area. The river Till, 5 miles south of the town and above Berwick Bridge, changes its name to the Breamish or the river 'of bright water', and to add to the existing confusion for visitors the river Glen, which rises in Scotland and flows east towards Millfield Plain, starts life as the Bowmont Water. On the opposite side of the valley, 3 miles to the north-east as the crow flies, lies Dod Law (196m, 654ft). Historically, Wooler has not a great deal to offer. In the 1715 Jacobite rebellion the Earl of Derwentwater operated ineffectually in the area for some weeks and was defeated at Preston.

Excursions from Wooler

1) The Harthope Valley

A pleasant walk (although some parts may be driven) starts by following Cheviot Street out of the market-place and along the hillside lane above Wooler Water. At the fork the left-hand lane goes to the **Happy Valley**, a favourite picnic spot. Keeping right for the Harthope Valley, continue through the farmstead of Earle to Middleton Hall (1½ miles). Turn right along a steeply climbing road, passing the Shining Pool and then the narrow tributary valley known as **Hell's Mouth**. On our right is **Spear Hill** (341m, 1,135ft) with **Cold Law** 445m (1,484ft) looming behind it and the **Langlee Crags** (417m, 1,390ft) on the opposite side. After passing a plantation, the grand prospect of the Harthope Valley opens up, with **The Cheviot** (803m, 2,676ft) on the right and **Hedgehope** (704m, 2,348ft) just seen to the left. The way up to The Cheviot crosses the Carey Burn and ascends on the right bank (heading upstream) of the Harthope Burn. Beyond the farm of Langlee the road crosses the Hawsen Burn and passes through pinewoods to reach the farmstead of Langleeford tucked away amongst the trees across the burn. Here the road ends, about 5½ miles from Wooler, though a cart track continues up the valley to Langleeford Hope farm and Harthope Linn. A track leads on up towards The Cheviot, and on the ridge at the end of the valley, several tracks lead off to **Cairn Hill** (764m, 2,545ft) and other peaks in the neighbourhood, including the **Pennine Way** through to Yetholm. (*For*

further information on climbs in this area see the section on the Northumber-
land National Park, page 215.)

2) Doddington, Dod Law, Roughting Linn, Melmin and Millfield (approx. 14 miles)

Three miles along the B6525 (A6111) from Wooler brings us to **Dodding-ton**, where stone is quarried. The church is interesting in having its altar at the west end. On the north side of the church is an aisle separated by an arcade of 13th-century arches. Doddington is at the foot of **Dod Law** (196m, 654ft). From the summit to the south-west lie Hedgehope (704m, 2,348ft) and Bloodybush Edge (600m, 2,001ft) directly behind it. To the right is The Cheviot (803m, 2,676ft) and due west the conical shape of the Yeavering Bell (355m, 1,182ft) on the edge of Millfield Plain itself. In the valley the river Glen joins the Till to flow down past Ford and Etal to the river Tweed. To the south-east can be seen Chillingham Castle with the summit of Ros Castle (311m, 1,035ft) behind it.

On the summit of Dod Law are several ancient earthworks and enclos-ures. On the south side is **Cuddy's Cave**, traditionally associated with St Cuthbert, who in his early days was an itinerant preacher. Nearby is a large block of stone with Bronze Age vertical groovings on it. To the north-east of the summit there is an earthwork known as **Ringses Camp**, probably from the number of stones bearing cup-and-ring markings. These inscriptions are very numerous in the area and lie in a line across Doddington Moor in much the same direction as that taken by the Devil's Causeway (see page 49).

From Doddington turn left off the B6525 (A6111) in the village itself and follow the unclassified road to Fenton, reached in 2 miles. (*For the continuation past Barmoor to Ancroft and Berwick-upon-Tweed see page 121.*) Turn right at the junction for 1½ miles, turning right again at White Hill. A mile along this road brings us to a junction where a farm track comes in from the right. In the trees is the confluence of two streams, and close by the waterfall of **Roughting Linn** (sometimes spelt Rowting Linn). On the right-hand side of this junction are the finest series of cup-and-ring-marked rocks in the country, all dating from the Bronze Age between 1800 and 1000 BC. On the other side of the road to the west is a late prehistoric promontory fort between the two streams with three main banks and a ditch.

Returning along the way we have come, we follow the road towards Millfield. In 1 mile to our right is Fordwood House, some 105m (350ft)

Cheviot Hills, near Alwinton

above sea-level, in front of which are the prehistoric earthwork remains of the cliff-fort of **Fordwood**. Continuing through the village of Kimmerston, the river Till is reached at Redcar Bridge, and after crossing it we keep to the right at the junction towards the A697 and the town of Millfield. On our left are the remains of a disused airfield.

Just after crossing the bridge over the Till, the site of **Melmin** lies close to the river on our right. Melmin was the royal residence of King Oswald of Northumbria (633–41). It has not yet been fully excavated, and it is doubtful if much remains. However, it has close associations with Gefrin (Yeavering), another Saxon royal residence close by (see page 46).

A right turn at the junction with the A697 brings us quickly into the town of **Millfield**. Set on the edge of the Millfield Plain, once a prehistoric lake, it has been the scene of many feuding encounters between Scots and English and became known as the 'Ill Road' for that reason. At **Millfield House** the 19th-century Northumberland social reformer Josephine Butler was born. General Monck, the founder of the Coldstream Guards, is also reported to have waited here for reassuring news

45

prior to his famous march south to London in 1660. The English army led by the Earl of Surrey also came this way *en route* to Flodden.

The return to Wooler follows the A697 southwards with views to the Yeavering Bell (see below) and The Cheviot Hills to the right. In 2½ miles the river Glen is crossed, with the B6351 road coming in from the right at Akeld. A mile past this latter village, on the left, is the site of the **Battle of Homildon Hill**, fought in 1402 between the Scots and the English, which resulted in an overwhelming victory for the English, led by the Percies. A further 1½ miles brings us back to our starting-point.

3) Yeavering, Kirknewton, Kirk Yetholm, Morebattle, Kalemouth, with optional return via Roxburgh, Kelso and Coldstream (approx. 57 miles)

Taking the A697 north from Wooler, we reach Akeld in less than 3 miles and turn left at the fork on to the B6351 for Kirknewton. The road runs parallel with the river Glen and in ½ mile we pass the hamlet of **Yeavering**. A mile beyond this the Saxon site of Gefrin is on the right, marked with a plaque. Opposite us is the conical hill known as the **Yeavering Bell** (355m, 1,182ft), the largest Iron Age fort in Northumberland. Inside the surrounding stone wall are the foundations of a large number of circular or oval huts, some with evidence of paving. The cairn at the east end may be the remains of a medieval beacon.

Gefrin, or ad Gefrin, was first discovered in 1955 and excavated by Brian Hope-Taylor, revealing a complex of timber hall structures with a stockaded defence work. There is a suggestion that one building was a pagan shrine and another a Christian church, reflecting possibly the transitional state which occurred at that time. In 625 Paulinus, one of the original companions of St Augustine at Canterbury, was ordained bishop and accompanied Ethelberga on her marriage to the heathen king, Edwin of Northumbria. Edwin became converted in 627, and some time after Paulinus went to Ad Gefrin and remained there thirty-six days constantly occupied in instructing and baptizing people in the river Glen. Bede tells us that this royal residence was later abandoned and Melmin took its place.

A mile along the road lies the village of **Kirknewton**, where the river Glen is joined by the College Burn flowing down from the foot of The Cheviot itself. A highly vulnerable Border town in the past, thickly built walls predominate. The church, which dates from Norman times, has a fine chancel and a small south transept. There is a remarkable carving, thought to be Saxon in origin, known as the 'Kilted Magi', where in the representation of the Virgin and the Three Wise Men the latter appear to be wearing kilts. In the churchyard is the grave of Josephine Butler, the Northumberland social reformer.

On the opposite side of the river Glen lies **Coupland Castle**, built after the Union of Crowns, the grounds of which are occasionally open to the public. A mile beyond the church a road leads off left at Hethpool at the foot of **Great Hetha** (339m, 1,129ft), the start of the valley of the College Burn leading into The Cheviot Hills. At the far end, close to The Cheviot itself, are two spectacular ravines known as **Henhole** and **The Bizzle**, where ravens and wild goats abound.

From the junction of the College Burn and the river Glen the latter changes its name to the Bowmont Water. Our road follows this along the northern edge of the hills, until 3 miles further on the B6351 turns right over a bridge and crosses the river. At this point we continue straight on along the unclassified road to Pawston and Kirk Yetholm, remaining on the left-hand bank of the stream and circling round past Pawston Hill. Ignoring a right-hand turn after 1 mile, we carry on around the steep rock escarpment through woodlands for another mile, crossing a small stream which leads into the Bowmont Water and marks the Border with Scotland.

Kirk Yetholm is reached in 1 mile. There is an inn and a youth hostel, as well as the parish church on this side of Bowmont Water, but the main part of these two villages lies over the river bridge less than ½ mile away at **Yetholm**, or Town Yetholm as it is sometimes known to distinguish between the two. Yetholm is the end of the famous Pennine Way, the 250-mile walker's route from Edale in Derbyshire, and it is a well-known centre for walking and climbing. There are hotels, guest-houses, caravan and camping sites and facilities for fishing and riding.

The B6401 runs through the town, and at the far end the road to Morebattle bends to the right, swinging away from the range of hills to the south. Less than 1 mile from the town a right-hand turn leads off to **Yetholm Loch**, where there is a nature reserve. The road to Morebattle continues straight on for a further 2½ miles, crossing the Kale Water, just past which is a left-hand turning up to Hownam and the Capehope Burn, deep into The Cheviot Hills. This latter road leads up the valley of the Kale Water for several miles into the deep ravine by **Woden Law** (416m, 1,388ft). Over the Border it leads on through to a series of Roman camps high in the hills at Chew Green.

Bowmont Water, near Kirk Yetholm

Morebattle itself is a small village on the Kale Water, where numerous prehistoric forts and settlements lie on the surrounding hills. A left-hand turning $2\frac{1}{2}$ miles beyond the town leads up to the now ruined **Cessford Castle**, which up to 1650 was the ancient home of the famous Border family, the Kers.

Following the Kale Water down towards **Kalemouth**, the B6401 continues for a further 3 miles before reaching the T-junction of the A698, where the stream joins the river Teviot. A right-hand turn leads into Kelso in $4\frac{1}{2}$ miles, and from here the excursion can follow either the north or south bank of the Tweed to Coldstream, thence via the A697 to Wooler. Alternatively, if a visit to nearby Roxburgh is to be included, turn right on the A698 for $\frac{1}{4}$ mile, then turn left over the Teviot bridge to Ormiston and Roxburgh, following the road through modern Roxburgh to the A699 (the Selkirk–Kelso road). Turning right again, almost immediately Roxburgh Castle appears on the right. The return journey continues into Kelso, thence as above.

4) Fowberry Tower, Chillingham, Ros Castle, Old Bewick and Lilburn Tower (approx. 21 miles)

From Wooler the B6348 leads off eastwards towards the coast at Bamburgh. In little more than 1 mile it bends sharply to the right, and within $\frac{1}{4}$ mile again a left-hand turning leads to **Fowberry Tower**, close to where the road crosses the river Till. The Devil's Causeway also crosses the Till close to this point.

To avoid a return to the junction continue on the same road for a further mile, turning right towards Chatton. In the village turn right again and take the next left to Chillingham, reached in $1\frac{1}{2}$ miles. Just before the main entrance to the castle a lane turns off left into **Chillingham** itself. At the end of this lane is the church. The basic 12th-century structure remains with an aisleless nave, chancel and south chapel, and within the modern porch is enclosed the Norman doorway. The chapel contains the richly carved table-tomb of Sir Ralph Grey (d. 1443), the first owner of Chillingham Castle, and his wife, Elizabeth Fitzhugh.

Close to the churchyard is the east gate of **Chillingham Castle** (*not open*). Sadly, the castle, which is one of the best specimens of its kind, is now falling into decay. With a central courtyard, four massive 14th-century corner towers and connecting wings rebuilt in the 17th century, its exterior is most impressive. It was first fortified in the 14th century and passed into one of Northumberland's leading families, the Greys, and thence to the Bennets who were the predecessors of the present owner, the Earl of Tankerville.

The main attraction nowadays is the herd of **Chillingham wild cattle** which roams the 365-acre parkland walled in to contain them in 1220 (*open 1st April to 31st October, weekdays, Saturdays and bank holidays 10–12 and 2–5, Sundays 2–5, closed Tuesdays*). Some 260 acres are rough grass, the remainder pasture and woodland which still largely retains its pristine wildness and grandeur. The cattle, who were there before the wall, have evolved in a state of semi-isolation which has helped to prevent

49

disease, and of the five herds of horned white cattle which remain in Britain today the Chillingham one can claim to have the purest surviving members of the wild white cattle which roamed the forests of northern Britain in prehistoric times. These cattle have remained uncrossed for centuries, and their intensive inter-breeding has been undisturbed by man.

From Chillingham we turn left at the top of the lane, following the park walls along to the first turning on the left, a lane leading to Hepburn in about 1 mile. A steep ascent of the Great Whin Sill formation (an area of volcanic rock intrusion that lies across the country from Hadrian's Wall to Bamburgh and the Farne Islands) follows, and in about 1 mile, leaving the lane, we follow the park wall round to Ros Castle.

Ros Castle (311m, 1,035ft) dominates Chillingham Park and is well worth the ascent. It is crowned by the traces of a double-ramparted Iron Age camp, and some 7½ acres were vested in the National Trust in 1936 by Viscount Grey of Fallodon. The views from the top include The Cheviot Hills, Lindisfarne, the Farne Islands, Chillingham and Bamburgh Castle.

Retracing our road through Hepburn, we turn left at the T-junction towards Old Bewick, reached in 2 miles. On our way there are some splendid views towards The Cheviot Hills, with The Cheviot and Hedgehope predominating.

The church in **Old Bewick** is reached by a path across fields. It has an early Norman nave and apsidal chancel. On a hillside to the east ¼ mile away is the late prehistoric cliff-fort of Old Bewick. Two adjacent crescents of strong ramparts with stone-cut ditches abut on to the cliff edge to form an unusual Iron Age stronghold. In the enclosure hut circles can be seen at the western end, and the whole is contained within a semicircular bank and ditch some 60m (200ft) to the north. Several rocks at the south-eastern end of the fort bear cup-and-ring markings, and one of these, from within the fort itself, is now in Alnwick Castle Museum and dates between 1600 and 1000 BC.

From Old Bewick a secondary road leads north-westwards towards **East Lilburn**, where the Devil's Causeway passes through the village. This leads on to **Lilburn Tower**, now a ruin, but dating from the time of Edward II. Joining the A697 main road at the junction beyond Lilburn Tower, a right turn brings us back to Wooler in 2½ miles.

3 The coastline from Berwick-upon-Tweed to Alnmouth
(Including Holy Island and the Farne Islands)

The north-east coastline of England, running some 70 miles from Berwick-upon-Tweed to Tynemouth, is an area of immense attraction to the holidaymaker. With its bracing air and fine stretches of open sand beaches it is little wonder that the small tucked-away fishing villages of prewar days have now turned themselves into major resort areas, catering for every type of visitor.

Fortunately, much has been done to protect the natural state of its inherent charm, and the 40 miles from Berwick-upon-Tweed to the mouth of the river Coquet at Warkworth harbour have been designated 'an area of outstanding natural beauty'. The formation of nature reserves and the acquisition of large areas of dune-land, together with those covenants already give to it, have enabled the National Trust to continue with this good work. Apart from the traditional holiday activities of bathing, fishing, sailing and golf, there is also much scope for the walker and the naturalist. There are countless rockpools to explore, one of the largest bird sanctuaries in Europe lies on the Farnes, and close to the offshore islands the grey seal comes to breed.

The coastline of Northumbria has been a haven to many migratory stirrings, and one cannot go far without hearing stories of those early Northumbrian saints – Aidan, Cuthbert, Wilfrid and Oswald – all of whom had associations with this region, and it has played host to their cause in Holy Island.

As an unprotected and vulnerable flank of England, it suffered countless invasions from Viking and Dane, pirate and smuggler and the inevitable and dreaded Scots. Its welcomes of the past have not always been cordial, and in a relatively deserted land it has learnt how to stand at bay. To some a graveyard and others a sanctuary, the coastline of Northumbria can still tell some epic tales.

From Berwick-upon-Tweed the A1(T) crosses the Tweed, heading south to Scremerston which is reached in 3 miles. From here a left-hand turn leads through to the coast just north of the Cheswick Sands, a long bar that runs almost to Holy Island and protects the lagoon from the north. Two miles beyond Scremerston a road leads off left to Cheswick itself and on through to the Berwick-upon-Tweed Golf-Club at Goswick, where Charles I is reported to have stayed on his way to Berwick. It is possible to walk from Goswick across the South Low Burn to Beal Point and the start of the causeway to Holy Island, and the whole of this area, from Goswick to Budle Bay (see under Bamburgh), is now a nature reserve.

We pass **Haggerston**, 7 miles from Berwick, with its castle and lake, now the centre of a caravan site. Only the castle tower remains, dating from 1345. Less than 2 miles beyond this point we reach the junction at West Mains, where on an open stretch of the main road by a lonely inn a left-hand turn indicates the way through to **Beal** and **Holy Island** (Lindisfarne). After traversing the level crossing carrying the main London–Edinburgh line, the road drops down in 1½ miles to Beal Sands and the start of the causeway to Holy Island. A wide expanse of tidal flats opens out in front of us, with Goswick Flats to our left, Holy Island Sands sweeping round the curve of the island itself in front and the wide expanse of Fenham Flats to our right. The whole forms a naturally enclosed basin and it abounds in duck and wading birds. The curious geological formation which has given rise to such islands as Lindisfarne is caused by the volcanic intrusions of basaltic dolerite which traces its way across Northumberland from west to east and which is known as the Great Whin Sill. It consists of jagged upthrusts of darker rock against the lighter limestone, and other examples can be seen in the Farne Islands and the mounds on which Lindisfarne Priory, its castle and both Bamburgh and Dunstanburgh Castles were built.

Care should be taken in crossing to Holy Island. (Crossing times can be obtained from tourist information centres and the Northumbria Tourist Board.) The causeway is 3 miles long, although for the last 2 miles it curves round the lee of the island. It is quite easy to drive across, but every year, in spite of warnings, motorists get caught by the rising tide and have to seek the sanctuary of the 'refuges'. A large notice is displayed at the start of the causeway giving the safe times for crossing, but in calculating the trip it must not be forgotten that you wish to return. The general rule is not to cross between two hours prior to high tide and up to three and a half hours afterwards, that is the five and a half hours when the causeway is covered by water at an average high-tide depth of 12m (39ft). For example, if high tide is at 10am, then it is safe to cross from 1.30pm (but not at 8.30am). Since there are two tides daily and the next high tide would be about 10.30pm, you can safely stay on the island up to about 8pm, crossing back again no later than 8.30pm, that is two hours before the next high tide. Tide tables can be purchased locally, in Berwick-upon-Tweed and also at the post office on Holy Island. But don't forget to reckon with British Summer Time!

The modern causeway with its hard surface is vastly different from the series of stepping stones which marked the 11th-century pilgrim's way, the line of which, still marked by stakes, is clearly visible. The island is 2¼ miles long and about 1½ miles broad at its widest part and has a long, low spit of land running to the west, aptly named the Snook. Its circumference is about 6 miles, and a pleasant walk can be made around the main part of it, starting from the village and taking in the priory, the castle and the limestone cliffs at the north end which form a nature reserve for the many sea birds.

Lindisfarne Castle

Once across the causeway the road leads into the village of **Holy Island**, the name which replaced the earlier one of Lindisfarne in the 11th century, although the two are still in current use. From the mainland the island appears generally rather featureless, but in the summer season the village itself is a pleasant surprise for the visitor with its rows of tiny cottages, gardens, shops and post office and a regular community life for the 200 souls who derive a living mainly from fishing and agriculture. Apart from catering for the many visitors, Holy Island enterprises include a flourishing mead factory, the production of a local liqueur and the sale of honey, with much revival of those Celtic-style trinkets which hark back to its earliest days.

In the little square at the south end of the village is the **Market Cross** built in 1828 but placed on an earlier, medieval socket. A pathway leads from the square towards St Mary's Church and Lindisfarne Priory, and behind them, protecting the southern flank of the island, is a rib of basaltic rock known as the **Heugh**. In earlier times it afforded a natural shield to the priory and its inhabitants and had a small fort for defence. A mile away, clearly visible from the village, Lindisfarne Castle stands on a similar pinnacle of rock which is known as the **Beblowe**. A pathway links the two and continues beyond the castle to the nature reserve at the northern end, where the low dunes are rich in bird life.

Historically, Lindisfarne must start with St Aidan and the growth of Celtic Christianity in Northumbria. Edwin, the first Christian king, was killed in battle in 633, and the pagan victors Penda and Caedwalla devastated Northumbria after contemptuously placing Edwin's severed head in the church at York. Edwin's nephew Oswald, who had been educated and raised as a Celtic Christian by the monks of Iona, regained the throne next year. In a battle at Heavenfield in 634 he vanquished the invaders. The next year he asked the Iona fathers for a bishop to restore Christian teaching in Northumbria, but the first to come made no impression at all. Aidan then came and although he might have chosen York, where Edwin's church was nearing completion, he chose Lindisfarne instead. Oswald himself was also later to be canonized and spent much of his time at Bamburgh. Thus, king and prelate combined their efforts to establish the new monastery and spread the word of the Gospels. Oswald reigned for nine years, dying in battle at Oswestry in 642, but his head was returned to Lindisfarne and his hand and arm to Bamburgh where they became sacred relics. He was succeeded by Oswy, who shared the throne with Oswin whom he later had murdered, but meanwhile Oswin became a close confidant of Aidan. The latter foresaw the death of Oswin and they both died within a few days of each other. After sixteen years in his episcopate, Aidan died on the 31 August 651, and his body was taken to Lindisfarne for burial. He was succeeded by Finan, a Scot from Iona, at a time when the controversy which existed between the Celtic and the Roman sides of Christianity was beginning to come to a head. King Oswy was very much pro-Celtic, but his son Alchfrid, who became a pupil and close confidant of Wilfrid and to whom he had given land at Ripon for a monastery, leaned the other way. After Finan died, his successor, Colman, attended the famous Synod of Whitby, called by the king to finalize the matter in 664. Colman and Wilfrid were the main speakers, but Wilfrid, who had travelled widely on the Continent and been to Rome, easily prevailed, and the king made the final decision in favour of the Roman side, which submitted to the heirarchy of Rome.

For a while after this time there was much interplay between the two sides, and Northumbria became the watershed between the work started by St Augustine from Canterbury in 547 and the teachings of St Columba from Iona in 565. Overnight the character of Lindisfarne changed, with Bishop Colman and many of his followers going back to Scotland and taking with them some of the relics of Aidan. With the rise and growth of Hexham under Wilfrid's leadership the episcopate of Lindisfarne was diminished in size and it came for a while under the influence of Melrose, from which foundation some of the succeeding bishops came, the most important being Cuthbert.

Tradition has it that Cuthbert, who started life as a shepherd on the Lammermuir Hills, rode up to the Abbey of Melrose in 651 (after seeing a vision of St Aidan) and demanded entry with a spear in his hand. Here he was trained under Boisil and made prior after the latter's death. He was a skilful speaker who toured the country and preached in the villages, eventually being transferred to Lindisfarne to train other monks. He yearned, however, for the solitary life and spent much time on Inner Farne, where the brothers helped him to build a tiny dwelling, surrounded, so Bede tells us, by an embankment so high he could only look up at the sky. It is said he spent eight years there alone, grew crops where none had flourished before and by his faith and prayers discovered a spring of pure water.

In 684 the king of Northumberland, Egrid, sent an army into Ireland and brutally devastated the churches and monasteries there and the next year, ignoring the advice of Cuthbert, he led an army against the Picts and was killed. Just before his death a synod was held under Theodore of Tarsus, appointed Archbishop of Canterbury in 669, in the presence of the king at Twyford-on-Aln to decide on the next bishop of Lindisfarne. Cuthbert was elected unanimously, but nothing would induce him to accept, until the king, with the whole company of monks, went to Inner Farne and begged him on their knees. Cuthbert consented and was made bishop the following Easter at York, first of Hexham and then later of Lindisfarne. He remained so for only two years until 687, then begged to return to the island. He foretold his own death, which occurred shortly afterwards, and in spite of his wishes to be buried on Inner Farne eventually agreed to Lindisfarne. Eleven years later, when the monks wished to place his coffin in a more honoured place within the church, his body was disinterred and was found to be still whole. From that time on it became a sacred relic of the Lindisfarne community.

Wilfrid, exonerated by his church from accusations made against him previously, returned to Northumbria in 687 and held the see of Lindisfarne for a year. It was a time of great trial for Northumbria, but although disorder reigned throughout the land, Lindisfarne survived and produced much of its finest work. St Cuthbert's Cross, now in Durham Cathedral, is a masterpiece of Celtic art, and two magnificent manuscripts – the Lindisfarne Gospels, a breathtaking work of supreme importance, and the *Liber Vitae*, an illuminated list of names – emanate from the period around AD 700. They lay for centuries in Durham Cathedral but are now in the British Museum. Superbly decorated with figures of men, animals and plants and the most intricate and complex designs in their borders, the Lindisfarne Gospels' pages stand out as one of the most painstaking works of art of this period. A modern facsimile is in the church on Holy Island.

In 789 there was a period of thunderstorms and gales, followed by famine, and Lindisfarne was attacked by the first inroads of the Vikings. In June 793 a major force arrived, sacked the monastery and murdered most of the inhabitants. In spite of this the monastery was revived and carried on its work until 873, when they fled before the second main Danish onslaught, taking their treasures, including the body of St Cuthbert, the head of St Oswald and their Gospels with them. For seven years they wandered around Northumbria, eventually settling at Chester-le-Street in 882 where the see was established for the next 113 years. In 995 the Danish threat again forced them to move, and their bishop, Aldhun –

twenty-fourth in line from Aidan – led them to Durham, where they have remained since that time and where a church was dedicated in 999.

Curiously enough there was a short return to Lindisfarne after the Norman conquest, for no sooner had William established his presence than the Northumbrians revolted and massacred the Normans in Durham under their leader, Robert de Commines, in 1069. Aware of the revenge that would follow, the population fled to Lindisfarne, taking the body of St Cuthbert with them, but they were back within a year to find their church desecrated and the countryside laid to waste. A huge army of Danes was on the Humber, but, fortunately, William was occupied elsewhere and they were left in peace.

In 1082 Benedictine monks from Durham, sent by the new Norman Bishop of Durham, William of Saint-Calais, founded a new monastery at Lindisfarne, and from that time onwards the ecclesiastical affairs of the two establishments were intertwined. It became known as Holy Island and remained a monastic foundation until the dissolution of the monasteries in 1536, when it fell into disrepair. The work of excavating the priory was begun in 1888 by Sir William Crossman, and its care is now in the hands of the Department of the Environment.

At **Lindisfarne Priory** (*open daily, charge*) no traces of the early church or monastery remain, apart from a few carved stones of a date later than the time of St Cuthbert. The ruins we see today belong entirely to the period after the Norman conquest, and the church, begun in 1090, was completed by 1140. Building went on right through the 12th century, but by 1300 it was mostly complete, although later bishops made fresh additions again in the 14th and 15th centuries.

The church is entered by the west door, a fine example of the Norman style, with a zigzag-moulded arch and triple shafts on either side. The interior of the very fine west gable – in four stages, with a gallery over the doorway – is well-worth noting. Of the crossing the north-west and south-west piers remain, but all that survives of the tower is a single, very graceful rib known as the 'rainbow arch'. Of the choir a considerable part remains with the complete frame of a large perpendicular east window, built about 1140. Also, towards the east end, is a trefoiled piscina, somewhat mutilated. From the south transept the way leads through to the cloister and most of the buildings here were completed at a later stage than the church. In the priory grounds stands a modern statue of St Aidan.

Adjacent to the priory is the ancient **St Mary's Church**. Founded

Lindisfarne Priory

about 1140, any of the original structure that might have remained was carefully disguised in the restoration of 1860 when the walls and nave were plastered over. The west front may be partially original, and the exceptionally stout buttress in the form of an arch, designed to carry the 18th-century bell turret, is certainly unusual. The interior is mainly late 12th or 13th century in origin, the piers of the north arcade being ornamented with alternate courses of red and white stones. In the south aisle are a large trefoiled piscina and an aumbry, a closed recess in the wall, indicating possibly a former chantry chapel.

In keeping with the local custom, shared by both Bamburgh and Tweedmouth, the brides at Holy Island weddings jump over the 'petting stool', sometimes known as the 'louping stool', and the higher the jump, the better their luck. Traditionally, shot-guns are still fired in salute.

From the village an unfenced road leads eastwards towards Lindisfarne Castle, or as an alternative a path from the priory circles round to join it close to the harbour. Just offshore, to the south-west of the priory, lies **St Cuthbert's Isle**, where the saint is said to have lived prior to seeking greater seclusion on the Farne Islands. It can be reached at low tide, and a cross marks the site of his chapel.

Lindisfarne Castle (*open daily April to September, 11–1 and 2–5 except Tuesdays and Good Friday*; the green National Trust flag will be flown if the castle is open at other times) was built as a Border fort about 1550, using a great deal of the stone from the priory after Henry VIII had conveniently dissolved the monasteries. It withstood a siege in the Civil War by Parliamentary forces, and in 1715 was briefly occupied by two of the Jacobite rebels. By the 19th century it had fallen largely into disrepair but was bought in 1902 by Edward Hudson, the then owner of *Country Life*. Sir Edward Lutyens was persuaded to make a superb restoration into a private residence, completed in 1903. It was given in 1944 to the National Trust. There is an interesting collection of Ridinger and other prints and some 17th-century Flemish and English oak furniture. As a vantage point on this part of the coastline, its position is superb, linking together visually some of the most important sites of early Northumbrian history.

Returning to Beal and the junction of the A1(T), in 6 miles Belford is reached. Six miles south-east of Belford lies Chathill, where Preston Tower is open to the public on Saturdays, Sundays and public holidays from the end of May to 25 September (2–6pm). From Belford a left-hand turn at the end of the village (B1342) leads through past land-locked Budle Bay to Bamburgh in a further 5 miles.

Bamburgh

Buses To Alnwick, Beadnell, Belford, Craster, Morpeth, Newcastle and Seahouses.
Camping and caravanning There are many sites along this coastline. The nearest is Glororum, 1 mile from Bamburgh on the B1341.
Distances Alnwick, 17 miles; Beal, 12 miles; Berwick-upon-Tweed, 20 miles; London, 324 miles; Morpeth, 36 miles; Newcastle, 51 miles; Wooler, 16 miles.
Early closing Wednesday.

Golf *Bamburgh Castle Golf-Club* on Budle Point to the north-west.
Hotels *Lord Crewe Arms, Mizen Head, Victoria, Sunningdale*.
Population 458.
Post Office In the village.
Sailing (and water-skiing) From Beadnell.
Sea-fishing trips From Seahouses.
Skin-diving Locally and at Seahouses and Beadnell.
Swimming Good bathing from the beach.

Bamburgh is a small but attractive and very busy coastal resort in the season with fine white sands. Its single main street slopes down to the foot of the castle rock, where it turns and runs along the coastline southwards. The main attractions are the castle, St Aidan's Church and the Grace Darling Museum.

Bamburgh Castle (*April to September daily at 2pm, charge*) is Northumbria's most prominent landmark and is visible for many miles. It stands on the 45m (150ft) high basalt rock which attracts as much interest today as it did when Ida the Flamebearer, leader of the Anglians, landed here in AD 547 and made it his base.

The historical record is none too clear until the reign of Ethelfrith, King of Northumbria from 593 to 616, who according to Bede was Ida's grandson. Having united for the first time the adjacent kingdoms of Bernicia and Deira to form a united Northumbria, he gave the fortress to his wife, Bebba, who renamed it Bebbanburh (or Bebba's town) and hence the Bamburgh of today. At this time York became the capital of the united kingdom, but Bamburgh continued as a royal residence and was the place where many of the early Northumbrian kings were crowned. Its life was precarious, and three times between 933 and 1015 it was stormed and pillaged by the dreaded Norsemen, sometimes aided by the Scots. In 1095 it sustained a siege by William II (Rufus) during a revolt by Robert de Mowbray, Earl of Northumberland, who was at that time the guardian of the Northern Marches. Mowbray escaped and fled to Newcastle, then to Tynemouth Priory, where he was captured. The king threatened to put out his eyes if Bamburgh was not surrendered, so the young Countess Matilda, his wife, who still held out in the castle, threw open the gates and capitulated. Mowbray was later pardoned.

Bamburgh

Restorations were carried out by Henry I (1100–35), and Bamburgh became a possession of the English Crown. Henry III and Edward I both visited it on their journeys to Scotland. During the Wars of the Roses Bamburgh suffered from more than one important siege, though it remained in Yorkist hands for most of the time. In the reign of James I (1603–25) the castle was in the care of a well-known Northumberland family, the Forsters, who owned it for 200 years, but the buildings grew more dilapidated. It was left to Lord Crewe, the Bishop of Durham, who married into the family, to restore the castle to its former glory, and in 1704 he purchased the Bamburgh estate. He entrusted the work to Dr John Sharp, the Archdeacon of Northumberland at the time, and later a trust was formed to continue the restoration. In 1894 the castle was purchased by the first Lord Armstrong, one of the great inventors of his age who was connected with the Armstrong works at Scotswood on Tyneside and who spent thirty years on a second great restoration. The Armstrong family still own the castle, parts of which are now leased off as separate flats.

Bamburgh Castle

On the north side of the Inner Ward we find the remains of **St Oswald's Chapel**. (St Oswald was King of Northumbria from 631 to 642 and died at the Battle of Oswestry fighting the Mercians.) Only the foundations belong to the original Norman building, the walls above having been built after 1770. The principal room, known as the **King's Hall**, is panelled with teak and hung with paintings and rich tapestries. Adjoining the dwelling house is the **Armoury**, with a large collection of weapons and armour, including some on permanent loan from the Tower of London. The **Keep** was built by Henry II about 1164 but probably also was restored by Dr Sharp.

From the north end of the village a road leads out to **Harkness Rocks**, with a lighthouse, and thence by path across the golf-course to land-locked **Budle Bay**, now controlled by the Nature Conservancy and a haunt of wildfowl. On the opposite side of the bay are **Ross Links**, and northwards can be seen the castle on Holy Island. The track continues round to Heather Cottages, and from here the Belford–Bamburgh road (B1342) can be regained about 1½ miles from Bamburgh, the whole round trip taking in about 4 miles.

St Aidan's Church is one of the largest parish churches in Northumbria, and the 13th-century chancel is one of the most beautiful in the country. The original church was erected some time after St Aidan's arrival here in 635, and he used it as a home when he was not travelling about the countryside preaching. A Norman church was later erected on the site, an aisleless structure, of which some parts of the transepts are thought to be incorporated in the existing church begun in the reign of Henry II (1154–89). There are numerous reminders of the lives of Northumbrian saints and heroines in the stained-glass windows and many memorials, including St Cuthbert in a modern one. One unusual feature is the 'low-side' window, where people afflicted with plague could still receive communion. On the south side of the chancel is a tomb niche containing the effigy of a cross-legged knight dating from the 14th century. Hanging from the north wall are the helmet, cuirass, gauntlets and a wooden sword said to have belonged to Ferdinando Forster (see below).

In 1837 the crypt was discovered and revealed the coffins of several members of one of Bamburgh's most notable families – the Forsters. Apart from Ferdinando the bodies of Dorothy Forster (1686–1767) and her brother Tom were also found. (Tom Forster, MP for Northumberland, took part in the 1715 Jacobite rising. He was imprisoned in Newgate, but Dorothy eventually freed him. He sailed for France and died in Boulogne in 1737, but his body was brought back to Bamburgh. Dorothy was the niece of the Forster who had married Lord Crewe, and she herself became an Armstrong, marrying the blacksmith who had helped her.) There is also an effigy in the church to another of Northumberland's heroines, Grace Darling, and a monument to her in the churchyard.

In keeping with the local custom on this part of the coastline, Bamburgh brides also jump over the 'petting stool' when they are married.

The **Grace Darling Museum** (*April to October, 11–7, free, but donations appreciated*) lies close to the church and was opened in 1938 by the Royal National Lifeboat Institution. It contains pictures, documents and various other relics of the heroine, including some of the many appreciations and gifts made to her from all parts of the world after the rescue of the crew of *Forfarshire* in 1838. The actual boat – a coble, 6·3m (21ft) by 1·8m (6ft), of a type still seen along the Northumberland coastline – is also there.

Three doors away is the cottage in which she was born in 1815 – the year of Waterloo – and when she was ten years of age, her father, who belonged to a family of traditional lighthouse keepers, was made keeper of the Longstone Light at the outer edge of the Farne Islands. She lived there for a number of years, a rather withdrawn, shy girl who already was sickly and ailing. She learnt to handle a boat, however, and was twenty-two at the time of the famous rescue, when nine lives were saved. For four years after this she was inundated with offers of marriage, invitations and patronizations of every kind. After a spell of convalescence for her growing consumption she died at the age of twenty-six in the house now occupied by the Post Office, overwhelmed, perhaps, not only by her illness but by the sudden and unexpected fame she had achieved.

South of Bamburgh and less than 3 miles away along the B1340 lies Seahouses. On the way we pass a point known as **Monks House Rocks**, the site of a house built on a piece of land given by Henry II (1154–89) to the monks of the Farne Islands as a storehouse for their provisions. The house is still in existence and since 1964 has been covenanted to the National Trust.

Seahouses

Buses To Alnwick, Bamburgh, Beadnell, Belford, Craster, Morpeth and Newcastle.
Camping and caravanning There are many sites along this coastline. The nearest are ½ mile north of Beadnell and at Beadnell itself.
Distances Alnwick, 15 miles; Beal, 15 miles; Berwick-upon-Tweed, 23 miles; London, 321 miles; Morpeth, 33 miles; Newcastle, 48 miles; Wooler, 19 miles.
Early closing Wednesday.
Golf *Seahouses and North Sunderland Golf-Club* (9 holes) is to the south of the town close to the sea.
Hotels *Dunes, Olde Ship, Bamburgh Castle, Beach House, Links*.
Information centre Main car park (April to September).
Post Office In North Sunderland.
Sailing (and water-skiing) From Beadnell.
Sea-fishing trips Mr D. T. Shiel, 7 Beechcroft, Seahouses.
Skin-diving Farne Diving Lodge, 146 Main Street, North Sunderland.
Swimming Good bathing from the many beaches.

Seahouses is the nearest point of embarkation for the **Farne Islands**. It has grown out of the clumsy name of North Sunderland Sea Houses and expanded as an offshoot of the older village in its own right. Once it was simply a small herring-fishing port, but now its hotels and guest-houses cater for the many yachts that frequent the harbour during the season and for its regular week-end visitors. Along the shore northwards there is safe bathing from the sands protected by St Aidan's Dunes. Twenty-four hectares (60 acres) of these – stretching from Monks House to just north of the village – now belong to the National Trust and were given in 1936 by the 1st Viscount Runciman.

From the sea front the view takes in the Farne Islands, often the main attraction for visitors to these parts. On the extreme left lies lonely **Megstone**, distinguished by its white rocks; then **Inner Farne**, topped by a lighthouse; **Staple Island** to the right and back a little, with **Brownsman** immediately behind it. The farthest island is **Longstone**, again slightly to the right, with a red-and-white-striped lighthouse. Lastly, tiny **Crumstone**, away to the right, can just be seen.

The actual number of islands varies with the state of the tide, with twenty-eight at low water and fifteen at high tide, and they lie between $1\frac{1}{2}$ and $5\frac{1}{4}$ miles offshore. One of the finest sea-bird breeding colonies in Europe, the islands are formed from the upthrust of the Whin Sill formation to provide fragments of barren rocks and cliffs which make ideal nesting-places for eiders, gulls, kittiwakes, terns, guillemots and puffins. With a total area of some 32 ha (80 acres) they are also the only breeding-place on the north-east coast for the grey seal.

The islands are divided into two main groups by **Staple Sound**: in the

65

southern group are Inner Farne, the largest and nearest to the mainland, with a 14th-century chapel and a pele or light tower, and **Knock's Reef** adjoining it. The northern group comprises in the main Staple Island and Brownsman, which are joined at low water, the latter being the only fertile island. Close behind them are the **North** and **South Wamses**, which also are joined at low water. **Big** and **Little Harcar** then lead through to the Longstone group, and these are the farthest offshore apart from the small rocks of the **Knivestone**. Apart from these principal islands there are many smaller rocks in the area. At the south-eastern end of the latter island are three isolated columnar rocks, known as the **Pinnacles**, now largely weathered away from the island itself.

One of the earliest inhabitants of Inner Farne was St Aidan who, as Bishop of Lindisfarne from 635 to 651, often withdrew there for prayer and meditation. But it was his successor, St Cuthbert, who not only made the island more famous – he lived there from 676 to 685 and again for a short while just before his death in 687 – but also introduced the first rules for the care of the nesting eider ducks, and in many representations of the saint he is shown holding one of 'St Cuthbert's Chicks', as they have become known locally. In 1255 another attempt was made to turn the island into a hermitage by two Benedictine monks from Durham who established a cell there.

In the centuries that followed the island fell into private hands and suffered greatly from egg-collectors. In 1880 the Farne Islands Association was formed, and since that time watchers have been employed to protect the birds. In 1925 the National Trust took over the work and now administers them, with the exception of the Longstone Lighthouse. In 1964 a sanctuary order for the birds and their eggs was granted by the Home Office. Only Inner Farne and Staple Island are open to visitors from April to the end of September, and restricted access very much applies during the breeding season from mid-May to mid-July.

Information and landing tickets can be obtained from the Information Centre at Seahouses Harbour before sailing or from the watchers on landing. The round trip takes two hours approximately, and up to thirty boats regularly operate trips across. They leave generally at 10am and again at 1.30pm during the season and more frequently when numbers demand. It is *essential* to book a trip to suit your requirements – not all boat operators are licensed to land on the islands, and some do round trips without calling in. It is also wiser to secure a landing ticket before you leave.

There are some simple rules affecting all visitors: they may spend as much time and go where they wish on Staple Island and they can make a guided tour of Inner Farne, including the chapel and tower. Brownstone and Longstone are normally out of bounds, and so is the Longstone Lighthouse. The collecting of eggs, flowers or plants is prohibited, and visitors must at all times obey the directions of the official bird-watchers. Permission to land at any other time or place can only be obtained from the National Trust Warden/Naturalist in charge at *The Shieling, 8 St Aidan's, Seahouses; tel. Seahouses (066 572) 651*.

Inner Farne is about 6·5 ha (16 acres) in area at low water, most of which is virtually bare rock. The chapel, whose original date is not known, was extensively restored between 1369 and 1372 and again in 1848. The tower was erected about 1500 by Prior Castell of Durham, after whom it is still known. The first warning light on Inner Farne was established in 1673 by a timber and coal fire placed on top of the tower. The first lighthouse was built in 1809, and the present light there is automatic, requiring attention only once a fortnight. During the season the bird-watchers live in the pele tower, while some stay on Brownsman Island in an old lighthouse cottage. There is a nature trail on the island.

South from Seahouses and its close neighbour North Sunderland the B1340 passes the golf-course and follows the coastline for the 2 miles to **Beadnell**, the next port of call along this coastline. The village lies just inland and ½ mile from its own harbour, which fringes **Beadnell Bay**, where some of the best sailing is to be had along the whole Northumberland coastline. This is the hub of the holiday area, with several caravan parks and a skin-diving centre. In the village there is an 18th-century church, rebuilt in the Gothic style in 1860, and an 18th-century inn called the Craster Arms. Beadnell harbour is tiny, and from it the sands of Beadnell Bay stretch 2 miles across to **Snook Point**. Close to the harbour are the disused 18th-century lime-kilns, now owned by the National Trust. Eastwards from the harbour on a narrow rib of land known locally as **Ebb's Nook** are the remains of a 13th-century chapel dedicated to St Ebba. A footpath leads from Beadnell harbour to Long Nanny, one of the two streams that flows into the sea half-way across the beach, opposite Robin Wood's Rock and about 1 mile away. It continues across **Newton Links** to the other side of the bay. Here over 40 ha (100 acres) of sand-dunes and rough grazing were acquired in 1966 by the National Trust. This gives a marvellous stretch of unspoilt coastline right down to Dunstanburgh Castle, some 4 miles away. From the other side of Beadnell Bay it is possible to walk through to High or Low Newton-by-the-Sea, and thence round Embleton Bay to Dunstanburgh and on to Craster.

The road from Beadnell (B1340) turns sharply inland to **Swinhoe**, then runs parallel to the coastline about 1 mile inland to reach the junction between the B1340 and the B1339 in 4 miles. At this point the right-hand turn (the B1340) runs directly through Rennington to Denwick and Alnwick in 8 miles, while the B1339 becomes the coast road leading to Embleton in another mile. On the same junction a secondary road leads off left to **High Newton-by-the-Sea**, with a minor road leading north a mile to Newton Links and Beadnell Bay and through to **Low Newton-by-the-Sea**. Between the two a path leads off to **Newton Point**, with fine views across **Embleton Bay** and the rocky islands off Newton Haven, again to the Dunstanburgh Castle.

Embleton Bay shoreline is part of the National Trust preserve, and close to the hamlet itself lies **Newton Pool**, a freshwater pool protected as a nature reserve which was purchased in 1972 with grants from the World Wildlife Fund. Public access is permitted only to the edge of the reserve.

The walker can follow the path around Embleton Bay, across the Embleton golf-links, and either turn inland by the clubhouse towards Embleton itself or continue the 2¼-mile course to Dunstanburgh Castle on the next headland.

From the junction of the B1339 and B1340 a mile along the former takes us into **Embleton**, a small village with a mainly 14th-century church and a vicarage that includes a pele tower built between 1332 and 1334 with later crenellations. Minor roads lead to the golf-course and to Dunstan Sands on Embleton Bay, with the coastal footpath leading on to Dunstanburgh as already indicated.

The B1339 from Embleton continues on to **Longhoughton** in 5 miles and thence to **Lesbury** in a further 1½ miles to join the main road between Alnwick and Alnmouth, but a secondary road leads off left from the village to Craster and Howick, with access on foot to Dunstanburgh from the former.

A left-hand turn 1½ miles along this minor road leads into **Dunstan** (also reached by continuing straight on and taking the next left), said to have been the birthplace of John Duns Scotus (1265–1308), the celebrated medieval scholar who is more associated nowadays with the town of Duns in Scotland. His birthplace was at **Dunstan Hall**, a 15th-century farmhouse with a red-tiled tower dating from 1420, on the right just before reaching the village.

Less than ½ mile brings us into **Craster** itself, a typical fishing village, noted for its famous kippers which are cured by a secret oak-smoked process. Close to the car park in the disused Craster quarry on the edge of the village is a permanent outdoor exhibition which shows the wildlife, flora and fauna of the region, and there is also a shell museum.

The coastal scenery between Craster and Dunstanburgh (1½ miles north) is most impressive, with the rocks of the Great Whin Sill rising in columns from the sea-bed. From the north end of Craster a path leads along the cliff-line which is one of the most pleasant walks in England. The two little islands off the coast, **Little Carr** and **Muckle Carr**, are both almost covered at high tide, their lighter colour reflecting the limestone formation which changes the nature of the coastline further north in Embleton Bay and contrasts considerably with the darker rocks of the shore which are more dramatic. The footpath is the only means of access to the castle itself.

Dunstanburgh Castle (*open daily, charge*) occupies an extensive and isolated hilltop, some 4·5 ha (11 acres) in area. Although there is not a

Dunstanburgh Castle, the gatehouse keep

great deal left of this once formidable fortress, it is nevertheless a sight to see. When it was first built in the 14th century, it must have been almost impregnable, for at that time the sea came up to the foot of the cliffs, and the tiny harbour, large enough to take Henry VIII's men-of-war later on, was widened into a ditch – some 24m (80ft) wide and 4m (13ft) deep – which ran right round the hill through to Embleton Bay, affording it even greater protection. A drawbridge guarded by a small fort dominated this access, which the footpath from Craster crosses on its way.

The castle was built by Thomas, Earl of Lancaster, who started it in 1313 mainly as a personal refuge. Although an opponent of Edward II, he was made Commander-in-Chief against the Scots in 1315 but did nothing to control their incursions. Edward revolted against this indifference, marched north and defeated Lancaster at the Battle of Boroughbridge in 1322. The castle then became an English stronghold against the Scots, until it came into the possession of John of Gaunt (1340–99) who became the Duke of Lancaster in 1362. He enlarged the castle, blocking up the gatehouse and converting it into a great keep, and placed the main entrance on the north-west side. It is no surprise, therefore, to find that Dunstanburgh became a stronghold for the Lancastrian side in the War of the Roses.

In 1462 it withstood a siege from Margaret of Anjou, Henry VI's Queen. The Earl of Warwick was campaigning heavily at this time against the Lancastrian forces in the north of England and finally defeated her forces at the Battle of Hexham in 1464. Margaret is reported to have fled back to Dunstanburgh or Warkworth before taking ship for the Continent, and both castles claim the privilege of harbouring her.

Much damage was done to the castle at this time from artillery bombardments, and it was never restored again. After Warwick had taken possession, it quickly fell into ruin. It has remained a magnificent one, now under the guardianship of the Department of the Environment, and the surrounding land with some 200 ha (496 acres) of foreshore and dune-land, including the Embleton golf-course, is now part of the National Trust holding. The monumental **Gatehouse-Keep**, one of the finest examples of its kind in England, was the original entrance. It consists of two semicircular towers separated by a vaulted entrance passage.

As an alternative to returning to Craster by the same path the excursion may be continued by crossing the golf-course ahead to Embleton Bay. In about 1 mile a road leads off left from Dunstan Sands to Embleton, or ½ mile further on at the clubhouse an alternative route occurs. Beyond this point another 1¼ miles takes the path into Low Newton-by-the-Sea in the reverse of the route already described on page 68.

South from Craster a cliff path leads in just over 1 mile to **Cullernose Point**, where the rising lines of the upthrusting Whin Sill are clearly seen and where there is some fine coastal scenery and a view of Dunstanburgh Castle. The path leads into Howick ½ mile beyond this point.

Less than ½ mile from Craster by road, taking the left-hand fork (the Alnwick road) on leaving, stands **Craster Tower**. About 90m (100 yards) from the junction a Georgian farmhouse on the left has incorporated into it a medieval turret, built around 1415, and the building has been the home of the Craster family for over 500 years. A left-hand turn 90m (100 yards) beyond this point leads through to the tiny hamlet of **Howick** in 1½ miles. There is a cliff path in both directions from this point, the one northwards past Cullernose Point to Craster, and in a southerly direction past Howick Haven – with fine rocks and some caverns – for the 2½ miles to Boulmer. Half-way along a small stream flows down the valley from Howick Hall into the sea, and just inland – less than ¼ mile – are the remains of a prehistoric settlement.

The road from Howick leads inland past **Howick Hall** (*gardens open April to September, 2–7, charge*) built in 1782, with the later house succeeding the 15th-century tower. It has long associations with the Northumberland family of Grey and was the home of the second Earl Grey, the Prime Minister at the time of the Reform Bill. The house is now the home of Lord Howick of Glendale who married Lady Mary Grey. From the house the road runs through a fine avenue of beech trees for another mile before joining the B1339 1½ miles north of Longhoughton.

Longhoughton nowadays is just a quiet agricultural village. The church, with its low square tower, is worth a visit: the nave, chancel arch and tower arch are all Norman. Its best claim to notoriety, however, comes from the fact that it was once the storehouse for much of the contraband brought ashore at nearby Boulmer. From Longhoughton a direct road runs inland directly to Denwick and then Alnwick, while the B1339 continues south to reach Lesbury in 3 miles on the main road between Alnwick and Alnmouth (A1068). It is also possible to make a circular tour by following the minor road to Boulmer and continuing through to Lesbury by the coast road.

Boulmer, 3 miles north of Alnmouth, used to be a quiet fishing village and was at one time a notorious smuggling centre, but its character has somewhat altered with the building of an RAF station there, and spread along the flat rocky shoreline, it now really extends to two villages.

The coast road from Boulmer leads south past **Seton Point**, and in another mile a left-hand junction goes directly into Alnmouth passing its principal golf-course on the way. Straight on the road leads into Lesbury, where it joins the main road (A1068) to Alnwick.

4 Alnwick and the Vale of Whittingham

Buses To Alnmouth, Bamburgh, Beal (for Holy Island), Berwick-upon-Tweed, Boulmer, Chillingham, Craster (for Dunstanburgh Castle), Embleton, Seahouses, Warkworth, Whittingham and Wooler.

Camping and caravanning Nearest sites Beadnell (9 miles) or Rothbury (12 miles).

Distances Bamburgh, 17 miles; Berwick-upon-Tweed, 30 miles; Coldstream, 32 miles; London, 308 miles; Morpeth, 19 miles; Newcastle upon Tyne, 33 miles; Rothbury, 12 miles; Wooler, 18 miles.

Early closing Wednesday.

Freshwater fishing Salmon and trout in the river Aln. Details from the Tourist Information Office.

Golf *Alnwick Golf-Club*, Swansfield Park (9 holes) and at Alnmouth.

Hotels *Hotspur, White Swan*.

Information office The Shambles (summer only).

Population 7,300.

Special events The ancient Alnwick Fair has been revived and is held for a week at the end of June. On Shrove Tuesday an outsize football match is held on the castle meadows.

Swimming-pools Swansfield Park Road.

Tennis Public courts in Prudhoe Street.

Half-way between Newcastle upon Tyne and Berwick-upon-Tweed **Alnwick** (pronounced locally as 'Annick') is a charming, walled town conveniently set on the river Aln less than 4 miles from the sea. Strategically an important defence position of bygone days against the incursions from the north, it has retained much of its medieval appearance as a fortified town. Not only is it a good centre for touring the Northumberland countryside but it responds to the visitor with its week-long Alnwick Fair, described as the 'Best Costumed Event in Britain', where everyone in the town seems to take part, as well as other special occasions.

Some of these revivals date back to the time when Alnwick, the centre of a prosperous agricultural area, was semi-autonomous with its own courts and rules for the organization of fairs and guilds. Like Berwick the town of Alnwick learnt by bitter experience that it was a long way from London and had to defend itself, and with much effort, shortage of money and labour it took fifty years to erect its own town walls, starting in 1433.

Much of its loyalty has been to the Percies, the Earls and Dukes of

Northumberland, who have made the castle their historic home, but there have been times when dissension reigned and not always have the policies of Northumberland and its traditional leaders agreed with those of the English Crown.

From the time it created its first market in 1291 Alnwick has also been a great commercial centre for its surrounding villages and farms, famous even today for its fishing-tackle industry and its rum, and the fourth largest of all Northumberland towns. On the old coaching route from London to Scotland its ancient inns and public houses have catered extensively for the traveller, and there are still over thirty of them, one in particular – The Nag's Head – dating back to 1598. Set in the vast castle estates on the outskirts of the town lie the ruins of Alnwick Abbey and Hulne Priory, and there are many pleasant walks both through this park and along the riverside.

Around the town

The A1(T) bypasses the town, but a link road joining the A1068 bisects Alnwick from north to south. The road from Rennington and Denwick (B1340) enters from the north-east, while that from Rothbury (B6341) comes in from the south-west. From the south, approaching Bondgate Without, the Denwick road (B1340) bears off to the right, leading to the **Denwick Bridge**, which was designed by John Adam and built in the 18th century when the 1st Duke of Northumberland extended his park and which replaced an earlier ford more to the west. At this junction stands the first monument of note – the **Percy Tenantry Column** – opposite the old railway station. This fluted doric column, 25m (83ft) high, magnificently topped by the Percy lion with tail extended stiffly and with four lions *couchant* at its base, was erected in 1816, it is said by 1,000 grateful tenants as a mark of their respect after the Duke had reduced their rents. However, there are many unkind stories about what actually happened, including the one that the rents had only been reduced after they had been doubled and quadrupled in the first place and even that the Duke had to top up the contributions to get it finished. For this reason it is now generally known as the 'Farmer's Folly'.

Bondgate Without leads through the narrow medieval archway of the **Hotspur Tower,** built by the 2nd Earl of Northumberland in 1443–50 as part of the town fortifications and the only one of the four original gates to have survived. Bondgate Within, now usually referred to as Bondgate, is one of the main streets of Alnwick, leading through to the junction of

Market Street (which in turn becomes the B6341 Rothbury road) and the adjacent market-place, once the scene of bull-baiting. In Bondgate itself is the interesting **Bondgate Gallery** which regularly exhibits the work of living artists.

In one corner of the market-place is the stepped **Market Cross** and the **Town Hall**, the latter built by the corporation of freemen in 1771. The **Northumberland Hall**, fronting the market-place and Market Street, was built in 1826 and presented to the town by the 8th Duke in 1919. The **Shambles** lie below and to the side – not so well known as the one in York – but originally used for the same purpose as a medieval meat market. Just to the left of the square at the foot of Clayport Street is the quaint fountain of **St Michael's Pant**, dating from 1765, the upper part of which depicts St Michael and the Dragon.

From the fountain Fenkle Street leads back to Narrowgate, the continuation of Bondgate. In Narrowgate is the 18th-century **Old Cross Inn**, with its famous collection of dirty bottles in the small bow window. It is said that 150 years ago the innkeeper died while dressing this window, and no one has dared or been allowed to try again. At the bend in Narrowgate Pottergate leads off to the left towards some of the older buildings of the town. At the far end is the **Pottergate Tower**, erected in 1768 and originally with a spire on top. At the end of Narrowgate is the tree-lined and still partly cobbled **Bailiffgate**, where one is immediately confronted by the great barbican guarding the gateway to Alnwick Castle.

Continuing the walk around the town, Bailiffgate leads from the castle entrance to **St Michael's Church** at the junction with Cannongate. The parish church is mainly Perpendicular in style, dating from the 14th century, but is first mentioned as early as 1147. Parts of the nave may date from Norman times, and there is some zigzag work on the west side of the chancel porch obviously out of its original position. The chancel and aisles were completely rebuilt in the 15th century in the time of the 4th Earl, the capitals showing unusual carvings and the floor being paved with old gravestones. At the extreme south-east corner of the aisle is a curious stair turret leading to the chamber of a chantry priest (seen from outside) which was also probably used as a lookout post towards Hefferlaw Pele Tower, 2½ miles north of the town, where a beacon signalled incursions by the Scots. In the vestry is a 14th-century Flemish chest, decorated with carved dragons, a hunting scene and foliage, one of the earliest known to exist in this country.

Continuing along Cannongate, Rattan Row leads off as a left-hand fork along the beech-shaded avenue to **Forest Lodge**, the principal entrance to Hulne Park. On the left, just before the lodge, behind a railed gap in the wall is **William the Lion's Stone**, marking the spot where the Scottish king was captured in 1174 whilst besieging Alnwick Castle. Cannongate itself leads down to **Cannongate Bridge**, crossing the Aln, with another entrance to Hulne Park near the ruins of Alnwick Abbey. The road then continues towards Eglingham and Wooler as the B6346.

On the right in Cannongate is Walkergate, which leads back to the Peth and the Lion Bridge. Half-way along Walkergate on the left stand the remains of **St Mary's Chantry Chapel** with a 14th-century doorway. Turning left at the top of Walkergate and linking up with the Peth leading from Bailiffgate, the river is reached at the **Lion Bridge**, built in 1773, the east side of the parapet surmounted by a leaden lion with the traditional stiff Percy tail. Across the bridge on the north side there is a lay-by for motorists to enjoy the view of the castle. Below the bridge are the pastures, with a footpath following the river bank to the Denwick Bridge downstream, and this is the site of the famous Shrovetide Football Match.

From the Lion Bridge the road runs north about a mile to rejoin the A1(T) at **Malcolm's Cross**, where Malcolm Canmore, King of Scotland (1057–93), was killed along with his eldest son, after invading England in protest against William the Conqueror's attempts to make him a vassal. A cross stood here from early times but was replaced in 1774 by the Duchess of Northumberland in the form of the present monument. Just to the south, before reaching this point, on either side of the road are the remains of **St Leonard's Hospital**, an aisleless chapel with a ruined chancel arch and a small doorway. It was founded between 1193 and 1216 by Eustace de Vesci for the repose of the soul of the foregoing King Malcolm and of his wife St Margaret but fell into decay long before the Restoration.

Alnwick Castle (*open May to September, daily except Friday 1–5, charge*) has been the home of the Percy family since the 14th century and the time of Edward II. With its bold towers, stout encircling walls and the great mass of the keep dominating the steep bank of the river Aln it has served to offer a formidable challenge and defence to any invaders from the north. The construction was started in 1135 by a Norman knight, Ivo de Vesci.

From 1309 onwards Alnwick became the Percy stronghold. From the ransom money received from Scottish prisoners after the Battle of Neville's Cross (near Durham) in 1346 it is said the two tall towers guarding the entrance to the Inner Bailey were built. But it was not until the reign of Richard II, when at his coronation in 1377 he created Sir Henry de Percy the 1st Earl of Northumberland, that the Percies came into their full prominence in their chosen county as prodigious warriors and clever statesmen. This first Earl was the father of Harry Hotspur, a redoubtable, likeable and hot-headed character, hero of the populace, whom Shakespeare shows in *Henry IV* as also being impetuous, impatient and sometimes rash.

The new Earl and his son reconstructed the keep, the postern and the Constable's Tower. Part of their duties was acting as Wardens of the Marches, and their traditional enemies were the Douglases from over the Border.

It is mainly for the Battle of Otterburn in 1388 that the name of Percy is recalled today. Although the Scots won, the Earl of Douglas was killed. Harry Hotspur and his brother Ralph were taken prisoner but subsequently ransomed themselves.

The Percies gained their revenge at the famous Battle of Homildon Hill (near Wooler) in 1402. After the battle the alliance between the Percies and King Henry IV, whom they had helped to secure the throne, broke apart, and the King annoyed them by refusing to ransom Mortimer (Hotspur's brother-in-law), demanding the handing over of all Scottish prisoners and being unwilling to pay them their dues as Wardens of the Northern Marches. The Percies entered into a fantastic scheme to join Edmund Mortimer and his Welsh ally Owain Glyndŵr to divide the kingdom between them. They even made an alliance with their former enemy, the Scots, and marched with them to join the other rebels, but Henry intercepted them at Shrewsbury before they could. Harry Hotspur (1364–1403) was killed, while his uncle the Earl of Worcester and their ally the Earl of Douglas both fell into the king's hands. It was a disastrous turning-point for the family which set them back for many years.

In spite of the loss of his famous son, however, the 1st Earl of Northumberland, who was pardoned by the king within six months, revolted again in 1405, helped this time by the Archbishop of York, the saintly Richard Scrope, who was one of his kinsmen. Reviving his treaty with Mortimer, he rose with the northern lords but was defeated at the Battle of Shipton Moor. The Archbishop was betrayed and executed, but

Northumberland escaped and remained at large until 1408 when he was defeated and killed at the Battle of Bramham Moor, thus ending the danger to the throne from the north for a while. These are the events recounted in *Henry IV* (Part II).

But the plots continued, and in 1415, when Henry V set sail for France, a conspiracy was uncovered at Southampton in which some Northumberland gentlemen were involved and which foreshadowed the later Yorkist claims. It seems fairly certain that Harry Hotspur's son went on this expedition, for a year later we find him restored as the 2nd Earl of Northumberland to his grandfather's estates. In 1440 he added the entrance gateway and the barbican to the castle, from which time onward – externally at least – the buildings appeared much as they do today.

In the War of the Roses the Percies now turned against each other at the Battle of Stamford Bridge in 1453. The Northumberland adherence to the Lancastrian cause continued into the next generation at the Battles of Towton (1461) and Hedgeley Moor (1464). With the accession of the House of York, however, all appears to be forgiven, for during the reign of Edward IV (1461–83) the Percies were restored to the Earldom of Northumberland once more, and in the latter part of the 15th century they shared the supreme judicial authority in the north with the Duke of Gloucester, later to become Richard III. With the entry of Tudor times a measure of peace came to Alnwick.

In the late 16th century the castle at Alnwick began to fall into ruin, for with the cessation of the Border raids it served less purpose as a fortress. Most of the Percies had already made Warkworth Castle their home instead and Alnwick was mainly the defensive fortress. A tragic episode occurred at Alnwick during the Civil War when, after Cromwell's troops had beaten the Scots at the Battle of Dunbar in September 1650, 6,000 prisoners were brought to Alnwick and confined within the bailey. Half of them died from starvation within eight days, with a further 2,000 perishing on their journey from Alnwick to Durham.

Alnwick Castle remained a ruin after this time, and the original Percy line also became extinct when the 11th Earl died in 1670. In 1750, however, the new Earl of Northumberland began restoring the castle using the services of James Paine and Robert Adam. He was made the 1st Duke of Northumberland in 1766, and it is from this source that the present line continues. The 4th Duke (1847–65), much influenced by Italian ideas, decided to sweep away the pseudo-Gothic style of Robert

Adam and carried out a second large restoration in 1854, using the services of Anthony Salvin, with the intention of restoring the outward medieval quality of the castle but making the interior a comfortable residence. Much of Adam's work was removed and a Renaissance style adopted, which converted the castle into the magnificent and stately mansion it is today.

Frequently known as the 'Windsor of the North', Alnwick Castle is now a treasure house of paintings by Titian, Canaletto, Van Dyck and other famous artists, some very fine furniture, Meissen china and many other historical heirlooms. It is the home of the present 10th Duke of Northumberland. Visits are permitted to the **Keep**, the **Armoury**, **Guard Chamber**, **Library** and other principal apartments, which are lavishly decorated in the Italian style, the **Dungeon**, **State Coach** and the **Museum of British and Roman Antiquities**.

Excursions from Alnwick

1) To resorts along the Northumbrian coastline from Alnwick to Berwick see page 51

2) To resorts from Alnmouth to Seaton Sluice see page 87

3) Hulne Park and Priory

This is really the castle estate, comprising some 1,200 ha (3,000 acres) of landscaped park on either side of the river Aln towards the north-west side of the town. Surrounded by a wall 9½ miles long, it was laid out partly by Lancelot 'Capability' Brown. *Normally open to the public on Wednesday afternoons and Sunday*, visitors are at other times admitted only by permit, obtainable from the Estates Office in Alnwick Castle. (*No dogs or cars are permitted.*) Apart from being a quiet place for a walk there are three interesting buildings within its enclosure: Alnwick Abbey, Hulne Priory and the Brislee Tower.

The main entrance is at Forest Lodge, but to reach the abbey there is another entrance just across Cannongate Bridge on the other side of the river. Just inside the park are the remains of the **Gateway of Alnwick**

Abbey, all that is left of the house founded by Premonstratensian Canons (a reformed order of the Augustinians) in 1147, but a plan of the buildings has been marked out on the ground. The gateway is 14th century, with four projecting towers and battlements.

There are a variety of onward paths leading from the abbey ruins towards the remains of **Hulne Priory**, but generally following the river line for just over 2 miles will get you there. A record shows that John de Vesci's father granted the site to the Carmelite Order of White Friars in 1240, and it is the only foundation of this order in the country to remain so well preserved.

Approaching the site, the massive curtain wall is still complete although it has lost its turrets and battlements. Entering by the south-west gate and following the west wall, we come to the **Tower**, added in 1488, which is the best-preserved part of the ruins. Sometimes known as the Lord's Tower, it was built by the 4th Earl as a refuge for the friars against Scottish attacks. To the right of the tower and connected with it by a bridge is the pseudo-Gothic **Summer-house**, erected by the 1st Duke in 1777. It stands on part of the earlier cloisters.

Close by is the **Church**, of very great length (36m, 119ft) compared to its width and like other churches of the order without aisles. The west gable, the south wall and the remains of the north wall are all original, but the east end is post-medieval and the east window is 18th century. The windows in the south wall are in the Early English style with double grooves for glass and wooden frames. There is a representation of a Tau-cross, a pre-Christian symbol based on the Greek letter Tau, in a gravestone set in the floor.

Facing the west door of the church is the wall of the former **Cloisters**, which were originally surrounded by the Vestry, Chapter House, Dormitory and Dining Hall, and some of these on the east side have been preserved. There were also a farm and a granary, which was later converted into a dwelling-house. The remains of fish-ponds can also be seen. The buildings suffered to some extent by the restorations of the 18th century in an attempt to tidy up their appearance.

From the priory one can cross the river by the ornamental iron bridge and walk to **Brislee Tower**, about 1 mile away to the south, joining up with the farm drive which comes into the park from Forest Lodge. This ornate structure 27m (90ft) high, was built by Robert Adam, in the pseudo-Gothic style of 1781, as part of the 1st Duke's restorations to enable him to survey all his estates from south of Alnwick to near the

Scottish border. From the tower ¼ mile to the south is a cave known as the **Nine-Year-Old Hole**, guarding the entrance to which is a stone figure of a hermit placed there in 1765. It lies next to a field once known as Moss-trooper's Field, the picturesque 17th-century name given to Border freebooters and raiders. From either point a return can be made by path to Forest Lodge in a little over 1½ miles, thus completing the circuit of the park.

---

4) To Eglingham, Powburn, Ingram, Linhope Spout and Glanton (approx. 33 miles, with an optional 3-mile walk)

Taking the B6346 road from Alnwick towards Wooler around the northern side of Hulne Park, **Eglingham** is reached in just over 6 miles. Like many Northumberland place-names ending in 'ham' it is pronounced locally as 'jum'. On the left just before the crossroads in the village is the **Church of St Maurice**, much restored but with a Norman chancel arch which has been rebuilt. Turning left at the junction on to the road signposted to Beanley and Powburn, a glimpse is caught of **Eglingham Hall**, an early 18th-century house with some parts from the 16th century and later additions. In 1¼ miles at the fork keep right on to the Beanley road, reached in ½ mile. The road now parallels the Breamish Valley, and 1 mile beyond the hamlet, keep left at the fork to Hedgeley Hall and Powburn. The hall is on the right, and ½ mile beyond it a right-hand turn leads to **Crawley Tower**, a 14th-century tower house, much repaired and restored, and with a later house added on. The road descends the escarpment, joining the main A697 Morpeth–Wooler road at **Powburn**. Turn right into the village and cross the river Breamish. It was at this point that the Roman road, known in medieval times as the Devil's Causeway, also crossed the river, taking an almost direct straight line to Berwick from here on, and some traces of it can be found in the village in the garden of the Plough Inn. Beyond the bridge turn left in ½ mile for Brandon and follow the river line westwards below **Brandon Hill**, where Bronze Age relics have been found. Brandon is reached in 1 mile, and a further 2 miles along the valley leads into **Ingram**, one of the main gateways for access into The Cheviot Hills. There is a National Park information centre here, open between Easter and the end of October, and a mountain rescue post. Ingram is on the edge of the National Park area, and the authority runs a large camping site here also.

St Michael's Church has some vestiges of its early Norman construction but was burnt down by the Scots in the 13th century and later stripped of its lead roof. The tower was rebuilt, and while some of its earlier work has been saved, the present chancel and aisles are Victorian.

Beyond Ingram we plunge into the purer air of the National Park, the road taking on a moorland character. On either side of the valley are some of the hilltop settlements with which this area abounds. In 1½ miles a bridge crosses the river Breamish, and the road leaves the glen and climbs up past **Greenside Hill** (253m, 843ft) to reach the hamlet of **Hartside** in a further 1½ miles. From here on the road is gated, but walkers may continue on to **Linhope Farm** (¾ mile) and on to **Linhope Spout** (a further ¾ mile), one of Northumberland's most attractive waterfalls. The path, on private ground, turns north from Linhope, rounding the slope of **Dunmoor Hill** (558m, 1,860ft), and crosses the bracken slopes and pastureland to the top of the waterfall, splashing down some 17m (56ft) into its pool in the cleft of the valley. Another path from Linhope Farm leads on up the valley of the Breamish past **Shill Moor** (520m, 1,732ft) to **Low Bleakhope**, where the ancient **Salter's Road** from Alnham is joined, continuing into Scotland. From Hartside also a track leads south to **Alnhammoor Ford** on the Breamish, which in turn leads to the farm at Chesters and one of the other major early settlements in this area, before leading on to Alnham.

Just north-east of Linhope, set on a platform below Greenshaw Hill and some 270m (900ft) above sea-level, is one of the major prehistoric sites of the area – **Greaves Ash**. The fortified part consists of double ramparts, joined at intervals by cross-walls, with the foundations of some twenty huts and paddocks clearly visible. Several other similar sites can be found on the opposite side of the valley – at **Megrim's Knowe** and along the ridge of **Hartside Hill**.

As far as Powburn the return to Alnwick reverses the outward direction, but on reaching the village we take the right-hand fork at the far end towards **Glanton** instead of following the A697 southwards. Set 150m (500ft) above sea-level, the village commands good views over both the Breamish and Aln Valleys and is famous for its **World Bird Research Station** (*open June to mid-October, 2–6, charge*).

From Glanton turn left at the crossroads, taking the road to Bolton which very shortly crosses the A697. About 1½ miles along this road the interesting old house of **Shawdon Hall** lies back on the left, dating from 1799 and emulating the style of Robert Adam. At Bolton, reached in another mile, turn right by the church to Bridge End, crossing the river

Aln and almost immediately turn left again around the side of Broome Park. At the T-junction turn left again, and keeping left the road leads through Lemmington and up the escarpment to join the B6341 Rothbury–Alnwick road, from which point it is 3½ miles to Alnwick.

5) Callaly Castle and the Vale of Whittingham (approx. 36 miles, with optional 2-mile walk)

Leaving Alnwick by the B6341 road towards Rothbury, a steady climb leads up to **Aydon Forest** (Alnwick Moor). At the top, some 3 miles from Alnwick and 180m (600ft) above sea-level, the crossroads at **Banktop** are reached, with impressive views northwards to The Cheviot Hills and Ros Castle. A right-hand turn on to an unclassified road signposted Whittingham leads down the Lemmington Bank into the valley of the Edlingham Burn, a tributary of the river Aln. At the foot of the slope a diversion can be made by taking the first road on the left to view **Lemmington Hall** (½ mile away), where there is a 14th-century tower house incorporated into a Georgian house of 1746 and a large memorial column in the grounds. Otherwise, continue on the road towards Whittingham and in 3 miles cross the A697 Morpeth–Wooler road at the Bridge of Aln Hotel, a crossing-point of the Aln also used by the Roman road known as the Devil's Causeway. In just over 1 mile the village of **Whittingham** is reached, set on both sides of the river Aln. Before making a visit here, a short diversion is made towards Callaly by taking the left-hand turning in the village (and before crossing the river) and following this for just over 2 miles. **Callaly** itself is a small village set below the sandstone **Callaly Crag** (275m, 918ft) on which there are traces of an early settlement and a priest's cave, hewn out of the rock by a former chaplain of the castle, probably in the 17th century, as a hiding-place. The valley itself carried the former Roman road linking High Rochester in Redesdale with the Devil's Causeway, which it joins close to Bridge of Aln. At the west end of the village the name Street Way commemorates this, and part of an *agger* can be traced in plantations to the west of these cottages and along the line of their gardens.

Callaly Castle (*open June to September, Saturdays, Sundays and Bank Holidays 2.15–5.30, charge; other days on application*) is one of the most interesting buildings in the county. Before the main house was built there had been an earlier pele tower on the site, probably 13th century, and it was a recognized Border fortress in the early part of the 15th century. Today the house is a gracious home in a beautiful setting, with a range of styles from the classical through Georgian to Victorian. The entrance hall of 1750 is richly decorated in the Italian style, similar to that found at Wallington Hall. There is an interesting collection of paintings and furniture, and the gardens are also a feature.

The road south from Callaly continues to Lorbottle and Thropton, passing Cartington Castle on the way, and thence to Rothbury from which point a return to Alnwick can be made by the B6341 to make a shorter tour. Returning to Whittingham, however, we cross the Aln and take the first turning left to the church. There are still some remains of its original Saxon workmanship, but the church was disastrously restored in 1840 when the upper part of the Saxon tower was replaced by the present pseudo-Gothic structure. At the same time the whole of the Norman north arcade was demolished and replaced by a matching reproduction of the late 13th-century south arcade. The west angles of the pre-Conquest nave, together with the west jamb of the former north arcade, remain, showing the characteristic Saxon quoining with alternating short and long stones which also features in the lower part of the tower.

On the opposite side of the road from the church lies **Whittingham Tower**, a former pele tower, which has been converted into a series of almshouses. The village itself has often been described as a model village and is the scene of the Whittingham Games and Fair (usually in August), a gathering of all the inhabitants of the Vale of Whittingham of which the village is a natural centre. A mile to the south-east of the village several Bronze Age weapons were discovered in 1847 at Thrunton Farm and one – the Whittingham Sword – is now in the Black Gate Museum in Newcastle.

From Whittingham the road westwards beyond the church follows the Aln Valley into the Vale of Whittingham, as this upper part is known. In 1½ miles a right-hand turn leads down to the river line and follows it through the estate of **Eslington Hall**, a fine old stone mansion of the early 18th century. At the T-junction turn right across the stream, heading for The Cheviot Hills. Cross the Mere Burn and keep left at the next fork, heading for Great Ryle. A footpath ¼ mile past this hamlet climbs up towards the long ridge of **Cochrane Pike** (329m, 1,096ft). On a good day **Long Crag** (314m, 1,048ft) and **Shirlaw Pike** (303m, 1,010ft) 6 and 10 miles respectively to the south-east, can easily be picked out.

For walkers the climb may be extended by following the path until it joins the main one coming up from Prenderwick, less than 1 mile from the start, where there is a choice of route. To the right a main path leads down the valley of the Fawdon Dean Burn to Ingram in just over 2 miles, skirting the edge of the National Park area. Alternatively, a walk can be made across **Alnhammoor** by keeping straight on in a north-westerly direction for 2 miles to the farm at **Chesters**, where there is a good example of a late prehistoric settlement on the edge of the Breamish Valley. The path continues to the Alnhammoor Ford and joins up with the road from Ingram to Linhope. On the way there are fine views to **Comb Fell** (640m, 2,132ft), **Shill Moor** (520m, 1,732ft), **Hedgehope** (704m, 2,348ft) and **Dunmoor Hill** (558m, 1,860ft) away to the north-west.

The road continues through the hamlet of Predwick, skirting the slopes of The Cheviot Hills and in 2 miles reaches **Alnham**, usually pronounced locally as 'Yelnham'. This is the source-point of the river Aln which rises just behind the village, and in former days the village was an important meeting-place for the many tracks and drovers' roads which led over The Cheviot Hills from Scotland.

A lane leads off to the small but well-restored **St Michael's Church**, which has some late Norman features. Opposite the church lie the few grassy mounds which are all that is left of **Alnham Castle**, which existed in 1415 but was destroyed in the early 16th century. Also close to the church is the former vicarage, dating from 1541, which is now a youth hostel and which incorporates a vicar's pele tower with a barrel-vaulted basement. A track leads off westwards at the end of this road into the hills, and ¾ mile away is the hill-fort of **Castle Hill**, relatively small in area but a typically contoured oval-shaped fort with triple banks and ditches, probably originating in the late Iron Age period a few centuries BC. There is another similar fort 1¼ miles up the valley at a point below **High Knowes** (388m, 1,292ft) and two earlier village sites in Alnham itself.

South-west from Alnham the road continues in 1 mile to the farmstead-hamlet of Scrainwood and on to Elilaw, rounding the slopes of **Ewe Hill** (238m, 793ft), to reach **Biddlestone** in 3 miles from Alnham, so named from the medieval Biddle Stones located along the driveway of **Biddlestone Hall**. The hall itself, which has now been demolished, is said to have replaced the pre-1796 building which Sir Walter Scott called Osbaldistone Hall in *Rob Roy*. Biddlestone lies under the lee of **Cold Law** (387m, 1,289ft) in which there are quarries working the hard red granite so favoured in road-making. From Biddlestone an unclassified road follows the Netherton Burn to Netherton and on to Thropton and

Rothbury, joining the B6341 road at Flotterton *en route*, and from Rothbury this road continues back to Alnwick.

If a longer excursion is required, from Biddlestone the road continues on to Alwinton, from which point a return can be made to Rothbury by way of Harbottle, Holystone and Hepple, thence onwards to Alnwick. (*See also the excursion to Harbottle and Upper Coquetdale under Rothbury.*)

5 The coastline from Alnwick and Alnmouth to Seaton Sluice

From Alnwick, following the A1068 eastwards along the river line, a run of 5 miles leads into **Lesbury**. The B1339 leads off left towards Long-houghton and the northern coastline and forms the main street of the town, with St Mary's Church set off it. A side-road from Lesbury also leads through to the Alnmouth Golf-Club at Foxton and circles back to Alnmouth itself.

There is a fine bridge over the Aln here, and crossing it, in $\frac{1}{2}$ mile, the B1338 branches off to the left, leading into **Alnmouth** over the river estuary in less than 1 mile. The town was formerly the port of Alnwick, with the river navigable up to Lesbury Bridge. The corn trade reached its peak here in the 18th century, the grain being stored in large granaries, distinguishable by their height and small windows, which have long since been converted into private houses. Alnmouth makes an attractive holi-day resort, with one hotel and several guest-houses, and is also a sailing centre with good sands both north and south of the estuary, sheltered by long dunes. It boasts two golf-courses, one at the village club and the championship course at Foxton, 1 mile to the north, founded in 1869.

To all except Northumbrians Alnmouth's name is unpronounceable, and attempts to reproduce it range from 'Yelnmouth' to 'Alunmouth' in clipped, indecipherable tones. From the north Alnmouth appears to be on an island, full of red roofs and solid, grey-stone houses built to withstand the inevitable winter gales from the north-east. It was one of these – appropriately enough on Christmas Day, 1806 – that changed the river's course, the sea breaking through the north-east bank of the river and turning its course around the north side of Church Hill, where previously it had flowed round the south. At the same time the Church of St Waleric, Norman on Saxon foundations, which had been a ruin since 1738, was also finished off by the gale, and only traces of the foundations remain. In 1789 a Saxon cross was unearthed on this site. A new church

Alnmouth

was built in the town and opened in 1876. Alnmouth claims to have been the scene of the Synod in 684 when St Cuthbert was unanimously elected Bishop of Lindisfarne.

In the 18th century Alnmouth was sometimes disturbed by several offshore naval encounters during the war with France. Three years after American independence, in 1779, an American ship, the *Ranger*, fired one cannonball at the church which missed and bounced into a farm-house. The attacker was commanded by the notorious freebooter John Paul Jones, a former pirate-turned-naval officer in his country's service and allied with the French.

A good spot for both sea and river fishing, a passenger ferry operates across the Aln estuary giving easy access to the beaches on the southern side. It is quite possible to walk along the sands southwards at low tide, past a group of rocks known as the **Birling Carrs**, and continue the 3 miles to Warkworth. Alternatively, a footpath also runs just inland, passing **Northfield** and emerging on to the Warkworth golf-course, and thence into the village.

From the junction of the B1338 the A1068 leads southwards the 3½ miles to **Warkworth**, lying near the coast some 7 miles from Alnwick. The main road crosses the river by an imposing modern bridge, but close to it is the 14th-century one, of two bold arches, with the remains of a fortified gatehouse at the southern end. It bears the Percy arms and is now used by pedestrians only. Bridge Street then leads into the market-place. In the nearby Mason's Arms an inscription commemorates the fact that the Jacobite rebels of 1715, led by the Earl of Derwentwater, stayed here in October of that year.

At the north end of the market-place lies **St Laurence's Church**. Though perhaps less impressive externally, it rivals those of Alnwick and Bamburgh in the beauty and interest of its interior and is one of the few fairly complete Norman ones in Northumberland. It is reputedly based on a Saxon foundation of the 8th century, built by King Ceolwulf of Northumbria who was a devout Christian and later gave up his throne to retire into the monastery at Lindisfarne. The present church was built in the early part of the 12th century by Richard de Aurival, chaplain to Henry I, consisting only of nave and chancel. The three lower stages of the tower were added in the 13th century, and a century later it was heightened by the addition of a rare stone spire.

The nave, 27m (90ft), is one of the longest in Northumberland. At the west end is the remarkable effigy of a cross-legged knight, dating from about 1330. Several fragments of medieval glass, one showing the figure of St Hilda, Abbess of Whitby, are in the east window.

When William the Lion invaded Northumbria in 1174, the church was the scene of a dreadful massacre by the Scots, most of the villagers being put to death. Like Alnmouth, Warkworth is tightly packed on to a small peninsula which it shares with the predominant mass of the castle. Close to the mouth of the Coquet there is a golf-course and a sandy beach about 1 mile away. The river provides possibilities for fishing and boating. The grey-stone houses are mainly 18th and 19th century in character, and there are several guest-houses. From the market-place Castle Street, the main street of the village, climbs up to the castle.

Warkworth Castle (_open daily, Sundays—afternoons only, October–March, charge_) enjoys a carefully sited position on the last of the numerous bends of the river Coquet. The original Norman motte-and-bailey construction was erected by Robert de Mowbray, Earl of Northumberland and guardian of the Northern Marches under William II (Rufus), in the early part of the 11th century. The castle was further

Warkworth Castle

strengthened by Henry, the son of King David of Scotland, in 1139. He built the outer wall around the existing bailey and the hall on the east side. At the end of the 12th century Robert Fitz-Roger added the gatehouse and the Carrickfergus Tower. After the expeditions led by the three Edwards against Scotland, the castle came into the possession of Edward III, who bestowed or sold it in 1331 to the Percies whose property it then remained. About 1400 the impressive keep was added, the chapel was built and a new front made for the hall. Between 1480 and 1489 the hall porch was heightened into what is now known as the Lion

Tower. The Percies maintained Warkworth as their home, with their fortress at Alnwick, until the 17th century, but when the family returned to Northumberland in 1750, the choice was reversed. Alnwick became the main home, although some rooms are still maintained at Warkworth for their use. No great effort has been made to restore this castle, therefore, and it is now in the care of the Department of the Environment.

Below the castle in the steep-sided river valley there is a pathway along the 'Butts' which leads upstream 1 mile to the **Hermitage**. Alternatively, boat trips are offered in the season, and you can also row yourself. Cut out of the solid sandstone rock is the **Chapel**, which has a vaulted ceiling. Next comes the **Sacristy**, with a shield over the door bearing the emblems of the Passion. Reached from the sacristy is the **Solar**, which is also open to the west. It was in use until the end of the 16th century and is now cared for by the Department of the Environment. From Warkworth the A1068 follows the river estuary the mile to Amble along the south bank.

Amble is a coal-exporting port 25 miles north of the Tyne, set at the northern end of the Northumberland coalfield. From here, the coal seams radiate south and south-eastwards to form a huge triangle down to the rivers Tyne and Tees, and although coal has been worked in Northumberland since the 13th century, most of the developments took place in the 19th century after the railways had provided the necessary transport. Now, by contrast, with modernization and amalgamation, some former mines have been closed or worked out. At Amble the seams run so close to the sea that in winter gales they are sometimes unearthed and sprinkled gratuitously along the shoreline for collection by grateful inhabitants. Nevertheless, some attempt has been made to cultivate the town into both an industrial area and a holiday resort, and there is a sandy beach with good bathing. It is also a centre for sailing and fishing.

A mile offshore lies **Coquet Island**, known as 'Cocwaedae' in Saxon times when a monastic foundation was established there. Apart from being a haunt of eider ducks the island has been notorious as a ship's graveyard. A Benedictine monastery also existed there from the 12th century but is now in fragments and has been replaced by a lighthouse.

From Amble the A1068 runs southwards to **Togston** in 2 miles, but there is also a coastal path which runs along the length of **Druridge Bay** through Hauxley to Druridge and Cresswell, subject only to the exigencies of the Danger Area by Hadston Carrs, where there is a Ministry of

Defence range, with warning notices. In $3\frac{1}{2}$ miles the road reaches **Widdrington**, with a side-road leading through to **Druridge** and on to **Cresswell** where there is a 14th-century fortified tower and the remains of Cresswell Hall. The next village, reached in a further $2\frac{1}{2}$ miles, is **Ellington**, the home of Ellington Colliery which shares with adjacent Lynemouth the largest undersea coalmine in the world, and one of the most modern and efficient. A side-road leads off from Ellington to Cresswell at the southern end of Druridge Bay, then follows the coastline 2 miles into Lynemouth itself. There is also a direct road to Lynemouth from Ellington, which continues on to Newbiggin-by-the-Sea. **Lynemouth** is largely industrialized with a power station and a huge aluminium works. It stands at the outlet of the small river Lyne and has some sands, with a footpath across the golf-links to Newbiggin-by-the-Sea. In the cliffs near Lynemouth the winter gales sometimes expose the stumps of fossilized trees from the primeval forest which went into the making of the coalfields.

The A1068 leads on in $2\frac{1}{2}$ miles to **Ashington**, which with its close neighbours Bedlington and Newbiggin-by-the-Sea forms the District of Wansbeck between the rivers Wansbeck and Blyth. Ashington is a large town with a population of 26,000, and much has been done in this area to relieve the former 'mining area' look. Less than 4 miles from Morpeth and 15 miles from Newcastle itself Ashington has made some real attempts to attract visitors to the area with the award-winning creation of the **Wansbeck Riverside Park**. Set along a 2-mile stretch of the only beck in the county, there are facilities for caravans and campers on riverside sites, fishing and walking, picnic sites and sailing and boating. In the centre of Ashington itself there is also a leisure centre. What was once the largest mining village in the country has now given way to a large shopping complex, swimming-baths, squash-courts and every kind of modern facility.

Less than 3 miles away, reached by either the A197 or B1334 from Ashington, is the fishing village and holiday resort of **Newbiggin-by-the-Sea**. The coastline is rocky with a sandy beach, and there are excellent views from Newbiggin Point. In spite of some minor pollution worthwhile attempts have been made to maintain Newbiggin's status as a holiday resort: there is a promenade, golf-course and a caravan site and a paddling-pool, tennis and bowls in Milburn Park. There is plenty of fishing and sailing, and a sports centre with squash courts. Close to the sea is **St Bartholomew's Church**, externally less interesting than the interior which is mainly 13th century. Like Warkworth it has one of those rare 14th-century Northumberland spires. There are several medieval tombstones in the north wall.

Between Ashington and Newbiggin on the A197 road is the famous **Woodhorn Church**, (*open from Tuesday to Saturday 10–12 and 1–4*), reputed to be the oldest in Northumberland. It is reached by circling around the northern side of Newbiggin less than 1 mile from the sea. Originally the Saxon building consisted of a chancel, an aisleless nave and a tower, and remains of the traditional alternations of long and short stones can be seen in the base of the tower. Just above this is the line that shows the original roof line. Norman and Early English features were added later. An extensive restoration was carried out in the early 19th century, and further repairs were carried out between 1974 and 1975, when the church was taken over by the Wansbeck District Council for use as a museum and cultural centre.

Within the church the most interesting relic of all is a 13th-century effigy of Agnes de Valence, wife of Hugh Baliol, who was the brother of that short-lived Scottish monarch, Edward Baliol. This sculpture has been described as one of the best specimens of monumental sculpture of its period in Northumbria. Two fine medieval bells also form part of the collection of historical relics, along with other memorials and stained-glass windows.

From Ashington the A1068 reaches **Bedlington** in under 4 miles, the third main centre of the Wansbeck District and the former capital of Bedlingtonshire when it formed part of the County Palatine of Durham until 1884. It is a typical, yet famous, mining village, where every June the Miner's Gala or Picnic takes place in Attlee Park. This is the great annual gathering of the miners and their leaders, with brass bands, beauty contests, jazz-band contests and other colourful events, attracting a large crowd which includes many politicians.

One of the main centres of the coalfields, Bedlington also once produced iron and rolled the first rails for George Stephenson's new railway. It is also famous for its Bedlington terriers, originally bred for badger-baiting. The main street of the town – the broad Front Street – leads down to the river Blyth, and so varied are the styles in some of the older buildings in this street that it has now been designated as a conservation area. There is also a market cross in the form of an obelisk. The principal **Church of St Cuthbert** is pre-Conquest in origin, but little if anything remains of the early church, apart from the late Norman chancel arch, and most is now 19th-century and later restoration. To the south of the town there is an eighteen-hole championship golf-course with a modern clubhouse.

The A193 road leads off from Bedlington to reach **Blyth** in 4 miles, a small town on the south side of the river Blyth estuary. Apart from its colleries it is also a major shipbuilding area and coal-exporting port which passed its peak a century ago. Now Blyth attracts other industries to replace the closing pits and tries to turn itself into something of a seaside resort as well, for there is a beach, a golf-course and a camping and caravan site, run by the local corporation at the south end of the town, and sailing is also popular here. The town spreads over both sides of the river, using two passenger ferries, to reach **North Blyth**, its main suburb. The old town of Blyth centres about Northumberland Street, where an old 18th-century lighthouse now stands well inland behind a terrace of houses.

Three miles south of Blyth is **Seaton Sluice**, now the most southerly coastal point in Northumberland. Seaton Sluice, once the haven of artists and very picturesque, has been given a face-lift in recent years with many new houses, but its original cottages, with their red roofs, and the **Octagon** (perhaps designed by Vanbrugh) remain. The early harbour was created by Sir Ralph Delaval in 1628 to provide a way out to sea for the Seaton Burn through the tidal sand, but this was improved by the cut through the solid rock made in the 1750s. The charming little harbour was a thriving port for nearly two centuries and regularly exported coal. Its history is very much tied up with that of the Delaval family (see below).

A mile inland, reached by the A190 from the north side of the Seaton Burn, is **Seaton Delaval Hall** (*open May to September, Wednesdays, Sundays and Bank Holidays 2–6*). One of the showpieces of Northumbria and a masterpiece of John Vanbrugh, Seaton Delaval stands as a fitting memorial to his talent. Admiral George Delaval, whose family claimed a direct line of descent from William the Conqueror, gave him the commission in 1720 without, it seems, any limitations on expense. It took ten years to build and became not only his own memorial but also that of his patron, for they both died before it was finished, the Admiral from a fall on a horse. Built in the Palladian style with a central block and huge Tuscan columns with a portico above, the building has long projecting wings on either side, one of which houses the stables. The house was unfortunately damaged by fire in 1725 and again in 1882, and fell into a

Seaton Delaval Hall

derelict condition for many years. Restorations began some twenty-five years ago when the present owner, Lord Hastings, married a descendant of the 'Gay' Delavals, as they had become known, after the male line had ceased. Visitors are admitted to the inhabited west wing which contains fine furniture, portraits and ceramics, the centre block with its statuary and historical records, and also the gardens and stables. In the grounds close to the house is a tiny 14th-century church, originally the family chapel but used as a parish church since 1891. It was first consecrated in 1102 and retains the Norman chancel and the original west door. There are memorials to the family inside and two 13th-century effigies of a knight and his lady. To the east of the house are an orangery and a mausoleum. Medieval banquets are now a feature of the Hall's activities and are held nightly in the west wing.

(*For continuation of the coastline from Seaton Sluice to Tynemouth see under Tyne and Wear.*)

6 Rothbury, Coquet Dale and The Cheviot Hills

Buses To Alnwick, Alwinton, Harbottle, Newcastle upon Tyne and Thropton.
Caravanning Coquet Dale Caravan Park, Whitton, on south side of river.
Distances Alnwick, 12 miles; Alwinton, 10 miles; Berwick-upon-Tweed, 41 miles; London, 304 miles; Morpeth, 15 miles; Newcastle upon Tyne, 30 miles; Otterburn, 15 miles; Wooler, 20 miles.
Early closing Wednesday.
Freshwater fishing Salmon and trout in the river Coquet. Information from the Tourist Information Centre.
Golf At Whitton, on the south side of the river.
Hotels *Coquet Vale, Queen's Head.*
Information centre Tourist Information Centre at United Travel Office, High Street; National Park Information Centre, Church House, Church Street.
Population 1,818.

Rothbury, the capital of Coquet Dale, lies in a most picturesque setting on the river Coquet and is an ideal centre for walking, touring and fishing holidays. Above all it is in easy reach of both The Cheviot Hills and the Northumberland National Park. It faces the heathery slopes of the Simonside Hills to the south, while to the east the dale narrows down to the densely wooded heights of Cragside, the estate of Lord Armstrong. The town is therefore set in a natural gap where the river Coquet forces its way through the sandstone fells by means of a narrow ravine known as the 'Thrum', with the Rothbury Forest area running north and south of it.

The town is one of the busiest market towns in the county and in summer attracts a high number of visitors. In 1205 the manor of Rothbury was granted to Robert Fitz-Roger, who was the Baron of Warkworth at that time, and like that establishment it passed into the hands of the Percies in the time of Edward II. The proclamation of James III was also read here in the Jacobite rising of 1715.

The town, on a steep sloping green on the north bank of the river, is geared for tourists with its boarding-houses and antique and gift shops. From the foot of the green, on the south side, Church Street leads through to **All Saint's Church**, the greater part of which was restored in

1850. Of the original 13th-century church only the chancel, its arch and the east wall of the south transept remain. The outstanding feature is the font pedestal, a section of the renowned **Rothbury Cross** discovered when the nave was rebuilt, which is topped by a bowl dating from 1664. It is undoubtedly one of the finest surviving examples of early Saxon Christian carving in the country and is dated to about AD 800. The most interesting of the two broader faces depicts an Ascension scene. On the other broad face there is a typical Saxon close-meshed 'basket-weave' or 'endless knot' design much favoured in this period. Both the narrow faces reflect on the nature of man before and after the Fall, one showing a feature of other early Northumbrian crosses – the vine scroll with animals and birds feeding on it, while the other, with its representations of writhing serpents devouring helpless quadrupeds and a naked figure struggling in their coils, would appear to show the state of Hell. Parts of the head of this cross are now in the Black Gate Museum in Newcastle.

Excursions from Rothbury

1) Summerville and Allerdere

Rothbury is a good walking centre, and there are many pleasant strolls in the neighbourhood. A mile to the west of the town a track leads down to **Lady's Bridge** and across the river Coquet towards **Summerville**, whence it is possible to circle round along the road towards **Allerdere**, the site of a former medieval hospital run by the Hospitallers of St John. Just before the hamlet is reached a footpath leads back to the river and over the bridge to **Thropton**, 2 miles west of Rothbury on the B6341.

2) Rothbury Terraces

Either from Thropton or Rothbury a walk can be made along the **Rothbury Terraces**, so called because of the parallel effect produced on the sandstone from glacial action. There are several prehistoric forts and early settlements along this north side of the valley. One of the most important of these forts is **Old Rothbury**, half-way between Thropton and Rothbury, defended by a double ditch and ramparts and outworks on the south and east sides. There is another ½ mile to the west of this camp on **West Hill**, again with circular ramparts and ditches.

3) Cartington Castle

From the eastern end of the Rothbury Terraces, close to **Debdon Lake**, there is a footpath which leads in just over 2 miles to the ruins of **Cartington Castle**, which was founded in 1441 and built on to an earlier pele tower. It is possible to reach it by road from Thropton, taking the Lorbottle–Whittingham road for 2 miles.

4) Great Tosson

Across the river from Rothbury is **Whitton**, where the former rectory incorporates a 14th-century pele tower. A side-road turns right after the bridge, off the B6342, leading past this and also the caravan site and continues on to **Newton** and **Great Tosson** (which also has a pele tower) in less than 2 miles. Both are small hamlets at the foot of the Simonside Hills, and from Great Tosson it is possible to climb to the top of the ridge, some 224m (748ft) above sea-level, where there are the remains of a late prehistoric encampment known as **Tosson Burgh**.

There are several other tracks leading along the top of this ridge. **Simonside** (422m, 1,407ft), a peak which in fine weather gives a view over the whole Northumberland coastline, lies 1¼ miles to the south. Slightly south-west of this and again at a distance of 1¼ miles is **Ravens Heugh** (415m, 1,384ft), and ½ mile beyond this in the same direction is **Tosson Hill** (433m, 1,444ft), the highest peak in the Simonsides. This is a popular area with climbers.

On the east side of the ridge at **Lordenshaw**, which can also be reached in under 3 miles by following the B6342 through Whitton, a path leads up to one of the major prehistoric sites in the area on the ridge overlooking **Garleigh Moor**. This is the hill-fort of Lordenshaw (264m, 879ft), oval in plan and like Tosson Burgh relatively small. Inside a number of circular hut formations can be seen, with some later medieval additions in the inner ramparts. There are some groups of Bronze Age cup-and-ring-marked rocks on the site, and several cairns in the neighbourhood. Several forestry tracks lead through from this point to **Chantners** and the **Fallowlees Burn**, with the **Fontburn Reservoir**, and parts of the hills and forest area fall within the boundaries of the Northumberland National Park area. Some of the hills, especially Great Tosson, are marked with the deep ruts from former cattle trails along the drovers' roads. In addition there is a great deal of forestry plantation in the area.

5) The Thrum

About ½ mile downstream from the four-arched bridge that spans the river Coquet is **Thrum Mill**, just below which the river forces its way through the narrow strip similar to the one at Bolton Abbey in Wharfedale. The chasm is about 54m (180ft) long and about 1·5m (5ft) wide.

6) Cragside

Just to the north of Thrum Mill, at the east end of the town, are the grounds of **Cragside** (*Grounds open 1st April to end September, daily 10–6, October, Saturdays and Sundays 2–5. House open 1st April to end September, daily except Monday, open Bank Holiday Mondays – then closed Tuesdays, 1–6, October, Saturdays and Sundays 2–5*).

This mansion, founded in 1870 and built as the home of the 1st Lord Armstrong (1810–1900), combines elements of mock Tudor with cupolas and Norman archways in a decided hotchpotch of styles. The grounds are a fine blend of woodland and formal garden with views of the house, over Rothbury and Coquet Dale to the Simonsides. The complete walking circuit amounts to about 7½ miles, but cars are allowed within the grounds.

7) Brinkburn Priory

Set in a loop of the river Coquet, 5 miles east of Rothbury, are the remains of Northumberland's best Gothic church. Following the B6344 Morpeth road along the valley through **Pauperhaugh**, the entrance is 1 mile beyond this latter village.

Brinkburn Priory was founded by William Bertram, 1st Baron Mitford, in 1135. After the dissolution of the monasteries, it passed into secular hands with religious services continuing for a while. By 1858 it was completely roofless, and the south-west angle of the nave had also collapsed. The remainder of the building, however, was still in a fair state of preservation, and in that year an extremely skilful restoration was begun by Thomas Austin of Durham. There is little doubt he succeeded well: the church of St Peter and St Paul stands today as a restored and almost perfect specimen of Norman transitional architecture. Some of the original medieval fittings are still to be seen, including a double piscina and the altar stone with its five consecration crosses. The church is now used on occasions for organ recitals.

99

Externally the superb north-west doorway is perhaps the most satisfying feature of the whole building, with its horizontal chevron moulding, dog-tooth ornament and row of beak-heads on the inner arch. No other part of the priory has survived, and undoubtedly its stones were used to build the adjoining house, which is part Georgian and part 19th century. Just to the east of the church is a ruined water-mill.

8) Elsdon, Grasslees Valley and Wallington Hall (approx. 34½ miles)

The first 10 miles of this route, crossing from the valley of the Coquet to that of the Rede, passes through some of the most isolated country in Northumberland. Leave Rothbury by the B6341 road west through **Thropton**, which is reached in 2 miles. Thropton is divided by the Wreigh Burn and has a foot-bridge over the river Coquet. The road northwards out of the village leads to Cartington Castle (2 miles) and on to Lorbottle and Whittingham. A left-hand fork from this leads through to Netherton and Alwinton. In the village is **Thropton Tower**, an early 15th-century fortified house, and there is also an attractive 18th-century inn. The church, relatively modern, is noted for its screen of three arches with pendants, separating the chancel from the nave.

At **Flotterton**, 2½ miles further up the valley, the road bears left towards **Hepple**, 2 miles away, where there are the ruins of a 14th-century pele tower. After crossing the river Coquet, we enter the National Park area with **Harehaugh Hill** (176m, 587ft) ahead and slightly right. The road bends right, then reaches the junction which turns right to Holystone following the river Coquet. Ignoring this, we continue on the B6341 into the glen of the **Grasslees Burn**, the entrance to which is guarded by the ancient fort on top of Harehaugh Hill. On the opposite hillsides are the remains of the prehistoric fort of **Witchy Neuk**, where Romano-British finds from the 3rd century AD have been made. The road passes several stone-built farms, old mines (for this also was a coal area) and the ruins of the 18th-century **Grasslees Mill**. At **Bilsmoorfoot**, 3 miles along the valley, there are the remains of an old deer park with a 7-mile wall around it. There is a camping and caravan site here now. A mile up a track northwards leads to **High Shaw**, where there are several ruined pele towers guarding the approaches from the north. The road begins to climb and, reaching a height of almost 270m (900ft) above sea-level, drops down into the valley of the **Elsdon Burn** and on to the Norman capital of Redesdale at Elsdon in 3 miles.

Elsdon, like Otterburn and Harbottle, is set in a strategic position. Tucked into the side of The Cheviot Hills, it guarded the two main routes which crossed the Border from Scotland and descended into Redesdale – the long valley of the river Rede running south from the Border to join the North Tyne near Bellingham. One of these was the line now followed by the A68 road to Carter Bar, and the other followed the line of the old Roman road Dere Street from High Rochester through to Chew Green. From early times Redesdale has been an area of small population, and it is not surprising to find that it was regarded as an area of lawlessness, where justice and administration, together with defence, were left in a semi-autonomous state. In Norman times the two main areas grew into the Liberties of Redesdale and Tynedale, with much confusion over the actual ownership of these Border provinces. At the end of the 12th century Tynedale belonged to Scotland and Redesdale to England, and it was not until the time of Edward I, when he declared war on Scotland in 1296, that both provinces came under the English Crown. The fixture was seldom permanent, however, for when Robert the Bruce crossed the Border in 1314, Tynedale immediately acknowledged him, and much of the lawlessness which pervaded the area grew out of the almost continuous Border warfare which went on from the 14th to 16th centuries. The number of fortifications on both sides of the Border greatly increased during this time, with the many pele towers dotted close to farms and churches to give some form of protection.

At the northern end of Elsdon are two curious **Mote Hills**, said to have been used by both the Romans and the Saxons as a place for dispensing justice, but although the name might come from the 'moot' or meeting-place of the Saxons, it is more likely to be derived from the 'motte' of the Normans. Certainly, there was a Norman castle here from about 1080 which the two mounds now cover, the southern circular one being the main defence work, while the other formed the outer bailey. From about this time until the early 14th century the de Umfraville family were Lords of Redesdale, but some time between 1160 and 1174 the main defence work was shifted to Harbottle, and a castle built there as well. In 1287 Edward I granted a charter for a weekly market at Elsdon, and by 1297 Gilbert de Umfraville was exacting market tolls in both Elsdon and Harbottle and taking a 'crossing tax' from Scots who came over the Border.

Elsdon's principal feature is its large village green, used as both a meeting-place for the Redesdale clans and as a cattle-holding area, and a circular pinfold or cattle-pound for strays exists in the southern corner. In former times the practice for farmers was to build little huts in the high mountain pastures in summer and stay up there with their cattle and sheep. This was known as 'schealing', and the places where the shepherds lived were known as 'shiels', which has given rise to many place names both north and south of the Border. Elsdon was also on the cattle drovers' road from Scotland and would have made a convenient stopping-point *en route* for the collection of various dues and taxes. Elsdon's position as the capital of Redesdale remained long after the defence had passed to Harbottle, but by the end of the 18th century the distinction had passed to Otterburn where it now remains. On the green stands **St Cuthbert's Church**, named so it is said as one of the many resting-places of St Cuthbert's body on its varied travels after the monks' flight from Lindisfarne. Mainly 14th century, with a characteristic bell turret of the 17th century, there are two pilasters in the west gable of an earlier Norman building. The aisles of the nave and transepts are exceptionally narrow and have half-barrel-vaulted ceilings extending directly from the outside walls above the arcades. Against the west pier of the north arcade stands a Roman tombstone tablet which was found at nearby High Rochester. In 1810 a mass grave was found against the north wall of the church and was presumed to be the resting place of English soldiers who died at the Battle of Otterburn in 1388.

To the north of the church is a fine example of a fortified tower house, formerly used as the vicarage and dating from around 1400. It is a very handsome building with a spiral staircase leading to the battlement roof. In more recent years Elsdon has revived stone-quarrying in the sandstone fells and coalmining as part of its daily activities.

From Elsdon the B6341 continues west for a further 2 miles, joining the A696(T) Newcastle–Otterburn road 1 mile south of Otterburn. For the continuation to Wallington the route turns south out of Elsdon by an unclassified road leading to Steng Cross and crosses the Elsdon Burn and Bridge before climbing steeply up the escarpment to the moorlands of Harwood Forest and the Ottercops Moss. This is the line of the old drovers' road which for the 2 miles to Steng Cross marks the boundary of the National Park area on the left. At **Steng Cross**, at a height of 312m (1,040ft) above sea-level, there are extensive views in all directions as we cross the stark scenery of the **Ottercops Moss**. Here a medieval socket-stone shows where some guiding cross once stood. Nowadays, interest in the site is more centred on the **Winter's Gibbet** where William Winter

Wallington, near Cambo, the central hall

was suspended in chains after his hanging in Newcastle in 1791 for the murder of an old lady in the neighbourhood. There is another wayside cross – the **Manside Cross** – 1½ miles to the south close to which is an impressive earthwork known as **Manside Camp**, which can be reached by a forest road further south, opposite Harewood Head.

The road continues dead-straight for a further 3½ miles, crossing the **Harwood Burn** and passing the old smithy where drove cattle were shod, before reaching the junction at **Gallows Corner**. At this point the B6342 road is joined, turning right for Cambo, which after crossing the Hart Burn is reached in another 2½ miles. **Cambo** was built in 1740 as a model village associated with the Wallington estate and consists mainly of rows of cottages in terraces, with its 19th-century church on top of the hill.

Wallington Hall (*open April to end of September, Mondays, Wednesdays, Thursdays, Saturdays and Sundays 2–6; October, Sundays 2–5*) lies 1 mile to the south. (*Gardens open April to end of September, weekdays 10–6, weekends and Bank Holidays 10–7; October, Saturdays and Sundays 10–5.*) The woodlands are always open. Set in the valley of the river

Wansbeck, the hall is now the largest property owned by the National Trust. The elegant sandstone house was built in 1688 by Sir William Blackett, a Newcastle merchant, on the site of an earlier one owned by the Fenwicks, and then practically rebuilt by his grandson in the 1740s. Much of the interior decoration was carried out by Italian experts, but English woodcarvers added to the adornment. The property passed to the Trevelyans in 1777, and the house has been associated with two famous historians, G. M. Trevelyan and Macaulay. In the mid-19th century the central hall was added by covering the courtyard and decorated by Ruskin and William Bell Scott, the Northumbrian artist, who also painted a number of huge, coloured murals depicting some outstanding episodes in Northumbrian history. There is also a collection of porcelain, needlework and interesting books.

The gardens were partly laid out by Lancelot 'Capability' Brown, who was born at nearby Kirkharle in 1716 and went to school in Cambo before embarking on his career. One of the famous sights at Wallington is the collection of four mythical beasts' heads which decorate the edge of the front lawn by the road. They came from London's old Aldersgate when it was demolished in 1761 and are reported to have been used as ballast by Sir William Blackett's ships on their way from London to the Tyne. The property was given to the National Trust in 1942 by Sir Charles Trevelyan, Bt.

From Wallington the B6342 returns to Cambo, but to vary the route back to Rothbury a right-hand turn is made here on to the B6343 leading in 1 mile to **Scot's Gap**, where a left-hand turn leads up to **Rothley Crags** after crossing the Hart Burn. This is still part of the Wallington estate, once a deer park, and after climbing into the wilder countryside we pass the crags themselves, some 198m (660ft) above sea-level, where the twin towers of **Rothley Castle** lie. These must be amongst the few man-made ruins in the country, for they were created by Sir William Blackett in the 18th century purely for decorative effect. A mile further on the route continues straight on across Rothley crossroads, past the lake created by 'Capability' Brown with the **Codger Fort** on the right, part of the National Trust holding, but without access.

The road, now the B6342, continues north towards Rothbury in a series of switchback ups and downs, first dropping into the valley of the river Font (with Fontburn Reservoir 1 mile to the left), where there are several prehistoric enclosures and quarries. There is a caravan park in the valley of the Font. At **Forestburn Gate**, 5 miles from Rothley crossroads, we reach the edge of the National Park area once more, the B6342 forming the eastern boundary along the edge of the Simonside Hills, and in a further 4 miles the bridge at Whitton leads back into Rothbury.

9) Harbottle and Upper Coquet Dale (approx. 20 miles)

As an alternative to taking the most direct route (see excursion 8), we cross the river at Rothbury and turn right off the B6342, passing through Whitton, and making another right-hand turn at the next junction by the caravan site. Here stands **Whitton Tower**, a fortified 14th-century former rectory, similar to the one at Elsdon. Following the valley of the Coquet under the lee of **Tosson**, keep right through **Newtown** farmstead towards Allerdene and then left around the hillside to **Little Tosson** and **Bickerton**, reached in 5 miles from Rothbury. Across the river from Bickerton is Hepple, and less than 1 mile on the road narrows into the gap below the prehistoric fort of Witchy Neuk, then bends right around the hill and is joined by the B6341 from Rothbury and Hepple. In less than ½ mile take the right-hand junction to Holystone, crossing the Grasslees Burn and winding round Harehaugh Hill towards Holystone Grange, where yet another pele tower stands behind the house. We continue up Coquet Dale, crossing **Holystone Common**. The road drops towards **Holystone Burn**, but ½ mile south of the village on a ridge to our left is the prehistoric site of **Five Barrows**, an important cairn cemetery dating from 1600 to 1000 BC. The cairns that have been opened yielded urns, flint tools, bone pins and evidence of both cremations and inhumations. The grave goods are now in the British Museum. A mile to the south of this point there is an alignment known as the **Five Kings**, about ¼ mile north-east of the **Beacon** (296m, 988ft). This consists of an alignment of standing stones, four of which are still standing.

Holystone itself is a pleasant village which draws many visitors to the renowned **Lady's Well**. A track behind the Salmon Inn leads through to it. It is rectangular in shape and as large as a small swimming-pool, with a stone cross set in the middle and a statue dedicated to St Paulinus by the side. It is now owned by the National Trust, who wisely make no claim for it except that it is traditionally associated with St Ninian, and it is always open, without charge, during daylight hours.

It is extremely unlikely that St Ninian visited the spot himself and that any Christian monks came through this way during his lifetime. But by the 6th century, when Christianity first came into Northumberland, some of his disciples may have followed the old Roman road from High Rochester through to Bridge of Aln and commemorated his name *en route*, as there are other wells bearing his name on other Roman roads.

Myth apart, what is certainly true is that the Romans used this as a watering-place, and their link road between Dere Street and the Devil's Causeway passed close to the well. There is also much evidence of its earlier use amongst the hill-forts and other encampments close by. The Lady's Well took its name naturally from the time when the Augustinian canonesses founded a medieval priory here, the only one of their order, some time before 1124, but of this there are now scant remains. There is some suggestion that **St Mary's Church** originated out of the chancel of the priory church, but it was rebuilt in 1848, and although some medieval work remains, it is difficult to discern this.

Holystone had a much larger population in earlier times than today, for like its close neighbours Harbottle and Alwinton it was linked by one of the main routes from Scotland. A side-road leads off westwards, following the line of the old Roman road for some of the way, towards Rochester in Redesdale, and about 1½ miles up the glen there is a beautiful natural oak-wood. The whole of this area is part of the Redesdale Artillery Range, and due attention should be paid to warning notices. From Holystone the road continues north and in slightly less than 1 mile meets the direct Rothbury–Harbottle road coming in from **Sharperton**. A left turn at the junction leads into Harbottle in 1½ miles.

Harbottle is one of the most pleasant Coquet Dale villages. Renowned as a healthy spot, it has a riverside situation, with the hills rising sharply to the west and undulating pastureland to the east. Like Elsdon and Alwinton to the north, it guarded the approaches across the Border from Scotland. **Harbottle Castle** stands on a mound (or knowe) and was built in 1160 at Henry II's instigation, when he transferred the main defence here from Elsdon. It was the second one on the site and was built on land held by the de Umfraville family. William the Lion, the Scottish king who joined the revolt against the English Crown in 1174, came this way and captured it, but after his capture at Alnwick and the subsequent Treaty of Falaise, Northumberland again came under the English Crown, and the castle reverted to the de Umfravilles who were here until 1415. It grew more important from the middle of the 14th century when it became the headquarters of the new Lord Warden of the Middle March.

There is another castle in Harbottle, a relatively modern one built in

View from Drake Stone towards Harbottle

1829 and now a private residence, housing a crafts centre. To the west of the village, where the river loops into a tight bend, a pathway leads up into the **Harbottle Hills** and a small lake about ½ mile away. On the left just before the lake is a 9m (30ft) high rock known as **Drake's Stone** or, probably more correctly, the **Dragon Stone**, a massive boulder where it is said Druidic rites took place. To the south of the village another path leads up to **Cold Law** (387m, 1,289ft) and **Harbottle Crag** and continues on to **North Yardhope** where the track from Holystone to Rochester is joined.

Just over 1 mile north of Harbottle at **Angryhaugh** the road crosses the Coquet just below the point where the river Alwin joins it, and bearing right, we find **Low Alwinton Church** between the two streams. It is a curious church, built on a slope so that the chancel is well above the height of the nave and the altar higher still. Norman in origin but mainly built in the 13th century, it was completely restored in 1851.

Just before crossing the Alwin, the road from Netherton comes in from the right, and in $\frac{1}{4}$ mile we enter **Alwinton** itself, the last village up the Coquet Valley before ranging off into The Cheviot Hills beyond. Alwinton is a good starting point for walking and fishing expeditions and is partly enclosed by the green Cheviot Hills to the north. Here, the igneous Old Red Sandstone granite of The Cheviot Hills meets the Fell Sandstones, which circle right round to Rothbury and beyond as the Simonside Hills, so that to the south there is different vegetation with the heather-clad slopes of the Harbottle fells making a contrast.

The area abounds with old camps and fortified enclosures dating from the Iron Age, and there are several on either side of the entrance to the Alwin Valley, notably **Clennell Hill** where there is a conspicuous promontory fort $\frac{1}{2}$ mile north-west of the tiny hamlet of **Clennel**, reached by a riverside path from Alwinton in just over $\frac{3}{4}$ mile. The hamlet took its name from a family called Clennell living here as early as 1245, and the famous **Clennell Street**, a green ridge road which crosses over the Border from Yetholm, also derives from this source. Opposite Clennell Hill lies **Lord's Seat** (386m, 1,286ft) where primitive cultivation terraces of several periods can be traced.

A road leads on north-westwards from Alwinton into Upper Coquet Dale for at least 9 miles to **Blindburn** with an onward single track to the great Roman earthworks at Chew Green. On occasion it is possible to circle right through to **Burness** by this road, crossing the Redesdale Artillery Range. An offshoot of this road leads through to **Windy Gyle** (610m, 2,034ft) on the Border, $3\frac{1}{2}$ miles away, where **Russell's Cairn** marks the spot where Lord Francis Russell was murdered by the Scots at a Border meeting in 1585. Another track follows the river Alwin into the denser reaches of the Kidland Forest area, named so it is said from the many wild goats living here. Much of the area is unfortunately restricted by the Redesdale Artillery Range area activities, but it is excellent for walking otherwise. Alwinton is also famous for its annual shepherds' show held usually in October.

From Alwinton a road leads eastwards to **Netherton**, reached in 3 miles. At Netherton Park Farm, Stannington, the north of England Equestrian Centre is situated. It provides full facilities for instruction in riding, show and social activities. A diversion can be made on the way to visit Biddlestone Hall and Alnham. Turning right in the village, an unclassified road proceeds towards Thropton. Just past Trewitt Hall, $1\frac{1}{2}$ miles beyond the village, the line of the old Roman road traces its way along the valley towards Callaly Castle, and the *agger* can be traced about a mile east of this point between High Trewitt and Lorbottle Weststeads. Thropton is reached in 4 miles, where the B6341 leads back to Rothbury in 2 miles.

10) Edlingham and Alnwick (12 miles)

From Rothbury the B6341 road curves round below Cragside and heads north-east through Rothbury Forest. In a few miles the landscape changes to moorland, the road climbing steadily to its highest point, some 3½ miles from Rothbury, at just over 270m (900ft) above sea-level. The peak of **Shirlaw Pike** (303m, 1,010ft) lies 1 mile to the right at this point. The mass of The Cheviot Hills are away to the left, and the Kyloe Hills, Bamburgh and Holy Island indicate the direction towards Berwick. A mile further on the crossroads on Rimside Moor are reached, with the A697 Morpeth–Wooler road crossing our path and the mound of **Wellhope Knowe** (255m, 850ft) marking the spot. As we begin to descend the ridge, and about 1 mile beyond the crossroads, the line of the Devil's Causeway, an old Roman road, crosses from right to left and drops down into the valley of the **Edlingham Burn**. Another mile brings us to the Edlingham turning on the left, where the church and castle can be seen on the other side of the burn.

Edlingham, pronounced with the traditional 'jum' at the end, is a small village marking the crossing of early routes over the moorland, sited half-way between Rothbury and Alnwick in one direction and close to the line of the old Roman road between Bridge of Aln to the north-east and Brinkburn and Weldon Bridge on the Coquet to the south. **St John's Church** has a square tower and is predominantly Norman, although a Saxon church is reputed to have existed here from the 8th century, and fragments of a sculptured cross from this period are in the church. The west wall is 11th-century work, but the church was rebuilt in the 12th century with a Norman nave and chancel and there is a Norman doorway. The narrow slit windows suggest it was built with defence in mind. The remains of **Edlingham Castle** lie to the north-east of the churchyard, close to the Edlingham Burn. Basically, it was a mid-14th-century tower house rather than a castle, but the remains of a large hall are still visible where the original tower was extended, with lofty rib-vaulting and an interesting fire-place. The village is a good point from which to explore the open moorlands and the Vale of Whittingham, and there is a caravan site here now.

From Edlingham the road crosses the line of the **Corby Crags** to reach the crossroads at Banktop in 2 more miles. The views are extensive from this point on as the road descends in a straight line across Alnwick Moor, reaching Alnwick in a further $3\frac{1}{2}$ miles.

To make a circular tour back to Rothbury the route of excursion 5 from Alnwick to Callaly Castle and Whittingham may be followed, making a round trip of some 36 miles. Alternatively, excursion 4 from Alnwick to Eglingham and Ingram may be followed, returning to Rothbury from Glanton on the A697 and the B6341, making a round trip of approximately 41 miles.

7 Through route, the Great North Road
Newcastle upon Tyne – Morpeth – Alnwick – Berwick-upon-Tweed (63 miles)

N.B. All mileages shown in brackets are from Newcastle upon Tyne

(From Newcastle upon Tyne to Seaton Burn see under Tyne and Wear, page 259.)

Just north of **Seaton Burn** (6½ miles) the A108 **Tyne Tunnel** road rejoins the A1(T) going north. From this junction also the A1068 leads off north-eastwards to the Plessey Woods Country Park and on to Bedlington. The heavy industrial area of Tyneside begins to give way to a more agricultural scene, with the southern boundary of Northumberland commencing at Seven Mile House Farm. On the left just after **Shotton Grange** (8 miles) is **Blagdon Hall**, the home of Viscount Ridley, a member of the well-known Northumberland family whose name is linked with that of Nicholas Ridley, Bishop of London, who died as one of the Oxford martyrs. The house was built in 1735 and restored in 1949 after a fire.

The Great North Road crosses the river Blyth at **Stannington Bridge** (9¾ miles). At **Clifton** (12½ miles) the A1(T) bypasses Morpeth (15 miles) and crosses the river Wansbeck on the western side of the town, linking up again with the northern exit from the town at Fairmoor. The A197 leads into Morpeth itself.

Morpeth is situated on a low peninsula formed by a U-bend in the river Wansbeck. It is a busy market town with agricultural and cattle markets still in existence. It has a population of about 15,000, growing steadily because of its proximity to Newcastle, and it is a junction point for roads leading to the moorlands to the north and north-west.

Historically, it has never been so important as either Alnwick or Berwick, and probably because it was close to Newcastle it was never a walled town. Its 14th-century castle did little to prevent its share of depredations both from the English as well as the Scots. In 1216 King John, furiously trying to get to grips with his revolting barons, burnt the town down, and in Elizabeth's time the Scots, it was said, continued to ride into the town to plunder as though they were coming to market.

Approached from the south, the A197 leads past **High Church (St Mary's)**, originally the parish church and one of the largest and most interesting in Northumberland. The chancel is the finest part of the church, with the tower, nave and aisles all dating from the 14th century. The east window noted for its 14th-century glass, although renewed, is still the finest example of such medieval work in the county. There is also a carved sedilia with curious figures on it, one holding a jug. Decorating the priest's door is some fine ironwork which also appears on the vestry door and the door to the aumbry on the north side. In the west wall of the vestry is a small circular window, taken to indicate that it was once used as an anchorite's cell. At local weddings the custom prevails of tying the church gates together until the bridegroom pays a toll to be let out as a married man.

Castle Hill is just to the north of the church opposite a huge battlemented **Courthouse** and police station, built in 1822 by the Newcastle architect, Dobson, with a gatehouse formerly used as a gaol. Opposite stands the mound where the remains of **Morpeth Castle** lie, consisting mainly now of a well-preserved gatehouse which is now a private residence. The castle was originally a Norman motte-and-bailey construction, restored in the 15th century, but the gatehouse is probably 14th century.

From the south side of the river two bridges cross the Wansbeck: the old, original 13th-century one has been largely destroyed but now carries a foot-bridge, and the main road crosses Telford's bridge built in 1831. At the north end the junction to the right (A197) leads off to Ashington and Newbiggin-by-the-Sea. To the left the A192 Alnwick road follows Bridge Street. In the angle between the road and the river is the **Bridge Chantry**, formerly **All Saint's Church**, founded in the 13th century and remodelled in the 18th with an arcade which has long been adapted to business and commercial use.

Bridge Street leads through to the central part of the town at the market-place in which the **Town Hall** stands. Designed in 1714 by Sir John Vanbrugh, it was rebuilt in 1870. Northwards from the market-place Newgate Street leads along to the 19th-century **St James's**

Church, in the neo-Norman style and set back behind a screen of columns and arches. Westwards from the market-place is Oldgate, in the middle of which is the **Town Steeple**, 15th century in origin with later additions. Further along Oldgate on the north side lies **Collingwood House**, the former home of Admiral Lord Collingwood, who took over at Trafalgar after the death of Nelson, and to whom a memorial stands at Tynemouth as one of the greatest of all Northumberland's sailors. Besides also being a major shopping centre, Morpeth has a park with tennis-courts and bowling greens and a common to the south-west of the town where there is also a golf-course. It is the scene of a miners' gala, similar to the one held annually at nearby Bedlington, and is a good centre for several interesting excursions along the Wansbeck Valley.

A mile to the west, along the river bank, lies **Newminster Abbey**, reached by following Newgate Street through into **Dogger Bank**, where it becomes the B6343 Cambo road. It descends to the river bank and crosses **Grange Bridge**, and shortly afterwards a track leads off left to the ruins standing on an elevated plateau as the valley begins to widen. Newminster Abbey was a Cistercian foundation of 1137, and became a daughter house of Fountains Abbey in Yorkshire. Unfortunately, within a year of its completion the buildings were ravaged by the Scots. However, after rebuilding, the new monastery grew very powerful. The ruins now hardly reflect this past, with only a single doorway arch, formerly the entrance to the north aisle of the church, and the arcades of three sides of the cloisters re-erected in 1913.

The B6343 continues westwards along the Wansbeck Valley, and in 2 miles reaches **Mitford** at the confluence of the river Font. A lane leads south from the west side of the village to cross the river. Parts of the church date from Norman times. It lay for a long time in ruins but was restored between 1874 and 1875, the south aisle being rebuilt and a new tower with a spire provided. This replaced the original Northumbrian-style bell turret and the two aisles of the former Norman church. Mitford was another village burnt during the ravagings of King John in 1216. Certainly, it is known that the castle was attacked the following year by Alexander II of Scotland, and it is possible that the church was first destroyed at that time. The chancel was reconstructed about the 13th century with the north wall of the nave. The transeptal chapels are a 14th-century addition, and there is a fine triple window at the east end. Outside the priest's doorway is some fine chevron-moulding decoration, part of the original building.

On the opposite side of the lane are the ruins of **Mitford Castle**. There are the remains of a five-sided keep at the highest point. The castle was built in 1138 by William Bertram (who also founded Brinkburn Priory) and it remained in this family until 1275. It was captured by the Scots under Alexander III (1249–86) and suffered repeated assaults until it finally became useless by 1323. It then passed into the possession of the Mitford family, who lived here until the early part of the 17th century and then discarded it for the greater comfort of the **Manor-house**.

The remains of this latter building are just along the lane to the north-west, now in private grounds. The battlemented gate-tower bears the date 1673, and the ruins of the house lie to the north-east. Back to the main road (B6343) and a little to the west of the village lies **Mitford Hall**, built in 1823. This house became the final home of the family and still is in their possession.

From Mitford an unclassified side road leads in 5 miles along the river Font to **Netherwitton** where **Netherwitton Hall**, an early 18th-century mansion, can be viewed and where a Georgian mill also lies. On the same road, 2 miles beyond this village there is another interesting house at **Nunnykirk**, where **Nunnykirk Hall**, one of the finest of Dobson's works, was built in 1825.

From Mitford westwards the B6343 continues to Hartburn in just under 6 miles, passing **Meldon Park**, built by Dobson in 1832, a mile before reaching the village. The line of the Devil's Causeway, the old Roman road to Berwick, runs through the village and crosses the Hart Burn here. The road then continues to Cambo and Wallington Hall.

To the east of Morpeth the A197 Newbiggin-by-the-Sea road leads to the coalmining town of **Pegswood** in 2 miles, and thence on to Ashington. A right turn at Pegswood leads through in 1 mile to **Bothal**, a model village, very similar to Ford or Chillingham. **Bothal Castle** was built in 1343 by Robert Bertram and later became the seat of the Ogle family. It has an elevated bailey, or courtyard, surrounded by an outer wall and defended by a heavily fortified gatehouse. The greater part of the wall has gone, but the **Gatehouse** has now been converted into a guest-house.

Close by is the **Church of St Andrew**, 13th century but enlarged in the 14th and again restored later on, which contains the tomb of Ralph, Lord Ogle, and his wife, who died in 1516. In the chancel there are fine Jacobean altar rails, with a squint on the south side of the chancel arch. There are also some fragments of medieval glass and a notable bell turret.

Another former property of the Ogle family is at **Cockle Park Tower**, reached from Morpeth by following the A192 northbound and turning off right in 1 mile towards **Hebron**. The tower is a mile past the village. Built about 1520, a fine Tudor building which was restored in the late 18th century, it is now the Agricultural Research Station of Newcastle University, and the pele tower is incorporated into the farmhouse.

North from Morpeth the A192 leads in 2 miles to the junction at **Fairmoor** (16½ miles) where the A1(T) is rejoined. In just over ½ mile the A697 Morpeth–Wooler–Coldstream road diverges to the left, while the Great North Road continues across the Floodgate Burn and the river Lyne to descend into **Felton** (25 miles) on the river Coquet. Here the barons of England met in 1215 to transfer their loyalty from King John to King Alexander of Scotland, an unforgiveable insult which John repaid the next year by burning the village down. **St Michael's Church**, although originally 13th century with some 14th-century additions, has had excessive alterations. Close to the village is **Felton Park**, a large house used in the 1715 Jacobite rising as a temporary base. From Felton also the B6345 road runs eastwards to **Acklington** (where a wartime fighter airfield existed) thence through to Togston and Warkworth. To the west the same road provides a link to Longframlington on the A697. The main road climbs steeply away from Felton, and in 2½ miles, just before Newton-on-the-Moor, a right-hand unclassified road leads through to **Guyzance** on the river Coquet, where the ruins of **St Wilfrid's Chapel** lie. At **Bank House**, just to the north of here, there is a caravan site, and by following secondary roads it is possible to work one's way down river to Warkworth.

A left-hand side-road which parallels the main A1(T) leads off 2 miles north of Felton to an obelisk erected to Lord Nelson by Alexander Davison, who was the victualler to the Royal Navy during the Napoleonic Wars. The same road leads on to pass **Newton Hall**, originally an Elizabethan farmhouse in the possession of the Widdringtons, who gave their name to the village 8 miles away to the south-east. A steady climb up to **Newton-on-the-Moor** (28½ miles) over 120m (400ft) above sea-level gives the first glimpses of the Northumberland coastline away to the north-east. There is another large house known as **Newton Low Hall**, built in the 18th century, close to **Newton Burn** on the right as the village is left behind. In a mile a right-hand turning leads off to **Shilbottle**, where another vicar's pele tower, dating from 1415, is attached to the vicarage. There is a modern 19th-century church with some Norman antecedents in the two small remaining windows in the north wall of the nave and the south doorway. This road continues on to Lesbury and Alnmouth.

On the left-hand side 2 miles north of Newton-on-the-Moor lies **Snipe House**. The A1(T) drops down to cross the Cawledge Burn, a tributary of the river Aln, and reaches Alnwick in 34 miles from Newcastle upon Tyne. The town is bypassed by the A1(T), but a link-road leads into the town via the A1068, rejoining the Great North Road at Malcolm's Cross.

From Alnwick the A1068 leads out of town northwards to **Malcolm's Cross** (35¾ miles) where it rejoins the A1(T), and in 2 miles from this point are the remains of **Hefferlaw Tower**, built as a look-out tower for the town and Alnwick Abbey in the 15th century. It stands at the highest point of **Hefferlaw Bank** (138m, 459ft) above sea-level, and bears both the arms of the Percy family and the crossed croziers of the Abbot of Alnwick Abbey.

The road drops down towards the Charlton Bog, and at aptly-named **Charlton Mires** (39 miles) the Great North Road is crossed by the B6347 leading eastwards to Embleton and High Newton-by-the-Sea, with a link-road continuing through to **Fallodon Hall**, the former home of the Grey family and, in particular, Earl Grey, the Prime Minister at the time of the 1832 Reform Bill. In the other direction the B6347 leads through to **South Charlton** and then links up with the B6346 to Eglingham and Wooler. **North Charlton** (41 miles) has a caravan site, and a mile past the village a side-road leads off right to **Ellingham** (pronounced with a final 'jum'), home of the Haggerston family at **Ellingham Hall**.

The main road begins to climb again across Rayheugh Moor, with views now to the Kyloe Hills to the north-west. It drops down to cross the Waren Burn at **Warenford** (45 miles), and a mile ahead there is a right-hand junction on to the B1341 leading directly to Bamburgh through Adderstone. The B6348 turns off left ½ mile on across Chatton Moor to Chatton, Chillingham and Wooler. **Belford** (48 miles), a famous coaching stop of the past, is reached in 2 more miles. Today, it is a thriving market town situated at the junction of the B1342 leading to the popular Northumbrian coastline through Bamburgh. **Belford Hall**, built in 1756 and partly remodelled in 1818, lies just outside the village. To the west the B6349 crosses Belford Moor to Wooler with extensive views to The Cheviot Hills and along the coastline.

Just up the road lies **Middleton** (49¼ miles), a good access point to explore the Kyloe Hills and their woodlands. The main road is now less than 1 mile from the coastline, with Holy Island and Fenham Flats to the right. At **Fenwick** (52½ miles) the B6353 turns off left leading to Lowick and Ford. A mile to the west along this road at **East Kyloe** there are the remains of a 14th-century pele tower in the farmyard.

The road drops down from the north-eastern slopes of the Kyloe Hills to reach the isolated junction at **West Mains** (54 miles), where the road to the right leads off to the causeway for Holy Island. At **Haggerston** (55½ miles), 1½ miles further on, there is a caravan park in the grounds of the former **Haggerston Castle** with the remains of a pele tower dating from 1345. In 2 more miles the B6526 comes in to join the A1(T) from the left, bringing in the Wooler road, close to Scremerston Hill. From Scremerston village (60 miles) the road leads straight into Berwick-upon-Tweed in 3 miles (63 miles).

8 Through route
Newcastle upon Tyne – Morpeth – Wooler – Coldstream (61 miles)

N.B. All mileages shown in brackets are from Newcastle upon Tyne

(From Newcastle upon Tyne to Seaton Burn see under Tyne and Wear, page 259; from Seaton Burn to Morpeth see under Northumberland, page 111.)

North from Morpeth the A1(T) road leads to the junction at **Fairmoor** (16½ miles), where the A697 forks left, crossing Longhorsley Moor to **Longhorsley** (21¼ miles) spread out from its crossroads which link to Netherwitton and Nunnykirk to the west and across to join the A1(T) Great North Road to Thirston on the east. The village has a well-preserved pele tower, built in the 16th century. The church, although thought to be Norman in origin, was restored in the early 18th century. There is one genuine Norman window and a famous trefoiled chancel arch. The A697 road climbs out of the valley towards Swan Hill. In 1 mile a lane to the right leads off to **Linden**, built by Dobson in 1812.

Dropping down steeply into the valley of the river Coquet, the road crosses it at **Weldon Bridge** (24 miles) by a new bridge, with a side-road leading off into this famous fishing village with the old 18th-century bridge and the Angler's Arms close by it. The B6334 leads off west along some of its reaches to Brinkburn Priory in just over 1 mile and on to Rothbury in 5½ miles, thence along the dividing line of the Grasslees Valley between the Simonside Hills and The Cheviot Hills to Otterburn. The line of the Roman road, the Devil's Causeway, crosses the river Coquet ½ mile to the west of the village.

The road climbs up the slopes of the Rothbury Forest, reaching in 1½ miles **Longframlington** (25½ miles), over 150m (500ft) above sea-level. There is a 12th-century church in the Transitional style and an 18th-century house at **Embleton Hall**. The B6345 road strikes off to the east through to Felton on the Great North Road, and ½ mile to the west of the village the lane marks the line of the Devil's Causeway which passes close to **Framlington Villa**.

Crossing Longframlington Common, the A697 road continues to climb, and 1 mile north of the village at Besom Barn the modern road joins the line of the Roman road and they run together for 1 mile to Framlingham Gate, crossing the Gate Burn at the same point. A mile to the east of this point is an old earthwork known by the odd name of **Canada Camp**, close to where the Millstone Burn joins the Gate Burn. To the left is **Shirlaw Pike** (303m, 1,010ft) and rounding this the road bears west opening up views to Thrunton Crags and The Cheviot Hills beyond and reaching almost 210m (700ft) above sea-level before dropping down to the cross-roads at **New Moor House** (30 miles) which is reached in another 3 miles. The B6341 Rothbury–Alnwick road crosses from left to right in the midst of Rimside Moor.

The A697 continues north-west, dropping down into the valleys of the Edlingham Burn and then the **Coe Burn** (32 miles), with numerous ancient earthworks on both sides and **Thrunton Wood**, a Forestry Commission fir plantation, on the left. There is a steady drop down to the valley of the river Aln, where at **Bridge of Aln** (34 miles) a side-road leads off left to Whittingham, Callaly Castle and The Cheviot Hills. Crossing the river, in 2 miles a left-hand turn leads to Glanton with its World Bird Research Station, while the main road curves down to **Powburn** (37 miles) where the river Breamish (later to become the Till) is crossed. Just across the river the first turning on the left leads up the valley of the Breamish to Ingram, one of the natural gateways into the National Park area. The Roman road also crosses at this point, and for the next 1½ miles the A697 follows its line almost exactly, skirting the easternmost slopes of The Cheviot Hills to **Hedgeley Moor**, where, as the road bears away to the left, there is one of the several Percy crosses marking the spot where Sir Ralph Percy fell at the Battle of Hedgeley Moor in 1464.

A mile further on at **Wooperton** (40 miles) the B6346 turns off right to **Harehope Hill** (194m, 646ft) and Alnwick, and in another mile at **Roseden** (41½ miles) a left-hand turning leads through to Roddam Burn and the famous **Roddam Dene**, where one of the best examples of the boulder conglomerate brought down from The Cheviot Hills by torrents in the geological formations of the Carboniferous period can be seen. Close by is **Roddam Hall**, an 18th-century house.

The main road is now close to the easternmost slopes of the Cheviot range and sweeps round in a right-hand curve towards Berwick, following the line of the river Till and the river Tweed. From Roseden a fork to the right in ¼ mile leads off to East Lilburn and Lilburn Tower, and a diversion can be made circling back to the main road in 2 miles. Three miles from Roseden the Harthope Burn appears on the left, and at **Haugh Head** (45½ miles) there is a ford on the left leading through to the Happy Valley and on into the Harthope Valley, one of the principal entry points into The Cheviot Hills and the National Park area. The valley leads up to Langleeford and to the highest point in the range, **The Cheviot** itself (803m, 2,676ft). A more convenient method of approach, however, is from **Wooler** (47 miles), 1½ miles further on. (*For Wooler and excursions from Wooler see page 42.*)

From Wooler the B6348 road leads eastwards to Belshill on the Great North Road, and an offshoot, the B6349, leads through to Belford on the

Flodden Field

same road. The B6525 (A6111) turns north-east to Barmoor and Berwick-upon-Tweed.

Two miles north of Wooler is the site of the **Battle of Homildon Hill**, the overwhelming revenge inflicted by the English under the Percies against the Scots in 1402 for their previous defeat at Otterburn. At **Akeld** (49½ miles) the B6351 forks left towards the Yeavering Bell and Kirknewton, circling the northern edge of the main Cheviot core and on into Scotland at Kirk Yetholm. The A697 swings right at this point across the Millfield Plain to **Millfield** (52½ miles) with a view to Ford Castle in the distance. The B6352 branches off left 1½ miles further on, passing the south side of **Flodden Hill**, where the Scots first waited for the English before the Battle of Flodden Field, and joining the B6351 at Kilham before continuing on directly to Kelso. In ½ mile the B6354 turns off right to the model village of Ford, and at **Crookham** (56 miles) the B6353 road comes in on the right from Fenwick and Lowick, joining the A697 towards Coldstream.

After Crookham, the first turning left leads through to the site of **Flodden Field** and the village of Branxton, while the main road curves west past the imposing avenue leading to **Pallisburn House**, an 18th-century mansion with later additions. Just past this point on the right is the **King's Stone**, a shaft 2m (7ft) high, set in a field.

The road drops down towards the valley of the river Tweed, first entering **Cornhill-on-Tweed** (60 miles). From Cornhill-on-Tweed the B6350 turns off left to Wark Castle and Carham on the south side of the river, before the main road crosses the fine bridge for the last mile into **Coldstream** (61 miles).

9 Through route
Newcastle upon Tyne – Otterburn – Carter Bar – Jedburgh (61 miles)

N.B. All mileages shown in brackets are from Newcastle upon Tyne

(From Newcastle upon Tyne to Newcastle Airport see under Tyne and Wear, page 258.)

The Northumberland boundary crosses the main A696 road close to Newcastle's airport at Woolsington. **Ponteland** (7½ miles), once a rural Northumberland village, is now a major dormitory area for Newcastle with a large estate and a busy through road. Set along the vale of the river Pont, its history dates back to pre-Conquest days. The **Church of St Mary**, although extensively altered, still has a Norman tower and west doorway, and there are some vestiges of Norman remains inside. It dates from the 12th century with alterations in the 14th and again in the 19th centuries. Probably the most interesting building in Ponteland is the old inn, the **Blackbird**, expertly restored from a 17th-century manor-house which itself was built on to a 14th-century pele tower. Just to the north of the village there are some rifle ranges, and one of the Northumberland Colleges of Education is situated on the Small Burn. There is also an agricultural college at **Kirkley Hall**, the original home of the Ogle family. Built in the 18th century, it was destroyed by fire and rebuilt in 1928. In the grounds is an obelisk, dated 1788, commemorating the landing of William III in 1689. From Ponteland the B6323 road circles round the west side of Newcastle, through Throckley, to reach the river Tyne at Newburn Heddon.

Beyond Ponteland the scenery changes into a more tree-covered agricultural landscape, climbing slowly towards **Higham Dykes** (10 miles), where a 17th-century red-bricked house, unusual in these parts, is tucked away in the trees on the right. An entirely different village aspect appears at **Belsay** (13 miles), where the village was re-created in the 1830s into an arcaded street of sandstone houses in the Italian style. It was designed by Sir Charles Monck, a member of the local Middleton family, who also built **Belsay Hall** (*not open*) in 1810, assisted by John Dobson. The hall is to the west of the village and is built in the Greek Doric style. In the grounds are the ruins of **Belsay Castle**, a most impressive 14th-century ruined tower house, designed like a keep with adjacent wings. This is best seen from a side-road, the B6309, which runs west then south towards Stamfordham, crossing the line of Hadrian's Wall eventually to reach the river Tyne at Bywell. To the east the B6524 links the A696 through Whalton and on to Morpeth.

From Belsay also an interesting excursion can be made to the **Bolam Lake Country Park** area. At the northern end of the village where the A696 bears left take the unclassified road straight on, crossing in $\frac{1}{2}$ mile the diminutive river Blyth. In $1\frac{3}{4}$ miles from the village a track leads off left, following the How Burn, to **Shortflatt Tower**, which can also be seen from the road. Though restored, it is a fine example of an early 14th-century pele tower with a later house attached to it. The road continues to **Bolam Lake** in $\frac{1}{2}$ mile, artificially created by John Dobson. Just beyond it a right-hand turn runs along the ridge into **Bolam** itself, where nothing remains but **St Andrew's Church** and **Bolam Hall**, now a most comfortable guest-house. However, the church is well worth a visit for it is one of the few, well-preserved Saxon ones in Northumberland, and the tower has survived unbuttressed since the year 960. The interior is mainly Norman 12th-century work with some vestiges of the original Saxon church in the north wall of the nave. The main part of the chancel is also 12th century with the previous apse altered to the present square structure a century later. The south doorway is adorned with dog-tooth moulding. In the east wall of this chapel is a curious trefoiled niche with hinges for double doors. A small window on the south wall marks the spot where a bomb, dropped by an enemy aircraft in 1942, broke through but did not explode.

To continue the excursion a return is made to the road junction on the western side of the village, where a right turn (straight on from the original direction) leads towards High Angerton and Hartburn. However, in less than $\frac{1}{2}$ mile a left-hand junction leads off west towards **Bolam Houses**, where a second diversion can be made. Just to the west of this hamlet a lane leads through to the standing stone known as **Poind and his Man**, approximately 2m (6ft) high and close to an ancient round barrow with which it may be associated. The line of the Roman road, the Devil's Causeway, also crosses the high ground close to this point on its way north-east to cross the river Wansbeck west of Low Angerton. The track continues through westwards as a public footpath towards **Shaftoe Crags** (209m, 698ft). There are early earthworks and the remains of a prehistoric fort here. To the south-east lies **East Shaftoe Hall**, a tower house with a later building attached.

Returning to Bolam Houses and thence east to the junction of the diversion, a left-hand turn puts us back in the direction towards Hartburn, the road zigzagging down to cross the little stream of the river Wansbeck at **Low Angerton** and on through the grounds of **Angerton Hall**, an early 19th-century house by Dobson in the Tudor style. **High Angerton** is at the other end of the estate, the road bearing left towards Hartburn. In a ¼ mile turn right, with a further right-hand turn in ½ mile more, to lead into Hartburn. **St Andrew's Church**, originally Norman, was rebuilt in the 13th century. The south doorway has dog-tooth moulding down to the ground and rows of similar moulding on either side of the jambs. The cup-shaped font is supported by a central pillar and three detached shafts. In the nave the arcades have very slender columns, with capitals that appear too small for the arches they sustain. There are also a triple sedilia and a large trefoiled piscina and the matrix of a brass, with the head and shoulders of a priest, on the chancel floor. It also has a monument to John Hodgson, the Northumberland historian.

To create a circular tour and a return to Belsay drop down across the burn and follow the B6343 eastwards for 2 miles, passing **Meldon Park**, a house built by Dobson in 1832, and then on to the Dyke Neuk Inn, where a right turn is made into the hamlet of **Meldon** itself. (*For the route straight on to Morpeth see page 114*.) The small 13th-century church was restored in the 19th century. Continuing south for 2 miles leads on to **Whalton**, with the Bolam road coming in from the right after ½ mile, where a left-hand turn is made at the T-junction. There is a dearth of signposts in these pleasant open lanes amidst fine agricultural surroundings, and it is very easy to take a wrong turn. Whalton's brown stone houses have a number of pele towers incorporated into them. A left turn leads past the Belford Arms into the broad main street. This is one of the two villages which traditionally hold a Baal fire ceremony on Midsummer's Eve, with sword and folk-dancing and a huge bonfire in memory of a custom brought in long ago by Northumberland's Viking ancestors, and similar events still take place in Scandinavia today. At the eastern end of the village is the **Manor-house**, converted in 1908 from four local houses by Sir Edwin Lutyens, who was also responsible for the conversion of Lindisfarne Castle. **St Mary's Church** lies about 200 metres along the right hand turning from the main village street on the road to Ogle. Unusually wide for its length, it was Norman in origin, reconstructed in the 13th century and again restored in 1908. Between the chancel and the chantry of the Ogle family from Kirkley on the north side is a remarkable pier made up of four widely spaced filleted shafts connected by huge dog-tooth mouldings.

The road south past the church leads on to **Ogle** in 1½ miles, crossing the river Blyth again just short of the village. There is a 14th-century tower house here with a manor-house added on later. A road south from the village leads in 2 miles to **Kirkley Hall**, the traditional home of the Ogle family, now an agricultural college. To return to Belsay follow the road west out of the village for 2 miles, joining the A696 south of Belsay.

Continuing north, the A696 leads in 2 miles to a right-hand turning signposted Harnham, which leads through to **Harnham Hall**, a medieval tower house, altered again in the 17th century. A mile beyond Harnham the Devil's Causeway crosses the line of the main road on its way to Shaftoe Crags just off on the right. At **West Shaftoe** (17 miles) a drive on the left leads through to **Capheaton Hall** (*not open*), the ancestral home of the Swinburne family since the 15th century. Half a mile along the main road a left-hand turn leads into the village of **Capheaton** and on past the grounds of the hall. Capheaton Hall is a masterpiece of 1668, built by Trollope, the Newcastle architect who also built Newcastle's Guildhall. It is in the Baroque style with fine ornamentation, and the gardens and lake were laid out in the mid-18th century by Lancelot 'Capability' Brown, who was born in the next village (see page 126).

At **Kirkharle** crossroads (19¾ miles) the B6342 leads off right to Wallington Hall and Cambo, thence through to Hartburn and along the river Wansbeck to Morpeth. In the westward direction the same road leads through to **Great Bavington** and **Bavington Hall**, the former home of the Shafto family, confiscated by the Crown for their part in the 1715 uprising. The present house was built by Admiral Delaval and building began at the same time as Seaton Delaval Hall. Close by is **Thockrington**, where many members of the Shafto family are buried in the isolated churchyard. The B6342 continues west past Hallington Reservoir, in an area rich with ancient earthworks and camps, to cross the A68 and carry on to Hexham.

The main A696 crosses the parkland of the Kirkharle estate, but it is possible to find the tiny 14th-century **St Wilfrid's Church**, rebuilt on an earlier Norman foundation, on a side-road through a farm. This is the hamlet where 'Capability' Brown was born in 1716. An old manor-house lies to the south-east of the church, and close by is the present **Kirkharle Hall**, a modern Victorian building. On the other side of the main road, to the north-east and close to the line of the river Wansbeck, is another manor-house, known as **Little Harle Tower**, a medieval building modernized in the 18th and 19th centuries and now used as a private residence.

At **Kirkwhelpington** (22 miles) the village is bypassed by the A696 as it crosses the river Wansbeck. **St Bartholomew's Church** has Norman traces but it is mainly 13th century with later additions and a Perpendicular tower. In another mile the road climbs up to **Knowesgate** (23 miles), with the rolling farmland giving way to the wilder and more stark countryside of the Ottercops Moss. At the crossroads here the left-hand turning leads through to **Sweethope Loughs**, where there are many traces of early settlements, some of them identified as post-Roman in date. One of the most important of these is **Great Wanny**, a promontory fort 300m (1,000ft) above sea-level. On some occasions the distant skyline of The Cheviot Hills shows clearly to the north, with the Harwood Forest and the Simonside Hills to the north-east. The road reaches a height of 307m (1,024ft) in a further 4 miles and then begins to drop into the valley of the river Rede by Blaxter Lough with Blaxter Quarry on the left. The view now opens up into Redesdale. At **Raylees** (29 miles) the Raylees Burn is crossed 2 miles to the east of the point where it joins the Rede, and from here also a side-road to the right crosses the dominating spur to the north-east to reach Elsdon in 1½ miles. On this spur lie the remains of an earthwork overlooking and guarding the junction of the two valleys. A mile further on the Elsdon Burn is crossed by Monkridge, and less than ½ mile further on the B6341 road comes in from the right. The combined routes then lead in ½ mile into Otterburn (32 miles).

Otterburn is situated in the valley of the Rede and makes an attractive holiday area for those who enjoy walking, fishing or wildlife, and its importance has grown in recent years largely through the growth of interest in both the National Park and the Border Forest areas just away to the north. It is also on one of the main routes through to Scotland. Here, the river Rede changes direction from south to south-west, running down to join the North Tyne at Redesmouth. Much of the history of this area has already been recounted under Elsdon, the original capital of

Redesdale, which Otterburn replaced in the 18th century partly owing to the opening-up of turnpike roads as distinct from the traditional pack-horse routes over The Cheviot Hills along the old drovers' roads. Part of its fame also centres on the 150-year-old **Mill**, which has now ceased producing. It lies close to the river at the south end of the village, where the B6320 road turns off, bridges the Rede and leads off across Corsenside Common to Bellingham in North Tynedale.

Otterburn is also famous for the **Battle of Otterburn** in 1388, when the Percies were defeated by the Scots under Douglas, and this story has already been told under Alnwick. About ¾ mile beyond the village, following the A696 north, there is a strip of wooded plantation on the right about 100 metres from the road, where Percy's Cross lies, a cross socket and shaft most probably put there several hundred years after the battle but reputedly marking the spot. However, no Percy fell at the battle, for Harry Hotspur and his brother Ralph were taken prisoner and it was the Earl of Douglas who died. Douglas's body was taken back to Scotland, and it has been suggested that the stone should more appropriately mark the spot where his funeral procession started from, following the medieval custom of putting down a cross each night to mark the homeward journey. Some historians have also associated the line of similar markings, known as the Golden Pots, which cross The Cheviot Hills on the route back to Melrose Abbey where the Scottish leader was buried as being a part of this route, but they are much more likely to have been Roman marking-points along their own road, Dere Street, leading to Chew Green.

Traditionally, the site of the battle was just behind this cross, towards **Otterburn Hall** (which can also be reached by a side-road from the village), a late 19th-century building, now a hotel. However, some evidence points more towards the slopes of **Fawdon Hill**, 1 mile to the north-east, which would have made a better strategic position for a waiting army. Close by also is **Otterburn Towers**, now also a hotel, where there are the remnants of a medieval tower house in the later Victorian building.

The A696 continues up the valley of the Rede, reaching the junction at **Elishaw** (34 miles), where the A68 road from Corbridge comes in from the left. This has been a junction since time immemorial, for the A68 follows the line of the old Roman road, Dere Street, which, unlike the modern road, continues straight on to join up again 1 mile further on. From this point on, as we enter the National Park area, the A696 becomes the A68, and at **Horsley**, a mile further on, the Roman road crosses through the village to reach the Roman fort of Bremenium, $1\frac{1}{2}$ miles away at High Rochester. In Horsley itself, **Holy Trinity Church** was erected in 1844 as a chapel of ease and contains a Roman altar in its porch found at the fort at Featherwood. Half a mile along the road at **Rochester** (37 miles) (Rochester meaning 'camp on the high rock') a lane leads off to the right to **High Rochester**, where the old village lies within the original bounds of the Roman fort of Bremenium, with its adjacent camp $\frac{1}{4}$ mile to the north-west in the Redesdale Camp area, part of the large army complex.

Bremenium, which means 'place by the roaring river', was one of the major strongholds of the northern border area, linked by a second Roman road that runs across the Redesdale Artillery Range through Holystone which eventually joins the Devil's Causeway at Bridge of Aln. The history of Bremenium is linked with the successive attempts made by the Romans to subdue and conquer Scotland. The first foundation here was probably in AD 81. In the insurrections of the northern tribes some of the defeats suffered by the Romans were so bad that one whole army legion was wiped out and its name erased from the army list. Hadrian to some extent stabilized the position with the building of the Wall, and in AD 138 the Emperor, Antoninus Pius, ordered a fresh advance into Scotland under Lollius Urbicus, who built the Antonine Wall between Firth and Clyde. High Rochester was probably rebuilt also at this time. It was rebuilt again in the time of Severus, between AD 205 and 208, when he also advanced deeply into Scotland, and many of the forts associated with Hadrian's Wall were also rebuilt at this time. The heyday of High Rochester was probably in the 3rd century AD when it was garrisoned by a cohort of the Roman army, with cavalry for patrols and its famous spring guns (ballistae) for defence. Two of the stone balls which this missile used can still be seen at the old village schoolhouse, the porch of which is largely built of Roman stones. It is also likely that the fort was rebuilt for the last time about AD 247 when it became for a while the most northerly of any Roman garrison, but within a century its usefulness was over. The so-called Barbarian Conspiracy of AD 367 brought overwhelming defeat for the Romans, and this was the end of this frontier outpost. Today, the walls and towers can still be picked out, and the most interesting remains are those of the west gateway and part of the surrounding wall.

The line of the Roman road, Dere Street, can also be traced on its way across the Sill Burn, proceeding north-westwards in a dead straight line for 3 miles to Featherwood Farm, but since this part of it is now in the Redesdale Artillery Range, access times are limited, and permission to cross must be obtained from the Range Liaison Officer at Redesdale Camp. The road runs from the camp over the line of the Roman road up to Featherwood Farm and ¼ mile beyond to the fork, where the road bears left. There are the remains of two Roman camps – **Featherwood East** and **Featherwood West** – on either side of the road, and 1½ miles further on at Foulplay Head the road swings abruptly westwards to Cottonshope Head, where the junction is marked by the first of the Golden Pots, and descends to Byrness as a forestry road (see below). On occasions, when the Range is closed, it is possible to turn right on to Foulplay Head, following the low broad mound across the moor northwards which marks the line of Dere Street. In 1½ miles at Harden Edge there are extensive views of the Cheviot range, the Coquet Valley and Chew Green itself, with two superimposed fortlets, the second with triple ditches and the adjacent labour camps associated with them. The single track road now follows the line of the medieval **Gammel's Peth**, noted even in the 13th century as a point for settling Border disputes, the line of which was presumed once to have been marked with stone crosses, with which the middle and outer Golden Pots are associated, and they can be seen as one passes along the track. The road drops down steeply in 2 miles to reach the miniature river Coquet, and from here a return can be made to Blindburn and Alwinton. The path continues northwards close to the forts of **Chew Green**, near Coquet Head, where the Pennine Way also comes in from the west. The Roman signal station site was on nearby **Brownhart Law** (499m, 1,663ft) just behind Chew Green and marking the Border. Dere Street then follows the natural ridge line, making for **Woden Law** (416m, 1,388ft) before leading down to the ford on Kale Water and on to the former Roman camp at **Newstead**, close to the Eildon Hills between Melrose and Newton St Boswells. (*See also the chapters on the National Park area and on Roman roads.*)

From Rochester the A68 continues past Redesdale Camp, just beyond which, at **Bellshiel**, a track leads off left across the river Rede to the remains of two early native settlements at **Birdhope**. On Birdhope Crags also is a Presbyterian church which was once the centre for many of the Scots who came over the Border seeking religious freedom. A mile to the right of the road at Bellshiel lies **Bellshiel Law** (320m, 1,068ft) with a prehistoric cairn long barrow of some importance. It is thought to date from around 2000–1500 BC. There are also a group of round barrows lower down on the slope.

The activities of the Forestry Commission now become more apparent as the borderline between the National Park area and the Border Forest narrows down to meet at **Byrness** (42 miles), less than five miles from the Border. At **Cottonshopeburn Foot,** 2 miles before Byrness, there is a camping and caravan site close to the river Rede. Next to it is the unmarked road leading up to Cottonshope Head and Chew Green. The Pennine Way also comes in here from the west and follows the river line for about 1 mile, before swinging off again up through the forestry plantations on its way to Chew Green (see above) by one of the best walking routes to that point. A Forest Drive Nature Trail (*toll*) also commences at this point, making its way westwards across the Border Forest area to Kielder.

Byrness caters extensively for the outdoor type of visitor with a National Park Information Centre, a picnic site and facilities for river

Eildon Hills

fishing, plus a small village built by the Forestry Commission for its employees. The 18th-century church is extremely small and contains a memorial to those who died in the construction of the **Catcleugh Reservoir**, which is situated 1 mile further up the road. Across the dam a track leads into **Chattlehope** and on to Chattlehope Spout. From the end of the reservoir a slow climb begins to the Border, a rise of over 165m (550ft) in little over 1 mile. At **Carter Bar** (47 miles), at a height of 419m (1,371ft), there is a lay-by where a stop can be made.

On a clear day the view stretches for 50 miles across the fertile parkland of Roxburghshire to Edinburgh and the Firth of Forth. Closer in, **Rubens Law** (9 miles as the crow flies) stands close to **Hawick**, while the triple mounds of the **Eildon Hills** (18 miles as the crow flies) mark the position of Melrose. On both of these the Romans had their signal stations which were in touch with the peak of Brownhart Law away to the right. This also is one of the points where the Wardens of the Middle Marches vainly tried to settle the many Border disputes between the Scots and English. On the slopes to the east of Carter Bar, known then as the Redeswire or col at the head of the Rede, the last of these meetings took place in 1575, some twenty-eight years before the Union of Crowns. Both sides started fighting all over again. It is said the Scots chased the English back 3 miles into England and helped themselves to 300 head of cattle on their way home. Ever since that day it has been known as the Redeswire Raid and is commemorated in a ride to the Border by local horsemen from both sides annually. The main A68 road continues down the Jed Water for 14 miles to the first of the Scottish Border towns at Jedburgh, while just below the col on the Scottish side the A6088 leads off left to Hawick in 16 miles.

10 The Middle Tyne Valley from Wylam to Hexham

N.B. For the sake of convenience the route along the north bank of the river Tyne is dealt with first. For the route along the south bank from Hexham to Prudhoe see under Excursions from Hexham, page 172.

(From Newcastle upon Tyne to Wylam see under Tyne and Wear, page 258.)

The A69(T) road emerging westwards from Newcastle upon Tyne to Corbridge and Hexham crosses into Northumberland at **Throckley**, 6½ miles from the city centre, where there is an interchange with the B6323 road from Ponteland which runs southwards to **Newburn** and **Scotswood** on the river Tyne.

Just under 1½ miles further on there is a slip-road left into **Heddon-on-the-Wall** from which point the B6318 road follows the line of Hadrian's Wall westwards while the B6528 links through to **Horsley** and **High Barns**, where it rejoins the main road again. Following the B6528 south-westwards for 1 mile, a left-hand turn by **Holeyn Hall** – a Georgian house added to by Dobson in the mid-19th century – drops down into **Wylam on Tyne**, now a suburb of Newcastle. Wylam lies on both sides of the river, with a part known as **West Wylam** very close to **Prudhoe** on the south bank, and a bridge links them here. Ten miles from Newcastle, one of its greatest attractions to visitors undoubtedly is linked with George Stephenson, the pioneer of early steam-engines, who was born here on 9 June 1781. Sadly, but true, his name is better known today than his predecessor William Hedley who also had links with Wylam, and whose memorial can be found in St. Oswin's Church built in 1887.

Wylam was once a famous colliery village, and **Wylam Colliery** is associated with the Blackett family who also had links with **Wylam Hall**, a late 19th-century building, and also with Wallington Hall. At Wylam some of the great inventive minds of the early 19th century began their work. The first of the early steam-engines was *Puffing Billy* designed by William Hedley and put into use in 1813 between Wylam Colliery and Lemington Staithes, the pier-head 4 miles to the east along the Tyne. At that time the prime use of locomotives was thought of in terms of moving coal underground and then later to places of shipment.

A mile to the east of present-day Wylam, along the northern river bank, lies the cottage where George Stephenson was born. It was given to the National Trust in 1949 by the North-East Coast Institution of Engineers and Shipbuilders but is not open to the public. At the age of twenty-three George Stephenson became engine-man at Killingworth Colliery, 6 miles north-east of Newcastle. He was already drafting out plans for engines including the later *Rocket*, but his first effort was the famous *Blucher* built in 1814 and used in the colliery where he worked. Meanwhile, Hedley had developed the *Wylam Dilly* which replaced his own first engine and this operated from Wylam up to 1862. In 1821 he was at Hetton Colliery where he built a locomotive to run to the river Wear. A company was formed with George Stephenson as their new engineer, and a railway line for passengers as well as coal was planned between Stockton and Darlington. The rails were made at Bedlington and on 27 September 1825 George Stephenson's *Locomotion Number One* operated the first passenger train service in the world from Witton Park Colliery (near Bishop Auckland) through Shildon to Darlington and Stockton (see also page 306).

These then were the pioneers of the railway age – William Hedley, whose home was at Burnhopside Hall just east of Lanchester, George Stephenson, his only son Robert, an outstanding civil engineer who built the Royal Border Bridge at Berwick-upon-Tweed and the High Level Bridge in Newcastle upon Tyne, and his nephew George Robert Stephenson, who also designed many railway bridges and was a director of the locomotive works. Some of the early engines which they designed are now in the North of England Open Air Museum at Beamish and the Museum of Science and Engineering in Newcastle.

In Wylam there is a caravan site to the west of the village, and the riverside road leads off in this direction past Horsley Wood to **Ovingham** in 2 miles. **St Mary's Church**, founded for Augustinian canons, has a late Saxon tower, but the interior is mainly 13th century, rebuilt and restored in the 17th and 19th centuries. South of the churchyard is the vicarage, the east end of which is 14th century, with additions in the 17th. There is a memorial in the church to Thomas Bewick (1753–1828), a wood engraver of some fame and the author of books on birds and animals. Some of his drawings are in the Hancock Museum of Natural History in Newcastle. Ovingham also celebrates an annual Goose Fair, usually held on the third Saturday in June with folk-dancing, Morris men, sword dancers and traditional Northumberland events. There is a caravan site to the north-east of the village and a bridge over the river at this point leading into Prudhoe. Over the Whittle Burn, a tributary of the Tyne, there is an old pack-horse bridge, passed on the road to Bywell.

Continuing west along the riverside road, the hamlet of Ovington is bypassed in 1 mile by keeping left at the fork and continuing straight on to **Bywell** in another 1½ miles, the road swinging off and following the river bank as a single-track lane. The B6309 road is joined just before entering the village, coming from Stocksfield on the south bank, and at the cross-roads a left-hand turn leads into Bywell with its castle, churches and hall all set close together.

Two ancient churches, sometimes known as the Black and the White, stand close together – the result of early manorial or parish divisions. **St Andrew's Church** was founded for the White canons of Blanchland and has a tall Saxon tower, the lower part of which is 9th century. The upper part, with the large bell opening, dates from about 1000. The interior is mainly 13th century with much restoration. **St Peter's Church** not only serves Bywell but also Stocksfield across the river and was founded by the Black Dominican monks of Durham. It is early Norman in origin, but the greater part is 13th century. The north chapel, built about 1350, was at one time used as a local school until the wall separating it from the nave was taken down and an arcade built into it in the 19th century.

Bywell Castle is an impressive 15th-century tower house, battlemented with four turrets and built mainly of Roman stones. It has been well preserved but is not open to visitors. In May 1464, after the second Battle of Hexham, Henry VI fled here after the Lancastrian defeat seeking sanctuary. **Bywell Hall**, one of the seats of the Fenwick family, was converted in 1760 by James Paine out of an earlier house and it was altered again by Dobson in 1817. It has a fine landscaped garden.

Across the river the bridge leads via the B6309 road into Stocksfield, linking up with the line of the old Roman road of Dere Street at Hindley and on to Ebchester and Durham. This is the last bridge over the river before Corbridge, and the road westwards from Bywell (after retracing one's steps to the crossroads) leads in 2½ miles to the A69(T) main road between Newcastle and Corbridge, from which point Corbridge is reached in 1½ miles. The road climbs out of the Tyne valley into parkland scenery with woodlands of spruce and larch. The run into Corbridge from this direction enters from the east past the pele tower at the entrance to the town.

The ancient town of **Corbridge** was once the capital of Northumbria and has played a leading part in its history, more so even than Hexham 3 miles to the west, which is now the capital of the Tynedale district. From about AD 81, when the Romans first came here and built their onward northern road towards Scotland (later known as Dere Street), it became a strategic crossing-point of the river Tyne and the junction with their lateral road east and west known as the Stanegate. By the 3rd century AD it was slowly evolving into more of a civilian town. King Ethelred I of Northumbria, expelled from his throne in 779, later recovered it but was murdered at Corbridge by a conspiracy of his nobles in 796, and this act of violation of an established Anglo-Saxon code of loyalty infuriated Charlemagne. In an attempt to stabilize this situation a close alliance was formed between Northumbria and the kingdom of the Franks. In 918 Regnald, a persistent Viking invader, defeated a joint army at Corbridge and by the next year had established his own Danish kingdom at York.

In 1138 the town was occupied by the Scots under David I as part of their campaign to detach Cumbria and Northumberland from the English Crown. A century later King John visited the town three times, more bent on reports of treasure hidden here than his customary destruction, but his men searched the Roman remains without success. In the Border struggles which went on throughout the 13th and 14th centuries the town was a frequent target for attack, but by medieval times Corbridge had become a large and prosperous borough. However, the town was seriously affected by the plague, and a period of decline set in. By the time it had built its first bridge – a seven-arched structure in 1674 – it had become little more than a village again. However, recovery was swift, for by the 19th century it became an attractive centre for Tynesiders. Today, it is a small but interesting town, beautifully set in the Tyne Valley on the edge of the Newcastle commuter belt and 17 miles away from the city. It attracts many tourists not only for the wealth of historic buildings in the town but also for the fascinating excavations and the museum associated with the Roman town of Corstopitum, 1 mile to the west. It also provides a convenient centre from which to explore Hadrian's Wall, 3 miles to the north. The driver should be wary of one of the most unexpected one-way systems, particularly when trying to find somewhere to park.

Close to the junction of Middle Street and Watling Street (a misnomer, for the real Watling Street is miles away) lies **St Andrew's Church**, without a doubt next to the Saxon crypt at Hexham the most important Saxon church in Northumbria and the only surviving church of four which once existed in the town. The lower part of the tower dates from pre-786, and judging by the remaining porch window there was also a porch here once. The upper part of the tower dates from the 11th century with the battlements being added later. Inside the church the most striking feature is the round tower arch, a former Roman gateway with huge square stones, transferred intact from Corstopitum. The church interior is mainly 13th-century work, but some traces of Saxon remains show in two window heads in the nave, while the north arcade dates from about 1200. The south doorway shows some Norman zigzag work, and the chancel, 13th century, has very fine lancet windows.

South of the churchyard there is one of the two fortified tower houses in the town. The vicar's pele, dating from 1318, has an overhanging parapet and again is built entirely of Roman stones from the local fort. It was officially re-opened in 1975 and is now used as the **Tourist Information Centre**. Close by is the market-place with the cast-iron **Market Cross** of 1814 bearing the Percy lion on its base. In 1332 the manor was given to the Percies of Alnwick (see page 77) for military service on the Border, and the Duke of Northumberland is still Lord of the Manor of Corbridge.

At the south end of the town lies the river bridge, built in 1674 with seven arches and the only one of the Tyne bridges to have survived the disastrous floods of 1771. It is doubled now by the use of an adjacent Bailey bridge for southbound traffic. When the river is low, it is possible to see a little further upstream the remains of the piers of the Roman bridge which brought Dere Street over the river to Corstopitum. A riverside footpath runs from the market-place along the north bank to the Roman site.

North of the bridge **Main Street** leads off eastwards to become the A69(T) road to Newcastle. At the corner is the **Angel Hotel**, an 18th-century inn but on much earlier foundations, where it is said some of the conspirators of the 1715 uprising held their secret meetings. At the eastern end of Main Street is the other fortified tower in the town, attached to the Jacobean **Low Hall** which dates from about 1600. There are many 18th- and 19th-century houses in the town, but through routes are none too easy for the motorist. There are a Victorian town hall and a number of interesting antique shops, including **Heron House**, built about 1700, now an art gallery. To the north-west of the town there was an Anglo-Saxon monastery but little of this remains. This is also the outward route northwards of the A68 road, following the line of Dere Street to Hadrian's Wall 3 miles away up Stagshawbank and continuing on to Otterburn.

To commemorate the proximity of Wylam the town holds a steam traction-engine rally usually in October, and country barn dances are a regular feature. For those interested in river fishing a stretch of water between Bywell and Wylam belongs to the Northumberland Angler's Association, with information on permits from the Tourist Information Office.

One mile to the west of the town (and reached by a signposted road off the town's northern A68 exit), close to where the Cor Burn joins the river Tyne, lies the Roman site of **Corstopitum** (*open daily, charge*), first excavated between 1906 and 1914 with a resumption in 1934. (The new bypass road – A69(T) – passes close to it, and Beaufort Castle is visible on approach.) About half the town has been uncovered. The main buildings include two buttressed granaries with underfloor circulation to keep grain dry, the remains of a fountain fed by an aqueduct, an enormous uncompleted storehouse with a large central courtyard, a group of small temples and two military compounds, one of which was a workshop. The **Museum** has probably the best collection of Romano-British sculpture in the country. Outstanding are the **Corbridge Lion**, depicting a lion devouring a stag, and a damaged pediment showing Romulus and Remus being suckled by a wolf. To the west of the site the line of the Roman road known as the **Stanegate** emerges on its way west towards Carlisle. It lies untouched, exactly as it was used 1,700 years ago.

To the north-east of Corbridge the B6321 road leads out from **Princes Street** to Wall Houses on Hadrian's Wall 4 miles away, almost immediately crossing over the new bypass road. About 2 miles along this road a left-hand turn leads towards **Aydon Castle**, following the road round for another mile. The castle is still in the course of restoration but is expected to be opened to the public shortly by the Department of the Environment. It is a fine example of an early 14th-century fortified manor-house,

Corstopitum, the east granary

battlemented and with an inner and outer bailey, set close to the wooded banks of the Cor Burn. The outer south wall shows a remarkable chimney breast topped with a small spire outlet, and close by there is a double lancet window with an apostolic head in the spandrel. Near to the castle is the 17th-century **Aydon White House**, now a private residence.

The return to Corbridge can be made by continuing along the same road in the direction of **Halton**, turning right at the fork into the village. **Halton Tower** is less than ½ mile from the line of the vallum and Hadrian's Wall itself with a track from the village leading on to them. Although marked on the OS maps as a castle, Halton Tower is really a well-preserved 14th-century tower house, with a fragment of a manor-house attached and a Jacobean house in addition. It is in private occupation and not open to the public. Close by is a rebuilt 17th-century chapel of Norman origin, said to have been on a site occupied by a church dating from the 8th century. Retracing the road out of Halton and continuing straight on at the junction, the A68 road is reached in just over a mile, where a left-hand turn leads back to Corbridge in 1½ miles crossing the new bypass road. The main A69(T) road from Corbridge to Hexham crosses the bridge to the south bank of the river Tyne and follows that bank westwards for 3 miles to Hexham, passing Dilston Castle on the left as the road crosses the Devil's Water. There is also a link-road off left to the B6307 to Blanchland.

(*For the route from Hexham to Prudhoe along the south bank of the Tyne see under excursions from Hexham, page 145. See also excursions along Hadrian's Wall, page 191; excursions to the North Tyne valley, page 152; excursions to the South Tyne valley, page 172; excursions to the Allendales, page 185.*)

Continuing the present route along the north bank of the river from Corbridge, a secondary road leads westwards from the town, passing the Roman site of Corstopitum and under the new bypass road to reach Hexham in 3 miles, but a diversion can be made to **Sandhoe** and to **Sandhoe House**, built by Dobson in 1850 in the Jacobean style. A little further south is **Beaufront Castle**, built by the same architect in 1837 in the Gothic style from an earlier Georgian house. The road linking these two hamlets on the north slopes of the terraces above the Tyne Valley circles round past Anick to come into Hexham from the north. The recently completed Corbridge bypass road, the A69(T), can be joined north of the town from the A68 and provides a quick road west past Hexham also, rejoining the former A69(T) road west of the town.

Hexham

Boating From Tyne Green.
Bowls Behind Hexham House, off Gilesgate.
Buses To Acomb, Allenheads, Alston, Bellingham, Blanchland, Blaydon, Carlisle, Chesters, Consett, Corbridge, Dilston, Falstone, Haltwhistle, Haydon Bridge, Keswick, Kielder, Morpeth, Newcastle, Penrith, Prudhoe, Wark. *Special Roman Wall bus services operate in the season.* (Bus Station in Priestpopple.)
Camping and caravanning Causey Hill Caravan Park, 1½ miles south; Trax Campsite, Hexham Race-course, 2 miles south; Lowgate Caravan Site, 2 miles west on the B6305; Riverside Caravan Site, Tyne Green, Hexham.
Distances Alston, 24 miles; Bellingham, 14 miles; Carlisle, 38 miles; Durham, 30 miles; Haydon Bridge, 7 miles; London, 282 miles; Newcastle upon Tyne, 20 miles; Rothbury, 32 miles.
Early closing Thursday.
Freshwater fishing River Tyne (Tynedale District Council permit). Information from the Tourist Information Office.
Golf *Hexham Golf-Club* on the A69(T) road 1 mile west of the town and a municipal golf-course (9 holes) on Tyne Green.
Hotels *Beaumont*, *Royal*, *County*.
Information centre Manor Office, Hallgate.
Library County Library in Beaumont Street; Borough Library in the Moot Hall.
Market Tuesday. Cattle/sheep market on Tuesdays and Fridays.
Population 9,820.
Post Office Battle Hill.
Tennis Public courts on the Seal.
Swimming-pools Indoor pool in Gilesgate.

With a population approaching 10,000, Hexham is the administrative centre of the Tynedale District, built on a terrace overlooking the river Tyne. Set in countryside of great beauty, Hexham is a main communication centre for the many unspoilt villages, castles and fortified towers in the neighbourhood and one of the best centres from which to explore Hadrian's Wall. Its old buildings, shops and markets provide much interest for the visitor, and Hexham's social life includes two night-clubs, frequent barn dances and the sound of the Northumbrian pipes, which are smaller than the Scottish ones. Local agricultural shows and sheep-dog trials are held here, and a music festival takes place usually at the end of September. Hexham also holds three steeplechase meetings annually at the race-course on Yarridge heights to the south-west of the town. Boating, canoeing and fishing are also possible on the river Tyne.

Hexham has had a long and turbulent history, which began with the grant of a large parcel of land to St Wilfrid in 674 for an abbey site. The gift was made by Queen Etheldreda (also known as Ethelthrith) of Northumbria, wife of King Ecgfrith, and caused immediate dissension between the king and Wilfrid. It was a time of some stress for the early church, for Theodore of Tarsus, appointed Archbishop of Canterbury in 669, was in the process of reforming the whole structure. On his arrival he had found only three bishops in office. Wilfrid, acting as Bishop of

Deira, was the only one properly consecrated in Roman eyes. Wilfrid was made Bishop of York and became the spiritual ruler of the whole Northumbrian church but almost immediately was dismissed from his see by the king. Theodore, at a time when there was almost a reversion to paganism, set about re-organizing his dioceses, and of the fifteen he created Hexham became one, but he recognized the patronage of the king and did not resist when Wilfrid was dismissed.

Wilfrid represented the Roman against the Celtic point of view in ecclesiastical affairs and became the main protagonist for the Roman point of view at the Synod of Whitby in 663. He went to Rome twice seeking justice for his dismissal and spent many years away from Northumbria, mainly in Sussex where he converted the South Saxons to Christianity, whilst his newly founded abbey at Hexham was developed by others. When he returned to Northumbria in 686, he found Bishop Eata at Hexham and although he was restored to his see in 705 after the death of Ecgfrith, he spent much of his time at Ripon and then at Oundle in present-day Northamptonshire. In spite of his difficult and highly individualistic life, however, his place as one of the prominent leaders in the early development of Christianity in the north became assured. Hexham, which he founded, and the community which grew up around it prospered. Together with the vast tracts of land which became 'Hexhamshire' it became similar to the later palatinate of Durham, an ecclesiastical kingdom with its own courts and justice and entirely self-contained. But with the advent in 876 of the Danes, who sacked the town and severely damaged the church, the see of Hexham ceased to exist and unlike Ripon was never revived.

It was not until the early 12th century that Augustinian canons refounded and enlarged the old church and added a gatehouse. Towards the end of the 12th century the building of a great new church began, and although it was to suffer from the frequent incursions of the Scots, the church seen today is in essence the one begun in 1190. In 1296 the Scots mounted a large-scale attack on the town and burnt down the first grammar school and destroyed many houses and the nave of the church. William Wallace descended on the town the next year and Robert the Bruce followed in 1300, with the result that the nave was not rebuilt until this century.

Hexham also played an important role in the War of the Roses, for in 1463 and 1464 there were several battles and skirmishes in the neighbourhood between the Yorkists and the Lancastrians. They took place on the Hexham Levels, close to Linnels Bridge 2 miles south of the town along the Devil's Water, the tributary that joins the Tyne between Hexham and Corbridge.

Many of Hexham's inhabitants also took part in the 1536 rebellion, known as the Pilgrimage of Grace, where many northern noblemen protested against the measures taken by Thomas Cromwell, the Vicar-General under Henry VIII, against the smaller monasteries. Led by Robert Aske with a banner showing the Five Wounds of Christ, they demanded the restoration of the monasteries, that the reforming bishops be turned out and that Cromwell be banished. Henry compromised until the rebels dispersed, then had the leaders seized and hanged them.

In the early 18th century the Riot Act was read in Hexham market-place after some Allendale lead-miners had protested against the conscription by ballot then being imposed. The troops opened fire and forty-five lives were lost, with some 300 wounded. Finally, the 1,300th centenary celebrations of the founding of Hexham Abbey were celebrated in 1964.

Around the town

The centre of Hexham's activities is in the **market-place**. On the east side stands the **Moot Hall**, a tower house built about 1400, which now houses the Borough Library and has exhibitions on its first floor. It once served as a court-house and bastion of the Archbishops of York, who exercised complete power over the 'Regality of Hexham', as it was known, until 1572. The archway of the Moot Hall leads through to the small square of the **Hallgate**, formerly known as the **Exchequer Fold**, in which stands the rather forbidding **Manor Office**. It was built in 1330 of Roman stone as a prison, but from the time of Elizabeth (although still used as a gaol until 1824) it became the administrative office of the Manor of Hexham. It now houses the **Tourist Information Office**.

To the south-east of the Manor Office is the attractive **Old Grammar School**, built in 1684 and now a private residence. Returning to the market-place, there is a small colonnaded building with Tuscan columns in the square known as the **Shambles**, dating from 1766, and nearby the **Temperley Memorial Fountain** of 1901. Also behind the colonnade is another alleyway leading through to **Meal Market**. Immediately through this is the site of **St Mary's Church**, built in the 13th century but in ruins by the 17th. Further along, at the first corner opposite The Grapes, is a plaque commemorating the Rev. J. Parker, D.D. (1830–1902), author of seventy-five books, including twenty-five volumes of the *People's Bible*.

Hexham's main attraction lies in its **Abbey**, opposite the Moot Hall, but the frontal sight is disappointing and was the second attempt by John Dobson in 1858 to extend the east end. The building reveals itself more stylishly from the rear in the abbey grounds, which now form part of the public park leading up to the **Seal**. The building of the abbey falls into three main periods: the Saxon remains dating from 675 to 680, from 1190 to 1296 and the later restorations from 1850 to 1910. From the earliest period all that remains is the **Saxon Crypt**, built mainly from Roman stones taken from Corbridge and undoubtedly the finest Saxon remains in Northumbria today. Many of the stones taken from Corstopitum have remains of inscriptions and ornamental designs. The tunnel vault of the relic chamber retains much of its original plasterwork. The crypt lay hidden for many years until its rediscovery in 1725.

In the main part of the church the **Choir** is the earliest part, built between 1190 and 1230 and showing the gradual change from the Transitional to the Early English styles. The church is rich in furnishings, and there are three rows of medieval misericords, the backs of which were removed and sold for firewood in the early 19th century. In the centre of the chancel stands **St Wilfrid's Chair**, tub-shaped and probably about 1,300 years old, which once stood in the Saxon church. It is also known as the **Frith Stool**, from the time when sanctuary could be claimed by sitting in it. The chair marks the site of the Anglo-Saxon apse or eastern chancel end and was also reputed to be used for the coronation of early Northumbrian kings. The magnificent **South Transept** reveals on the west wall the **Night Stair**, a wide and well-worn flight of steps by which the monks could return to their Dormitory along the rib-vaulted passage, or slype, which linked the two, and where there are two Roman altars. The transept also contains a Roman tombstone showing the standard-bearer Flavinus riding over the figure of a crouching Briton armed with a dagger. The slightly later **North Transept** is more elaborately decorated with trefoil arcading and some dog-tooth moulding.

The **Chantry Chapel** of Prior Rowland Leschman, who died in 1491, is adorned with a remarkable series of carvings, probably by local masons. Among the subjects depicted are St George and the Dragon, St Christopher, musicians and a jester, a fox preaching to geese, a monkey and a lady combing her hair. Some of them are grotesque caricatures with a touch of ribald interpretation, and many depict typical human attributes of piety, gluttony and so on.

144   *Hexham Abbey. The Choir, showing St Wilfred's Chair*

The **Nave** was rebuilt in 1908 by Temple Moore in the 14th-century style, though part of the south wall is original, and in the south-west corner the original Saxon floor has been exposed. A number of carved fragments may be seen in the south and west walls dating from Roman, Saxon and Norman times.

Only parts of the monastic buildings remain: they include the **Lavatorium** with its seven gabled arches, the 13th-century **Vestibule** to the Chapter House and, along Flag Walk, the **Priory Gate** which dates from about 1160. On the south side part of the buildings around the former **Cloisters** now house a magistrates' court and the Area Health Office.

Running south from the market-place, Hexham's modern shopping centre in **Fore Street** is now a pedestrian precinct. From the north-west corner of the market-place runs **Market Street**, with several Georgian buildings, which at St Wilfrid's Gate becomes Gilesgate. Along this latter street lies **Hexham House**, also Georgian, now used as council offices with the public park behind.

Hexham Bridge and **Tyne Green** lie to the north of the town. The bridge, built in 1785 after the floods of 1771 had washed away the earlier one 1 mile to the west, offers a good viewpoint over the whole of Hexham. Traditionally, the town has had a long association with tanning and leather industries, and some of its products are still on sale today.

The construction of a new bypass road on the north bank of the Tyne has now been completed and links the main A69(T) 2 miles west of Hexham, skirting the town and also Corbridge, and rejoining the existing A69(T) 3 miles east of Corbridge, thus offering a new and faster through route between east and west.

Excursions from Hexham

1) Hexham to Dilston Castle, Riding Mill and Prudhoe Castle (approx. 18 miles)

The A69(T) road eastwards from Hexham follows the south bank of the river Tyne past **Dilston Park** and in 2½ miles reaches the **Devil's Water**, a tributary of the Tyne which rises some 12 miles away to the south on Tedham Moss. The river's curious name comes from the Dyvel, later Dyvelstone, family who settled here in the 12th century; the name was modernized as Dilston.

Close to the river lie the scant remains of **Dilston Castle**. The home that James Radcliffe, 3rd Earl of Derwentwater was having built – a huge mansion – was never completed and was knocked down after his death following the 1715 rebellion. The modern **Dilston Hall** a short distance away, formerly the home of Viscount Allendale, now bears a sign naming it as an Advanced Social Training Unit. Otherwise, all that remains are an Elizabethan tower house and a chapel.

Just beyond the river the main A69(T) road continues into Corbridge in 1 mile, while a link road (the A6080), crossing the line of the Roman road of Dere Street in ½ mile from this junction, continues east to join the A68 road close to Corbridge station. Following the south bank of the Tyne, in 2 miles **Riding Mill** is reached, a rapidly-growing residential village from Newcastle's overspill. Apart from a 17th-century manor-house, it has an inn – the Wellington – from the same era. The village has also been recently chosen as the site of a new pumping station and pressurized pipeline to lift water from the river Tyne and carry it some 210m (700ft) up over the hills to the south as part of the new Kielder Water Scheme linking the supply with the three river valleys to the south.

The A68 road runs south from Riding Mill towards the Derwent Valley, while the A695 continues eastwards towards Newcastle along the south bank of the river. In 2 miles **Stocksfield** is reached with a bridge over the river here to Bywell. A unique agricultural and farm museum was opened at Easter 1979 at Westside, Newton, Stocksfield, the **National Tractor Museum** (*open April to September 10–6 daily, tea room and shop*). This collection has been assembled over the past 15 years. It contains over 100 tractors and over 4,000 different catalogued items depicting the development of farm life, work tools and machinery over the last century. Over 12,000 feet of covered display area is open and there will eventually be a total area of 30,000 sq. ft. The planned expansion will give a varied and interesting undercover exhibition. Scale working models and steam engines will also form an unusual display. Between Stocksfield and Prudhoe, 2 miles further on, was a former colliery area, but many of the old terraces of houses along the river banks have now been replaced by sprawling modern estates half-way up the hillside. **Prudhoe** is largely a dormitory area for the metropolis but also contains a large new industrial area. There is a single-track bridge here across the river to Ovingham, while the remains of **Prudhoe Castle** are at **Low Prudhoe** on a spur between the river and the main road. This castle, which once boasted its impregnability in the face of Scottish attacks, contains a keep which is probably amongst the oldest in Northumberland, built about 1173 in Henry II's reign. The rest of the castle was built by the de Umfraville family mainly in the 13th century but later came into the hands of the Percies. The most significant feature remaining is the **Gatehouse**, with Norman arches to the gateway and a barrel-vaulted ceiling which is most impressive. Here also is the 13th-century **Chapel** with an oriel window which is said to be one of the earliest in existence and which is reached by an open stairway. Alongside the gatehouse the 14th-century **Barbican** is also a very fine example of its kind. Although in fact the castle did hold out twice against the Scots, by 1586 it was in a semi-ruinous state, and Cromwell is said to have knocked down the tower with cannon fire. It was partially restored by the 2nd Duke of Northumberland between 1808 and 1818 with a house being added between the two baileys. At the present time only the outer parts of the castle are open as the Department of the Environment is restoring the site.

Less than 1 mile eastwards along the A695 beyond Prudhoe the road crosses the Stanley Burn, marking the boundary between Northumberland and the County of Tyne and Wear. Blaydon is reached in 6 miles and Newcastle upon Tyne in 10 miles. (*From Prudhoe to Newcastle upon Tyne see under Tyne and Wear, page 269*). An alternative route back to Hexham can be made by following the north-bank route along the river Tyne through Wylam to Ovingham, Bywell and Corbridge.

2) To Linnels Bridge, Blanchland, the Derwent Reservoir, Kiln Pit Hill, the Tyne Valley and Hadrian's Wall (approx. 47 miles)

Leaving Hexham by the B6306 road to the south-east, in 2 miles **Linnels Bridge** is reached. Originally built in 1581 by Humphrey Errington, whose somewhat indecipherable inscription remains there, the present bridge replaced it in 1698. Half a mile beyond the bridge is Dipton Wood, where the B6307 link-road from Corbridge comes in on the left. On the **Hexham Levels** to the west the two famous **Battles of Hexham** were fought in 1463 and 1464. A mile to the west of Linnels Bridge is the West Dipton Burn, and 3 miles along this, in remote and hidden countryside, is the reputed **Queen Margaret's Cave**, where it is said the warrior Queen of Henry VI, together with her small son, was sheltered by a bandit after the battle which so turned the fortunes of the War of the Roses.

A steady climb from Linnels Bridge past Wooley Hospital's turning leads in just under 3 miles to **Townhead**. Here, a side-road leads off to **Slaley**, where the gardens of **Slaley Hall** are occasionally open to the public. There is also a caravan site along this road which leads on along the moorland ridge through to Barleyhill and Kiln Pit Hill and provides an alternative means of reaching both Minsteracres Hall and Healey Hall, two of the larger houses in the neighbourhood.

From Townhead onwards the road drops down into the valley with neat farms and forest land, then climbs again to pass through the vast expanse of the Slaley Forest which spreads away to the west. The road continues to climb, reaching a height of 311m (1,036ft) above sea-level, before it clears the trees and turns along the ridge overlooking the Derwent Reservoir, with the great backbone ridge of Stanhope Common straight ahead on the Durham side of the boundary. The road drops steeply down a 1 in 5 descent, past the Kiln Pit Hill turning and on into **Blanchland**.

Once described as one of England's most perfect villages, Blanchland lies in the upper Derwent valley, surrounded entirely by moorland. It is right on the boundary between Northumberland and Durham, and the reservoir itself, theoretically at least, is shared between them. To the west of the reservoir the Beldon Burn marks the boundary line. Blanchland draws most visitors to see its famous **Abbey**, founded in 1139 by that reformed order of Augustinian monks known as the Premonstratensians, who already at that time had one house at Alnwick. They were also known as the White Canons, from which the village takes its name, and like so many other monasteries in the 16th century they were dissolved in 1539. The area was neglected for the best part of two centuries but eventually came under the influence of Lord Crewe, the then Bishop of Durham, in the early part of the 18th century. It was from this village that 'General' Tom Forster kept in touch with the Earl of Derwentwater prior to the 1715 uprising.

Lord Crewe's trustees kept up the good work after his death, skilfully restoring the abbey. They were also responsible for planning and building the village whose stone cottages were erected for the lead-miners who worked in the district. The square around which these are grouped is L-shaped, the main building being the renowned **Lord Crewe Arms** hotel which, although essentially Georgian, incorporates fragments of the former monastic buildings. The **Gatehouse**, dating from about 1500, forms one of the entrances to this square. In the hotel itself are portraits

Blanchland

of Lady Crewe (the former Dorothy Forster), her husband and her niece, the other Dorothy Forster, who rescued her brother from Newgate. Of the **Abbey Church** very little remains of the 13th-century building apart from the tower and north transept. The east end of the **Chancel** was renewed in 1884. In the churchyard John Wesley preached to the lead-miners during his missions in the area in 1747.

The **Derwent Reservoir**, 1 mile to the east of Blanchland, is 3½ miles long. It was opened in 1967, and most of the surrounding area has been turned into a tourist recreation area. It is possible to drive right round the reservoir, and the recommended route is anti-clockwise from Blanchland by the B6306 road to **Edmondbyers** (which passes through the old Abbey gateway), thence to the **Derwent Bridge** via the B6278 and on to make a left turn on to the A68. A mile along this latter road turn left on the unclassified road at the fork. This leads through to a T-junction where a left turn reaches **Barleyhill**. A left turn at this point for 2 miles returns you to the north shore of the reservoir by the **Millshield Picnic Area**.

From here the north shore road circles round back to Blanchland. The dam is at the south-eastern end of the reservoir with the administrative buildings below this, and there is a **Fishing Permit Centre** close by. At Edmondbyers also there is a caravan site.

At its western end the reservoir is a restricted nature reserve, and close to Blanchland itself is the **Carrick's Picnic Area**, set in a wooded valley close to the Beldon Burn, with access to the river allowed. On the south bank half-way round is the **Pow Hill Country Park**, a natural parkland setting with hides for bird-watching and space to roam around but no access permitted to the water's edge. On the north bank is the Millshield Picnic Area, a smaller site with parking facilities, picnic tables and so on, which does give access to the water. Close by is the **Derwent Reservoir Sailing Clubhouse** where various classes of dinghies operate, available to members only. They usually have an open week in August. Visitors to Derwent wishing to enjoy the reservoir's sporting amenities can obtain further information from the Utilities Building below the dam. Angling permits may be purchased here.

To complete our own excursion route take the B6306 road from Blanchland towards Edmondbyers but turn left in just over 1 mile by **Ruffside Hall**, passing the Carricks Picnic Area and following the unclassified new country road along the north shore of the reservoir marked out with miles of new white fenceposts. A number of lay-bys have been constructed along this bank and those nearer to the western end provide interesting viewpoints into the nature reserve area, but access is not permitted. Passing Winnowshill Farm, this scenic route continues to the Sailing Clubhouse, and then at the Millshields Picnic Area the road turns away from the reservoir and climbs the 2 miles to Barleyhill crossroads. Straight ahead are the grounds of **Ministeracres Hall**, a late 18th-century house with later additions, now used as a Passionist monastery. A right turn at this point leads in just over 1 mile to **Kiln Pit Hill**, where the main A68 road meets our own at the crossroads. Continuing straight across past **Greymare Hill**, close to the slopes of which will be sited some of the new installations relating to the Kielder Water Scheme, the road drops down steeply in 3 miles to **Whittonstall**. Here, a left turn brings us on to the line of the Roman road of Dere Street along the B6309 road towards Stocksfield.

From Whittonstall, with its fine views over the Tyne Valley to the north, the B6309 road leads down to Stocksfield from which point a variety of return routes to Hexham can be made. By turning left and following the A695 road along the south bank of the river Tyne through Riding Mill a direct route can be made via the A68, A6080 and the A69(T) past Dilston Hall making a round trip back to Hexham in 31 miles.

Alternatively, by crossing the river to Bywell the north bank route can be followed through to Ovingham and Wylam with an optional recrossing of the river again at Wylam to visit Prudhoe Castle. To complete a circular tour, from Wylam follow the road north out of the village past **Holeyn Hall** and straight across the crossroads of the B6528. The road crosses over the A69(T), and at the roundabout the right-hand fork leads in 1 mile to Vindovala, the Roman fort at Rudchester. Turning left at this point on to the B6318, we follow the course of **Hadrian's Wall** and in 2½ miles reach **Harlow Hill**. To the left are the reservoirs of **Whittle Dene**, close to which is the ruined 15th-century **Welton Tower**, built of Roman stones with a later manor-house attached. The B6318 is followed to Wall Houses where a left-hand turn leads on to the B6321 road. In 2 miles a right-hand turn follows the unclassified road towards Aydon Castle and also Halton Castle before circling round to approach Corbridge from the north, where a visit can also be made to the Roman site of Corstopitum. The return to Hexham can then follow either the north bank of the Tyne or the south according to choice.

Carter Bar

11 The North Tyne Valley from Hexham to Deadwater

By the time of the Norman Conquest Scotland's frontier rested on the line of the river Tweed, but in the turbulent era that followed she also claimed much of both Northumbria and Cumbria. In 1174 and again in 1189 parts of these lands were given away by English kings in attempts to secure allegiance, but frequently the treaties – such as that of 1189 – were not enforced, and the situation remained untidy and fluid. Attempts were made to fix proper boundaries in 1222 and in 1237 when Alexander II of Scotland resigned his claims on English land. In 1243 and again in 1249 further attempts were made to agree on a common boundary with six knights from each side appointed to fix a line between England and Scotland, but the ambitions of the first two Edwards undermined this action, and in 1314, when Robert the Bruce invaded England, the district of Tynedale immediately recognized him as their rightful monarch.

Following the Treaty of Northampton in 1328, the need to fix a definitive line was again recognized, but it was not until King David II of Scotland was released from eleven years of captivity in 1357 that something began to be done. Ten years later another treaty was made with the establishment of the Wardens of the East and West March, and in 1381 the Middle March was added with their respective headquarters at Berwick, Harbottle and Carlisle, with the great families of the north – the Percies and the Nevilles – mainly responsible for patrolling and regulating the frontier. Two of these Marches faced Northumberland with a great number of passages between the two countries, all of which were very convenient for local feuding or the traditional art of reiving, and probably the worst aspect was that the local inhabitants themselves were none too concerned where the actual line was drawn, for their allegiances were more often than not loyal to kith and kin on either side (and sometimes both sides) of the actual frontier.

Nothing authority in either London or Edinburgh could really do would establish a firm division, and in the spate of claim and counter-claim no area was more fluid in its line than upper Tynedale which remained basically Scottish up to the middle of the 14th century. In the Border struggles which followed into the next two centuries the Scottish line followed the Liddel Water, well to the west of the present line at Deadwater, but even then the English claimed it should have been the Tarras Burn several miles further west again, and the intervening portion became known as the 'Debatable Lands', a no-man's or everyman's area which became particularly lawless and a haven for reivers and refugees from both sides, subject only to local feudal power. By the Treaty of Norham in 1551 some attempt was made to rectify this, along the line of Liddel Water and then the river Esk down to Solway Firth, with the last portion west following the river Sark into the estuary, but again this became a cause of some dissension. On the Northumberland side both Tynedale and Redesdale remained liberties of their own for many years, and even after they were incorporated into the national structure, their autonomy remained by the sheer inability to control them. This state of affairs continued long after the Union of Crowns in 1603, when Border warfare officially ceased.

In Tynedale the great families were the Charltons, Robsons, Milburns and Dodds. The great names in Liddesdale were the Armstrongs and the Eliots, and the former clan became so numerous in the 16th century that they moved into the Debatable Lands by Wauchopedale. Originally, their name had been Fairburn, but in the 14th century, when they had first moved into Liddesdale, they were visited by the Scottish king who asked for assistance in mounting his horse and was lifted bodily into his saddle by one of them using only one arm. Thereafter they were dubbed Armstrong. But in time, they turned nearly everyone against them and became a doomed clan. In 1530 James V of Scotland, fed up with trying to keep peace on the Border, tricked Johnnie Armstrong into meeting him at Carlinrigg near Hawick and hanged him and his companions.

Known as the Robin Hood of Liddesdale, Johnnie Armstrong's death began the harrying of the clan by the Wardens of both sides, so much so that in 1549 several hundred of them moved over to the English side and were followed later by the remnants of the clan. By 1610 the handful that remained on the Scottish side were broken men, and as late as 1793 the 3rd Earl of Buccleuch cleared them from the Border again.

North Tynedale today, with its vast forests and extensive plans for future tourist development, is one of the most attractive of all Northumberland's holiday areas.

From Hexham the river Tyne is crossed by the bridge, at the far end of which is the new bypass roundabout at Bridge End. Turn left, and in ½ mile, a right-hand turn leads on to the A6079 road for Chollerford. A right-hand turn leads off to **Acomb**, where the lavishly appointed **Church of St John Lee** lies, built by Dobson in 1875 and enlarged in 1885. **Acomb House**, dated 1736, is also in the village. In 3 miles is the village of **Wall**, less than ½ mile from the Roman frontier after which it is named and with a hotel aptly named **The Hadrian**. On the opposite side of the North Tyne are the Warden heights. This village, with a large green and a 19th-century church, makes a convenient overnight point for explorations along Hadrian's Wall. A mile beyond the village at **Low Brunton** the crossroads of the B6318 are reached, where the **Military Way**, built by General Wade in 1752–3 as a rapid means of cross-country communication after the rising of 1745, follows the line of Hadrian's Wall and is actually built on top of it. The A6079 continues straight on to join the A68 road towards Otterburn in 4 miles. On the right 200 metres short of this junction a signposted footpath leads up **Brunton Bank** to Turret 26b, one of the best preserved of the fortifications on Hadrian's Wall, with a view across the river to Chesters House.

A left turn at the crossroads leads across the five-arched Chollerford Bridge into the village of **Chollerford**. The bridge was built after the great Tyne flood of 1771 had washed the previous one away. It is a single-track bridge controlled by lights, with heavy delays in summer months. Just to the south of the present bridge lie the remnants of the Roman bridge crossing (reached by a footpath by the modern bridge and signposted), following the line of Hadrian's Wall. A left turn after crossing Chollerford Bridge leads directly to the site of the Roman fort of Chesters in 1 mile along the B6318. The B6320 road continues north-west up the North Tyne Valley, but a right-hand turn on leaving Chollerford follows a side road to **Humshaugh** close to the river, with the red-bricked Georgian mansion of **Humshaugh House** nearby. The road continues on to **Haughton Castle** (*not open*) which is one of the great houses of Northumbria, a battlemented castle originally built in the 14th century with some even earlier stages. Sacked and burnt down in the 16th century, it remained a ruin until the restorations of the 19th century when a west wing, designed by Salvin, was also added. On the opposite bank is Barrasford.

The road continues along the west bank to **Coldwell**, passing **Wester Hall**, and then rejoins the B6320 road into **Simonburn**. The village is set slightly to the west of the main road, with the parish **Church of St Mungo** which once controlled the largest parish in England with an area ranging from Hadrian's Wall to the Scottish Border. Originally a 13th-century structure, little of this now remains, for a great deal of restoration took place in the 18th and 19th centuries, some of it by Salvin. It is a large church with its floor sloping down towards the altar, and there is some evidence to suggest that a much earlier church may have stood here in Saxon times. It is possible that the influence of the monks from Hexham penetrated as far up the North Tyne as this even in the 7th century. At St Mungo's a fragment of a Saxon cross-shaft lies in the porch.

The church also has monuments to two local families – the Allgoods who are associated with Nunwick (see below) and the Ridley family, one of whom – Cuthbert Ridley – was the rector here and died in 1625. The Ridley family are a well-known and widespread Northumberland family, among whose members was Nicholas Ridley, Bishop of London, who died with Latimer as one of the Oxford martyrs. Another member of the family, Nancy Ridley, is one of the best-known Northumberland authors, who has written several enlightening travel books about the area.

Simonburn's importance grew from its early outpost position where the Keepers of North Tynedale watched for the intrusion of Border raiders. The vicarage, although 17th and 18th century in style, had a much earlier tower house, and at **Simonburn Castle**, ½ mile to the west of the village, there was another 13th-century tower house. Reached by a track north out of the village leading to the ford on Hopeshield Burn, then taking the left-hand pathway until it meets the Castle Burn, the remains lie in densely wooded surroundings.

At the point where the village road rejoins the B6320 going north are the gates of **Nunwick House** (*not open*), with its parkland stretching to the river. It is an elegant 18th-century brown sandstone house, later altered by Bonomi. Just beyond this point a side-road on the left leads through to **Ravensheugh Crags** and into the denser areas of **Wark Forest**. A track leads off, 3 miles along it, to the left, ½ mile up a hill, to a group of stones known as the **Goatstones** – four stones equally spaced and facing a centre. One stone bears cup-markings which suggest a date of between 1600 and 1000 BC, and the slightly raised centre may suggest a burial place. They are sited close to the peak of the Ravensheugh Crags (252m, 840ft).

The forest road marks the boundary of the Border Forest Park and continues on to circle round to **Stonehaugh,** a postwar-created forest village of block terraces, which house both employees and the Forest Office for Wark Forest. Just before reaching the village the **Pennine Way** crosses the forest road from south to north at **Ladyhill,** and 1 mile to the south of this point lie the remains of **Comyn's Cross,** a reminder of the famous Scottish family who once occupied Tarset Castle and whose member, John Comyn the Red of Badenoch, was murdered by Robert the Bruce in Dumfries in 1306. They had met to discuss their respective claims to the throne of Scotland but quarrelled; Bruce acted hastily and had to fly into exile as a result.

Wark Forest is the southernmost unit of the Border Forest Park, and from Stonehaugh there are a variety of walks possible, including the **Warksburn Forest Trail.** There is also a caravan and camping site here, and examples of totem-pole carving created by the forest workers. It is also possible to follow forest trails right across Henshaw Common to Haltwhistle and the line of Hadrian's Wall, but only on foot, and cars are not permitted beyond Stonehaugh. However, a circular drive from Simonburn to Stonehaugh can return along the line of the Wark Burn back to Wark (see below), about 12 miles in all. (*See also the chapter on the Border Forest Park, page 222.*)

From Simonburn the main road continues north in just over 2 miles to **Wark,** a former market town, sometimes known as Wark-on-Tyne to distinguish it from its namesake on the river Tweed. For many years – up to the mid-14th century at least – Wark was not only the capital of North Tynedale but Scottish to boot, and Scottish kings held court here. Even after the English returned and began to garrison this area, there was some resentment of their presence. Some records show how they tried to suppress the constant lawlessness and reiving that went on but met with no assistance from the local populace and, in two instances, actually had their strongholds destroyed by them. Like its counterpart in Redesdale, Tynedale held its own liberty courts and was completely autonomous, where not only did the king's writ fail to run but it was doubtful if even the Percies' writ, as Wardens of the Marches, had any more effect. Justice was done on the **Mote Hill,** where the earlier Celts had also held their courts, and later on came the Norman motte-and-bailey **Castle,** the earthwork remains of which can be seen by the beautiful stretch of the

North Tyne river which is found here. There is a village green and an interesting 16th-century farmhouse converted into an inn with the attractive name of the **Battlesteads**. The church is an early 19th-century one. Wark's early history also indicates a Saxon presence, for it was the scene in 788 of the murder of King Alfwald of Northumbria.

There is a good viewpoint of the village from the bridge which crosses the river here, with a secondary road leading to Chipchase Castle and south to the village of Chollerton following the east bank.

The B6320 continues north and in 1 mile reaches **Houxty**, with views across the river to Chipchase Castle. Just to the north of here the Houxty Burn runs into the North Tyne. At the foot of Houxty Bank the naturalist Abel Chapman lived. He was the man who persuaded the South African president to set up the Kruger National Park, and some of his relics from here are in the Hancock Museum in Newcastle. Climbing the bank, the road swings away from the river, just as the latter bends north-east around the Birtley bluff, then crosses the fell 180m (600ft) above sea-level with an excellent viewpoint over the river valley. On the opposite bank the river Rede joins the North Tyne at Redesmouth. The landscape opens up into a more bare and tree-less aspect as the road drops down to Bellingham. A mile before the town is reached the **Pennine Way** comes in from the left and joins the road to make its crossing of the North Tyne by the bridge that leads into the town.

Bellingham (pronounced Belling-jum) is a busy market town and a typical Border centre, where farmers from both Northumberland and Scotland are attracted to its special lamb sales. Its population does not exceed 1,000 inhabitants, but it is the present-day capital of North Tynedale and one of the few towns of any size for many miles around. It is also the venue of the annual North Tyne Agricultural Show, usually held the last Saturday in August. It attracts many visitors, who rightfully see it as a centre for access to fine walking country, and it is also a gateway to both the Border Forest Park and the Northumberland National Park. In former days its activities included both coalmining and ironworking, and it is said that some of the ironwork founded here was used in the construction of the Tyne Bridge built in 1834.

St Cuthbert's Church, named after the traditional way of marking the temporary resting-place of the saint's body on his many travels around Northumberland before a final interment in Durham, is unusual in having one of the few stone roofs in the country. It was placed there in the 17th century, a massive structure with wagon-vaulting, after the church had been set on fire many times by Border raiders and probably as a means of deterring further efforts in this direction, but the weight was too much for it and it had to be buttressed later on. It is claimed a church stood here from the 11th century, but the earliest visible signs date from the 13th century. A great deal of remodelling took place in the early part of the 17th century, probably to conform to the new roof structure, and this late medieval style is essentially the one seen today. In the churchyard there is a curious gravestone shaped like a long pedlar's pack of the kind used in the early 18th century. It recalls a well-known local legend – the 'Long Pack' – a tale told by James Hogg, the Ettrick Shepherd, a poet and friend of Sir Walter Scott, from whom many border ballads have originated. There are many versions, but this one concerns a pedlar who called at one of the two great houses in the Bellingham area – Lee Hall – in the year 1723 and finding only a maid at home asked if he could leave his pack and call back later. The maid agreed, but later the other servants became suspicious of a movement inside the pack and one of them fired an old shot-gun into it. Inside they found a young man dying, put there to let his accomplices in after dark. A reception committee was set up and the intruders, signalled in by a whistle, met with a warm welcome and a fusillade of shots. It is claimed that several local robbers disappeared as a result of this, while the young man was buried in the churchyard, but others say his body was removed later on.

A pathway behind the churchyard leads to **St Cuthbert's Well**, or Cuddy's Well to give it its more colloquial name, the waters of which it is claimed have healing powers and are still used in baptisms today.

In the small market-place there is a **Boer War Memorial**, and to add to the relics from such days, outside the Town Hall is a mounted musket or Gingall, looking like a harpoon gun, from the Chinese Boxer Rising, which was brought back by a member of the Charlton family. The 19th-century Catholic **Church of St Oswald** also reflects some of the local influence of this family from Hesleyside Hall, one of the four great families in the area, who were members of this faith.

Bellingham also has a nine-hole golf-course, a youth hostel and a **Tourist Information Office** and is a good centre for riding and fishing as well as fell-walking. There is also a camping and caravan site here. Just to the north of the town lies the **Hareshaw Burn**, running south to join the North Tyne, which provides a favourite 1½-mile walk up the dene to **Hareshaw Linn** where the waterfall drops some 9m (30ft) into a wooded chasm. The **Pennine Way** also follows this route away from the town northwards but turns away before the falls, passing **Callerhues Crag** (335m, 1,118ft) and then close to **Hareshaw House**.

From the town the road which parallels this route is the B6320 which continues north-eastwards to cross **Hareshaw Fell** and the fairly desolate moorland between Troughend and Corsenside Commons on its way to Otterburn. The road crosses the track of the **Pennine Way** just before **Hareshaw Head** where it reaches a height of 306m (1,020ft) above sea-level. It then drops down to cross the A68 road – the Roman road of Dere Street – in 6½ miles and reaches Otterburn in 8 miles. A left-hand turn at the A68 junction leads through to Elishaw, High Rochester and Carter Bar.

A second, unclassified road from Bellingham follows the southern slopes of **Corsenside Common** north-eastwards along the line of the river Rede to reach **West Woodburn** in 4 miles, where it joins the A68 road close to the Roman fort of Habitancum. At **Hole**, 2 miles from Bellingham, is a well-preserved pele or bastel-house with outside steps, dating from the early 17th century, close to Hole Farm.

Finally, another unclassified road runs south-east from Bellingham, following the east bank of the North Tyne to **Redesmouth** and then circles round to Wark or provides the through route to **Green Rigg** and on to the **Sweethope Loughs**, a most scenic way along the **Wanneys**, as this area is known, by moorland roads.

Continuing north-westwards from Bellingham up the North Tyne Valley, there is a road on both sides of the river, and, with the advent of the Kielder Water Scheme, the one on the north side has now become the main one to Kielder, with a new bridge south of Lanehead, 3½ miles west of Bellingham, where it joins the south bank road by Bent House. Ignoring the Kielder signpost therefore and recrossing the bridge out of town, a right turn off the B6320 follows the unclassified valley road on the south bank, which almost immediately enters the National Park area. In 1½ miles, through some fine parkland scenery, on the left are the grounds of **Hesleyside Hall** (*not open*), a fine, mainly Georgian house, where the park was laid out by 'Capability' Brown in 1776. The house is still occupied by members of the Charlton family and one of its treasures is the great 'spur', said to have been carried into the dining-room on a salver whenever the lady of the house found her larder running low, and which immediately led to another spate of reiving. The incident figures in one of the paintings by W. B. Scott in the Wallington Hall collection.

The road continues to **Birks** where the **Chirdon Burn** flows into the North Tyne and marks the boundary of the Border Forest Park in this area. Half a mile along the burn lie the ruins of **Dally Castle**, a 13th-century bastel-house, occupied for a long time by the Lindsey family as a Scottish outpost on English soil, but it was destroyed in the 16th century, along with Tarset Castle on the opposite bank of the North Tyne, by local inhabitants after English garrisons had taken over, for they resented the watch-dog activities which spoilt their reiving. The Chirdon Burn continues deep into the forest area, past **Allerybank**, and there are some very pleasant walks in the area, with forest tracks leading through to **Hopehouse**, **Black Knowe** (485m, 1,615ft), **Rushy Knowe** (391m, 1,304ft), close to which the memorial to Lord Robinson is situated, before circling back to the Whickhope Burn and Emmethaugh. About 6 miles along the burn are a series of waterfalls known as the **Seven Linns**, best seen when the river is in spate.

On the opposite bank at Birks the **Tarset Burn** runs into the North Tyne, and there is a bridge across the river at this point where the north-bank road from Bellingham comes in. A mile along the road is **Greystead**, with an almost identical church to those of Humshaugh and Wark, built in 1818 along with the others by the Greenwich Hospital Commissioners as part of their development of the former estates of the Earl of Derwentwater and to break up the existing over-large parish at Simonburn which covered all this area. A track leads off left 2 miles beyond this hamlet to **Ridley Stokoe**, with a path on to the Linn of Ridley Stokoe, a waterfall dropping down from the **Stokoe Crags**. Less than a mile beyond this, also on the left and on the ridge, is the settlement of **Smales**, one of the many traces of primitive dwellings and former camp sites in the area, particularly of the Romano-British era. There is a signposted path on the left of the road. The **Smales Burn** joins the North Tyne at **Smalesmouth**, and the whole of this area is part of the Border Forest Park. The road has been improved very much in recent years, and 1 mile beyond here at **Stannersburn** there is a bridge across the North Tyne into Falstone.

Great activities are in progress at the present time throughout this last isolated part of Northumberland, for work has already commenced on the new Kielder Water Scheme which will not only divert the present road but also flood the whole area between Falstone and Kielder to create a new reservoir about 7 miles long. This monumental project will then become the largest man-made lake in the country, with two dams – at

Bakethin and Falstone – due for completion by 1980. As a direct result of this, some of the lower-lying areas presently used for recreational purposes will be covered over, and the following paragraphs should be therefore read with due circumspection. **Plashetts**, for example, one of the forest's coal-producing areas, set on the opposite bank, has a picnic site at the moment, which will be drowned, and there appears to be a stone-crushing plant in operation there now. **Mounces**, 2 miles on from Emmethaugh and which also has a picnic site, will be likewise affected, but great plans are already being outlined for replacements where necessary. Again, at **Lewisburn**, where the tributary of that name flows into the North Tyne, considerable alterations will have to be made.

The new road is already partially completed and is operating from Lewisburn. At the moment there is also a large camping site here, run by the Caravan Club and open from Easter to October, and the start of a forest trail. Two stretches of the North Tyne at this point are available for trout fishing, which again will be lost, but enthusiasts will be glad to learn that plans are being made for a new trout and salmon hatchery in the vicinity of Kielder village for stocking the new reservoir as well as the North Tyne.

Just beyond Lewisburn is **Kielder Camp** and ½ mile beyond this point the site of the new **Bakethin Dam**, the smaller of the two that will eventually control the water flow. **Kielder** village is reached 1½ miles further on. This is the main point of activity in this huge man-made forest area, the centre of **Kielder Forest** which is the largest forest in Great Britain and probably in Europe as well. Just before reaching Kielder, ½ mile to the south, is one of the best-preserved pieces of railway architecture in the country – the **Kielder Viaduct**, built in 1867 and designed by Peter Nicholson of Newcastle. Described as the 'finest example of a railway arch in Britain', it will soon mark the northern end of the artificial lake, its piers lapped by the water.

Kielder village has about sixty houses for its forestry workers, most of them built in the early 1950s. Additionally, there are information centres, adventure playgrounds, a tea-room, youth hostel, toilets, car parks, picnic sites and several forest trails and waymarked walks starting from this point. A 12-mile-long toll-road links Kielder with Byrness in Redesdale and climbs through the forest up to the 450m (1,500ft) mark above sea-level, past **Oh Me Edge** and through some of the more remote parts of the area. It is a single-track, unsurfaced road with passing places, and is maintained by the Forestry Commission to a reasonable standard.

Redesdale Forest

It has various observation points, forest walks and picnic sites *en route*. The road provides a very convenient way of linking Tynedale with Redesdale as part of a day's tour, the only alternative being to carry on into Scotland and return via Carter Bar. The Redesdale side with its much taller trees tends to be more interesting and there is a picnic site close to the river Rede.

One of the main attractions at Kielder is **Kielder Castle**, built on a hill above the junction of the North Tyne and the Kielder Burn, which was constructed in 1775 as a quadrangular shooting lodge in the new Gothic style for the Duke of Northumberland. Now, it is the administrative centre for the forest and houses a forestry exhibition and the **Information Centre** (*both open Easter to October, week-ends 2 to 5, also daily the last week in July and August 2 to 5, with a charge for the exhibition*). There is also a County Field Study Centre at Kielder, and the area is used in connection with the Duke of Edinburgh's Award Scheme.

Close by are many early settlements and camp sites inhabited by early man, but within striking distance is the **Devil's Lapful**, $\frac{1}{2}$ mile to the south-east, the medieval name given to the long barrow and Bronze Age cairn, dating from about 2000 to 1500 BC, which consists of a mound of boulders and large stones. There is another round cairn group, $\frac{1}{2}$ mile to the south of this point, constructed of natural boulders. Known as the **Deadman** or **Deadman's Currich**, it dates from about 1600 to 1000 BC. Both cairns form part of the dozen or so similar sites in the forest area. A variety of forest walks are carefully laid out from Kielder, waymarked to make them easy to follow, including the **Duchess Drive Forest Trail**, some 2½ miles long, and information on all of them is obtainable from the **Forestry Commission Information Centre**.

On the road that leads through to Scotland, 1½ miles beyond Kielder, is **Bellsburn Foot**, where a ½-mile walk along the burn to the left will bring you into Scotland at the nearest present-day point to Kielder itself. At **Bell's Linn**, a shallow waterfall, you can stand with one foot in each country. Another 1½ miles along the road, the main forest road reaches the Border at **Deadwater**, which, as the name implies, marks the watershed between the North Tyne Valley and that of the Liddel Water on the Scottish side, and every stream beyond this point flows westwards to join the latter. **Deadwater Fell** (560m, 1,866ft) stands 1½ miles to the north-east of Deadwater. To the north of the village runs the **Deadwater Burn**, leading up to the peak of **Rushy Knowe** (367m, 1,224ft) which marks the Border line and which is not to be confused with the other Rushy Knowe in the forest south of Whickhope. In the early 19th century Deadwater was also famous for its sulphur springs, and an attempt was once made to establish a spa here.

From the village a track leads northwards along the Border line to **Peel Fell** (593m, 1,975ft) in 3 miles, with a further 1½ miles leading to the **Kielder Stone**, an enormous sandstone block which not only marks the Border line but was also used in medieval times as a neutral post-box with messages and requests being left here in a small hole in the rock. Carved on two of its faces are the initials 'D' for Douglas and 'N' for Northumberland to mark the respective allegiances. From this point the track continues on to **Knox Knowe** (491m, 1,637ft), marking the Border line along the Carter Fells through to Carter Bar. It is also possible to circle round from the Kielder Stone southwards down the **Scaup Burn** to **Kielderhead**, thence along the **Kielder Burn** and so back to Kielder itself, making a round walk of some 12½ miles.

From Deadwater the forest road descends into the valley of the **Liddel Water** and on to **Saughtree**, set snugly on the north side of the **Larriston Fells**, in just over 3 miles, where it joins the B6357 road between Newcastleton and Bonchester Bridge. In a southerly direction the road leads through to Carlisle, while, northwards, it passes through the **Note**

of the Gate Pass (used by Bonnie Prince Charlie on 7 November 1745 as he marched towards Preston), then crosses the **Wauchope Forest**, which forms part of this Border Forest Camp and joins the A6088 at the fork south of Bonchester Bridge. From here a return can be made via Carter Bar into Redesdale, the diversion into Scotland adding some 12 miles overall to a round trip between North Tynedale and Redesdale, as an alternative to taking the toll-road through Kielder Forest.

Returning southwards along the North Tyne Valley from the Scottish Border, an alternative route back to Hexham can be made after **Yarrow Moor**, where a left turn over the bridge leads into **Falstone** and joins the road running along the north bank of the river. The village boasts two churches, a school and an inn, but as it will be at the foot of the new main Kielder Dam by 1980, with two new electricity generating plants close by, it is almost certain to expand. Falstone has very early antecedents, for an Anglo-Saxon cross, inscribed with runic characters, was found here and is now in the Newcastle Museum of Antiquities with some fragments remaining in the church. This is the point where the Border Forest Park and the Northumberland National Park meet. A church was built here in 1808 by the Greenwich Hospital Commissioners and restored in the 1890s as part of their attempts to split up the previously overlarge parish ruled from Simonburn, but the fact that a Scottish Presbyterian kirk was established here in 1807 may also have had something to do with it. Amongst other local interests for tourists is a pony-trekking centre and the remains of a fortified house incorporated in the farmhouse next to the church. From Falstone the minor road eastwards rises up over the fells and at times follows the line of the old railway. It is gated in parts, and after 4 miles, at **Rushead**, at the T-junction, the left-hand fork climbs up over **Thorneyburn Common** to the early 19th-century **Church of St Aidan**, another example of the work of the Greenwich Hospital Commissioners' architect, H. H. Seward. It is a small church with an embattled west tower.

Continuing right at the T-junction, the road crosses the Tarset Burn and reaches the crossroads at **Lanehead** in 1 mile. Close by lie the grass-covered remains of **Tarset Castle**, built in 1276 by John Comyn, father of Comyn the Red of Badenoch who was murdered by Bruce in 1306. After being garrisoned by English soldiers, it was burnt down in 1526 by local inhabitants led by a Charlton, ostensibly because they were interfering with the local sport of reiving, and, as if by way of an encore, they followed it up by burning Dally Castle as well.

A minor road runs up the Tarset Burn to **Greenhaugh**, with a link from there round **Hareshaw Common** to join the B6320 Bellingham–Otterburn road. A little further on, at **Burnmouth**, is a bridge across the Tarset Burn which leads (as an alternative route) through to St Aidan's Church at Thorneyburn. The Tarret Burn joins the Tarset Burn at this point and just north of here, at **Gatehouse**, there are two fortified bastel-houses, the local equivalent of a pele house, one of which is well preserved. Further up the gated road, near **The Comb**, as the road continues into the Border Forest Park area at Waterhead, there are also the remains of two others, one known as **Barty's Castle** and the other as **Corbie Castle**, and obviously this was a main infiltration route in medieval times. From **Waterhead**, just over the bridge, a 7-mile waymarked walk can be made through the forest area to Plashetts. To the south of this point is a picnic site at **Sidwood**.

From the Lanehead crossroads there is a road south across the river bridge to Greystead on the opposite bank of the North Tyne, now the main road up the valley from Bellingham. Eastwards, the road continues in 1¼ miles to **Charlton**, a small hamlet from which the leading North Tyne family took its name, above which, high on the slopes of Hareshaw Common, are the remains of an early settlement. In 2 more miles the road leads back into Bellingham.

Continuing south by the east bank of the North Tyne, the return route follows the unclassified road eastwards out of the town towards **Redesmouth**, where the river Rede joins the North Tyne flow. From Redesmouth a road runs eastwards across **Buteland Fell**, crossing the A68 road in 3½ miles and continuing eastwards along the line of the Wanneys to the Sweethope Loughs, a notable scenic drive. The road south out of the hamlet leads through the **Countess Park Wood** towards **Birtley**. On the slopes overlooking the North Tyne close to this point are the remains of many early settlements, some with highly suggestive names dubbed on them, possibly by bands of medieval gipsies long after the original inhabitants had left, such as **Good Wife Hot Camp**, **Male Knock Camp**, **Night Folds Camp**, **Carryhouse Camp** and **Shieldence Camp**. Medieval superstition abounds too in the legend of nearby **Holywell Burn**, where a rock can be seen with the Devil's footprints, when he tried to jump across the river to **Lee Hall** on the opposite bank but fell into **Leap Crag Pool** instead.

The road from Birtley joins the one from Wark to Barrasford, and just over 1 mile further south lies **Chipchase Castle** (*not open*), a striking combination of a large 14th-century tower joined to a fine Jacobean mansion of 1621, with Georgian additions. In the grounds is an 18th-century chapel which, along with a wing of the house, can be seen from the road. In the 16th century the original castle was the home of Sir George Heron, one of the Keepers of Tynedale, who was killed in the last Border affray at Redeswire on Carter Bar in 1575.

Gunnerton, the next hamlet southwards, tucked into the vale of the Gunnerton Burn calls for a slight diversion from the road towards Chollerton. Here is **St Christopher's Church**, built in 1900 by a young student-architect named Hall, who later took holy orders in both the Anglican and Catholic persuasions and ended his life as a hermit. Pevsner calls the design 'quite original if somewhat mannered' which is not bad praise for a student who won a competition to design a small moorland church and was later invited to build it using local stone and labour. On the heights surrounding Gunnerton and also between here and Barrasford there were many early settlements, and within $\frac{1}{2}$ mile of the hamlet are the mounded remains of a Norman motte-and-bailey castle, with several more earthworks and quarries on the escarpment. A minor road from Gunnerton leads eastwards towards the A68, joining it just north of Great Swinburne, passing **Barrasford Park** on the way, where there is a camping and caravan site, and close by the hamlet of **Pity Me**, a curious name which, if compared to the village of the same name outside Durham, may indicate a former mining area.

From Gunnerton, Barrasford is reached in $1\frac{3}{4}$ miles, with Haughton Castle on the opposite bank of the river. In a further mile the A6079 is joined at **Chollerton**, with a link-road turning north to join the same road on to the A68 at Robin Hood's Well. Chollerton is a hamlet noted for the interior of its church. The exterior, at first glance, seems unprepossessing, but the Norman south arcade (built in 1150) makes up for it, incorporating five monolithic Roman columns, probably taken from the fort at Chesters, which show signs of Roman tooling. The north arcade is 14th century, but the tower and the chancel were built in the mid-18th century and later Gothicized in 1893. Of the two fonts one is a reused Roman altar, while the other from the 13th century has a Jacobean cover. At **Cocklaw**, $\frac{1}{2}$ mile to the south-east and reached by a side-road off to the left, is a well-preserved 15th-century tower with a vaulted ground floor.

The A6079 leads in another mile to the crossroads at Low Brunton, completing the circuit along both banks of the North Tyne Valley, with the return to Hexham straight on for a further 4 miles.

12 Through route

Corbridge – West Woodburn – Elishaw – Carter Bar
(35 miles)

N.B. All mileages shown in brackets are from Corbridge

The present line of the A68 road from Corbridge mainly follows the line of the Roman road that led from here to the forts of Habitancum (Risingham) and Bremenium (High Rochester) and over The Cheviot Hills into Scotland, which later became known as Dere Street. The modern road varies little from this line as far as Elishaw, with the result that long stretches of it are dead straight with a characteristic flat-topped effect (more suited to carts than cars) in its series of undulating switch-backs.

Leaving Corbridge by the north-west exit, the newly constructed Corbridge bypass soon crosses the line of the A68 with its interchange point. The road then climbs **Stagshawbank**, passing **Stagshaw House** on the left, close to which the ancient Stagshaw Fair, held annually from 1204 to 1927, used to attract visitors from all over the country. Stagshaw church is silhouetted against the skyline close by. On the right there are side-roads to Halton and Aydon castles and one to Sandhoe on the left. The top of the bank is reached 3 miles from the town at a height of almost 210m (700ft) above sea-level on the edge of a spur along which the line of Hadrian's Wall runs. Now partially covered by the Military Way of General Wade, the modernized B6318 forms the crossroads here at a point known since Roman times as the **Port Gate** (3 miles). This is where the Roman road of Dere Street crossed the line of Hadrian's Wall. Less than 300 metres to the right is the closest milecastle point, known as No. 22, also often referred to as the Portgate.

Proceeding northwards, the tree-lined slopes give way to the open moorland ahead. Just over a mile north of the Portgate at **Beukley** (4¼ miles), where the tall radio mast now stands, a second Roman road,

Halton Castle

now known as the Devil's Causeway, branched off Dere Street to the right, passing close to Great Whittington and Ryal on its direct-line course to Berwick-upon-Tweed. The A68 drops down steeply towards the Errington Burn, passing on the left **Errington Red House** (5 miles). This house, built in 1704, was the home of one of Northumberland's great families, the Erringtons, two members of whom were responsible in the 1715 uprising for capturing Lindisfarne Castle and holding it for twenty-four hours. They were gaoled for their exploits but succeeded in escaping.

A mile beyond the house the road crosses the **Erring Burn** (6 miles) with, after climbing the far bank, a view to the right of the twin **Hallington Reservoirs**. At the A6079 (7¼ miles) the road to the left leads off to Chollerton in 2 miles, with a link-road through to Barrasford and the North Tyne Valley. To the right, past Robin Hood's Well and Colwell, the B6342 road passes the reservoirs to Little Bavington and reaches the A696(T) road in 7 miles at Kirkharle.

A mile beyond these crossroads a side-road on the left (8¼ miles) leads in less than a mile to **Great Swinburne** (*not open*), the 17th-century manor-house home of the Swinburne family, who took their name from the local burn. Unfortunately, there is nothing left of **Swinburne Castle**, but the family took part in the 1715 rising, and, of course, have connections with the poet Algernon Swinburne and also Capheaton Hall.

Half a mile to the south of Swinburne Castle ruins lies the largest standing stone in the county, a mass of red rock, 3·6m (12ft) high by 90cm (3ft) wide, covered entirely in grey lichen but deeply marked with incised grooves down the sides and some cup-markings as well. It lies near the Coal Burn in the midst of meadows which also reveal early attempts at agriculture: the 'lynchet' or low bank strips that mark the outline of terraced fields cultivated during the Middle to Late Bronze Age and date, as does the stone, from about 1600 to 1000 BC. About 350 metres away, closer to the farm road that runs through the estate, there are three barrows of the same period.

The A68 road continues north to cross the Swin Burn, the modern road swinging away to the right to descend the valley side, while the line of the Roman road of Dere Street ploughs straight ahead but is rejoined on the other side. Just over 1 mile from the Swinburne turning a lane leads off left (9¼ miles) to **Barrasford Park**, where there is a camping and caravan site, and through the tiny hamlet of Pity Me to lead on to Gunnerton.

On the right the **Colt Crag Reservoir** (10 miles), one of Newcastle's sources of water-supply, has the peak of **Colt Crag** (222m, 741ft) on the far bank with an ancient burial cairn on the top. Away to the left are views of the Pittland Hills. In another 1½ miles the **Tone Inn** (11½ miles) is reached, well-known as a coaching-stop in former days. The dead-straight road continues on for another ½ mile before taking one of those slight shifts to the right as the Roman surveyors corrected their line towards Chesterhope Common, and the modern road politely follows suit. At the crossroads (12¾ miles) just before Fourlaws the road from Redesmouth comes in from the left crossing the Buteland Fells and continues across to the right past Green Rigg and Great Wanney Crag to the Sweethope Loughs before continuing on to join the A696(T) at Knowesgate. This is a particularly scenic moorland drive through the area known as the Wanneys.

The site of the Roman camp of **Fourlaws** is on the left, $\frac{1}{2}$ mile beyond this point, close to the Broomhope Burn. Just beyond here the A68 swings right into Fourlaws village (13$\frac{1}{2}$ miles), away from the straight line of Dere Street, whose *agger*, or mounded base, can be seen as more lightly-coloured herbage across the fields. At Fourlaws a Bronze-Age barrow yielded a gold bead necklace now in the Black Gate Museum in Newcastle.

The modern road, now well over 300m (1,000ft) above sea-level, climbs across Chesterhope Common towards **Ridsdale** (14$\frac{1}{2}$ miles), where a side turning on the left leads down the slopes to the caravan site at **Chesterhope**. In the Broomhope and Rede Valleys away to the left are the remains of many former iron and coal workings now disused. Just beyond Ridsdale the road swings left away from the top of the ridge and works its way down into the Rede Valley. At **Broomhill** (15$\frac{1}{2}$ miles) the track of an old, now dismantled, railway crosses the road, part of the former industrial activity in the area, and its embankments can still be seen running down the Rede Valley towards Bellingham. Dropping down, a mile further on, the houses of **West Woodburn** (16$\frac{1}{2}$ miles) straddle either side of the river Rede bridge. On the south side a turning to the right leads to **East Woodburn**, 1 mile away, with a back road that follows the Rede Valley through to join the A696(T) at Monkridge, while opposite this turning is a track that leads into the site of the Roman fort at **Habitancum** (Risingham). Close to the bend in the river, $\frac{1}{2}$ mile away, the fort remains consist almost entirely of a few grassy mounds with some fragments of finely worked masonry at the north-east corner. Although on private land now, the remains can be viewed from the roadway. To the west the line of Dere Street passes on its way northward, close to where the stream flows into the river Rede. As at other forts in the area, Habitancum was rebuilt several times after its foundation in the middle of the 2nd century AD. The evidence shows that it was rebuilt in the time of Severus early in the 3rd, reconstructed and rebuilt again in the 4th and finally abandoned in 367, when the 'Barbarian Conspiracy' overran all the country north of Hadrian's Wall and there was treachery amongst the Romans themselves, with some of them joining the invaders. Never again did the Romans garrison such outpost points as these, and within sixty years their armies had left the country to its fate. The workmanship of the masonry has been highly commended at this site, and some of the stones are in the Black Gate Museum in Newcastle.

Across the river Rede, opposite the **Bay Horse Inn**, a left-hand turn follows the Rede Valley down to Bellingham. Continuing north, at **Woodhouse** the Roman road line rejoins that of the modern road. Less than ½ mile beyond this point on the left-hand side and behind a stone wall is a Roman milestone. Beyond this, in the open countryside of **Corsenside Common** (the start of the National Park area in this sector), lies the Artillery Range area, rising up to 360m (1,200ft) above sea-level. On the right, in ¾ mile (1½ miles from West Woodburn), at **Dykehead** (17½ miles) a gated track leads up to the Norman **Church of St Cuthbert**, isolated in an exposed position. The track continues on down to the Brig Burn, with a primitive rectangular enclosure there known as the **Brigg**, which suggests it may have been on one of the old drovers' roads from Otterburn, to where the footpath eventually leads.

The A68 crosses the Brig Burn from Dykehead and then, in 1½ miles, the **Miller Burn** (19 miles). Less than ½ mile beyond here the B6320 road crosses, the left-hand link coming in from Bellingham, while the right turns towards Otterburn in 1½ miles. On the left are the expanses of **Troughend Common**, and **Troughend Hall** lies on the left ½ mile beyond the crossroads.

The modern road diverges from the line of Dere Street to pass close to the house, then swings back again on to the Roman line ½ mile further on, continuing dead straight for ½ mile to cross the **Dargues Burn**, where the faint traces of another Roman camp lie on the left. It then continues to **Blakehope** (21½ miles), ½ mile before the junction with the A696(T) road at **Elishaw**. Here on the bend to the right lay the Roman fort of Elishaw, a less significant construction than either Risingham or High Rochester and built of turf ramparts. The line of the Roman Dere Street continues straight on at this point, and its *agger* can be seen making for the river crossing ahead on a direct line for High Rochester. A track also leads off left here up to **Rattenraw**, with the remains of a pele tower and further up the burn the traces of an early settlement.

From Blakehope the A68 curves right to cross the river Rede and joins the A696(T) from Newcastle to Carter Bar just north of Otterburn and at the medieval toll-point of Elishaw (22 miles). (*For the continuation of the route from Elishaw to Carter Bar (35 miles) see page 131; for the route from Newcastle to Elishaw see page 127.*)

13 The South Tyne Valley from Hexham to Whitley Castle and Alston

Although still an integral part of Northumberland, South Tynedale is characteristically so different from the remainder of the county that it might well be called 'North Pennine Land' instead. This is particularly true of the area south of Haltwhistle where the river South Tyne makes a sharp right-angled bend as it flows down from Alston and the Pennine dales before joining the east-west line more commonly associated with the Tyne Valley.

The river itself actually rises outside the county on the slopes of **Cross Fell** (880m, 2,930ft), the highest peak in the Pennine chain, within a few miles of the boundaries of Northumberland, Durham and Cumbria, and on this watershed height are also the sources of both the river Wear and the river Tees. Of the four great rivers of Northumbria only the Derwent fails to start its course so far to the west, but its tributary line along the Beldon Burn reaches almost to Allenheads, less than 10 miles to the east. Thus, within a small radius from the meeting-point of the three counties the main water-supply of the region has its beginning, and while, with such projects as the Kielder Water Scheme in the offing, today it may not be so important, it obviously had much to do with the early shaping of the country.

Undoubtedly, it is this proximity to both Cumbria and Durham which has changed not only the local dialect of South Tynedale but some of its local customs as well. Much of this may have been occasioned by a common working ground in the great mineral wealth of the region. The Romans, who mined the lead, felt the area important enough to build a fort at Whitley Castle not only to guard the route northwards but to protect the miners and workings as well.

Much of this high Pennine area is wild and bleak, littered with former workings and the deserted hamlets of shepherds and miners who once frequented the district more thickly than now. It is perhaps understandable that in their wanderings over the fells they would not be too concerned about the political or administrative separations marked by an invisible line along a mountain ridge, for such divisions were made in Saxon times when mountains made natural barriers. Today, they make excellent ground for the sport of fell-walking or even skiing in the winter.

The South Tyne Valley was amongst the last parts of Northumberland to revert back from Scottish to English rule, but its history is far less chequered than that of its counterpart in North Tynedale. In its lower reaches from Haltwhistle to Hexham there were both Border raiders and the usual reivers, who used the 'Busy Gap' by Thirlwall in medieval times to drive the stolen herds back north, but their penetrations seldom went further south. There was plenty of local feuding, but generally speaking the area was more peaceful with a hinterland largely uninhabited apart from the numerous small valleys cut out by its streams and rivers. Most of the land formed part of the 'Regality of Hexham' – later Hexhamshire – and was a major hunting area where kings and clerics pursued their game.

In its lower reaches along the Tyne Gap and where The Pennines finally peter out along their northernmost edge there are some wooded valleys and spectacular rock scenery. The best of this countryside lies in the area known as the Allendales, where many small peaty burns tumble down from the heights leading up to the Durham boundary, and the two main rivers of the East and West Allen induced our Victorian ancestors to call this area 'the English Alps'. Peaceful it is, and perhaps it is more appropriate in this day and age to note that a group of Zen Buddhist monks are at present building a new, as well as the first, training priory for their order in this country at Throssel Hall, high up in the Allendales on land riddled with former mine workings, where they are also hoping to reopen a former coal seam for their own use.

From Hexham the main A69(T) road west rejoins the bypass road 2 miles to the west of the town at **Westwood**, where a bridge across the South Tyne leads in 1 mile to Warden, an appropriately named hamlet by the Warden Rocks which marks the dividing line between North and South Tyne streams.

Haydon Bridge is reached 4 miles further on. It is a small, unpretentious town with a bridge built in 1773, originally with chains and bars to prevent reivers from Scotland and North Tynedale slipping across too easily, set next to the modern road bridge and still used by pedestrians only. Just before reaching the river crossing the A686 road slips off as a left-hand fork towards **Langley Castle** and across Whitfield Moor to Alston in Cumbria. It is also one of the main routes into the Allendales.

Haydon Bridge, or rather Haydon, has held its charter for a fair and a market since the 14th century, but this was the medieval village ½ mile to the north where the **Old Church** lies. Built mainly of Roman stones, it is a Norman edifice with a 14th-century chapel added. The nave was pulled down in the late 18th century, then rebuilt, and the whole restored again in 1882. The font is a former Roman altar. Closer to the river bridge is the **New Church of St Cuthbert**, built in the 18th century, with a tower and a pagoda-style pyramid roof. It is on Church Street, now the B6319 road to Fourstones (see below).

Much of Haydon Bridge's growth came after the railway line had been extended here from Hexham in 1836 as a first step in its approach to Carlisle. One of the streets has been named after John Martin (1789–1854), the artist and engraver, who was born here and painted many apocalyptic visions of Old Testament scenes but was hardly recognized during his lifetime. A grammar school was founded here in 1685, known as the Shafto Trust, later to become a technical school for farming. The Shaftos are a well-known Northumberland family, one of whose members gave rise to the song 'Bobbie Shafto's gone to sea'.

Along Church Street northwards on the B6319 a left turn at the T junction leads to **Newborough** and the site of the Roman fort on the line of the Stanegate. A right turn leads along the north bank of the South Tyne river past Allerwash Hall to **Fourstones** in 3½ miles, continuing on to join the B6318 at **Walwick** in 6 miles, along the line of Hadrian's Wall by the fort of Chesters and thence into Chollerford. From Fourstones a riverside road turns south and circles the mass of Warden Hill, past one of the oldest surviving paper mills in the county, dating from 1763, and on to **Bridge End**. Here, a left turn at the **Boat Side Inn** (a good spot for fishing) leads on to the hamlet of **Warden**. The whole area is dominated by **High Warden Hill**, almost 180m (600ft) above sea-level, on the top of which is an early Iron-Age settlement, its ramparts built of local sandstone.

St Michael's Church claims to be Saxon because its 11th-century tower was built just before the Norman invasion. It has a tower arch incorporating Roman stones. The large transepts were built in the 13th century, while the chancel is Victorian. The road continues northwards from the hamlet, winding upwards along a lane known as Homer's Lane and follows the valley of the North Tyne. Just over 1 mile north of the houses and ½ mile short of Walwick Grange is the presumed crossing and line of the Roman road of the Stanegate on its way from Corbridge to Carlisle, which continues west through Fourstones. At **Walwick Grange** the B6319 road is joined and in 1 mile northwards reaches Walwick. **Chesters House** is seen on the right.

From Haydon Bridge the A69(T) road westwards follows the north bank of the South Tyne river to Bardon Mill in 3½ miles. A mile short of Bardon Mill, at **Whitechapel**, a bridge across the river leads through to castellated **Ridley Hall**, close to the junction of the river Allen with the South Tyne. To the left a minor road climbs through thickly wooded countryside over the heights of **Moralee Wood** to emerge on the A686 by Langley Castle, and a diversion from here leads through to the beauty spot of Plankey Mill. A right turn after the bridge leads in 1 mile to the hamlet of **Beltingham**. **St Cuthbert's Church** claims a Saxon foundation, but the well-sited building by the Beltingham Burn probably dates from around 1500 and was built as a chapel of ease, though much restored in Victorian times. In the churchyard there are two Roman altar stones and a yew tree reputed to be over 900 years old. The elegant Georgian house next to the church belongs to the Bowes-Lyon family, to whom the present Queen mother is related.

The road, which has no outlet for through traffic, carries on for another mile to **Willimontswick**, an interesting Saxon name implying both a small village and a meeting-place of the said William. There is a ford close to here and a foot-bridge across the South Tyne to Bardon Mill. The massive **Gatehouse**, probably 14th century, leading into the present-day farm, marks the site of the medieval fortified manor-house of the Ridley family, known as **Willimontswick Castle**, and two narrow and ancient towers adjoin the later house. It claims to be the site of the birthplace of Nicholas Ridley, the Oxford martyr, but shares this privilege with Unthank Hall, 3 miles away along the south bank. The road ends at this point, and a return to the road bridge is made by the same route.

Bardon Mill, the closest communication point to the Northumberland lakes just north of Hadrian's Wall, is a small but busy semi-industrial village. It also serves during the season as one of the main thoroughfares to the Roman fort and civilian settlement at **Vindolanda** at Chesterholm, 1¾ miles to the north. For those without cars or for those who would like to park and walk along the Wall it is worth noting that a tourist bus service operates from Hexham to Housesteads and Steel Rigg in the season to the Once Brewed Information Centre from which point there are services of a mini-bus to Vindolanda. Details are available from **Hexham Tourist Information Office.**

It is quite possible to make a visit from Bardon Mill by the road leading north out of the village to Chesterholm and by using the car park on the eastern side of the hamlet. Here the line of the Roman road of the Stanegate passes through the hamlet, and the boundary of the National Park area commences on this sector. However, the normal signposted route from Bardon Mill to Vindolanda leads through to the car park on the western side, owing to the volume of seasonal traffic, and it is wiser to follow this.

It must be stressed that Vindolanda is not a wall fort but pre-dates the Wall by some forty years and was originally part of the defence line that guarded the east-west Roman road of the Stanegate, sometimes known as the Carelgate, which linked Corbridge with Carlisle. About AD 208 a stone fort was erected here, which curiously enough faced south – as though to protect the military zone from that direction against the remaining Brigantes in Yorkshire who had caused trouble in the past. The remains of the fort seen today are from the time of Constantius, who died at York in AD 306 and completely remodelled the fort to face north. There were also extensive repairs to it in AD 369, two years after the 'Barbarian Conspiracy' had overrun the Wall. During the 3rd and 4th centuries the garrison here belonged to the 4th Cohort of Gauls who renewed their allegiance at this time.

Whether approached from the eastern or western sides it must be stressed that there is, sadly, no through route along the road at this point, and the track is deliberately left unrepaired to deter this. You either use the eastern car park and enter by the museum, or the western and enter from the fort side, and walk between the two – some 400–500 metres and leave by the same route. Along the line of the Stanegate from Chesterholm there is a fine example of a Roman milestone between the Bradley and Brackie's Burns (where the museum now is), just north-west of the farm. The remains of another lie one Roman mile – 1,620 yards (1,458m) – to the west. Beyond Brackie's Burn, on the left, on a platform of land lie the remains of the fort. The outline includes the north and west gates, the west wall showing some of the repairs of AD 369, the east wall and gate and, in the centre, the headquarters building. This is one of the finest of such discoveries anywhere in the country, containing as it

Langley Castle

does record and paymaster's offices with a sunken pit for regimental funds, a tribunal and cross-hall, a regimental shrine, and besides a number of domestic rooms a courtyard and well. After AD 369 a conversion took place, with some of the rooms being turned into granaries and huge open hearths introduced into others, a sign of the changing pattern of life more associated with the adjacent civilian settlement. Some of the relics from this fort are now in the museum at Chesters. The fort which was excavated by Professor Eric Birley was presented by him to the nation and is now in the care of the Department of the Environment. It is open at standard DoE hours from 9.30 am with a charge made on entrance.

Undoubtedly, the greatest draw at Vindolanda at the present time is the excavation of the civilian settlement to the west of the fort. All Roman forts had their *vicus* outside the walls, with shops and inns. There is evidence to suggest that it became a self-governing community, which appears to have outlasted the Roman military occupation, and that it became a Romano-British (possibly Christian) settlement of the 5th century AD. It is being excavated by the Vindolanda Trust, founded in 1970, and is open daily from 10 am with a charge made on entrance. Buildings so far uncovered include the only example in Britain of an inn of this era, plus a bath-house and many dwellings. Across the valley to the east, reached by a steep path is the **Museum**, which holds one of the most important collections of Roman remains in the country and probably in Europe. The whole area is laid out neatly with tea-rooms and gardens. It is possible to walk along the line of the Stanegate westwards for 1 mile, turning right for a further ½ mile to the Once Brewed Information Centre on the line of Hadrian's Wall, passing the site of other Roman camps on the way, and this is the route into the western car park.

To the east of Chesterholm village lies **Barcombe Hill** (275m, 915ft) from which point an excellent view of the Wall, *Vallum* and the line of the Stanegate are visible. The Romans took some of their building stone from this hill, and on the top, close to the **Long Stone**, are the remains of an early British settlement and the site of a Roman signal station.

Returning to Bardon Mill, the A69(T) road continues along the river bank terraces the 4 miles to **Haltwhistle**, passing the hamlets of **Henshaw**, with its 19th-century **All Hallows Church** built in the Early English style, and **Melkridge**. The name Haltwhistle originates from the Saxon-Norman cross of haut wiscle or whysile meaning a 'high boundary' or 'bank', perhaps related to the sharp bend in the river ½ mile above the town. Haltwhistle itself lies between the Haltwhistle Burn and the South Tyne river at the top of a steep bank and is a small market town serving a large rural area. It has the distinction of being the nearest town to Hadrian's Wall just over a mile to the north, and a nature trail leads up the Haltwhistle Burn to a point where the Stanegate, *Vallum* and Wall close in on each other to within ½ mile. There are several Roman forts in the area – on the Stanegate itself, the fort at Haltwhistle Burn, while the fort of Aesica at Great Chesters is just to the north on the Wall – to name but two of the more visited. The Haltwhistle Burn is fed by the Caw Burn further up its course, and the latter comes all the way from Greenlee Lough.

Haltwhistle's position makes it a good centre for visits to the north or south, for with the new bus link through Alston a visit to the Pennine uplands is also a possibility. It caters for the visitor and has a nine-hole golf-course as well. It is the centre for the South Tyne Annual Show and has seasonal cattle and sheep markets, as well as a small town market on

Thursdays. There is an outdoor leisure pool and plenty of local excursions and walks. Formerly a coalmining area, its industries are now lighter, and it is noted as a paint-manufacturing town. It is a town of rather severe grey-stone houses, ranging in terraces up the hillside. To the west is an industrial estate dealing in chemicals and transport.

Behind the market-place lies the interesting 13th-century **Holy Cross Church**. There are claims that the earliest church here was founded by William the Lion, King of Scotland, in 1178. The exterior is plain, but the nave and aisles are extremely wide and virtually form a square. The chancel and the nave, with its painted roof, are also at varying heights, though originally they would have been level, and this may be due to some of the heavy restoration in Victorian times.

In the town the **Red Lion Hotel**, close to the market-place, has part of a former pele tower incorporated in its structure. Along **Central Place**, the old courthouse is now an antique shop. There is also a neglected 16th-century bastel-house on the north side of the Haltwhistle Burn.

Excursions from Haltwhistle

1) Unthank Hall, Plenmeller Common and Whitfield

Leaving the town by the South Tyne bridge close to the railway station, a left-hand turn after crossing leads into the hamlet of **Plenmeller** at the foot of the slopes leading up to **Plenmeller Common**. A left-hand turning at the end of the hamlet leads through to **Unthank Hall**, 1 mile down a side-turning from which there is no exit, apart from turning round again. The house, mainly 19th century, reveals little of its earlier history and is not open. Part of it dates from 1815 and is the work of John Dobson, the Newcastle architect. The earlier house on the site has the first claim (the other is Willimontswick) as the birthplace of Nicholas Ridley, the Protestant Bishop of London who died at the stake in Oxford in October 1555, two years after Mary Tudor had restored Roman Catholicism to England. He died, along with Latimer, rather than recant, and their names are commemorated in the Martyrs' Memorial outside Balliol College.

The country road continues up Plenmeller Common to join the ridge road that runs from Coanwood to Whitfield, 1 mile to the east of **Wolf Hills**, a significant enough reminder of the past on the top of this lonely moorland, nearly 360m (1,200ft) above sea-level and with extensive views across the South Tyne Valley to Hadrian's Wall. A left turn at the junction leads across the ridge past Beacon Hill and then drops down the steep incline of Dingbell Hill into **Whitfield** at its junction with the A686. From this point a left turn leads north to Cupola Bridge and Langley Castle, returning via Haydon Bridge or diverting into the picturesque scenery by Plankey Mill and the National Trust holding by Ridley and the river Allen. Alternatively, an extension can be made into the Allendales.

2) The South Tyne Valley: Bellister and Featherstone Castles, Lambley and Alston

With the cessation of the South Tyne Valley railway link from Haltwhistle to Alston in Cumbria, a new bus and road link has been introduced using the new Diamond Oak road bridge at Coanwood, which has made many trips down the valley more accessible. From Haltwhistle a second bridge, ½ mile to the west of the town, crosses the South Tyne, with a right turn leading almost at once to **Bellister Castle**, a ruined 16th-century square tower of the bastel-house kind, attached to a manor-house of 1669. Following the river bank, in 1 mile the junction at Park is reached by the Park Burn, where a left-hand turn climbs the steep riverside slopes and on to Rowfoot. A diversion to the right leads in 1 mile to **Featherstone Castle** (*not open*). Most of the house is Victorian Romantic in style with castellated towers, but the western end contains the remains of a 13th-century hall and there is a battlemented 14th-century strong tower, somewhat restored. The bridge opposite, which crosses the South Tyne in one span, dates from 1775.

A steep climb away from Featherstone leads up to Rowfoot, with a right-hand turn leading in 1 mile to Lanehead. The route eastwards from this point passes close to **Stonehouse** (where there is a caravan site) and then links up with the ridge road running across Plenmeller Common to Whitfield. Turning right, the road drops down the bluff to Coanwood, over the South Tyne river by the newly opened bridge and into **Lambley**, where it joins the main A689 Brampton to Alston road. Lambley is a good centre for some interesting walks in the South Tyne Valley. The Pennine Way passes on its way north ½ mile west of the village. Close by is the South Tyne Gorge with the disused Victorian railway arch spanning the river 33m (110ft) above the water with its thirteen arches. A 2-mile walk over the footbridge to Coanwood can return by the new road bridge at Diamond Oak. Alternatively, there is a footpath along the west bank of the South Tyne all the way to Featherstone Bridge, with a return

Lambley Viaduct

footpath along the east bank, a round trip of about 5 miles. From the east bank also a footpath runs south through Eals to Burnstones in less than 3 miles. The church at Lambley is a 19th-century one, and between there and Featherstone are the ruins of a Benedictine nunnery which was razed to the ground by the Scots in 1296.

The A689 road runs west from Lambley for 2 miles alongside Hartleyburn Common before reaching the Cumbrian boundary, close to the Black Burn, thence making its way to Brampton. Southwards, it follows the river valley, paralleling the courses of both the Pennine Way and the former Roman road of the Maiden Way. In 3 miles it reaches **Burnstones**, where the Thinhope Burn flows down from the slopes of Knarsdale Forest to join the South Tyne river. From here a track leads off west via the Gelt Burn and follows the Pennine Way round to Slaggyford in under 3 miles. **Knarsdale Forest** and **Common**, at the northern end of The Pennines, dominate the western side of the valley, with the Cumbrian boundary 3 miles away on the ridge.

Close to the village of Burnstones is 17th-century **Knarsdale Hall**, between the Thinhope Burn and the South Tyne, and the side-road which leads to it has Knarsdale church, an early 19th-century edifice, at the corner. This minor road leads to a river bridge which crosses to Eals

181

and follows the east bank back to Coanwood. **Slaggyford**, its name suggestive of some of the former mining activity, lies 1½ miles to the south. It is sheltered from the north-east by the mass of **Williamston Fell** ranging up to 457m (1,522ft) above sea-level. The Pennine Way also touches this village and it is possible to follow it southwards out to the Roman fort at Whitley Castle and on to Alston in 5 miles.

Two miles south is **Kirkhaugh**, a name showing both former Scottish and Viking influences, which could be translated as 'church mead'. Here, the **Church of the Holy Paraclete**, built in 1868, is said to have been designed by its vicar. It stands alone on the opposite bank under the lea of **Kip Law** (422m, 1,540ft). There is a Saxon cross in the church-yard. A little further along, close to **Kirkside Wood**, two Bronze-Age barrows were discovered in a field.

The remains of **Whitley Castle**, the site of a Roman fort on the Maiden Way, lie ½ mile south of Kirkhaugh, just off to the right. The area still remains to be excavated and, for this reason perhaps, no record has yet been found indicating its Roman name. It is believed that besides pro-tecting the route northward to Carvoran on the Stanegate the fort was sited to protect the lead-mining interests locally. The Gilderdale Burn marks the boundary with Cumbria ½ mile south of this point, and 1½ miles further south the road runs into Alston.

Alston, although not part of Northumbria, is a significant focal point for many of the routes emanating from there. Apart from the A689 from Brampton and Haltwhistle there is the A686 from Haydon Bridge, the A686 from Penrith and the A689 along Weardale to Stanhope and Durham. Finally, the B6277 follows the line of Teesdale to Middleton in Teesdale, Darlington and Scotch Corner. It is thus one of the most important crossing routes over the North Pennines and has been since very early times. Almost surrounded by some of the highest fells of The Pennines, Alston claims the distinction of being the highest market town in England, about 270m (900ft) at river-level, with the contours rising to over 300m (1,000ft) at the top of the town. It is a holiday centre offering numerous walks in high moorland scenery, but one must keep a wary eye on old pot-holes and mine shafts which still litter the area.

To the south-east **Cross Fell**, at 879m (2,930ft) the highest point in The Pennines, is the source of the South Tyne river, and across its western slopes comes the line of the Maiden Way, the minor Roman road from Kirkby Thore which is 4½ miles north-west of Appleby, on its way to the Stanegate and Hadrian's Wall. The Pennine Way, more boldly, touches the summit and then drops down to the river valley by Carrigil, 3½ miles south-east of Alston, thence to follow the river course northwards. The parish **Church of St Augustine** records a history dating from 1154, and the present mid-19th-century building is the third on the site. There is also a **Tourist Information Office** in the town.

A return to both Haltwhistle and Haydon Bridge can be made either by the A686 road or by following the A689 eastwards 4 miles to Nenthead and coming through the Allendales.

3) Blenkinsopp Castle, Greenhead, Thirlwall Castle and Gilsland

From Haltwhistle the main A69(T) road heads west for Carlisle, 19 miles away, following the line of the Tipalt Burn which creates the linking gap through to the western extremity of Northumberland at Gilsland, some 4 miles away. Again, it is a natural focal point leading from the South Tyne Valley over the watershed into Cumbria along the northern edges of The Pennines or, by turning north-west, it afforded in the past a quick route back to Scotland across the edge of the Spadeadam Waste. It is little wonder, therefore, that during medieval times it enjoyed such titles as the 'Busy Gap' and sometimes the 'Bloody Gap' as the reivers pushed their struggling herds past here.

In 1½ miles, on the right, are the grounds of **Blenkinsopp Hall** (the gardens of which are occasionally open), an early 19th-century house with some work put in by Dobson. A mile beyond this, on the left, stands the ruined shell of **Blenkinsopp Castle**, first mentioned in the 14th century, now partly in use as a private house. Just before this point, also on the left, where the Small Burn joins the Tipalt Burn, the line of the Roman road of the Maiden Way comes in from the slopes of Blenkinsopp Common and crosses the modern road close to the castle. It is now only ½ mile from its destination at Carvoran, and a fragment of its line can be seen on the slopes to the east of the road. The whole of this area was also formerly dedicated to mining, and some signs of this industry can still be seen on the steep hillsides.

Another ½ mile leads into **Greenhead** where the Military Way of General Wade, now the B6318, comes in from the right. The A69(T) main road swings away left from the village, turning south-west as straight as a die across Thirlwall's South Common towards Brampton and Carlisle. It crosses into Cumbria over the Temon Bridge where the line of the Poltross Burn running down to join the river Irthing at

Gilsland marks the boundary line, less than 3 miles west of Greenhead. About 1½ miles west along this road the line of the Pennine Way crosses at Gap Shields on its way towards the north.

At Greenhead, which has an elaborate church designed by Dobson in 1826 and also boasts a nine-hole golf-course, everything seems to come together, for ¼ mile north of the village the line of the Stanegate, the *Vallum*, Hadrian's Wall and its ditch, as well as the Roman Military Way, all cross the line of the Tipalt Burn on their way to the major crossing of the river Irthing at Willowford Bridge, just west of Gilsland and already in Cumbria. Some parts of the Roman remains are visible here, and there are several other temporary camps in the neighbourhood. Half a mile east along the B6318 a side-road leads to the site of the Roman fort of Carvoran (Magna), where the Maiden Way road joined the line of the Stanegate.

Thirlwall Castle lies ½ mile north of the village, guarding the entrance to the 'Busy Gap' from the north, and is close to a group of crags known as the **Nine Nicks of Thirlwall**, which quarrying has partially destroyed. The word 'Thirlwall' itself, from the Scottish word *Thirl*, suggests a break in the wall, and it has long been thought that this was the point where the Caledonians broke through Hadrian's Wall. Now a romantic ruin, it was built of Roman stone in the 14th century. Edward I stayed here on his way to Scotland in 1306. The Pennine Way passes close to this point before picking up the line of Hadrian's Wall.

From Greenhead the B6318 road curves round north-west in 1½ miles to reach **Gilsland**, the last western outpost of Northumberland, where Hadrian's Wall splits the village in two and where even the hotels commemorate the fact with names like 'Romanway'. The Haltwhistle golf-course is close by, and it is a convenient point from which to visit the line of the Wall and especially sites like **Willowford Bridge** and **Birdoswald** just over the boundary in Cumbria (see page 193). From Gilsland the B6318 wanders its way north-westwards touching the edge of Kershope Forest and into Scotland across the Liddel Water, close to Canonbie.

On the Northumberland side of the river Irthing a minor road runs north to Gilsland Spa, and the river line marks not only the boundary here but the westernmost edge of the National Park area. There are some interesting walks along this valley. The return to Haltwhistle can be varied slightly by taking the B6318 road from Greenhead and returning along the line of Hadrian's Wall, turning south by the Haltwhistle Burn.

14 The Allendales and North Pennine uplands

From the Tyne Valley there are two main routes into the scenic area known as the **Allendales** – from Hexham via Low Gate and across Stublick Moor to Langley, and from Haydon Bridge direct to Langley, from which point both climb East Allen Dale to Allendale Town and Allenheads. From Haydon Bridge the A686 road continues beyond Langley across Whitfield Moor to Alston in Cumbria, taking in some of the higher Pennine scenery. Between Ridley, opposite Bardon Mill, and Cupola Bridge a few miles to the south is a stretch of river, crag and woodland (of which the National Trust holds a large portion) particularly suitable as a walking and picnic area along the River Allen. A recent proposal has been made to create the North Pennine area as one of 'outstanding natural beauty'. Bus services operate from Hexham and Haydon Bridge to Allendale Town and Allenheads, allowing sufficient time for visiting these areas. As there are many routes criss-crossing the area, the following description has been sectionalized for ease of reference.

1) From Hexham to Langley (7½ miles)

Leaving Hexham by the A69(T) road westwards, the B6305 forks off left at the end of the town heading for **Low Gate** in 2 miles, where there is a caravan site. The road climbs up over the moorland past East and West Nubbuck on its way to Stublick. In 5¾ miles at Branch End, where some of the disused mines begin to appear, the B6304 turns off left towards Allendale Town, joining the B6295 coming up from Langley. However, by keeping right on the B6305, just over ½ mile beyond this point on the left is **Stublick Chimney**, a relic of the lead-mining days with its tall chimney and flue. In 7½ miles from Hexham the crossroads at Langley are reached. A right turn here leads into the A686 and another right turn leads in 1 mile to Langley Castle.

2) From Haydon Bridge to Langley (3 miles)

Across the bridge at Haydon Bridge an immediate right turn cuts the corner of the junction with the A686 and leads through to this road in ½ mile. Continuing south-west, this road passes Langley Castle now an entertainment centre in 1½ miles, and 1 mile further on the left-hand fork of the B6295 turns in past Langley and across the crossroads of the B6305 in 3 miles from Haydon Bridge.

3) From Langley to Allenheads and East Allen Dale (11 miles)

Both routes now follow the B6295 across the fells by **Emertley Hill** (310m, 1,033ft) to reach **Catton** in 2 miles, where there is a fell rescue post and one of the many field study centres in the area. The road is high above the valley of the East Allen river, and in another 1½ miles **Allendale Town** is reached on a steep bank above the water. Capital of the district and 240m (800ft) above sea-level, it was the former market town of the dales, at its busiest in the era before the lead-mining ceased in 1861. The industry was started by the Beaumont family, and one of them took the name Allendale when he was raised to the peerage.

Allendale Town is now a popular holiday centre with a well-kept air about its stone houses and gardens. It lives on hill-farming and holiday-makers, and there are many amenities for visitors. The river and hill scenery is varied, with plenty of good walks, some trout fishing and a nine-hole golf-course across the river at **Thornley Gate**. Further up the dale attempts are being made to introduce skiing in the winter and this is growing. Allendale Town claims to be the geographical centre of Great Britain, but in spite of its local sundial which it is said proves the fact, the system of determining how is not clear to most observers, although it is true that it is about half-way between Beachy Head and Cape Wrath.

A large and square market-place leads to the **St Cuthbert's Church** in the north-east corner, an early 19th-century edifice. One of the vicars of Allendale, known for ever afterwards as the 'Renegade Patten', was the chaplain to the rebel forces in the 1715 uprising but turned king's evidence and then wrote a history of the event. In his heyday John Wesley also preached in the area. Some of his influence remains and there are also strong Quaker elements in the neighbourhood. The great annual attraction of Allendale is the New Year's Eve bonfire, a hangover from an early Nordic custom, a pagan rite associated with the winter solstice. The town also holds its own agricultural show and sheepdog trials.

Beyond Allendale Town, climbing the vast slopes of Allendale Common, the scenery becomes less sylvan with more evidence of a past industrial activity. Through **Sinderhope**, where there is another field study centre, on past disused mines and quarries the road climbs in 6½ miles from the town to **Allenheads**, the former centre of the mining area and the estate village at the head of the dale. Here, the many small burns running down from **Killhope Law** (617m, 2,056ft) give rise to the source of the East Allen river. At one time almost 15% of all the lead in the country was mined here from mines first discovered by the Romans. The area was also used to test some of the guns invented by Lord Armstrong in 1856. A new lease of life has recently come into the area with the opening of a new fluorspar mine and the establishment of a small but flourishing winter-sports centre with ski tows in use.

At **Byerhope**, close by, is a small reservoir, next to a characteristically named site known as the Dirt Pot. At **Doddo**, on Allendale Common, there is another. Behind the village, over Rookhope Head to the east, the moorland road crosses the Durham boundary in ¾ mile and continues the 5 miles to Rookhope. The B6295 continues south across Allenheads Park crossing the Durham boundary at a height of 78m (1,926ft) above sea-level in 1½ miles, close to **Burtree Fell** (544m, 1,814ft), and then drops down into Cowshill in another 1½ miles. From Allenheads a return can be made via the West Allen Valley.

4) From Allenheads to Coalcleugh (5 miles)

A return north from Allenheads for about 1 mile is necessary to pick up this moorland road running west across the northern slopes of Killhope Law (617m, 2,056ft), the ridge of which marks the Durham boundary. The source of the West Allen river also rises on these slopes less than 1 mile from its twin stream. Passing the many shafts on Coalcleugh Moor, the road joins the one coming over **Black Hill** (600m, 1,998ft) from Nenthead at **Coalcleugh** itself, where a right turn leads down the West Allen Dale. Once a former mining village, there is little left at Coalcleugh now apart from its claim to be one of the highest villages in the country at a height of 525m (1,750ft) above sea-level. The three county boundaries of Northumberland, Durham and Cumbria meet ½ mile to the south of the village.

5) From Coalcleugh to Whitfield and West Allen Dale (7½ miles)

From Coalcleugh, with the mound of the **Dodd** (604m, 2,014ft) on the left marking the Cumbrian boundary, the road runs down the secluded valley of the West Allen. In 1½ miles, at **Carr Shield**, another fell rescue post reflects the off-the-beaten-track sporting activities of the area, and ¾ mile further on a junction to the right leads by a high moorland road across Dryburn Moor to Allendale Town in 6 miles.

The valley road follows the river, which soon is augmented by the waters of the Wellinghope Burn and the Whitewalls Burn, the church at Corryhill marking the junction 3 miles further on. In another mile at **Ninebanks**, where there are the remains of a pele tower, another moorland road climbs the steep bank to the right and heads also for Allendale Town in 4 miles across the fell. Keeping left, the valley road crosses the West Allen river and heads straight for the junction with the A686 road at Carr's Burn. On the right just before the junction are the grounds of **Parmentley Hall** where there is a camping and caravan site. A right turn at the junction leads into Whitfield in 1 mile and back to Haydon Bridge in 8 miles.

6) From Haydon Bridge to Alston (16 miles)

Joining the A686 road on the south side of the Tyne bridge, **Langley Castle** is reached in 2 miles. This massive 14th-century structure was restored in the 1890s after lying since 1541 in a totally dilapidated state. Now it is a thriving centre for medieval banquets and other stimulating social evenings which attract many visitors to the area. Basically an oblong structure with four towers at the angles, the castle has at some time been associated with many of Northumberland's leading families – the Percies, Nevilles and the Radcliffes to name but a few. In 1882 it was bought and restored by the Northumbrian historian, C. J. (Cadwaller) Bates, who lived for a time at Heddon Hall, close to Heddon-on-the-Wall. The castle was one of the sequestrated properties of the ill-fated Earl of Derwentwater after the 1715 uprising and also passed with his other estates to the Commissioners of Greenwich Hospital for a while.

From beside Langley Castle a minor road winds its way past Moralee Wood and the hamlet of **Moralee** to cross the river Allen and emerge by the picnic site and car park of the National Trust holding by Ridley Hall. From here a bridge leads across the South Tyne into Whitechapel, close to Bardon Mill on the A69(T) road. A left-hand turn leads through to Plankey Mill 1½ miles along this road.

Continuing south-west on the A686, ¾ mile beyond Langley Castle, the B6295 road forks off left past Langley village, crosses the line of the B6305 road from Hexham to Alston and ascends the East Allen Valley to Allendale Town and Allenheads.

On the right, ¼ mile beyond this junction, a right-hand fork leads through to **Plankey Mill** in 2 miles. This is a favourite walking and picnic area beside the river Allen at the Allen Banks. A riverside path to the left leads along in 1 mile to the Staward Pele (see below), while, across a foot-bridge and off to the right, the footpath follows the river through the steeply banked and wooded glen, past **Raven's Crag** into the National Trust holding. This is an area of 79ha (194 acres) of hill and river scenery with walks amongst the wooded hills and crags, of which some 75ha (185 acres) were given to the Trust in 1942 by the Hon. Francis Bowes-Lyon, with covenants over 223ha (552 acres) of the adjoining Ridley Hall estate, once the home of the family of that name. The house also has a history as a College of Education in more recent times.

The footpath follows the river down past the grounds of the estate to emerge by the picnic site and car park run by the National Trust and mentioned above, close to the point where the river Allen flows into the South Tyne, opposite Whitechapel where there is a bridge. There are, then, several routes into the area, depending on how far you wish to walk or how close to drive and park.

Continuing along the A686, ¾ mile beyond this turning, the B6305 road comes in on the left from Hexham, and ¾ mile further on another footpath, again on the right, leads in less than 1 mile along the river Allen to the **Staward Pele**. This is one of the most scenic stretches of the river, and, of course, it is possible to walk right through to Ridley Hall. The remains of the Staward Pele are now rather scanty, but the site chosen for a defence point is a natural one on a promontory overlooking the junction of the Harsondale Burn and the river Allen. The tower was at one time held by the Friars of Hexham but after the dissolution of the monasteries came into private hands. A precipitous path leads down from it to a pool on the river below known as **Cypher's Linn**. A riverside footpath leads on from this point to Plankey Mill.

Back on the main road and almost opposite this point is a minor road off to the left leading to High Staward and across to Catton and Allendale Town in 4 miles. The A686 now drops down in less than 1 mile to the steep ravine by Cupola Bridge, where the waters of the East and West Allen rivers unite. There are some very fine views down the length of the deep ravine, and a convenient lay-by is provided. **Whitfield** lies 1½ miles beyond the bridge and is partly tucked away from the main road, with a right-hand turning leading up in ½ mile to the older part. This latter road leads on across Plenmeller Common to the valley of the South Tyne by Coanwood, and there are some fine views on the way. Whitfield has two churches – **St John's** at the top of the hill, built in the early 18th century and restored in Victorian times, and the new **Holy Trinity**, built in 1860, which lies beside the main road. Just beyond the village on the left, is a turning to Catton and Allendale Town which climbs steeply up to Hunter's Oak with some very fine views to the north. **Whitfield Hall**, built in the 1750s but with a history going back to the days of William the Lion, is just beyond this turning. It is now the home of the Blackett-Ord family, who were also responsible for the 'new' church.

A left-hand turn off the A686 1 mile beyond Whitfield climbs up the valley of the West Allen river past Ninebanks to Coalcleugh. The main road follows the line of the river also for 1 or 2 miles and then swings off right along the line of the Whitewalls Burn and climbs the steeper slopes of Whitfield Moor. Crossing the head of the burn in another 1½ miles, it reverts to its former direction with a left-hand swing, passing to the left of **Willyshaw Rigg** (489m, 1,631ft). In less than 4 miles the road has climbed 300m (1,000ft) from Whitfield, and in another mile the boundary into Cumbria is crossed. The road winds down again past Clargilhead and a farm with the strange name of Moscow, close to the Ayle Burn. The B6294 swings off left in 1 mile, following the north bank of the river Nent to Nenthead in Cumbria, while a minor road turns off right by Clarghill House and, crossing the Ayle Burn, follows the South Tyne Valley through to Slaggyford. The A686 continues its descent and in 1½ miles leads into the town of Alston.

The Pennines, near Alston

15 The Roman Wall from Heddon-on-the-Wall to Gilsland

Historical note

The major part of the Roman works in Northumberland stem from the arrival in Britain in AD 78 of Julius Agricola, who became the Governor at that time. The Romans, who had been here since AD 43, had spent their first thirty-five years of occupation in securing a frontier line along the Fosse Way from Exeter to York, then advancing into Wales and subduing it. But their traditional policy of 'divide and conquer' and the brusqueness of some Roman officials in collecting taxes from the populace brought on some serious revolts. In AD 71 a major battle was fought against the predominant tribe of Yorkshire and Northumberland, the Brigantes, at Scotch Corner, which threw this major fighting force of the Britons back to northern Northumberland and over the Scottish Border. From this point of time the Romans were now ready to advance north and into Scotland. Their three legionary headquarters were moved to York, Chester and Caerleon.

Their first line in the north was between Corbridge and Carlisle, along a Roman road known today as the Stanegate, much of which can still be traced. Along this were built the first series of forts: Corbridge, Newbrough, Chesterholm, Haltwhistle Burn, Carvoran, ending, as far as Northumberland is concerned, at Throp, just over the boundary into Cumbria, 1 mile south-west of Gilsland. By AD 81 Agricola advanced into Scotland, following the line of the Roman road of Dere Street from Corbridge to Chew Green and over the Border to Newstead by Melrose, with a secondary line of advance along the Devil's Causeway, which branched off Dere Street at the Portgate and led directly to Berwick-upon-Tweed, to which point his fleet moved up to support him. Linking these two routes was the lateral road from High Rochester which joined the Devil's Causeway by Whittingham at the crossing of the river Aln.

In four short years in Scotland Agricola reached the Moray Firth and

brought the Caledonians to a declaration of peace. He secured the highland line with a series of forts and created a new legionary headquarters
on the river Tay, but much of his effort was in vain for after AD 85, when
he had been recalled, there was a successive withdrawal again. The
Roman army was too extended, and the line was brought back to the
river Tweed. In AD 117, just as the Emperor Hadrian came to the throne,
there was a major revolt in north Britain, which resulted in the 9th legion
being removed from the Roman army list. As a result Hadrian himself
visited Britain in AD 122, took a look at the situation and immediately
envisaged the Wall, which he entrusted to the new Governor of Britain,
Aulius Platorius Nepos, to build. Hadrian was recalled in AD 126.

The original plan was to build a wall from Newcastle to Carlisle, 80
Roman (about 73½ modern) miles long, effectively sealing the Tyne–Solway line. The legionary soldiers and much local labour were impressed
into an effective work-force, and lengths of 40·5m (45 yards) were
entrusted to different 'centuries' as the various inscriptions show. There
were to be milecastle fortlets every Roman mile and two turrets or signal
stations in between each ⅓ mile.

The first step was to lay the foundations from Newcastle to the river
Irthing by Gilsland, wide enough to take the broad Wall planned. This
was to be 3m (10ft) wide, with a height of about 6m (20ft) and with the
rampart about 4·5m (15ft) above the ground. However, within a very
short time of commencing work a change in plan was made. The Wall
was reduced in width to 2·4m (8ft) and was now known as the narrow
Wall. This change can be seen after Turret 26B at Low Brunton, leading
up to the river North Tyne crossing by Chollerford and close to the site of
Milecastle 27, but more clearly, perhaps, on the other side by the fort of
Chesters. At the same time a decision was made to extend the Wall
eastwards from Newcastle to Wallsend, right on a bend of the river Tyne,
to guard against an outflanking river crossing, and the fort at South
Shields was also associated with this move. Thus, from Chollerford
Bridge the Wall extended right across country to Gilsland on the western
boundary of Northumberland as a narrow Wall on a broad-Wall foundation, and a good example of this can be seen in the Romanway Hotel
garden at Gilsland.

Much of the work was completed in the four years from AD 122 to 126,
but alterations and additions are apparent all along the line of the Wall
within the first ten years, with some early constructions being destroyed
to make way for later ideas. A number of forts were associated with the

original construction, projecting beyond the line of the Wall so that their north-east and west gates could open quickly on to the open country to deploy troops on the north side, the tactic formulated by Hadrian. Into this category fall Benwell, Rudchester, Halton Chesters and Birdoswald (just over the Cumbrian boundary) as well as Housesteads, which because of its position on the Whin Sill crags does not project. Following the change to a narrow Wall, additional forts were created with Wallsend, Greatchesters, Carrawburgh and Carvoran in the Tipalt Gap, the latter an intermediate post between the Stanegate and the Wall. Later still, outpost forts were added in front of the Wall, notably at Risingham and also Bewcastle, north-west of Birdoswald, just over the Cumbrian boundary and south of the Kershope Forest area.

Associated with the construction of the Wall was the Ditch to the north, running 6m (20ft) in front and 8m (27ft) wide, with the excavated earth formed as a counterscarp bank 18m (60ft) wide forward of the Ditch and sloping away, bringing any approach into an immediate silhouette, day or night. On the hard dolerite of the Whin Sill and other rock surfaces some of this is cut through the rock, but at other points, notably Limestone Corner, the rock proved too much and it has been left unfinished.

To complete their military zone the Romans also built a ditch behind the Wall, now known as the *Vallum*, which, unlike the Ditch to the north, does not attempt to parallel the Wall but marks off instead a series of sections to the south as a forbidden part of the frontier zone and would have acted as a deterrent to any surprise attack from the rear. The Brigantes were still active in Yorkshire, and the fact that the Romans were concerned about this in the early days of the Wall's history is demonstrated by their building some forts facing south, notably Vindolanda on the Stanegate, as late as AD 208. Later the *Vallum* became a kind of customs barrier through which civilian travellers were allowed to pass. Its line is constructed like a Roman road that seems, at times, to ignore its own close proximity to the Wall and at others to swing away for a good mile to the south. Generally speaking, however, it tends to keep reasonably close most of the way. Basically, its total width is that of the Roman surveyor's measure of 36m (120ft) – an *actus* – with a ditch 6m (20ft) wide, 3m (10ft) deep and, unlike the northern ditch which is V-shaped, with a flat bottom. The removed earth forms two mounds, 9m (30ft) north and south of the ditch, each of which is 6m (20ft) wide, originally edged in with turves. Occasionally, there is a third marginal mound,

The Roman Wall, Housesteads

where later cleaning-out of the ditch has occurred. In its original construction the *Vallum* had causeways across the ditch to the forts, which were controlled by an unmanned gateway, together with a gap in the southern mound by which public access could be regulated from the fort. However, no similar breaks occurred elsewhere at this stage, and although the milecastles also had narrower causeways, these were designed to give the garrison access to the south berm, between the ditch and the south mound, for use as a patrol track before the Roman Military Way was built. Later on, after AD 140, when the Romans had won control of southern Scotland again and the Antonine Wall was built along the Forth–Clyde line, the *Vallum* was thrown open, and 'crossings' were introduced every 40·5m (45 yards) across both mounds with causeways across the ditch, and examples of this can be seen in the stretch of *Vallum* behind Cawfield Crags, to the east of Haltwhistle Burn. With the reverses that took place towards the end of the 2nd century AD, the barrier of the *Vallum* was brought into use again mainly by reopening the ditch, but the mounds were frequently left untouched.

The need for a better road to service the line of the Wall brought the Roman Military Way, started after the *Vallum* had been thrown open in AD 140. With a width of 6m (20ft), it linked the whole military construction post by post with a branch to each turret. It ran independently of the Wall and in some places avoided the difficult terrain that the latter followed, notably between Sewingshields and Thirlwall where it can be seen as a fine example of Roman engineering. It was linked to the Stanegate road to the south, which in turn could be used to bring up reinforcements from as far afield as York via the Roman road from there through Binchester and Ebchester to Corbridge and also from Chester, the other legionary headquarters, through Lancashire to Penrith, thence using the Marian Way from Kirkby Thore to Carvoran.

There are many examples in the neighbourhood of quarries used by the Romans, some left with inscribed dedications. The milecastle fortlets were generally quadrilateral, 15m (50ft) to 18m (60ft) broad and from 19·5m (65ft) to 22·5m (75ft) in length. Their north faces were flush to the wall with gateways to the north and south, part of Hadrian's strategy, so that movements could take place hidden behind the Wall and troops could emerge from any two or more gateways to effect a pincer movement. Usually, the milecastles had one or sometimes two barracks, sufficient for fifty men. The turrets were generally about 4m (14ft) square and recessed into the south face of the Wall. They were manned by soldiers from all over the Roman Empire.

Following the death of Marcus Aurelius in AD 180, a tribal revolt in Scotland overran the Antonine Wall which was destroyed and not rebuilt, although some measure of peace returned. Power struggles were going on in Rome, and with the assassination of the Emperor Commodius in AD 193, Albinus, the Governor of Britain, withdrew most of the troops from Britain to fight for the throne. Meanwhile, the tribes had swept down from the north across Hadrian's Wall and reached York, where the legionary fortress of the 6th Victrix was left in ruins, and a trail of destruction followed their path. The new emperor, Severus, sent a new governor, L. Virius Lupus, to restore the situation, and he immediately bought the invaders off, at the same time rebuilding as fast as he could. The reconstruction work was carried on by his successor, Senecio, between AD 205 and 208. The latter's work has been noted at Chesters, Housesteads and Birdoswald as well.

Severus himself arrived shortly afterwards along with his son Caracalla, and in AD 208 advanced into Scotland and beat the Caledonians into final surrender. After the death of Severus at York in AD 211, Caracalla continued the campaign against the other Scottish tribe of the *Maeatea*, and a peace was imposed which lasted for eighty-five years. Roman troops were withdrawn from Scotland, and no more forts were maintained there. This is the period when tactics along the Wall were changed, with the milecastle gateways being blocked up and the use of some of the turrets discontinued. Larger garrisons were maintained at the forts, and the forward outposts were strengthened, particularly at Risingham and High Rochester. Long-range scouting patrols of cavalry regulated the tribal meetings and maintained the peace in the lowlands. The use of the *Vallum* was dropped, and the civilian population were now allowed to approach and even pass through, subject to search and interrogation. Roman soldiers were now given permission to marry, and a transition from fighting units to a kind of para-military force of soldier-farmers began to take place at this time. Both the forts at Chesters and Chesterholm (Vindolanda) reveal this transition.

Struggles between rival usurpers for the throne led to a draining off of the regular troops once more in AD 296, and the inevitable overrunning of the Wall followed automatically, with the tribes destroying both York and Chester on this occasion. Constantius Chlorus was nominated Caesar with the special responsibility of winning back Britain from Alletus, whom he quickly defeated. In nine years he had restored all the forts, and after advancing deep into Pictish territory to punish them, he died at York in AD 306. The main problems for the Romans at this time were the Saxon and Irish sea-borne invaders whose threats were growing, and over the next seventy years they held them with a new series of forts around the coastline along with the existing line of forts down the Cumbrian coastline to Ravenglass.

In AD 343 there was trouble on the northern frontier once again involving some of the Roman scouts, and both Risingham and Bewcastle had to be rebuilt, with High Rochester being left in ruins. This led to a whole series of raids by the Picts, Scots, Saxons and the Attecotti, which were a continual nuisance but contained. What happened next took the Romans completely by surprise – a combined operation against them known as the 'Barbarian Conspiracy' of AD 367 in which the Picts, Scots and Attecotti tribesmen, aided by both Saxon and Irish pirates and even some Franks from Gaul, made a concerted attack that swept all before it.

There was some treachery in the Wall garrison, all outposts and the Wall were overrun and the line only held at York and Chester by the intervention of the legionary forces. Among the many forts destroyed at this time was Corbridge.

Theodosius arrived in AD 369 to clear up the mess. He restored the Wall and rebuilt the forts, but his greatest task was the restoration of morale with free pardons to the Romans who had defected. The frontier scouts were disbanded, and the garrisons of the Wall now became a mixture of soldier-farmers and civilians. The guardianship of the forward zone was now entrusted to two local tribes – the Votadini of Lothian and the coastal area around Berwick-upon-Tweed and the Dannonii of Strathclyde. This lasted until AD 383, when one of the Roman military commanders – Magnus Maximus – revolted, conquered Gaul and Spain and set himself up as Emperor of Britain. Hadrian's Wall was swamped with invaders again as a result. This time no effort was made to restore it and it ceased to be an effective barrier. Roman soldiers were already being withdrawn from the country to fight the Goths who were attacking Rome.

The last Roman soldier was evacuated in AD 406, and almost at once the Saxons invaded. In 410 Honorius told the Romano-British *civitates* to arrange for their own defence, which they did by buying Saxon mercenaries to fight their own kin, paying them sometimes with land. There is a suggestion that the Romans may have briefly returned in AD 417, but by AD 429, when St Germanius led an army against the Saxons (the 'Hallelujah Victory'), they had gone. In 446 a last appeal was made by the *civitates* of Britain to Aetius, the Roman commander in Gaul, but Britain, not for the last time, was left on its own.

Places to see

Benwell (Tyne and Wear)	2 miles west of Newcastle	Fort on Wall, *Vallum* with causeway, temple
Birdoswald (Cumbria)	1 mile west of Gilsland, on B6318, then minor road	Fort and narrow Wall
Brunton	3½ miles north of Hexham on the A6079	Turret 26B embodied on Wall
Carrawburgh	On B6318 3 miles west of Chollerford	(Brocolita) fort on Wall, Mithraeum and Coventina's Well

Carvoran	½ mile east of Greenhead on B6318, then minor road	(Magna) fort on Stanegate
Cawfields	2 miles north of Haltwhistle on north side of B6318	Milecastle 42 on Wall
Chesterholm	1½ miles north of Bardon Mill; south of the B6318 close to Once Brewed Information Centre	(Vindolanda) fort on the Stanegate, Roman milestones, civilian settlement, museum, replicas of Wall, milecastle and turret
Chesters	Close to Chollerford	(Cilurnum) fort on Wall, bath-house, bridge, museum
Chollerford	3½ miles north of Hexham on the A6079	Roman bridge abutments ½ mile south of modern bridge
Corbridge	On A69(T) between Newcastle and Hexham	(Corstopitum) fort and supply base on the Stanegate, museum
Denton Burn (Tyne and Wear)	3½ miles west of Newcastle	Turret 7B embodied on broad Wall
Gilsland	5 miles west of Haltwhistle; 1 mile west of Greenhead on B6318	Milecastle 48, narrow Wall on broad foundation at *Romanway Hotel*
Great Chesters	2 miles north of Haltwhistle on north side of the B6318	(Aesica) fort on Wall, Ditch, Roman Military Way
Heddon-on-the-Wall	7 miles west of Newcastle on B6528	100m of broad Wall, rock-cut *Vallum*
High House (Cumbria)	½ mile west of Birdoswald	Turf wall
Hotbank Crags	¾ mile west of Housesteads	Differences in thickness of narrow Wall
Housesteads	8 miles west of Chollerford on B6318; 3 miles north of Bardon Mill	(Vercovicium) fort on Wall along Whin Sill ridge, civilian settlement, museum, Roman Military Way, *Vallum*, walks along Wall-line
Limestone Corner	2¾ miles west of Chollerford on B6318	Unfinished Ditch cut through rock, Turret 29A, *Vallum* with crossings

Newcastle (Tyne and Wear)		Museum of Antiquities, Black Gate Museum
Once Brewed	On B6318 2 miles north of Henshaw on A69(T) between Haydon Bridge and Haltwhistle	National Park Information Centre, access to Steel Rigg, Peel Crag, Winshields Crag, Vindolanda, bus-stop
Rudchester	8½ miles west of Newcastle on B6318	(Vindovala) fort on Wall
Sewingshields	6½ miles west of Chollerford on B6318; 4 miles north of Haydon Bridge	Turret 34A, Ditch, *Vallum* with crossings, Roman Military Way, views from crag
South Shields (Tyne and Wear)	9 miles east of Newcastle on A184/5	(Arbeia) fort and museum
Steel Rigg	½ mile north of Once Brewed on B6318	Car park, access to Wall on Winshields Crag and Peel Crag, Ditch, Roman Military Way, views
Wall Houses	4 miles north-east of Corbridge on the B6321 at junction of B6318 6 miles west of Heddon-on-the-Wall	2-mile length of Ditch and *Vallum* with crossings
Wall Town	1 mile north-east of Greenhead (footpath)	Turret 45A embodied on Wall, Roman Military Way, *Vallum*
Whittington Fell	¾ mile west of junction between A68 and B6318 at the Port Gate	Milecastle 23, Ditch, *Vallum*, Roman Military Way
Willowford (Cumbria)	1 mile west of Gilsland on B6318, then minor road ½ mile south	Bridge remains across river Irthing, narrow Wall on Broad foundation, milecastle 49, Ditch
Winshields	½ mile north of Once Brewed Information Centre on B6318; 2 miles north of Henshaw on A69(T) road between Bardon Mill and Haltwhistle	Highest point of Wall on Winshield Crags, 369m (1,230ft) above sea-level, views

Many of the foregoing places are served by seasonal bus services from Hexham, Haltwhistle, Bardon Mill and Newcastle. Details are available from the Tourist Information Offices in Hexham and Newcastle.

Note

Some concern has recently been expressed at the overselling of Hadrian's Wall to large influxes of tourists. A survey at the end of 1976, prepared by the Dartington Amenity Trust for the Countryside Commission, estimated an annual flow at present of 750,000 visitors and foresees this doubling by 1991. There are calls for some planned strategy to deal with the increasing congestion (very apparent in July and August already) and damage. It is notable that the Department of the Environment employ two full-time masons on reparation work at Housesteads, which tops the list for all National Trust properties in 1976, with 147,000 visitors, just over 4% of their overall total. Vindolanda comes a close second.

Undoubtedly, the finest stretch of the Wall lies between Chollerford and Gilsland, where it is seldom far away from the B6318 road, and easy approaches to it exist at Once Brewed and nearby Steel Rigg. There are plenty of other sites and stretches of Wall, some as yet totally unexploited, with no admission charges. For the walker the Pennine Way commends itself in the 8-mile stretch it follows, and for those other explorers it is hoped the following notes will be useful.

From Heddon-on-the-Wall westwards the Wall, hitherto in minor key, now begins to dominate the landscape. The line of the B6318 road closely follows its course, but although it is known as the **Military Way** (which it was), it has nothing to do with the Roman Military Way already referred to in the preamble. The Military Way was built after the Jacobite rising of 1745, when no lateral road existed between Newcastle and Carlisle and General Wade was unable to defend Carlisle at that time because of this fact. He had been waiting between Newcastle and Wooler with the Hanoverian forces for Bonnie Prince Charlie who attempted to deceive him about the Scottish plans and who then marched south down Liddesdale behind the line of The Cheviot Hills. After the defeat which followed, General Wade ordered the construction of the Military Way. It was built between 1752 and 1753 mainly by levelling the tumbled-down ruins of Hadrian's Wall.

Thus, between Heddon-on-the-Wall and the Portgate, a distance of 9 miles, the actual Wall is hidden except at a few points, but the Ditch to the north and the *Vallum* to the south are more distinct. The B6318 road makes a slight deviation from the Wall line to cross the A69(T) road just west of Heddon-on-the-Wall but quickly picks up the line again and follows it in ½ mile to **Rudchester**, where the fort of **Vindovala** lies. This was the fourth of seventeen forts along the line of the Wall. It traversed the line of the Wall so that the west and east gates were lined up with it. South of the modern road, the ramparts of the south and west sides can just still be seen, but otherwise not much remains. The *Vallum* lies 72m (240ft) to the south. A temple to Mithras, the Persian god of light, was located and excavated in 1953, and many shrines were also recovered from this site, some of which are now in Newcastle's Museum of Antiquities. Many of the nearby farmhouses, incidentally, bear evidence of building with Roman stones filched from the Wall, and some of these carry inscriptions.

At High Seat, ½ mile on from Rudchester, there is a view to Harlow Hill 2 miles away, with the Ditch to the north quite distinct. The line of the *Vallum* comes to within 30m of the Wall line at this point but then turns away again as the Wall makes a bend to the north to gain the higher ground. At Harlow Hill only a fragment of the Wall can be traced close to the site of Milecastle 16, with two small lengths of the *Vallum* visible at the rear about 400m away. The road crosses the Whittledean Reservoirs, from which point the Ditch is visible again. The minor road to the left leads through to **Welton Hall** which was built almost entirely of Roman stones, with a ruined 15th-century tower attached to a manor-house of 1614.

The sites of Milecastles 17 and 18 are passed coming up to **East Wallhouses** and **Wall Houses** where the *Vallum*, intent on keeping its own independent straight line, closes in on the Wall again. Parts of it are visible here, together with some crossings. The B6321 road branches off left to Corbridge, and from here on only the Ditch is visible as the B6318 passes **Matfen Piers**, the old gateway piers to the large estate to the north. Milecastle 20 lies by **Halton Shields** and was discovered in 1935. Here, close to Carr Hill, the B6318 road swings away from the line of the Wall and follows instead the line of the north berm between Wall and Ditch to the north. Here, a southward bend in the Wall line took place, aiming for Down Hill, with the *Vallum* swinging south to avoid it, and its line and some crossings can be seen here close to **Halton Red House** where a minor road turns off north to Great Whittington. Both alignments now make directly for the site of the Halton fort ½ mile away, known as **Onnum** or sometimes **Hunnum**, the fifth in line from Wallsend.

The curious thing about **Halton** is why it did not coincide with the line of the Roman road of Dere Street, emerging from the Port Gate ¾ mile to the west at the present-day junction of the B6318 and the A68. Halton is a fairly large fort with the northern third of the structure extended in front of the Wall line and it was enlarged in its rearward area later on. Excavations and some of the inscriptions here show that it was occupied by a regiment of cavalry. To the north an extensive bath-house was discovered in 1827, one of the largest along the Wall, but is not visible now. The road to Halton running south from the B6318 divides the fort area into two, and the line of the ramparts can be seen.

Between Halton fort and the Portgate the *Vallum* is visible once again, and close by a small portion of the Roman Military Way, virtually the first identifiable section to be seen coming from Newcastle. From the crossing of the A68 road the B6318 follows the north mound of the *Vallum* more or less all the way to Chollerford, and both *Vallum* and Wall keep fairly close together. Less than 1 mile beyond the crossroads at the top of Whittington Fell are the remains of Milecastle 23, where the line of the Roman Military Way recommences along the north mound of the *Vallum* which is plainly visible here. To the north the Ditch is cut through rocky ground. On **Errington Hill Head**, ½ mile beyond here, there are the outlines of several early British encampments. Opposite the track that leads in this direction is the site of Milecastle 24 on the south side of the road, the platform of which can be seen. The next one, Milecastle 25, is close to where the road comes up from Codlaw Hill 1 Roman mile further on. Between the two milecastles the Wall makes a slight turn southwards, and the modern road follows suit.

At **Hill Head**, ¼ mile further on, road and Wall change positions, with the B6318 crossing over to the line of the south berm of the *Vallum*, that is, between the *Vallum* ditch and its southern mound. Close to this point a centurial dedication stone was found, now incorporated in the nearby farmhouse face, while from one of the Roman quarries on **Fallowfield Fell**, ½ mile to the south, an inscribed rock bearing the name Flavius Carantius was found and is now in Chesters Museum. Opposite the minor road leading down to Fallowfield is a footpath, marked by a cross, which leads the way to the chapel behind the trees built to commemorate the Battle of Heavenfield in 634, where the Northumbrian king Oswald defeated the forces of Cadwallon, King of Gwynedd, and the Britons.

The chapel was built in 1737 and given a Victorian restoration. There is a Roman altar inside decorated with scroll-work, which formerly served as a socket for a cross. From the churchyard there is a fine view over Chollerford and the North Tyne Valley.

Descending Brunton Bank, the B6318 road swings back to the north side of the Wall and follows the line of the Ditch as far as Brunton House. Close to Planetrees Farm, on the south side of the road just past the site of Milecastle 26, is a stretch of the Wall, open at any reasonable time without charge and in the care of the Department of the Environment. It shows a junction between the broad Wall and a much narrower piece only 1·8m (6ft) wide. It was at this point that the broad Wall of 3m (10ft) width began to be changed for the narrow Wall of 2·4m (8ft), and this becomes more clear on the other side of the North Tyne river by Chesters.

The B6318 road drops steeply down Brunton Bank, but by Brunton House it swings away to the north-west to make its approach to Choller-ford Bridge. There is another fine stretch of the Wall just behind Brunton House, best approached by turning left at the crossroads on to the A6079 Hexham road for about 200m, where a signposted stile and path on the left lead up to it. This is the site of Turret 26B, first excavated in 1873, together with a fine stretch of the broad Wall on the western side and for about 3·6m (12ft) on the eastern side, when it abruptly reverts to the very narrow 1·8m (6ft) Wall seen at the previous site. This is the best-preserved of all the turrets and is recessed about 1·2m (4ft) into the Wall, which here stands to a height of about 1·5m (5ft). It is possible that with the proximity of the nearby bridge the turret and its flanking Wall to the west were constructed before the policy change in width occurred, with the section to the east being filled in afterwards. The site is open at any reasonable time without charge and is in the care of the Department of the Environment.

Between this site and the North Tyne river another milecastle (No. 27) stood, about 200m east of the river bank, on the Wall line to the Roman bridge crossing, which can be reached by a footpath along the disused railway line signposted from Chollerford Bridge. The remains of this striking bridge were excavated in 1860 by John Clayton who also did much of the work at Chesters on the opposite bank. Among other things discovered was the fact that there had been two bridges at this point, one prior to the Wall's construction and another at much the same time. The line of the Wall and its *Vallum* can be seen as they approach the river, together with the remains of the tower which stood upon the bridge abutment. When the water is low, some of the piers can be seen. It seems that the Romans used the river to operate a mill-race and a water-mill on this site, which again is in the care of the Department of the Environment and is open at any reasonable time without charge.

To reach **Chesters** on the opposite bank a return north is made on the A6079 with a left turn across single-track Chollerford Bridge and another left turn at the far end on to the B6318 road. The entrance to **Chesters Park** is just up on the left, where not only the line of the Wall can be picked up again but also the Roman fort of **Cilurnum**, one of the most accessible and important of all the forts along the Wall. The work of excavation here lies squarely to the memory of John Clayton (1792–1890), an amateur archaeologist and a contemporary of the Newcastle architect, Dobson, who also dabbled in sites along the Wall. Clayton devoted himself to solving some of the intricate puzzles of the Roman remains and lived in the 18th-century Chesters House also in the park. Built in 1771, it was enlarged by Norman Shaw in the 1890s.

The results of Clayton's work are more than interesting: a large Roman fort, covering an area of 2·33ha (5¾ acres), shaped in the usual playing-card plan with rounded corners to its 1·5m (5ft) thick walls. Standing on a platform, the mounds of its ramparts and the ditch that surrounded it are visible, and enough remains to identify the barrack blocks, granaries and the central headquarters administration block with the commandant's house. It had six gateways, parts of which remain, and from building inscriptions it is known to have been garrisoned by the 2nd Ala of Asturians, a Spanish cavalry regiment.

One curious thing about Chesters is that the fort overlies part of the foundations of the Wall itself, and there are several examples along the Wall of patching or bonding in afterwards. The fort was built in the early 2nd century AD sometime after AD 122 and before AD 146, the date of a remarkable diploma or certificate of honourable discharge for an auxiliary soldier, also creating him a Roman citizen, now in the Chesters Museum. There is also sufficient evidence to show that the fort was restored after the incursions of AD 197, 296 and 367 which affected so many forts along the Wall. An abundant water-supply was brought to the fort by aqueduct not only for drinking purposes but also to fill the splendid bath-house lying just away from the fort.

On either side of the fort the narrow Wall is now evident, and to the south the mound of the Roman Military Way can be traced to the river's edge where it joined the bridge across the North Tyne. At low water the foundations of the western abutments of this bridge can be seen.

The **Clayton Memorial Museum** is a treasure-house of recovered Roman relics not only from Chesters but from many other sites as well. There is a fine collection of Roman altars and inscriptions, pottery, glass and sculptures, including the collection from the shrine of the water-nymph goddess Coventina from Carrawburgh and the bronze corn-measure from Carvoran which was shown to have erred very much on the Roman side when it came to collecting taxes in kind. The site is in the care of the Department of the Environment and is open at standard hours with a charge.

Across Chesters Park the line of the Wall continues westwards but is now buried under the site of the house and its adjacent road. Returning to the B6318 road, it can be picked up again by Walwick where a short stretch of the *Vallum* lies to the south-east of the village and the site of Milecastle 28 lies. The B6318 bends south-west on leaving the village, swinging across from the line of the Wall to the north mound of the *Vallum*, and just past Walwick Hall another part of the *Vallum* and the Ditch to the north can be seen. Both the Ditch and the *Vallum* can be seen as the road approaches the **Tower Tye** crossroads, 1¾ miles west of Chollerford, where a small house of that name was built out of Roman stones in the 1730s. A minor road runs north here to Simonburn, while the southern link leads through to Fourstones. On nearby **Walwick Fell**, to the left of the road, are the remains of a Roman camp and also a native settlement. Half a mile beyond the crossroads on the northern side the site of Turret 29A, together with a fine section of the Wall, is preserved at **Black Carts**. It is in the care of the Department of the Environment and is open at any reasonable time without charge. Both the Ditch and the *Vallum* are still in sight here, with the latter showing crossings.

Climbing the hill towards Limestone Corner, another minor road leads off northwards towards Simonburn in the North Tyne Valley. Where the modern road bends is the site of Milecastle 30 with two small stretches of the Roman Military Way on either side, but the main attraction at this point is the unfinished Ditch to the north, where attempts to cut it through the hard rock have been abandoned. The *Vallum*, which together with the line of the Wall and the Ditch all make a 35° swing to the south, is also rock-cut through this section and shows the intermittent crossings every 40·5m (45 yards) which were effected after the formal eradication of the rearward military boundary.

The descent is made towards **Carrawburgh**, reached in another mile, where close to the site of Milecastle 31 the Roman fort of **Brocolita** stands. Most visitors come to Carrawburgh to see the **Temple of Mithras** and the site of **Coventina's Well** also to be found here. True, there is a large fort but it is as yet unexcavated. It was built as an afterthought by the Romans with its north side bonded into the narrow Wall, but in order to get it in they had first to refill the *Vallum* which had already been dug, and this dates it to well after AD 122. Inscriptions have been found here showing it was garrisoned by a force from the Low Countries, the 1st Cohort of Batavians, in the 3rd and 4th centuries. In 1873 John Clayton excavated a bath-house on the slope to the west of the fort, but his most original discovery was the site of Coventina's Well to the west, a spring bubbling from the swampy ground, which had become a shrine to the Celtic goddess Coventina. The altar and other sculptured stones are now in the Chesters Museum. Many votive offerings of jewelry were also recovered along with a hoard of 13,487 Roman coins. The garrison also practised a much more sophisticated religion with the bull-cult of the Persian god Mithras, and lying to the south-west of the site is the largest and best preserved of the three Mithraic Temples found along the Wall. It is quite small but contained three altars, the originals of which are now in the Museum of Antiquities in Newcastle along with a full-scale mock-up of the temple. There is some evidence to suggest that both the well-shrine and the temple were violently obliterated, possibly by a later Christian commander. The site is in the care of the Department of the Environment and is open at all reasonable times with no charge. There is a car park.

The B6318 road continues westwards, climbing in $\frac{3}{4}$ mile to Milecastle 32 on the south side of the road just past the crown of the hill. The *Vallum*, Ditch and Roman Military Way are clearly seen from this point, while $\frac{1}{2}$ mile to the south-west at the top of **Brown Moor**, well over 240m (800ft) above sea-level, lies another Roman camp. In 2 miles from Carrawburgh the bridge across the Settlingstones Burn marks a major change in the relative positions of the Wall and the modern road. Just before this point, at Shield on the Wall, Milecastle 33 appears on the right where the B6318 swings slightly left to follow the line of the *Vallum*. The site of Turret 33B is marked by a group of trees on the right. Both the line of the Wall and the Ditch turn slightly north and then come back again.

This is the start of what is probably the most dramatic and interesting section of Hadrian's Wall as the Whin Sill crags begin and the Wall swings to take in the higher ground, while the *Vallum* keeps below. Here also the B6318 swings south away from the Wall line and pursues an independent course for the rest of its journey to Greenhead. This is the spot to start walking, and the 2½-mile stretch from here to Housesteads along the line of the Wall can be very rewarding, as the line runs up and down the crags, followed by its Ditch (but only where necessary) and the Roman Military Way. Ahead and to the right is Sewingshields with the ruined site of **Sewingshields Castle** just below the site of Turret 34A. To the north lie Halleypike Lough and Folly Lake on Haughton Common with the southern edges of Wark Forest behind. To the left of the lakes are the **King's Crags** and **Queen's Crags**, two pinnacles of sandstone emerging from the plain, both associated with one of the many legends of King Arthur. The King's Crag is sometimes still known as 'Arthur's Chair' even today.

As an alternative to following the line of the Wall on foot it is possible to trace a way along the line of the Roman Military Way which here is fairly distinct. Otherwise, returning to the B6318 road, it is a fraction over 2 miles to the car park at Housesteads with a ¼-mile walk up to the site.

Of all the Wall forts **Housesteads** certainly has the most impressive position and probably still draws more visitors than any other. Its draw is its spectacular position, perched on the 300m (1,000ft) contour of the Whin Sill crags, overlooking both Broomlee and Greenlee Loughs and surveying the country to the north. It is a well-preserved site with good access to the line of the Wall in each direction along the crags. On the approaching slopes from the car park are signs of early cultivation terraces which could be associated with the *vicus*, or civilian settlement, outside the fort walls to the south-west or might just possibly be medieval. In the settlement the remains of shops and houses are still evident. This is the area that served the needs of the soldiers at the fort, and it has been estimated that up to 2,000 civilians may have lived here, living in the upper storey of two-storey houses and using the ground floor to display their goods and trade.

The main purpose of the fort, however, was to guard the way through the Knag Burn below it and to the right. In the Roman army list it was known as **Borcovicium**, but inscriptions found on the site named it **Vercovicium**, a not improbable transliteration between 'b' and 'v' often associated with Greek and Latin names. It was a largish fort, just over

2·02ha (5 acres). Both fort and its surroundings were presented to the National Trust, who also purchased Crag Lough and neighbouring farms to give a total holding of 3½ miles of Wall and some 469ha (1,159 acres) of land. Both J. M. Clayton and Dr G. M. Trevelyan were involved in these gifts and covenants. The museum, which is to the west of the site, was also built by the National Trust, but the whole area is in the care of the Department of the Environment, open at standard hours, charge.

Excavations have shown that the fort was built after the foundations for the broad Wall were laid sometime after AD·122 but before the narrow Wall reached this point. Discoveries have revealed the foundations also of Turret 36B, almost certainly demolished again to make way for the fort, here set lengthwise to the Wall without the usual projection forward for obvious reasons. The fort would have held up to 1,000 men.

There is plenty to see at Housesteads, and one of the most interesting points is the role the fort played as a Roman customs and frontier post after civilians were permitted to pass through the Wall late in the 3rd century AD. To the east and below in the Knag Burn a gateway was let

Housesteads Roman Camp

into the Wall, flanked by guard chambers and with a second door at the rear, to admit transit passengers a few at a time for interrogation and search. Beyond this, on the shelf of rock on the other side of the burn, a bath-house stood, but now only fragments remain.

In the museum are plans, photographs and models of the fort with some pottery and sculpted stones. The collection includes a relief of three hooded and cloaked deities from a shrine found in the *vicus*, a figure of Mercury and one of Hercules and the Lion. A whole symposium of gods has been located at Housesteads and its adjacent settlement from the Persian god Mithras, whose underground temple is found on **Chapel Hill** to the south-west of the fort with relics in the Museum of Antiquities at Newcastle, to the German deity Mars Thincus, attended by female Valkyrie spirits of pre-Wagnerian myth, whose shrine is now in the Chesters Museum where reliefs of both Victory and Mars, also found here, are likewise on show. From the *vicus* a series of seated mother-goddesses were found, now in Newcastle's Museum of Antiquities, which also houses a small altar to another German god known as Hueter.

From the fort it is possible to walk in both directions along the Wall: eastwards, Sewingshields Crags is reached in just over 1 mile, and one can either return to the same point or continue through for $2\frac{1}{2}$ miles to the point where the B6318 road meets the Wall by the site of Milecastle 34; westwards, the line runs along Cuddy's Crags, Hotbank Crags and Crag Lough to Peel Crag and the car park at Steel Rigg, a distance of $2\frac{1}{2}$ miles. The route passes the sites of Milecastles 37, 38 and 39, the first and last of which are identifiable. The gap between Cuddy's Crags and Hotbank Crags is known as the Rapishaw Gap, one of the many 'busy gaps' in the days of raiding and reiving but now the northern exit from the Wall line for the Pennine Way.

By Crag Lough the Wall line descends into Milking Gap, passing the site of Milecastle 38, where the Bradley Burn runs down in 1 mile to the fort of Vindolanda on the line of the Stanegate road. Beyond the lough the Wall climbs up Peel Crag past Milecastle 39, which can be identified, then past the hill of Steel Rigg into the gap by Peel, where connections with modern civilization again exist. In keeping with the changed tactics introduced by Severus, many of the turrets in this sector were demolished by the Romans themselves.

As an alternative to walking the Wall line in this sector it is possible to follow the Roman Military Way, which is less strenuous and eventually reaches the same point. For the motorist from Housesteads the B6318 road can be followed westwards, and in 1½ miles the line of the modern road rejoins the line of the *Vallum* just past Milking Gap, then follows it for another mile to the crossroads by Once Brewed, where a right turn will lead into the National Trust car park (known as the Steel Rigg car park) ½ mile to the north at Peel Gap. The minor road running south leads through to the A69(T) road between Haydon Bridge and Haltwhistle by Henshaw.

Once Brewed is the focal centre for much activity along the Wall. There is an information centre here, operated by the Northumberland National Park authorities, and a very modern youth hostel. It is the main calling point for many of the seasonal bus services operated from Hexham and Haltwhistle for visitors to the Wall. Mini-bus services also operate from here to Vindolanda. The names Once Brewed and Twice Brewed intrigue many visitors to the area: East Twice Brewed was the name of a farm used as an overnight stop by carriers from Newcastle to Carlisle in the days before railways, now transferred to a local inn as Twice Brewed; the other was a later addition in the competitive supplying of victuals and beer to travellers, but whether the 'brewed' relates to tea or ale no one seems to know.

From Once Brewed westwards is the most dramatic 3-mile section of the Wall, rising to its highest point on **Winshields Crag**, 369m (1,230ft) above sea-level. The Pennine Way follows this stretch, and the line can be walked from Peel Gap, passing Milecastles 40, 41 and 42, of which the last, at **Cawfield**, is one of the best preserved on the line. The Ditch is visible again by Peel Gap, and within ½ mile, by the Winshields Milecastle (No. 40), a stretch of the Wall is in the care of the Department of the Environment and is open at any reasonable time without charge. There is another stretch of the Wall visible across Melkridge Common with a section of Ditch covering the gap here. Passing along the Cawfield Crags, Milecastle 42 is worth an inspection, together with the section of Wall here, once again in the care of the Department of the Environment, open at any reasonable time without charge. The Wall line then drops down into Caw Gap, crossing the Caw Burn, the main tributary of the Haltwhistle Burn. Again, the use of the turrets was discontinued by the Romans along this sector.

For those who prefer the road the B6318 from Once Brewed westwards leaves the line of the *Vallum* again, as the latter changes direction and heads for the Caw Gap in its customary straight line sections and comes up to the line of the Wall there, while the Roman

Military Way snakes its way behind the Wall line, choosing its own convenience of route. In 1½ miles the B6318 is joined from the left by a minor road coming up from Melkridge on the A69(T) road, and just beyond this point a right turn leads up to Shield on the Wall, where access to the *Vallum* (here marked by many crossings), the Roman Military Way and the Wall is possible. At the junction of these two roads the line of the Stanegate coming west from Vindolanda swings to the north side of the B6318, and traces of it can be found in the fields to the north-west.

Half a mile further west the road from Haltwhistle crosses the line of the B6318. Just to the north of this junction is the site of the **Haltwhistle Burn fort**, associated more with the Stanegate line and not the Wall itself. Standing on a bluff above the stream, it is quite small but a reasonably well-preserved specimen of the earlier forts. Both its ditches and the line of the Stanegate road can be seen here, and it has been suggested that the Romans themselves demolished the fort when a change in their operational plan came with the moving of the forts on to the Wall line. It was occupied at one time by the 6th Legion, who more than likely used this base for much of the construction of the Wall itself, for there are several temporary camps in the area which may have housed some of the native work-force and there are also local quarries.

To the north of this point, with a right turn at the Milecastle Inn, there is a car park and picnic site from which visits can be made to the Cawfields Milecastle and also to the fort at **Great Chesters** (**Aesica**), which lies a little to the north-west along the line of the Wall. Although there is not a great deal to see, it is an interesting fort for the archaeologist, for it tells much of the early and later developments of the Wall construction. Like many forts, it was built as an afterthought, for it occupies the site of Milecastle 43, already constructed at the laying of the broad Wall foundation, and with the advent of the narrow Wall the fort was built and bonded into the latter, the milecastle being demolished. The south and west ramparts can be seen, and the west gate shows signs of the later blocking which reduced their overall size. On the more vulnerable western side there are four ditches, and to the north there are traces of a remarkable 5-mile long channel cut by the Romans to bring water from the head of the Caw Burn. The fort faced east with the Roman Military Way approaching this point and leaving again by the west gate. A branch road from the Stanegate entered by the south gate, and a pathway follows this link today. Much of the fort remains to be excavated, but a bath-house has been found as well as traces of a *vicus*, or civilian settlement. The 3rd-century garrison was the 2nd Cohort of Asturians. There are some signs of a post-Roman occupation, and a hoard of Celtic jewelry was discovered here. To the south-west the line of the *Vallum* is quite clear with several crossings.

From Great Chesters the line of the Wall follows the last series of crags known as the Nine Nicks of Thirlwall, but heavy quarrying operations in the past have destroyed some of their original shape. Past Cockmount Hill the line of the Wall can be followed along the Pennine Way for the 4 miles to Thirlwall Castle with some lengthy sections of it visible. There is a Roman milestone, removed from the Roman Military Way just west of Cockmount Hill with a section of the Ditch covering the gap. In another mile, as the Wall line snakes in and out of the small gaps in the Whin Sill ridges, Turret 44B is sufficiently identifiable with a section of the Roman Military Way to the rear. Across the next gap to the Walltown Crags much of the line of the Wall has been destroyed by quarrying, but a small section, including Turret 45A, is in the care of the Department of the Environment and is open at any reasonable time, without charge. Some repair work has been recently effected here. This is the last visible section before dropping down the escarpment line to Thirlwall Castle and crossing the Tipalt Burn.

Along the B6318 road from Great Chesters little remains to be seen before reaching Greenhead in under 4 miles. After the Haltwhistle Burn is crossed, there are several Roman temporary camp sites north and south of the road, and the line of the Stanegate runs parallel to the modern road, 200m to the north, crossing Haltwhistle Common. At Sunny Rigg, where the minor road comes in on the left from Haltwhistle, a series of footpaths leads off to the right, one leading through to a section of the *Vallum* which is visible here, the other past Peatsteel Crags to Low Town and then Walltown, where a stretch of the Wall and Turret 44B can be seen. The outline of a large temporary Roman camp, just to the north of the road and astride the Stanegate line, can also be detected just beyond this junction.

A mile further on a second road comes in on the left from Haltwhistle, and just beyond this a minor road turns off right, signposted to Low Tipalt, towards Walltown on the edge of the escarpment before dropping down the last ½ mile to Greenhead. Just along this turning on the left is the site of the Roman fort of **Carvoran**, a fort associated with the original defence line of the Stanegate, overlooking the Tipalt Burn gap, and the northern terminal of the Roman road of the Marian Way which led up the South Tyne Valley. Carvoran or Magna, to give it the Roman name, is thus a much earlier fort than those associated with the Wall, the original construction dating some time after AD 80 when Agricola built the Stanegate. However, judging from the few remains located here, it seems likely that a later fort existed after the Wall, for inscriptions have been found with the date AD 136–8, and it is known that a company of Syrian archers, the Hamians, were garrisoned here. Part of the north-west tower remains, and earlier observers reported a bath-house. A Roman bronze corn-measure, now in Chesters Museum, was found here as well as some shrines. It is believed a civilian settlement was formerly outside the walls. The site is extremely close to the line of the Wall, with the *Vallum* just to the north. Opposite Carvoran, by the first farmhouse, a lane leads off right past Walltown quarries towards Walltown.

Beyond Greenhead the B6318 road crosses the line of the Wall, with the line of the Stanegate, followed by the *Vallum* (with some crossings but without causeways), visible on the left. Just south of this point is the site of a large Roman camp, and, for the enthusiast, there are two more $\frac{1}{2}$ mile and 1 mile to the west. The Ditch line is also seen as the road and railway head through the gap, then turn west to parallel the line of the Wall to the north. At Gilsland $1\frac{1}{2}$ miles on, Milecastle 48, on the west side of the Poltcross Burn (which here marks the Northumberland boundary), is the first of several interesting sites which congregate around the river Irthing crossing. To reach it turn left just before the Gilsland railway arch, where a signposted road leads straight into the Station Hotel car park. A footpath from here leads along the railway down to the Poltcross Burn. It is a very good example and like the other sections of the Wall is in the care of the Department of the Environment. It is open at any reasonable time without charge. Close by, in the gardens of the **Roman-way Hotel** there is another section of the Wall, also in the care of the Department of the Environment. Both are technically in Cumbria.

Both the sites of **Willowford Bridge**, where the Roman Wall crossed the river Irthing, and the fort at **Birdoswald**, the junction point to the outpost fort at Bewcastle, are well worth a visit and easily reached from Gilsland across the bridge into Cumbria.

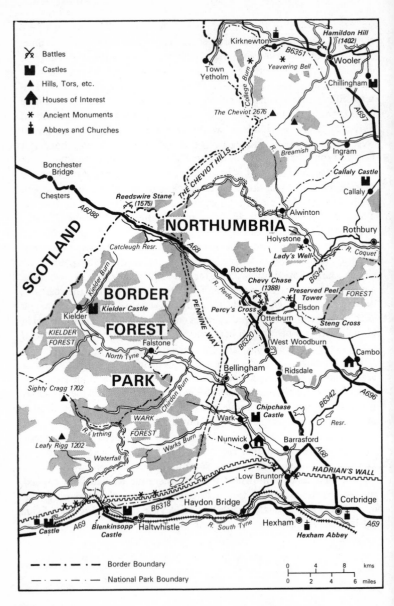

Battles ✗

Castles ◼

Hills, Tors, etc. ▲

Houses of Interest ⌂

Ancient Monuments ✳

Abbeys and Churches ⬙

Kirknewton

Hamildon Hill (1402)

B6351

Wooler

Town Yetholm

Yeavering Bell

Chillingham

College Burn

A697

The Cheviot 2676 ▲

R. *Breamish*

Ingram

THE CHEVIOT HILLS

Bonchester Bridge

Callaly Castle

Chesters

Reedswire Stane (1575)

A6088

Callaly

NORTHUMBRIA

Alwinton

Rothbury

Holystone

SCOTLAND

Catcleugh Resr.

Lady's Well

R. Coquet

BORDER

Kielder Burn

Rochester

R. *Rede*

Chevy Chase (1388)

B6341

FOREST

Preserved Peel Tower

Kielder

Kielder Castle

Percy's Cross

Elsdon

FOREST

A68

PENNINE WAY

Otterburn

Steng Cross

KIELDER FOREST

Falstone

R. *North Tyne*

West Woodburn

Cambo

PARK

Bellingham

B6320

Ridsdale

Sighty Cragg 1702 ▲

Chirdon Burn

A696

WARK FOREST

Chipchase Castle

B6342

Wark

Resr.

R. *Irthing*

Leafy Rigg 1202 ▲

Nunwick

Barrasford

Warks Burn

Waterfall

A68

HADRIAN'S WALL

Low Brunton

Corbridge

Haydon Bridge

B6318

Castle

Blenkinsopp Castle

Haltwhistle

A69

R. *South Tyne*

Hexham

Hexham Abbey

A69

▬ ▪ ▬ ▪ ▬ **Border Boundary**

▬ ▪ ▬ ▪ ▬ **National Park Boundary**

0		4		8	kms

0	2	4	6	miles

214

16 The Northumberland National Park

Of the ten national parks in England and Wales the **Northumberland National Park**, designated in 1956, has the added advantage of sharing a common boundary with the Border Forest Park (see page 222). Instead of offering the visitor a mere 398 square miles of really worthwhile countryside, it combines its open moorland scenery with that of the Border Forest Park to provide something approaching 574 square miles of open leisure space.

Its northern boundary, set along the Cheviot border ridge between Northumberland and Scotland, covers some of the wildest and least populated areas of the county, intruded upon by five or six deeply incised river valleys which penetrate its isolation. Southwards, 40 miles away and almost to the South Tyne Valley, it takes in 15 miles of the more interesting line of Hadrian's Wall between Gilsland and Walwick Fell. The western boundary traces the line of the river Irthing marking the Cumbrian border northwards to Wark Forest, where the two park areas then share a common line to the Scottish border at Carter Bar. In the east it takes in the quieter reaches of the North Tyne Valley north-westwards from Bellingham and finally, following the line of the river Rede to include Redesdale, it makes a large swing around the Simonside Hills almost to Rothbury and traces back along the river Coquet.

Thus the park falls into five distinct and separate areas. Amongst the least spoiled parts of the whole countryside in Britain today, each contributes towards an integrated whole, dominated by the Cheviot mass and surrounded by small villages and market towns that afford pleasing vistas to the eye. Its skyline is broken by a pattern of hill farms and remote shepherds' cottages.

Geologically, the whole area is fascinating: some 300 million years ago volcanic outbursts from a series of craters west of the present Cheviot line threw up the first agglomerate deposits in great showers of rocks and

215

boulders, some of which can still be seen, particularly at the head of the Coquet Valley. A laval flow followed, which formed the bulk of the Cheviot mass, cooling as andesite in purple and grey smooth-surfaced hills, today covered by grass and known locally as 'white land', good for grazing. It formed the prehistoric shoreline in a primeval sea, and its line can still be traced around the hills from Kirknewton through Wooler, past Ingram and Alnham to Alwinton and Elsdon. Later – much later – the sedimentary beds of the Carboniferous period formed around this igneous core of the Old Red Sandstone era pushing the coastline back but leaving a large prehistoric lake that stretched from Wooler to Berwick.

Later still, another upthrust into the solidified lava brought the central core of granite which formed the highest peaks of The Cheviot Hills – The Cheviot itself, Hedgehope and Comb Fell and an area of about 5 miles in radius around these. Here, it melted and pushed its way through the lava but elsewhere it lies underneath, and time and weather have gradually eroded away the surface layer to reveal exposed patches in other parts. A second upthrust of granite in the form of dykes also pushed up the lava later on, and as it has been weathered away, outcrops of this finer-grain granite appear at such places as Linhope Spout and Biddlestone, where it is quarried for road-building.

Through the long process of the evolutionary time scale glacial action followed by melting water streaming down the hillsides carved out the steep-sided valleys and brought down pebbles and boulders to form the conglomerate masses found in such exits from the higher slopes as that at Roddam Dene just south of Wooler. Meanwhile, on the shoreline successive layers of sandstone, shale and limestone were built up from tidal actions of the sea to form much of the surrounding countryside seen today. Eventually, some of these layers formed the Fell Sandstones of which the Simonside Hills, stepped up in waves of succession, are a fine example. Other such outcrops range north-westwards beyond Rothbury to the Kyloe Hills just south of Berwick-upon-Tweed, while the Harbottle Hills, just south of Alwinton, show the distinct break between the grass-covered 'white land' of the igneous Cheviot mass to the north and the sedimentary deposits of the later era which have led to the bracken and heather slopes of the 'black land' to the south, and its distinctive types of vegetation which have dictated in turn how the resultant grazing pattern would lie. To the west, and covering much of the National Park area in Redesdale, the North Tyne Valley and down to Hadrian's Wall, later layers of peat formed over the sandstones and in time formed thin

Snow covered Cheviot Hills, near Wooler

seams of coal. Some of this has been worked in the past with evidence of many small mines even from Roman times, and the outcropping sandstone has also been quarried for building as shown just north of Hadrian's Wall.

The last phase of the evolutionary pattern came with later earth shifts, forming dykes and faults, which led to upthrusts of molten basalt filling in the exposed gaps in a distinctive line right across the county. This extremely hard rock, known as whinstone, extends from Greenhead along the line of Hadrian's Wall (where its presence was put to good use) and through past Alnwick to the east coast to form the Farne Islands, then circles back inland south of Budle Bay to leave a hard ridge across country that meets the northern end of the Kyloe Hills. Its hardness led to its natural choice as a base on which Dunstanburgh and Bamburgh castles were built, and a thin sill of it runs long the southern edge of Holy Island to form the castle base there as well. At one time this rock was also used for road-building and shipped out from Craster harbour.

Thus, not only the pattern of land use, vegetation, drainage and inhabitation of the National Park area lies squarely to these geological successions, but to some outward degree at least so also do its early defences. Its river valleys provided the very earliest routes of occupation by man, with some minor Mesolithic infiltrations from the 5th millenium onwards moving in from the coastline towards the distant hills. Of these incursions, however, few traces remain. It is only from the Neolithic period about 3000 BC that examples of the long barrow burial cairns begin to appear, and there are two good examples at Bellshiel Law, close to Byrness in Redesdale, and also in the Border Forest Park by Kielder, where the Devil's Lapful lies. Around 2600 BC fresh incursions from the Continent brought the Beaker Folk from the Rhineland. These more sophisticated newcomers introduced the use of copper for weapons and tools, which led, in later developments, to the start of the Bronze Age. They also left their traditional beaker-shaped pots in single burial chambers covered by round barrows such as the one at Five Barrows on the hills by Holystone. Later sites, such as that at Lordenshaw south of Rothbury, reveal the stone-lined burial cists with capstones on top. There are many similar sites, generally falling into the period between 1600 and 1000 BC, for this was the era of Stonehenge and Avebury, with a wide-ranging civilization pattern that included a contact with the Megalith builders and knew the rudiments of mathematics and astronomy. Artefacts from this period include bone pine, pottery, metal weapons and tools, gold, amber and jet ornaments, some of which are on display in the Museum of Antiquities in Newcastle, at Alnwick Castle and also at the smaller museums of Lewisburn and Ingram. Part of the mystery of this period lies in the very prevalent and cryptic cup-and-ring markings found on so many sites, particularly along the line of the Devil's Causeway, and one suggestion made by archaeologists is that such markings may relate to copper-producing areas. To some extent this has been borne out by similar markings found in Scotland and Ireland.

By far the majority of the early inhabited sites within the National Park area, however, belong to the first waves of the Celtic invasions of the Iron Age. It was the Celts who brought the use of this metal with them from the Continent and infiltrated into the existing Bronze Age stock around 800 BC. Unlike areas more to the south, a distinctive Iron Age era hardly occurred in Northumberland, and the periods tend to overlap with the inhabitants continuing to live in Bronze Age conditions using iron only when they could acquire it, for it quickly became a form of currency which not every tribe could afford. The newcomers were prodigious builders of banked and ditched hill-forts, and there are many examples on the hills of the National Park area which have donated a variety of iron utensils, weapons, brooches, pins and weaving instruments to the local museums. Later Celtic invaders from about 400 BC onwards lived in timber huts within an outer defence work, and at one of the best examples – the Yeavering Bell site – as many as 132 hut foundations have been located within the outer stone wall. It is about this period that recognizable tribal patterns of Celtic stock, such as the Votadini of Northumberland and coastal Berwick, become apparent.

These conditions persisted through the Roman period of occupation. Although the Celts still built their forts on a defensive basis at first, they soon grew aware of their comparative ineffectiveness against the might of Roman arms. It will be recalled that after the terrible damage inflicted to Hadrian's Wall and other Roman defences in AD 367 by the combined northern tribes the guardianship of the forward zone up to the Scottish Border was entrusted to the Votadini. As a result, hill-fort sites became less strategically placed and turned into more peaceful settlements, and Greaves Ash, in the upper Breamish Valley, Lordenshaw, close to Rothbury, and Castle Hill at Alnham all fall within this category.

The post-Roman period is in many ways less precise, for there is little evidence to suggest that the Saxons settled the National Park area to any great extent. They, like their early predecessors, preferred the river valleys, and both the Tyne Valley and the valley of the Coquet reflect this in relics of this era. Apart from the two royal palace sites of ad Gefrin and Melmin, close to the Yeavering Bell, there is some evidence to suggest that Saxon places of worship may have been established at Whittingham, Ingram and Holystone, as far as the National Park area is concerned. At the height of its power the Saxon kingdom stretched to the west coast, and a remarkable Saxon monument was discovered close to Falstone in the Border Forest Park area of the North Tyne Valley. It is inscribed in both runic characters and Roman uncials and is now in the Museum of Antiquities in Newcastle. A similar monument was found at Bewcastle, west of the Wark Forest area, where the Romans had an outpost fort, and several Saxon crosses have also been discovered, notably the one at *Rothbury*.

In Norman times the 103,200ha (255,000 acres) of the National Park area became a kind of buffer zone in the ensuing struggles between England and Scotland, with semi-autonomous liberties guarding the few through routes in this wild and untamed land. Even up to the middle of the 18th century the northern half of Northumberland was considered a waste land, worthy of little or no effort to secure and farm on, and this state of affairs continued right through the medieval period. A few routes – pack-horse trails and drovers' roads – were established over The Cheviot Hills, and a few small towns and villages emerged where they descended again into the valleys, but the majority of the few inhabitants lived in a state of perpetual danger, where safety meant a pele tower or a bastel-house attached to a small farm and every stranger was viewed with suspicion.

It was a lawless era, where the continual Border struggles between the two kingdoms gave rise to a pattern of raid and counter-raid between individuals, families and the gangs of outlaws and reivers who frequented the area, and this was particularly true of the main areas of the National Park in Redesdale and North Tynedale, where the rule of law was one of force and every man's hand was on his sword. Danger and deceit were followed by treachery and swift justice.

The memories of these struggles lingered on for at least a century after the Union of Crowns, leaving a scar tissue of suspicion and resentment which took its time to heal. Slowly, the area began to open up to farming, sheep-rearing and, to some extent, industry as well. Nowadays, there are over 400,000ha (1 million acres) of farmland in the county, nearly half of which is described as 'rough grazing', and much of this falls within the National Park area and its surroundings. In the Park itself some 34,400ha (85,000 acres) fall into the category of hill grazing land, where 250,000 sheep now browse in the summer months. In adjacent sectors barley and corn are grown, and there is some of the finest fattening land in the country, catering for a large influx of cattle.

The economy of sheep rearing now dominates the area, and it is not surprising that the first sheepdog trials in the country were held at Byrness in 1876. Agricultural shows are part of the way of life in the National Park area today, and at the Border Shepherds' Show, held annually in October at Alwinton, one can hear the Northumberland bagpipes (smaller than their Scottish counterparts) played by the men who make them. Local shepherds are also noted for their carving of the handles of crooks, usually in the form of a fish or a bird, and some of these are on display.

As far as the visitor is concerned, the National Park area is essentially a place to enjoy leisure time in an unrestricted, open area. Basically, it is a collection of individual farms and hill land, where the owners have co-operated with the National Park authorities to form such an area in the first place. Unfortunately, although one of the main purposes of this object is the protection of wildlife and the natural environment with established rights of way for walkers and campers, such areas also seem to appeal to governments as suitable places to establish artillery ranges, and in the Redesdale Artillery Range, set smack in the middle of the Park area, a large area of land with particular interest for geologists is more often than not excluded from the accessible countryside.

The **Pennine Way** runs for almost 50 miles from Greenhead right through the Park area to Chew Green, thence following the Border ridge into Scotland, and is probably the best-known path through the area, but there are many more with youth hostels and camping sites *en route*. Sailing is possible on **Greenlee Lough** just north of Hadrian's Wall, and the ardent rock-climber can enjoy his sport in a variety of easy climbs in the **Simonside Hills** and in the more difficult Whin Sill crags. For the naturalist and lover of wildlife there is an abundance to see. Although under separate authorities and possibly with different objects in view, both the Border Forest Park and the National Park area should be viewed by visitors as one entity, for by doing so a much wider field of enjoyment can be obtained.

Note

There are information centres open between Easter and 31 October from 10 a.m. to 6 p.m. at **Byrness**, **Ingram** and **Once Brewed**, and at weekends and Bank Holidays in the season a mobile information van also operates in the area.

View of Simonside

17 The Border Forest Park

In the early 1920s with a newly established Forestry Commission the idea of growing coniferous trees for softwood timber production began in a small way with the acquisition of 1,416ha (3,500 acres) in the Newcastleton Forest on the Scottish side of the Border. This was followed by a 809ha (2,000 acre) plantation at Smales, near Falstone, on the hitherto tree-less and heathery moorland of the upper North Tyne Valley in 1926. The local scheme in this part of the world really got into its stride with the purchase from the Duke of Northumberland of his 19,029ha (47,000 acre) Kielder Estate in 1932, together with the former shooting lodge of Kielder Castle. Some plantations were already in existence on this estate and were formed mainly as shelter belts, but generally the area was bare hill-land which at that time supported very few animals indeed. Curiously enough, this had not always been the case, for all the prehistoric evidence shows that there once was a thickly forested area in the vicinity which constant grazing had slowly destroyed.

Encouraged by the possibilities of reviving this, the Forestry Commission persisted with its early efforts, and much of the vision of those days rests with Lord Robinson, the Chairman from 1932 to 1952, who took the name Kielder as part of his territorial title. When he died, his ashes were scattered in the forest itself, with a memorial cairn to his memory deep in the forest 3 miles south of Whickhope. Today, in the Border Forest group covering the three counties of Cumbria, Northumberland and Roxburghshire in Scotland there are at least nine separate forests covering an area of 300 square miles on either side of The Cheviot Hills. Two-thirds of this are within the boundaries of Northumberland and are formed into five main forests: **North Kielder**, **Falstone**, **Mounces**, **Wark** and **Redesdale**, which from 1955 onwards have formed the Border Forest Park. Of these Kielder is by far the largest man-made forest in Britain, and probably in Europe as well. Additionally, on the Northumberland side there are smaller units at Thrunton, Holystone, Harwood and Hepburn, which, although technically outside the Park area, do also cater for visitors with waymarked forest walks as well. Some 20,234ha (50,000 acres) of the Border Forest Park area lie within the confines of the Northumberland National Park, for the two are fairly closely integrated with their aims, while another 20,235ha (50,000 acres) are set aside as tenanted hill farms as part of a planned development economy to make the best overall use of the land. Trees and sheep do not always mix, but the sheep will go higher in this hilly region in search of nourishment and can do so without harming the trees.

Some 38,040ha (94,000 acres) have already been planted up, and over the years the cycle of planting, thinning and cutting is now well established. Generally speaking, planting ranges up to the 450m (1,500ft) mark, which is why the landscape frequently reveals an etched contour line of trees well below the peak of a hill. Once planted, the trees are fenced only against sheep. Timber production now runs at the rate of 984·2 tonnes (1,000 tons) per day. In 1970 the total production amounted to 86,000cu m (112,488cu yards), and this is expected to rise to 108,000cu m (141,264cu yards) by 1980. Most of the resultant timber goes to paper and board-making mills.

Some 230 forestry workers are employed in this industry, and they live with their families in six forestry villages around the forests. On the Northumberland side the main ones are at **Byrness** in Redesdale, **Kielder**, and **Stonehaugh** in Wark Forest, and there are schools at the former two for the children. To assist in their own work the Forestry Commission have built over 500 miles of rough forest roads and in many cases have turned these into pleasant walks or drives for the public. The whole area caters extensively for the walker and the camper as well as the casual day visitor, and at **Kielder**, **Lewisburn** and **Stonehaugh** forest trails are laid out which are easy to follow. Additionally, there are a great number of waymarked forest walks with coloured route indicators throughout the region, not only in the main Border Forest Park area but also in the smaller forests within the county. At Kielder also there is a 12-mile-long forest drive linking that village with Byrness in Redesdale. A modest toll charge is made, and it has the advantage of saving mileage if one is making a circular tour. Scattered throughout the Park are picnic sites, adventure playgrounds, exhibitions of forestry work and the local flora and fauna, youth hostels, mountain rescue posts, camping sites and, occasionally, refreshment facilities and toilets. In some parts permits can be obtained for trout fishing and even deer stalking or game shooting in the relevant season, the latter, fortunately, under some supervision.

The whole area was inhabited by very early man, and the remains of early settlements, long cairns and round cairns are among the many archaeological sites to be found. Some interesting finds have also been made, such as the Bronze Age sword, now in the British Museum, dating from 1000 BC to 450 BC. A prehistoric trackway – the Wheel Causeway – can still be traced from **Deadwater**, running north through the Wauchope Forest. At **Smales** there are the remains of a Romano-British camp, and close to Kielder itself such odd medieval names as the **Devil's Lapful** and **Deadman's Currich** reveal prehistoric burial sites. Such natural oddities as the **Kielder Stone**, a 6m (20ft) high sandstone block marking the line of the Border, provide much interest for the visitor, as do the old drovers' roads which came this way. The one that crosses the Border at **Bloody Bush** still marks its authority with a list of toll charges. Undoubtedly, it is the wildlife that does more to attract visitors than any other factor and the variety is so great and the pattern so shifting that any attempt to list either animals or birds would be incomplete.

The fifty years of work in the area to date has produced not only a thriving industry but a refreshingly pleasant environment which cannot fail to attract the average visitor. The simple drive through the Border Forest Park from Bellingham to Deadwater and on into Liddesdale has up to now been an experience not to be missed, for until one has seen this vast man-made forest for the first time and stopped long enough to sample its complete and natural surroundings, its emptiness and (in some parts) its complete silence, it is almost inconceivable that such an area exists in these overcrowded islands today. Whether this pleasant state continues remains to be seen, for, undoubtedly, there are going to be many great changes over the next few years with the advent of the Kielder Water Scheme, and much of its hitherto remoteness may disappear.

This highly ambitious idea has already completed its groundwork, and one of the first casualties is the former road from Falstone to Kielder, which lay along the valley floor where the huge new reservoir will form. An alternative route is already operational. The intention is to flood an area of some 1,093ha (2,700 acres), stetching the 7 miles from Falstone to Kielder and forming a lake about as big as Lake Ullswater or two-thirds the size of Lake Windermere. Either way it will become the largest man-made lake in Britain. Two dams will hold back this new water-head, the main one by Yarrow Moor, close to Falstone, while the smaller, topping-up dam will be constructed at Bakethin, just south of Kielder. In its early days this latter dam will be submerged until the operating level of 180m (620ft) above sea-level is reached, and the complete scheme, which will include two electricity generating plants, can come fully into operation by 1980.

The Northumbrian Water Authority will thus be able to control the flow of water into the North Tyne and the river Tyne at a rate to suit its own extraction purposes, and this wide-ranging scheme is intended to serve all the four great rivers of Northumberland – the Tyne, Derwent, Wear and Tees – by means of a pipeline. The first stage will be constructed at Riding Mill, and from here the water will be pumped up 210m (700ft) above sea-level and then flow by tunnel into an interim reservoir at Airy Holm, close to Kiln Pit Hill. It will then be led by tunnel to the Derwent, Wear and Tees Valleys in succession, discharging into the two latter streams but with a provision for a flow into the Derwent as well at a later stage. The construction will take place up to 1980, and in the initial stages some disruption will obviously take place in the upper North Tyne Valley.

The Duchess Drive forest trail at Kielder will fortunately escape the rising waters which should lap around the piers of the Kielder Railway Viaduct at the northern end. The Lewisburn camp site as well as the picnic site at Plashetts will also be submerged in due time, but, according to the published programme, great new plans are in preparation for creating a new nature reserve, picnic areas, sailing, canoeing and fishing facilities, camping and caravanning sites to replace those to be lost. Additionally, holiday cabins and some new forest walks will be introduced, all of which should be completed by 1980.

It is to be hoped that in their exuberance for a great new playground area the planners will not overlook the value of silence which up to now has been the strongest feature of the Border Forest Park. Recent years have seen a large influx of visitors, tending to overcrowding at times which, by implication, can turn even the most beautiful area into one of devastation. This is the real problem for the planners – not to concentrate but to disperse their visitors so that some of the remoteness of the Park is not lost. Silence does not always appeal to the modern tourist, but for the wildlife and all nature lovers it is still the greatest attraction of the Border Forest Park.

18 The Pennine Way

The longest footpath in Britain, the **Pennine Way** runs for 270 miles from the village of Edale in Derbyshire's Peak District to the village of Kirk Yetholm just over the Border line of The Cheviot Hills into Scotland. It links a procession of old drovers' roads, miners' tracks, footpaths and bridleways, plus a Roman road or two to provide the walker with a challenge to his skill and stamina.

Nearly a quarter of the route lies within Northumberland – from the Gilderdale Burn close to Alston in the South Tyne Valley to the lofty ridge heights of The Cheviot Hills along the Border line past Chew Green to The Cheviot which, although slightly off-track, is officially part of the route and, next to Cross Fell in Cumbria, is the second highest peak on the way. This last northern sector, signposted most of the time, entails some pretty tough walking conditions and should not be attempted by anyone without proper dress and equipment and the ability to read a map and steer a course by compass.

It is only fair to add that many of the shorter southern stretches are relatively easier, and this is true of the area along Hadrian's Wall and in the South Tyne Valley, where one of the great attractions of the route is this ability to pick a short sector for an afternoon's stroll without getting too far from civilization. The 15-mile stretch from Hadrian's Wall to Bellingham in the North Tyne Valley presents a fair challenge for a day's outing, as does the similar length from Bellingham to Byrness in Redesdale, but it is the final challenge of a Cheviot crossing which is probably the most rewarding sector of all.

It is largely the result of much work put in by the Countryside Commission, together with local authorities, that its right of way has now been formally recognized. Both the National Parks and Access to the Countryside Act of 1949 and the Countryside Act of 1968 have contributed much towards this definition, and of the eleven recognized paths

The Cheviot Hills

so designated three at the moment, including the Pennine Way, have their rights of way established throughout their lengths. But this does not mean a free-for-all over private property, and a countryside code has been established and reparation projects undertaken to keep the peace between irate farmers and inveterate hikers.

From its north-westward track up the Tees Valley in Durham the Pennine Way makes a wide swing westwards through the Lune Forest to enter Cumbria by **Cross Fell** (789m, 2,930ft), the highest peak in The Pennines. It then drops down to Carrigill following the infant South Tyne river to Alston and less than 10 miles further on it crosses into Northumberland, close to Whitley Castle by the Gilderdale Burn. Here also the Roman road of the Marian Way comes in from the west, and the two tracks intertwine along the South Tyne Valley. For those who want a diversion into the Allendale country there is a track up the Ayle Burn leading in under 5 miles to the nearest youth hostel to this point at **Keirsleywell Row**, close to Ninebanks in the West Allen Valley.

As far as Lambley the two routes run together, the Maiden Way continuing northwards from a point ½ mile west of the village along the line of the modern road. The Pennine Way turns north-west across Hartleyburn Common to the east of **Cross Rig** (850m, 2,834ft), virtually along the line of the Northumberland–Cumbrian boundary. On past Wain Rig it reaches the southern side of Thirlwall Common, passing Black Hill to gain Gap Shields Farm, very close to the A69(T) main road, then swings east to parallel this towards Greenhead. It crosses the A69(T) road at Bank Top, ½ mile west of the village, making for Longbyre, then, turning east, crosses the B6318 road, then the railway and across the footbridge over the Tipalt Burn, close to Thirlwall Castle, where it joins the line of Hadrian's Wall. From Gap Shields a minor road leads north straight into Gilsland, and from here it is possible to trace a path back to Longbyre or Greenhead, both possible sources of overnight accommodation.

From Thirlwall Castle the Pennine Way follows the line of Hadrian's Wall for the next 8 miles, starting along the **Nine Nicks of Thirwall** which, although sadly mutilated now by quarrying, are the start of the impressive line of dolerite outcrop that forms the Whin Sill ridges. The Northumberland National Park (see page 215) has its western boundary at this point, and the line of the Wall between Thirlwall and Sewingshields is amongst the most dramatic and revealing stretches to walk along. For those who join this sector only the Pennine Way can be followed for most of the way, but if the overall distance of 11 miles is too far, then the shorter but infinitely more impressive part from Peel Crag by Steel Rigg, along past Housesteads Fort and on to Sewingshields will cut this to about 4 miles.

Climbing the slopes towards Walltown and once past the quarry, the first glimpse of Hadrian's Wall soon appears with Turret 45A, and in this sector the Pennine Way tends to follow the line of the Roman Military Way over the 3-mile stretch to the partially excavated fort of Aesica at Great Chesters. The path turns slightly southwards to cross the Caw Burn, close to its junction with the Haltwhistle Burn, and from here it climbs the Whin Sill ridges along Cawfield Crags and Winshields Crag, where some fine stretches of the Wall are apparent and the highest point (369m, 1,230ft) above sea-level is reached. In another ½ mile the path reaches Peel where a minor road leads down to the **Once Brewed Youth Hostel** and the Northumberland **National Park Information Centre**, once again a good stopping place for walkers, for there is little beyond this point and the next staging-post is Bellingham some 16 miles away.

The next section eastwards is the most spectacular part of Hadrian's Wall, with the Pennine Way continuing along the line of Peel Crag and Highshield Crags, the latter overlooking Crag Lough. This mile-long stretch of the Whin Sill attracts many rock climbers. Dropping down to Hotbanks Farm, the Pennine Way then follows the ridge again along Hotbank Crags, with the Northumberland loughs just to the north. The nearest of these, **Greenlee Lough**, is where the West Northumberland Sailing Club have their headquarters. Between Hotbank Crags and Cuddys Crags is the Rapishaw Gap where the Pennine Way leaves the line of the Wall and turns north again, but with the Roman fort of Housesteads only ½ mile further on a diversion here is often made. (*For additional information on this sector of Hadrian's Wall see page 209.*)

From the Rapishaw Gap the Pennine Way heads north into what was once a waste land, but prodigious efforts by the Forestry Commission have begun to decorate the horizon with growing trees. The path passes between the Greenlee and Broomlee Loughs, reaching the Jenkins Burn in ½ mile, then past the farms of Cragend and Stonefolds to reach the southernmost edges of Wark Forest. A forest road leads in amongst the tightly packed spruces, but the Pennine Way swings off this and emerges fairly quickly again in a north-easterly direction, heading for Comyn's Cross 3 miles from the Wall. Then, re-entering the forest area, another mile brings it through to the forestry road from Simonburn to Stonehaugh at Ladyhill on its way to the North Tyne Valley. From Ladyhill northwards the Pennine Way marks the boundary of the Northumberland National Park area along the edge of the northern sector of Wark Forest and in just over 1 mile crosses the Wark Burn, thence through Leadgate and Lowstead in a further mile to join a farm across Wark Common to a T-junction. It continues straight across as a path again towards Esp Mill and the Houxty Burn which it crosses by a foot-bridge, then circles round past Shitlington Hall. Heading north to the Shitlington Crags, an easterly turn is made towards Shielafield, and finally the northerly line is resumed out towards Fell End, where the B6320 road from Wark to Bellingham is joined 1 mile short of the town. The total distance from the Rapishaw Gap to Bellingham is close on 15 miles, and there is a youth hostel at **Bellingham** as well as accommodation and food in the town.

The penultimate stretch of the Pennine Way runs from Bellingham to Byrness, with the outward route along the West Woodburn road (where the youth hostel is situated), and turns left by the camping and caravan site, north-eastwards towards Blakelaw Farm, where the path traverses the eastern slopes above the Hareshaw Burn below the Callerhues Crags. However, before starting on this sector, there is a strong draw for overnight visitors to walk up the western side of the Hareshaw Burn to Hareshaw Linn to view one of the local beauty spots, but since there is no onward link, this means a return to the start. Continuing along the Pennine Way, in just under 3 miles Hareshaw House is passed, and ½ mile further on the path crosses the B6320 road from Bellingham to Otterburn. This sector of the way is fairly open moorland, with a 14-mile slog most of the way to the river Rede and a further 2¼ miles on to the youth hostel at **Byrness**. Crossing Troughend Common, the route follows the line of the peaks past **Lough Shaw** (330m, 1,102ft), then **Lord's Shaw** (350m, 1,167ft), across the track of a moorland road and on to **Padon Hill** (372m, 1,240ft), with the line of the Tarret Burn 1 mile away in the valley to the west. On top of this hill stands a monument, built in the form of a cairn, to a Scottish Covenanting preacher, Alexander Padon, who, exiled over the Border as a refugee, held meetings in the neighbourhood. Padon Hill is the high point of the route before the descent into the Redesdale Forest area begins, past **Brownrigg Head** (357m, 1,191ft) and Black Hill. Entering the forest area at Rookengate, the Pennine Way follows the forest road for the last 3 miles, emerging by the river Rede at Blackehopeburnhaugh, the inhabitants of which rival those of nearby Cottonshopeburn Foot for the claim to the longest place-name along the route. The Pennine Way then follows the river line north-westwards to Byrness, where there is a youth hostel and a National Park information centre. The last northerly sector of the Pennine Way from Byrness in Redesdale over The Cheviot Hills into Scotland and on to Kirk Yetholm amounts to 26¼ miles, plus 2½ more to make the necessary detour to include The Cheviot, and due acknowledgement is given to A. Wainwright's pleasurable *Pennine Way Companion* for this precise measurement and some of the background material for this part of the route. It is not tough in a mountaineering sense but can be arduous and tricky in bad weather and should never be attempted without adequate food and equipment. There is plenty of good advice to be had locally, but it must be remembered that there are few beds and no inns along this stretch, and the aim should be to do it between dawn and dusk or be prepared to spend a night bivouacked down half-way. It is certainly not the easiest route over The Cheviot Hills into Scotland, but with 12¼ miles along the Border ridge line at heights ranging from 390m (1,300ft) to 750m (2,500ft) there is nothing more spectacular or rewarding if the weather is kind. At times the path is not well defined (although signposts do exist in places), but with a good map and a feel for the contours, this should present no problem. Should the weather turn sour, there are a number of well-known paths leading off the ridge and a few shepherds' cottages in upper Coquet Dale where sometimes accommodation can be pre-booked, and here again Mr Wainwright's guide offers some useful advice as well as precisely drawn maps of his own making.

From Byrness a 2¾-mile climb up along the forest edge by **Ravens Knowe** (519m, 1,729ft) takes the Pennine Way past Ogre Hill to pick up the line of the Border fence and continues to Coquet Head on the Scottish side. From here the path tracks back again along the boundary of the Redesdale Artillery Range (to be avoided at all cost) and into England again to reach **Chew Green**, the major Roman encampment on the line of Dere Street. A series of star markers indicate various sites of antiquarian interest in the area. There is a road from here leading down to Blindburn and Alwinton. From Chew Green the Pennine Way follows the Roman road northwards for a mile, picking up the Border fence line again just past **Brownhart Law** (499m, 1,664ft), the site of a Roman signal station. The Pennine Way turns north-eastwards here, taking a short cut below the ridge and leaving the Border fence until it picks it up again 1¼ miles further on by **Lamb Hill** (503m, 1,676ft), a tricky section if the weather is misty, when it is easier to follow the Border fence all the way round. The route then continues along the Border fence, past **Beefstand Hill** (553m, 1,844ft) and **Mozie Law** (543m, 1,811ft) to **Windy Gyle** (610m, 2,034ft). Roughly 13 miles from the start, this is the half-way mark. Here also the line of the old drovers' road known as **The**

Street crosses the border, coming up from the Coquet Valley by the junction with the Barrow Burn above Alwinton and making its way down to Hownam on the Kale Water. An old tumulus cairn, marked with a star marker and now known as **Russell's Cairn**, is close to this spot and indicates the former meeting-place along the Border line between the English and Scottish Wardens. Such meetings were not always peaceful, and the cairn is a memorial to Lord Russell who was murdered here on a day of truce in 1585. Over the next mile the Pennine Way follows the Scottish side of the Border fence to where the next cairn marks the medieval crossing known as the Hexpethgate, now the Border Gate. Here, the track of **Clennell Street**, another drovers' road, comes up from Alwinton through Wholehope and Davidson's Linn to cross the Border on its way down to the Bowmont Water and Yetholm.

At this point the Pennine Way crosses back to the English side of the Border fence before continuing on past the **King's Seat** cairn (523m, 1,743ft) and then on to **Score Head** (573m, 1,910ft), sometimes known as Crookedsike Head. Still climbing, in another mile the path reaches the west side of **Cairn Hill** (726m, 2,419ft), where the Border fence makes an acute turn to the north-west. This is the point of diversion to climb the nearby **Cheviot** (803m, 2,676ft), the highest peak in The Cheviot Hills. The secondary path leads round the ridge line past another **Cairn Hill** (764m, 2,545ft) above Scotsman's Knowe and on to the flat-topped peak. This detour, which adds 2½ miles to the overall distance, is officially part of the route, but most experts tend to agree, especially with mist or rain about, that it is a pleasure which can be safely missed.

Returning to the point on the west side of Cairn Hill, the Pennine Way follows the Border fence north-westwards to **Auchope Cairn** (715m, 2,382ft) which lies on the west shoulder of The Cheviot. The route now overlooks one of the most eerie of all Cheviot ravines – the Hen Hole – the source of the College Burn running down to Kirknewton. The path parallels the ravine along its western side towards **The Schil** (594m, 1,979ft), then turns through a gate in the Border fence into Scotland, the route running between the **Black Hag** (540m, 1,801ft) and the **Curr** (555m, 1,849ft) to descend the last 4 miles along the Halterburn into Kirk Yetholm. There is a youth hostel here, and in adjacent Yetholm further accommodation is available.

Part II: Tyne and Wear

The Metropolitan County of Tyne and Wear was formed in 1974 from the former county boroughs of Newcastle upon Tyne, Tynemouth, Gateshead, South Shields and Sunderland, plus a small number of urban districts from Northumberland and Durham, and was the first new county in the country to be formed from a close similarity of industrial development rather than a natural geographical area. Nearly everywhere in the new county already had a close and long history of working together in the commercial growth of the huge conurbation between the Tyne and Wear industrial regions, and so its unification under one title was a natural one.

Bounded on the north and west by Northumberland with Durham to the south and the North Sea on its eastern flank, it has an area estimated at 20,235ha (50,000 acres) and next to its new neighbour of Cleveland to the south it is now the second smallest of the English counties. Yet, what it may lack in space it makes up for in density, for the 1971 census gave it a population of 1,209,000, and it is probably nearer to $1\frac{1}{2}$ million today. Thus, of the four counties making up present-day Northumbria it contributes something like 45% of the combined populations in less than 3% of the available total space.

Although its commercial history began with the wool trade, its real reputation lies with the exploitation of coal, begun in Roman times and then after a long gap resumed in the 12th and 13th centuries. At first it started in a small way from the surface-exposed fields to the west of Newcastle not too distant from the river, and by medieval times the export of 'sea-cole' to London was firmly established. In Elizabethan times, with the general shortage of wood as a fuel, this trade increased over twelve times, and between 1565 and 1625 the area held a monopoly. This was broken by the Civil War, when Newcastle took the Royalist side of Charles I and attempted a blockade of London's coal supplies. Sunder-

233

Tynemouth and sands

land, however, cashed in and promoted its own export of coal from
Wearside, and by the time of the Restoration in 1661 not only the two
but, within a few years, three coal-producing areas were at work.

The Tyne and Wear area led the Industrial Revolution, for already the coal-dependent industries here of glass-making, pottery, chemicals and iron were firmly established before the rest of the country followed. By the middle of the 18th century, using cheap coal for power and empty returning colliers for raw materials, a high state of economy was achieved. Later on, the development of steam-engines allowed a deeper exploration for coal, and the coalfield to the east of Newcastle was opened up. Wallsend household coal became world-famous, and the supremacy of this trade was not seriously challenged until the 19th century. It was the age of invention and great industrial growth, and the work of William Hedley, George Stephenson and the first Lord Armstrong together with their fellow inventors of the 19th century entirely changed the industrial pattern. Both heavy engineering and shipbuilding grew from then on, with coalmines going deeper and deeper towards the sea and in some cases well under it. It opened up the railways which gave the necessary mobility, and a world-wide export trade followed. At the same time the older industries declined and were replaced by shipbuilding and repairing as more and more demand came for the new 'iron ships'. The production of coal became intensely specialized with grading into different types for smelting, gas or steam production, and some of the older pits began to close.

By the present century the major industries were the heavy ones, with shipbuilding, repairing, marine and heavy electrical engineering predominating the scene and some minor activity in soap and paint, but in the 30s a great period of industrial depression brought on the attempts to diversify this structure by the creation of urban industrial estates geared to lighter industries. To some extent this continues up to the present day with attempts to attract different kinds of manufacturing industries and the creation of modern 'new towns' to replace some of the mining villages of the past.

In spite of the high density of population, there is ample open space in the new county with some really worthwhile efforts being made in the creation of parks, nature trails and the re-establishment of riverside promenades, all of which are within a few short miles of the heart of the metropolis. There is a fine stretch of coastline both north and south of the Tyne estuary, quickly reached by urban railways and well-developed resorts such as Whitley Bay, South Shields, Roker and Seaburn to provide the necessary breath of fresh air in an intensely working area. The 'Geordies', as the locals are known, are amongst the most friendly in Britain and will go out of their way to make a stranger welcome.

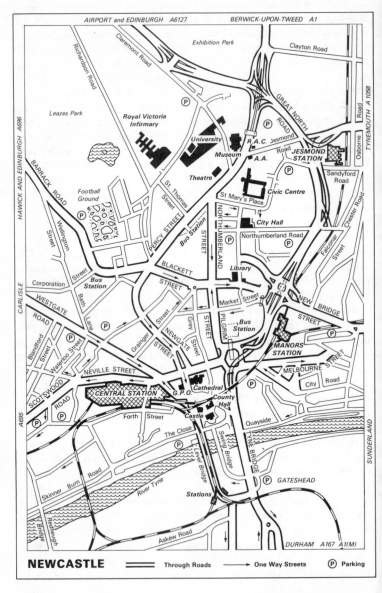

AIRPORT and EDINBURGH A6127   BERWICK-UPON-TWEED A1

Claremont Road

Exhibition Park

Clayton Road

Richardson Road

GREAT NORTH ROAD

Leazes Park

Royal Victoria Infirmary

University

Museum

R.A.C. Jesmond

A.A.

Road

JESMOND STATION

Osborne Road

TYNEMOUTH A1058

Sandyford Road

Theatre

Civic Centre

Chester Road

HAWICK AND EDINBURGH A696

BARRACK ROAD

Wellington Street

Football Ground

St. Thomas Street

St Mary's Place

City Hall

Falconar Street

PERCY STREET

Bus Station

STREET

NORTHUMBERLAND

Northumberland Road

CARLISLE

Corporation Street

Bath Lane

Bus Station

BLACKETT STREET

Library

NEW BRIDGE

WESTGATE ROAD

Grainger Street

Grey Street

STREET

Market Street

Bus Station

PILGRIM STREET

STREET

MANORS STATION

Blandford Street

Waterloo Street

NEVILLE STREET

NEWGATE STREET

MELBOURNE STREET

City Road

SCOTSWOOD ROAD

CENTRAL STATION

G.P.O.

Cathedral

County Hall

A695

Forth Street

Castle

Quayside

The Close

Level Bridge

Swing Bridge

TYNE BRIDGE

Skinner Burn Road

Redheugh

River Tyne

Stations

GATESHEAD

SUNDERLAND

Bridge

Askew Road

DURHAM A167 A1(M)

NEWCASTLE   ═══ Through Roads   → One Way Streets   Ⓟ Parking

19 Newcastle upon Tyne

Bowls There are numerous greens in the parks.

Buses Frequent buses operate within the city with long-distance coaches to and from the main cities of England and Scotland. Main terminals: Gallowgate – express services including London; Haymarket – north and east of the city and express services including Scotland; Marlborough Crescent – south and west of the city and express services including Lancashire, Yorkshire and the Midlands; Worswick Street – east and south of the city.

Camping and caravanning Trax Campsite, Newcastle Race-course, Gosforth, 4 miles north of A1(T) (March–Sept.); Marsden Bay, 2 miles south of South Shields on the A183 (April–Oct.); South Foreshore Site, ¾ mile north of South Shields by the pier (April–Oct.).

Cinemas *ABC*, Haymarket; *ABC One and Two*, Westgate Road; *Apollo 1–3*, Shields Road; *Jesmond*, Lyndhurst Avenue, West Jesmond; *Odeon*, Pilgrim Street; *Queen's Cinerama Theatre*, Northumberland Place; *Royalty*, High Street, Gosforth; *Studio 1–4*, Waterloo Street; *Tyneside Film Theatre*, Pilgrim Street.

Cricket Northumberland County Cricket Ground, Jesmond.

Distances Alnwick, 34 miles; Berwick-upon-Tweed, 63 miles; Carlisle, 57 miles; Durham, 15 miles; Edinburgh, 106 miles; Hexham, 20 miles; London, 274 miles; Morpeth, 15 miles; Otterburn, 32 miles; Rothbury, 30 miles; Scotch Corner, 41 miles; South Shields, 11 miles; Wooler, 46 miles.

Early closing Wednesday; some shops also close on Mondays.

Football Newcastle United, in the 2nd Division, play at St James' Park. Of the many rugby clubs the best known is Gosforth, who play at New Ground, Gosforth.

Freshwater fishing Coarse fishing is available in both the rivers Wansbeck and Blyth.

Golf *Gosforth Golf-Club*, Broadway East, Gosforth; *John Jacobs Golf-Centre*, High Gosforth Park, Wideopen; *City of Newcastle Golf-Club*, Three-Mile-Bridge, Gosforth; *Newcastle United Golf-Club*, Spital Tongues; *Northumberland Golf-Club*, High Gosforth Park, Gosforth; *Westerhope Golf-Club*, Whorlton House.

Guided tours On application to the City Information Service.

Hotels *Airport, Avon, Cairn, Centre, County, Europa Lodge, Gosforth Park, Holiday Inn, Imperial, Northumbria, Osborne, Royal Station, Royal Turk's Head, Swallow.*

Information centre City Information Service, Central Library, Princess Square.

Museums and art galleries See list on page 255.

Population 212,430.

Post Office The GPO is in St Nicholas Street.

Racing Horse-racing at Newcastle Race-course, High Gosforth Park; speedway and greyhound racing at Brough Park Stadium, Fossway.

Sailing Tynemouth and Whitley Bay.

Sea-fishing Tyne estuary piers and resorts north and south along coastline.

Sports centres Wide range of sports at the Eldon Square Recreation Centre and the Lightfoot Sports Centre, Wharrier Street, Byker.

Swimming-pools Northumberland Road Baths, city centre; Jesmond Baths, St George's Terrace, Jesmond; Gosforth Baths, Regent Farm Road, Gosforth.
Tennis Numerous public courts.
Theatres *Theatre Royal*, Grey Street; *People's Theatre Arts Centre*, Stephenson Road; *Balmbra's Music-Hall*, Cloth Market.
Tourist Information Centre Northumbria Tourist Board, Prudential Building, 140 Pilgrim Street; Newcastle upon Tyne Tourist Information Centre, Princess Square.

Historical note

By the time the Romans started building Hadrian's Wall in AD 122 a bridge, dedicated to the Emperor Hadrian's family name of Aelius and known as the *Pons Aelii*, already lay across the river Tyne, and to this was added the Roman fort on the site now occupied by the remains of the castle. After the Roman withdrawal in the early part of the 5th century, the place fell into some obscurity but was known in Saxon times as Monkcaster from the number of monastic foundations reported here. Several more centuries were to elapse before the Normans came and took a look at the strategic importance of Newcastle and realized its value in dominating the northern defence.

In 1080 William the Conqueror's eldest son, Robert Curthose, a frequent rebel against his father's authority, built a wooden castle here on his way back from an incursion into Scotland and dubbed it the 'New Castle'. His brother, William Rufus (1087–1100), reconstructed it in stone against the many rebellions in the area, and the name 'Newcastle' remained henceforth. During the reign of Stephen (1135–54) Newcastle was for a while a part of Scotland but after the capture of William the Lion at Alnwick in 1174 it reverted back to Henry II. The town, by this time also walled, suffered from further Scottish attacks, notably in 1342 and 1388 when Harry Hotspur defended it before the Battle of Otterburn. During the troubled years of medieval Border warfare the city acted as a natural bulwark for England against Scottish inroads.

Because of its importance in defence it earned itself many royal favours and early charters. By 1216 the burgesses gained the right to have their own mayor and in 1400 they won a charter turning the town into a county with its own sheriff and law courts. During the Wars of the Roses it managed to stay fairly neutral but during the later Civil War it became a Royalist city, refused to send its coal to London and endured a three months' siege by Scottish soldiers, led by the Earl of St Leven, fighting on the Parliamentarian side. Sir John Marley, the Mayor, with fewer than 2,000 men defied a Scottish force of much greater strength until they finally broke through the walls and he was forced to capitulate.

The city's commercial prosperity has steadily increased throughout its long history through wool, coal, salt, lime and glass-making, which gradually grew into the far more heavy industries of the Industrial Revolution. Newcastle has always been a pioneer and from 1850 onwards its reputation rested on shipbuilding and railways and it became the centre of the great new era of steam, 'iron ships' and bridge building where the geniuses of such men as the Stephensons and Lord Armstrong could have full fling. The pace of industry was matched by a change in architecture, for up to the early 19th century the city was still very medieval in character. Three men were responsible for the innovation that turned all this into one of the best-planned city centres in England with elegant stone-faced buildings and gracious streets: John Dobson, the Newcastle architect, Richard Grainger, a builder, and John Clayton, the Town Clerk of Newcastle, later associated with Chesters and excavations along Hadrian's Wall. Richard Grainger first built thirty-one houses in Blackett Street, then in 1826 began his first big enterprise in Eldon Square, followed in 1831 by Leazes Terrace and Crescent, starting work there on 7 March 1831.

The three men worked out a scheme for rebuilding the centre of Newcastle with new markets and a new theatre, submitting models on public display on which the public voted 5,000 for, 300 against. Dobson designed the imposing Central Railway Station, opened by Queen Victoria in 1850, and such fine streets as Grey Street, Grainger Street and Clayton Street, as well as the markets, the Royal Arcade and the Theatre Royal all commemorate the work of these three men and their associates. The whole scheme was completed in five years, and there are many interesting buildings still to see.

In recent years many howls of anguish have greeted the current plans to rebuild the heart of the city. To drive a motorway through the middle of a city to relieve the pressure of through traffic from the Tyne bridges is clearly an ambitious solution to Newcastle's main problem, but the irony is that it is now bringing traffic back again from the Tyne Tunnel road, and the approach roads, particularly on the south side, breed congestion. Sadly, Eldon Square has gone and has been replaced by an immense shopping centre; the city is being burrowed right and left for the stations of the new metro railway; there are art galleries, museums, a new civic centre, university, supermarkets, multiple stores, cinemas, night clubs and a new central library; and an inexhaustible network of subways, flyovers, walkways linked by escalator and flights of iron staircases. Unless you are a local, it is extremely difficult to drive or walk around, but the modern trends reflect some of the need to maintain Newcastle as the largest shopping and commercial area in the north-east.

Nevertheless, the city is a place of great interest to the visitor, and there is plenty to see, from the early 19th-century centre to the surviving ancient buildings close to the river together with the cathedral and castle close at hand. The city's tremendous drive and energy reflect in innumerable ways in the many restorations and conversions of older buildings and the deconsecration of some of its churches for secular use, its creation of new museums and cultural centres and its enterprising housing developments such as the Byker Wall. Yet it manages to retain some of its traditional character and historic past in its music halls, its ancient inns and city walls and its outlying open spaces and broad avenues of elegant and stately houses.

The river line

Since all orientation within the metropolitan area centres on the river Tyne, it is best to put this in perspective first. From Ryton to Tynemouth the 20-mile stretch of the river is tidal and within the new county of Tyne and Wear and is managed by the Port of Tyne Authority. Within this stretch there are eight bridges, five of them centred between Newcastle and Gateshead, and soon there will be a sixth bridge close by to carry the new Metro railway line.

Upstream the furthest west is the Newburn Bridge, almost 6 miles west of the city. At Scotswood, 2½ miles further downstream, road and rail bridges lie close together, and the new road bridge, opened in 1968, replaced the earlier suspension bridge dating from 1829.

From Newcastle to Gateshead the five bridges are:

The Tyne Bridge: Forming part of the A1, it was built between 1925 and 1928. The two main piers are of steel and granite, and from their base springs an imposing parabolic arch of steel lattice framework. The bridge served as a model for the Sydney Harbour Bridge which was constructed two years later.

The Swing Bridge: This was built in 1876 on the site of the first Roman timber bridge. Two stone bridges followed the latter, but a swing bridge was required to allow tall ships to pass up the Tyne. Designed by Lord Armstrong, this low-level bridge uses hydraulic machinery to pivot the central section.

The High-Level Bridge: A combined road and rail bridge built by Robert Stephenson between 1846 and 1849, this is the oldest bridge now standing. It has six cast-iron arches between stone piers and was opened by Queen Victoria in 1849.

The Redheugh Bridge: Built in 1901, this bridge is due to be replaced by a new concrete bridge slightly downstream from its present site.

The King Edward VII Bridge: This bridge carries the main London–Edinburgh railway line and was constructed in 1906.

The New Metro Bridge: Due to be opened in 1979, this bridge will cross the river on a three-span steel bridge, linking the two tunnel systems from the Newcastle and Gateshead sides.

Apart from bridges there are two tunnels under the river, a pedestrian tunnel opened in 1928 which runs from Harrow to Howdon-on-Tyne, 5 miles downstream from the city centre, and which boasts the longest escalator in Britain, and close by the Tyne Tunnel, a mile-long vehicle tunnel opened in 1967 to divert traffic around the eastern side of Newcastle and to provide a more immediate link between industrial areas north and south at this point. A toll charge is made. Ferry services operate between North and South Shields, Hebburn and Walker and also between Hebburn and Wallsend. There are also river sightseeing trips, operated by Mid-Tyne Ferries of Hebburn, during the summer months. A round trip of 2½ hours can be made to the harbour from No. 7 berth, Newcastle Quay, a short distance from the Tyne Bridge. Also from North Shields and Hebburn there are return trips upstream to Ryton.

From its early trading days, when the keelmen took their loads of coal out to the waiting colliers from the Old Quayside, the port's focus of activity has shifted bodily downstream. The Port of Tyne now deals in a wide range of traffic, mainly in fuels and coal, as well as passenger services. The Tyne Dock between Jarrow and South Shields deals mainly with fuel oils, while on the north side of the river at North Shields are the Albert Edward Dock and the Tyne Commission Quay, both less than 2 miles from the sea. The latter dock handles the important passenger and car ferry services to Denmark, Norway and Sweden. Shipbuilding and repair work are now concentrated mainly at Wallsend, Hebburn and North and South Shields.

Walks around the city

With the advent of the newly built city centre and the great number of subways and pedestrian walkways which abound, perambulations around the city are becoming more complex, and constant reference to a street plan is essential. These can be obtained from the City Information Service at the Central Library in Princess Square. The City now naturally falls into four main areas, namely: tour A (western city walls area); tour B (eastern city walls area); tour C (central Victorian Newcastle); tour D (modern Newcastle). From these four itineraries most visitors will be able to choose a personal one to suit themselves. In many instances they overlap, but since each section can take the most part of a day, a choice can be made dependent on time available. Parking in central Newcastle is extremely limited, but there is a multi-storey car park (Manors Car Park) off the first roundabout by Swan House, reached via Pilgrim Street coming north over the Tyne Bridge – A1(M) – which will give a good starting-point.

Tour A (western city walls area)

Probably the best place from which to start a tour of the older part of the city is from the **Old Quayside**, now virtually a deserted area, but some of the steep flights of stairs, known as 'chares', remain between the 17th-century houses and warehouses. This was the point from which the early exports of coal were handled by the keelmen who manned the shallow lighters and whose trade went back to the time of Henry VIII.

Opposite the Swing Bridge lies the **Guildhall**, built in 1658 by Robert Trollope, a local architect, on a 14th-century site. The Tuscan columns on the east side were added by John Dobson in 1823 after a refacing of the entire building in 1796. The interior, including the **Great Hall** with its double hammer beam roof and the **Merchant Adventurers' Court** with its finely-carved chimney, has seen little change since the 17th-century, however. The ceremony of calling the guild still takes place here occasionally. (*To view the interior application must be made to the Estate and Property Surveyor's office in the new Civic Centre.*)

Opposite the Guildhall is **Sandhill**, with a group of fine old houses. At No. 41, **Bessie Surtees House**, there is a plaque recording how Bessie descended from an upper window of this 17th-century house to elope in 1772 with John Scott, who later became Lord Eldon and Chancellor of England, with a square named after him as one of Newcastle's favourite sons. In 1815, after the Corn Law, his house in Bedford Square in London was attacked by a mob and he was forced to flee into the grounds of the British Museum.

Along the same street No. 43 is a five-storeyed structure dating from the 16th century, and both No. 33 (Derwentwater House) and No. 23 (The Red House, now a restaurant) deserve a mention. Behind these houses lies **Castle Hill**, access to which is via **Castle Stairs** which climb the steep-sided river embankment through the Norman **Southern Postern,** the only remaining fragment of the castle wall. On the right is **Moot Hall,** where the Crown Court meets, built in 1810 in the Grecian style by William Stokoe. Close by is the rather disappointing **Northumberland County Hall**, built in 1910.

Crossing **Castle Garth** and through the railing's gate, the **Keep** appears. This is a splendid example of Norman military architecture. Built by Henry II between 1172 and 1177, it stands 25·5m (85ft) high on a bluff overlooking the river. It is one of the best examples of Transitional architecture of its kind in England and consists of a principal apartment on each floor, surrounded by walls 3·6 to 5·4m (12 to 18ft) thick, honeycombed with smaller rooms, passageways and staircases. There is a forebuilding on the east face, and for extra defence the walls were carried right up above roof level. The upper parts and battlements have been restored, and the height to the top of the turret is 32m (107ft).

The curtilage walls have long since gone, and after the castle had ceased to be 'the bridle of the Scots', it was put to various uses, including that of a prison after the roof had fallen in. Fortunately, the Newcastle Society of Antiquaries rescued it in 1848, along with the Black Gate, and it is now under their protection.

The **Chapel** is one of the best-preserved and most interesting parts of the keep. The Norman rib-vaulting is irregular in some places, with some of the diagonal ribs almost missing their supporting brackets. (*Open Mondays 2–4, Tuesdays to Saturdays 10–4.30, with closing October to March at 3.30; charge.*)

Just to the north of the keep is the **Black Gate**, added to the castle's defences by Henry III in 1247, long after the rest of the castle was finished. Its intention was always to act as a barbican-gatehouse on the west side, the only side where a level approach was possible. At first it was constructed beyond the moat with an open roadway between it and the castle walls, with a gateway in the latter for connection. Then, side walls were added joining the two and blocking the moat, which was then led round the outside of the new edifice and spanned by a drawbridge. A deep pit was dug in the old moat which was also spanned by a drawbridge and later on, in 1358, a smaller barbican was constructed beyond the second moat to defend that in turn, but of this latter building no trace remains. Thus, any attacker would have a long line of moats and guard-chambers to pass through before gaining the castle proper. It is believed that part of the Roman fort lay under this western side, and new excavations are taking place at the present time. The medieval pattern of defence reflects in the ground-plan we see today, consisting of a central passageway, flanked by semicircular towers containing guard-chambers.

Inside the Gate is a staircase built in 1883 when the building was converted into a museum. Originally, it housed the fine collection of the Newcastle Society of Antiquaries, much of which has now been moved to the Museum of Antiquities, but it is now the world's only Bagpipe Museum, opened in 1972, with a collection of over 100 sets of bagpipes from all over the world, a shepherd's room, recordings, displays and so on. (*Open Tuesday to Saturday 12–5, charge.*)

From the castle remains, and passing under the railway line that is cut right across its bailey, the next point of interest is **St Nicholas' Cathedral** just to the north along St Nicholas' Street and into the square of the same name. Although the first church here was erected by the Normans, the date is uncertain. The first mention is in 1122 when Henry I included it in a list of Northumbrian churches assigned to the monks of Carlisle, and its first association with St Nicholas appears to be in 1194.

Destroyed by fire in 1216 and again in 1248, the reconstruction of the church must have been immediate since a 13th-century pillar remains embedded in later masonry. The new church, Early English in style, was complete by 1350, except for the tower with its famous spire and the choir arcades, the latter being finished by 1400. The lower part of the tower was also completed by then, but the belfry, vaulting and crown took at least another fifty years. The organ was installed in 1676 and enlarged in 1710. In keeping with the period, in the late 18th century the parishioners decided to convert St Nicholas into a more fashionable church, and a great number of drastic alterations took place at that time. In the 19th century a large amount of restoration work was undertaken with the complete refacing in the Perpendicular style. In 1859 the east gable was rebuilt with its present large single window, while Victorian stained glass was inserted in other windows. Gilbert Scott carried out a further large restoration in 1867, and in 1882 the church, which up to that time had been the fourth largest parish church in England, was raised to cathedral status. As a result the main fittings of the church were refurbished with a new reredos, choir and stalls, bishop's throne, sedilia and chancel screens to change the dignity of the setting.

The Central Arcade, Newcastle

The crowning glory of the cathedral is the west **Tower** with its original and beautiful spire, often known as the 'Scottish Crown' type, but it certainly antedated and served as a model for the one at St Giles in Edinburgh (1495), also at King's College in Aberdeen (c. 1500) and the cross steeple in Glasgow (1637). It consists of a remarkable 'lantern' supported in the air by four flying buttresses, and the tip of the spire is 58m (194ft) above the pavement. Every evening after dusk a light burns here.

The cathedral is entered by the north-west porch, where there is a memorial to Admiral Lord Collingwood, Nelson's friend and his successor at the Battle of Trafalgar. Along the north aisle part of the Norman arch can be seen in the masonry of the north-west pier at the crossing, one of the few remains of the 12th-century church. On the other side of this pier a piece has been cut away to reveal the 13th-century pillar.

In the **Nave** there are interesting carved heads of people in late 13th- and early 14th-century costume, as well as original carved bosses on the roof which are worth noting. The brass eagle lectern, early 16th-century work, is the only pre-Reformation lectern in the north of England. Below the north end of the **Transept**, reached by steps, is the tiny **Crypt**, one of the church's most interesting features. Consisting of a narrow chamber with a barrel-vaulted roof of large stones supported by segmental ribs, it is a fine example of a medieval charnel chapel, of which few now remain. On the rear wall of the **Reredos** is the huge painting of the Washing of the Disciples' Feet, now generally accepted as a copy of the Tintoretto original in Madrid.

In the south **Choir** is the magnificent German brass of Roger Thornton (d. 1429) and his wife. Adorned with ninety-two figures it is the only 15th-century specimen surviving in England. Roger Thornton was the 'Dick Whittington' of Newcastle who, arriving penniless in the town, became Mayor ten times and the Member of Parliament four times. This brass was recently transferred to the Cathedral from All Saints' Church.

In the east window of **St Margaret's Chapel** is a roundel of 15th-century glass with a representation of the Virgin and Child, the only surviving fragment of medieval glass in the cathedral. Against the walls are a number of medieval grave covers with some interesting designs: one shows a pick and hammer depicting the early history of coalmining.

Under the tower at the west end is the octagonal 15th-century **Font** of Frosterley marble, its face carved with shields. The fine **Font Cover** is almost contemporary with the font itself.

From the cathedral walk northwards along St Nicholas Street, turning left into Collingwood Street towards the **Central Station**, the huge single-storey structure built in 1850 from John Dobson's design. Easily the largest 19th-century building in Newcastle, with innumerable arches along the two miles of platforms, it is a fine monument to the start of the railway age. At the Westgate Road turn half right along it. Immediately on the left is the **Stephenson Monument**, a bronze statue of the great engineer (1781–1848) by John Lough, a native of Newcastle. Westgate Road follows the line of the ancient Roman Wall of the Emperor Hadrian, and a plaque on the wall of **Neville Hall** commemorates this fact.

About 100m along Westgate Road on the right-hand side lies **St John's Church**, close to the corner of Grainger Street. The body of the building dates from the 14th century and possibly earlier, and the church shows the influence of the cathedral in its later restoration work. Part of the chancel and also possibly the main walls of the nave may be Norman, but the nave arcades with their octagonal columns as well as the main part of the north transept belong to the 14th century. Both the west aisle of the north transept and the south transept, however, are 15th-century work. The font has a cover similar to those both in the cathedral and St Andrew's Church. There is a fine 17th-century pulpit, and a window on the north side of the chancel has a mosaic mainly of medieval glass.

Passing Grainger Street and continuing along Westgate Road, the graceful **Assembly Rooms** are tucked around the corner close to the junction of Finkle Street. They were designed by William Newton in 1774 after the style of Nash, with four splendid Ionic columns in the centre. The magnificent ballroom once rivalled those of Bath and York. At present the building is being redeveloped as an entertainment centre. Some 200m further along the Westgate Road, passing Clayton Street's intersection, continue on to Bath Lane, with a half turn right into it, where there is an attractively restored section of the city wall, known as the **West Walls**, where the most interesting feature is the **Durham Tower**.

Turn right into Stowell Street, where just a little way up on the right is Friars Street leading through to the 13th-century **Black Friars**, a Dominican house founded in 1239 by Peter Scott, the first Mayor of Newcastle, which flourished until 1539. It was acquired by the corporation and leased back to the local craft guilds in 1552, the remains being granted to the nine 'most ancient trades of the town'. The building now seen is the **Refectory** with the **Cloister** behind, and in spite of much alteration over the years, the outline can be still traced. The Black Friars is again, at present, undergoing extensive restoration, and the first phase has already been completed. The building is being adapted as a craft centre.

Returning to Stowell Street and crossing over, behind the west side the narrow lane of West Walls continues northwards. At the foot of the street lies **Heber Tower**, part of the massive fortifications erected in the 13th century and added to by Edward III (1327–77). They stretched for about 2 miles, strengthened with towers at regular intervals and look-out turrets between them. Half-way along the lane **Morden Tower**'s medieval base was built up in the 17th century to provide a hall for the guild of plumbers, glaziers and pewterers. At the top end of West Walls a turn right into St Andrew's Street, past the Northumberland Arms, leads through to Newgate Street, where a left turn reveals **St Andrew's Church**, which claims to be the oldest church in Newcastle, built during the second half of the 12th century. The original nave with its fine arcades remain, but the aisles were rebuilt and widened in the 15th century, the north aisle being as wide as the nave. The transepts have also been modified to open from the nave by taller arches, and the chancel was lengthened some time after 1250. The chancel arch is partly original and embellished with zigzag mouldings and is unusually tall for its width. The opposite holds true for the tower arch which is remarkably wide for its height. There is some 12th-century masonry here in the tower base, but the tower itself dates from the 13th century. A fine Perpendicular font cover resembles those in the cathedral and St John's Church, already mentioned, and dates from the 15th century. On the floor of the north chapel is the matrix of a double brass over 3·3m (11ft) long. There is also an impressive fragment of the city walls in the churchyard.

A right turn at the top of Newgate Street leads into Blackett Street towards **Grey's Monument** at the northern end of Grey Street and thus back to the centre of the city.

Tour B (eastern city walls area)
The other half of the circular tour of the walled city also starts from the **Old Quayside**. Walking eastwards along the quay from the Tyne Bridge, at King Street on the left there is an impressive view of **All Saints' Church**, a graceful Georgian building of elliptical shape built on the hilltop in 1786–96 by David Stephenson. Unfortunately, it has now been deconsecrated and is at present closed with its future use undetermined. The famous Thornton Brass which used to lie inside has now been removed to the cathedral. Continuing eastwards along the quay, the **Customs House**, built in 1766 and restored in 1840, is passed. The visual interest along this stretch is divided between the river traffic and the many narrow lanes, known as 'chares', where the medieval warehouses lay. In one of these – **Broad Chare** – a left turn leads to the picturesque **Trinity House** on a site occupied since 1492. The oldest part of the present building dates from 1721, and the courtyard behind the mock-Tudor facade has a definite Dutch atmosphere. The hall and

chapel face on to this courtyard, the latter having an attractive interior with fine Jacobean stalls and a double-decker pulpit. The fraternity, founded in the 16th century, was originally known as the Fellowship of Masters and Mariners of Ships of Newcastle but later became the Master Pilots and Seamen of Trinity House, who maintained the lighthouses built along the coastline and also provided a school and an almshouse, which adjoins the building. (*Access to the courtyard is allowed during the daytime, and tours of the interior can be made by special arrangement.*)

Returning to the Quayside, continue eastwards, turning left into Milk Market, which in turn leads into **Sandgate**, an area associated with the keelmen, who operated the small lighters that ferried out the coal to the waiting colliers. At the corner is a granite **Fountain**, close to the site where John Wesley delivered his first sermon in Newcastle in 1742. At the top of Milk Market lies the **Keelsmen's Hospital**, which was built by the men themselves in 1701 and has recently been restored.

Steps to the left of the **Corporation Weigh-house** lead through to **City Road** (the A186 to St Anthonys and Walker). Cross here to Causey Bank where there are more steps leading up to the **Sallyport Tower**, also known as the **Wall Knot Tower**, which not only marks the eastern line of the medieval city walls but is the point where they crossed the Roman wall. In 1716 the Ship's Carpenters' Company converted this tower into a meeting-hall, and above the east entrance is the relief of a ship's keel, which has given it a third name of the **Carpenter's Tower**. Return to City Road and turn right, where there is another surviving tower known as the **Corner Tower**. This also has some 18th-century additions.

Westwards along City Road, towards the city centre, and on the south side which can be reached by subway, there is the **John Joicey Museum** (*open weekdays 10–5.45, free*) which is very close to the line of the new central motorway east. This recently renovated building, originally dating from 1681, was formerly the Holy Jesus Hospital founded by the corporation for the care of freemen. It has a fine collection of models relating to Newcastle's early history, weapons and armour and *tableaux* illustrating the development of furniture.

From the museum walk back along City Road a short distance to Trafalgar Street, turning left and continuing through to Manors Station. Turn left past this, over the foot-bridge which crosses over the new central motorway east, and continue past the Centre Hotel to Market Street. The first on the left is Croft Street in which stands the **Plummer Tower**. The building, which dates from 1265, originally formed part of the medieval defences of Newcastle but was converted into a hall by the masons' guild in 1750. Its main displays are of 18th-century period furniture in the two main rooms with appropriate pictures. (*It is open only occasionally, and all enquiries regarding visits should be directed to the nearby Laing Art Gallery to which it is affiliated.*)

Returning to Market Street, a left turn leads through to the centre of the city at Pilgrim Street.

Tour C (central Victorian Newcastle)

The following itinerary will take in most of the Victorian parts of Newcastle, including the work of Dobson and Grainger.

Starting from the **Central Station**, turn left into Neville Street, walking alongside it to the roundabout where a right turn leads into **Clayton Street**. Here, some of the well-proportioned Georgian houses immediately stand out. On the right the **Roman Catholic Cathedral** was built in 1844 from a design by Pugin, and the tall, slender spire was added in 1872. Passing Bewick Street on the right, the next junction is that with the Westgate Road. Continue straight on, past Finkle Street, to the Newgate Street junction. After crossing it, the road becomes pedestrianized. On the left is the new **Greenmarket**, part of the Eldon Square Shopping Centre, and on the right are **Grainger's Markets**, a covered shopping precinct designed by John Dobson and erected by the builder in 1835 as part of the bargain struck with the corporation when rebuilding the city centre. It lies between Nun's Street and Nelson Street, and at the time of its opening was considered to be 'the most spacious and magnificent market in Europe'. It is still one of the largest covered markets in England, and the exterior with its many bays and pilasters is most impressive.

Turn right into Nelson Street and through to Grainger Street, with a left turn to the point where it meets the intersection of Blackett Street and Grey Street by the Grey Monument. Here probably is the heart of Newcastle, both old and new, and one of the busiest areas of the city. To the left is the huge complex of the **Eldon Square Shopping Centre**, while to the right, a short distance away, is the busy, pedestrianized shopping street of **Northumberland Street**.

The **Grey Monument**, marking perhaps the northern limit and focal point of Victorian Newcastle, is a 40·5m (135ft) high Doric column, designed by Benjamin Green, and was erected in 1838. It is surmounted by a statue of the second Earl Grey (1764–1845), the Prime Minister at the time of the Reform Bill in 1832. The statue was made by Edward Baily, who also designed the one of Nelson for Trafalgar Square. A spiral staircase, with 164 steps, leads to a platform with an excellent view over the city. Normally open, it is closed at the present time owing to the construction of the underground Monument Station as part of Tyneside's new metro rapid-transit system.

Continuing eastwards, Blackett Street becomes New Bridge Street after passing Northumberland Street on the left. Here, **Broadcasting House** was originally built as a hospital by Dobson in 1826. The

Balmbra's Music Hall, Newcastle

architect's own house, with three bays, is at No. 49. To the left now are the frontiers of the more modern city to the north in the shape of the new **Central Library** in Princess Square and the **Laing Art Gallery** dealt with in the next itinerary. Continue to the end of the street and circle back into Market Street or cut through Croft Street to make the return. On the left-hand side of **Market Street** is a block of eleven houses in Dobson's style dating from about 1880. Still moving west, cross over Pilgrim Street to the next junction at Grey Street, where across the road, half right on the far corner, is a large block decorated with columns and domes, known as the **Triangle**. Continue straight on into Grainger Street, where once again the Grainger Market appears.

To finish the tour return to Grey Street and walk the length of it, both up and down, for this is the finest of all Newcastle's streets and the centre of its Victorian grandeur. Although there is much of Dobson's work at hand, it was not exclusively his entire conception, and others had a hand in it, notably Benjamin Green, who designed the **Theatre Royal**, with its great jutting Corinthian portico. From the lower end the whole street curves gracefully up towards the Grey Monument. Just above the Theatre Royal is the **Lloyds Bank Building**, while opposite is the **Exchange**. Below Market Street is a block of twenty-seven bays with an elaborate centre of Doric pilasters and Ionic columns. Below that again is a block of fifty-seven bays, on the west side, enriched by Corinthian columns.

For those who have the time a walk down Grainger Street may be included, to the junction with the Westgate Road, where the **Trustee Savings Bank**, built in 1861, has a particularly fine interior, then a left turn along Collingwood Street and Moseley Street back to the foot of Grey Street. There are many fine commercial buildings along this latter stretch, four of them banks. Off Moseley Street on its north side runs the **Cloth Market** where **Balmbra's**, one of the most famous of all Tyneside music-halls, has its home.

Some northern areas of the city also have attractive residential suburbs with buildings of the same style as the centre. One of the best examples is at **Leazes Terrace** to the north-west of the city, while **Jesmond Road** also has some elegant terraces, with a parish church and cemetery lodge both by Dobson.

Tour D (modern Newcastle)
Up to the 1960s the new city of Newcastle referred mostly to the graceful

central area inside the city walls. Now, however, an ultra-modern category has come into being with many examples of contemporary architecture, but there is little doubt that for every new creation some destruction has taken place.

The key to most of the recent development lies in the A1 main road coming into the city over the Tyne Bridge which leads into the new roundabout by Swan House. This was the site of the old **Royal Arcade**, a Grainger building of 1831, designed as a covered shopping centre with commercial premises above it, but demolished to make way for the new point of entry to the city's main commercial area. **Swan House**, named after Joseph Swan, the Gateshead inventor who in 1880 demonstrated his early experiments with electric lighting, now contains a replica of the Royal Arcade underneath it, and the building is linked by subways to the surrounding streets. Close by is the new **Bank of England** building, and to the south-east is an area known as the **All Saints Office Development** with the multi-storey **Manors Car Park** in between. The Church of All Saints has been deconsecrated but preserved, possibly for some secular use.

The Swan House roundabout is also the start of the central motorway east, opened in 1975 to carry the main through flow of traffic from the A1 coming across the Tyne Bridge, and this circles around the eastern half of the city. Part of it is underground, which entailed some radical changes to streets and traffic flows. Northwards, along Pilgrim Street the city's main commercial offices remain, but at the top end, where it joins New Bridge Street and Blackett Street, a left turn past Grey's Monument leads directly into the new **Eldon Square Shopping Centre**, and the original Eldon Square, an integral part of Dobson and Grainger's scheme, has gone.

The line of Pilgrim Street continues northwards along **Northumberland Street**, now a traffic-free shopping precinct which attracts large numbers of shoppers. Passing the junction with Northumberland Road, the way leads up to the **Haymarket Bus Station** on the left. At the corner, by St Mary's Place, the scene opens out to some of the new buildings to the north.

St Thomas's Church, designed by Dobson in 1825, stands firmly in the middle of the green. Behind it, half left, the **University** at Barras Bridge has expanded enormously with a plethora of modern buildings, and the **University Theatre** also lies here. Barras Bridge leads out northwards along the line of the A1 to Morpeth, and the bridges bringing the central motorway east around the city cross it just north of this point. Beyond the University is the **Hancock Museum**, while the **Museum of Science and Engineering**, soon to be moved to new premises in the city centre, is some way up the Great North Road in the **Exhibition Park** on the edge of the Town Moor.

Undoubtedly, one of the most striking of the new buildings in Newcastle is the new **Civic Centre**, which lies on the north-east side of the green. Designed by George Kenyon and completed in 1969, it has won a civic trust award. Striking in its isolation amidst the constant traffic flow around it, it is certainly the most impressive new building in Newcastle today.

To the east of this area are the buildings of the **Polytechnic** which stretch from Ellison Place to the Sandyford Road. By turning south from the Civic Centre and descending College Street these are on the left-hand side. At the corner of Northumberland Road are the **City Hall** and **Baths**. Turn right at this corner and left at the next junction into **John Dobson Street** where, if you are tired of walking, there are some convenient bench seats. Further down, the street turns into an underpass by the new **Princess Square** complex, a near-skyscraper building by the junction with New Bridge Street. Around the corner on the left is the **Laing Art Gallery** while on the opposite side is the new Central Library. To reach this it is necessary to climb the stairs over the road, emerging on to a platform known as Princess Square, Upper Level, which, with its seats and nicely set-out plants, affords a pleasant haven in the midst of a busy city and seems indicative of the shape of things to come.

The new **Central Library** was opened by Sir Edward Boyle on 17 April 1970, according to the plaque just inside the main entrance. It is a formidable building and a massive library. A word of praise must be said for the efficiency of the **City Information Service** which it also runs and which handles an enormous number of visitors dexterously. Besides information leaflets on most of the places of interest in the county of Tyne and Wear, competent and intelligent comments can be obtained on most aspects of Northumbrian life.

From the Central Library a short distance westwards on New Bridge Street leads back to the centre of the city by Grey's Monument.

Museums and art galleries

The county of Tyne and Wear runs a comprehensive museums' service, and up-to-date information on current exhibitions can be obtained from the City Information Service. The areas covered by Gateshead, South Tyneside and Sunderland are dealt with under their respective headings. Newcastle itself offers an excellent choice of museums and art galleries covering a wide range of subjects, and while some of these have already been referred to in the text, a list and brief description are given below.

Greek Museum Department of Classics, Percy Building, The Quadrangle, University of Newcastle. (*Open Monday to Friday 10–4.30 and by appointment.*) Greek and Etruscan art. Collections of vases, bronzes, gems, terracotta and armour ranging from the Minoan to the Hellenistic periods.

Hancock Museum Great North Road, Barras Bridge. (*Open weekdays 10–5, Sundays (April to September) 2–5, charge.*) Run jointly with the Natural History Society of Northumbria. Mainly natural history but also a large ethnographical collection. Comprehensive collections of British birds, mammals, plant and animal fossils. Aquarium displaying British freshwater fish.

Hatton Gallery Department of Fine Art, University of Newcastle. (*Open weekdays 10–6, Saturdays 10–5.*) Permanent collection of paintings, particularly of the Italian schools. Frequent loan exhibitions.

John George Joicey Museum City Road. (*Open weekdays 10–6.*) Formerly the Holy Jesus Hospital, the building was converted to museum use in 1972. Fine displays of costume, paintings, engravings, models, Roman relics and local applied art. The Town Hutch, Period Rooms, Armour, Weapons and Military Section are particularly interesting.

Keep Museum The Keep, Castle Garth. (*Open Mondays 2–4, Tuesdays to Saturdays 10–4.30, with closing from October to March at 3.30, charge.*) Part of the former castle.

Laing Art Gallery Higham Place, New Bridge Street. (*Open weekdays*

10–6 (Tuesdays and Thursdays open until 8), Sundays 2.30–5.30.) A splendid range of water-colours of the British schools, also collections of 18th- and 19th-century costumes, English pottery, glass and pewter. Paintings of local scenes and of events in Newcastle's history. Prints and drawings of Thomas Bewick.

Museum of Antiquities Department of Archaeology, The Quadrangle, University of Newcastle. (*Open weekdays 10–5.*) Run jointly with the Society of Antiquaries. Prehistoric, Roman and Anglo-Saxon antiquities mainly from Northumberland. Large numbers of finds from sites along Hadrian's Wall and scale models of the Wall. Reconstruction of the Temple of Mithras and of Roman arms and armour.

Museum of Mining Engineering Department of Mining Engineering, Queen Victoria Road, University of Newcastle. (*Open Monday to Friday, 9–5.*) Exhibits depicting the history of mining. Large collection of mine safety lamps. Water-colours of Northumbrian mines in the mid-19th century.

Plummer's Tower Croft Street. (*Open only occasionally, in association with the Laing Art Gallery to which it is affiliated.*) Main displays of 18th-century period furniture and paintings.

Science Museum Exhibition Park, Great North Road. (*Open Easter to September, weekdays 10–6 (Tuesdays and Thursdays open until 8), Sundays 2.30–5.30; October to Easter, weekdays 10–4.30, Sundays 1.30–4.30.*) Exhibits showing the early history and development of engineering, shipbuilding, mining and other industries in the north-east.

Society of Antiquaries Bagpipe Museum Black Gate, Castle Garth. (*Open Tuesday to Saturday 12–5, charge.*) Also known as the Black Gate Museum, it now houses the world's only collection of bagpipes, with recordings, displays and a shepherd's room.

20 Environs of Newcastle upon Tyne

North of the Tyne

1) Elswick, Scotswood, Newburn and Throckley

Westwards from the Tyne Bridge the A695 road leads along the north bank of the Tyne towards the Scotswood Bridge. A circuitous route around the one-way system past the Central Railway Station finally emerges on to the Scotswood Road. Along the north bank large apartment blocks and high-rise flats predominate before the road runs into the heavy industrialized areas of **Elswick** and **Scotswood**. Elswick is the home of Vickers-Armstrong, set up in 1846 by the 1st Lord Armstrong, which became one of the major armament and heavy engineering works of the country and spread right along this bank. There is fairly heavy river pollution along this stretch of the Tyne, and the area is undergoing redevelopment. Scotswood appears to have been named from earlier intrusions of the Scots working their way eastwards along the river line. In $3\frac{1}{2}$ miles the Scotswood roundabout and bridge are reached. Across the river the A695 continues to Ryton and Prudhoe, while the A694 turns south through Blaydon and follows the Derwent Valley. The new Scotswood Bridge has also opened up a bypass route to the west of the city for the A613 running north from the A1(M) at Birtley. On the north side of the river the A191 circular road links Scotswood with Denton and Kenton Bar acting as a ring road around the western suburbs of the city. Continuing along the river bank, the A6098 leads on through Lemington, where from the 'staithes' some of the early coal exports were made, and on into Newburn, past the Tyne Cattle Auction Mart and the Stella North Power Station.

The road turns inland and winds up **Newburn**'s curving main street. On the right the **Church of St Michael** has an early Norman tower and arcades with a chancel dating from the 13th century. George Stephenson,

257

born 3 miles up the Tyne from here at Wylam, was twice married in this church and also first tried out his famous *Rocket* in the village. The A6085 continues on through **Throckley**, where it crosses the line of Hadrian's Wall, then crosses the main A69(T) road leading west to Hexham. Northwards from this point it becomes the B6323 providing an outer ring road link through to Callerton, Newcastle Airport and Ponteland.

2) Benwell, Denton, Throckley and Heddon-on-the-Wall

From the Central Station the Westgate Road, the A69(T), links Newcastle with Hexham and Carlisle, following the line of Hadrian's Wall. In 2 miles at **Benwell** there are the remains of a Roman fort. Another mile reaches the roundabout where the A191 inner ring road crosses. Just past here at **Denton Burn** and **West Denton** are more Roman remains, and close by is **Denton Hall**, a Jacobean house of 1622. At the West Denton roundabout the B6528 continues straight on, following the line of Hadrian's Wall and leading into **Throckley** and **Heddon-on-the-Wall**, where the start of the more visible parts of the Wall occurs. The A69(T) main road swings slightly northwards, bypassing both these villages and continuing into Northumberland just north of Heddon-on-the-Wall.

3) Kenton Bar, Woolsington (Newcastle Airport) and Ponteland

The original A696 Jedburgh road left Newcastle close to St Andrew's Church and followed Gallowgate into Barrack Road. Gallowgate, just outside the city walls, was the scene of public hangings, the last of which took place in 1844. Just to the north is Newcastle United's Football Ground and Leazes Terrace, where Grainger built some very fine houses, on the edge of Leazes Park. It is still possible to work a way through to Kenton Bar following this route, but with the new motorway central east, the A696 through route follows the motorway around the east side of the city and emerges north-westwards along the line of Claremont Road crossing the former Town Moor. By the time you have worked your way past the complexities of slip-roads and tunnels the 3-mile steady climb to **Kenton Bar** is past. The A191 road from Scotswood comes in on the left just before this point and from the roundabout at Kenton Bar continues eastwards around the northern suburbs to Gosforth, Longbenton and Whitley Bay.

From Kenton Bar the A696 continues north-westwards 2 miles to **Woolsington Hall,** an early 18th-century mansion-house, close to the edge of **Newcastle's airport** and on the line of the Northumberland boundary. The airport buildings and the Airport Hotel are on the right on a high plateau overlooking the surrounding countryside. In 2 more miles **Ponteland** is reached, with the large residential estate of Darras Hall.

4) Newcastle to Gosforth and Seaton Burn (The Great North Road)

The old line of the A1 along Pilgrim Street, Northumberland Street and Barras Bridge northwards along the Great North Road has been superseded for through traffic by the central motorway east which now links up by Brandling Park and rejoins the main road to Morpeth, Alnwick and Berwick-upon-Tweed at this point. From this junction on either side are Exhibition Parks – on the left forming part of the former Town Moor, on the right Brandling Park and some of the suburbs of West Jesmond with the Royal Grammar School and Jesmond church.

Less than $\frac{1}{2}$ mile north of the junction, where the slip-road feeds into the A1(T), is the Museum of Science and Engineering. One mile north the B6339 road comes in on the left at the roundabout and continues eastwards as the A189 into West Jesmond and along the line of Jesmond Dene to Gosforth Lake and Woods. Here also is the golf-course at **High Gosforth Park,** a caravan site and Newcastle's race-course, where the famous Northumberland Plate is usually held in June and known to everyone as the 'Pitman's Derby'. **Gosforth** is largely a residential suburb 3 miles north of the city but hardly separated from it nowadays. Gosforth Park is to the north of the built-up area and includes also a squash club and a nature reserve. The **Gosforth Park Hotel** lies on the edge of the park. From Gosforth the A189 links up with the A188 coming north from Heaton and continues through Dudley and the new town of Cramlington to Bedlington. The road crosses into Northumberland just north of Dudley, where a link-road (A190) leads off eastwards to Seaton Delaval and Seaton Sluice.

The A1(T) road continues north, and in another mile the A191 lateral road from Scotswood, linking through to Whitley Bay, crosses its path and also leads into Gosforth and Longbenton. Four miles north of Newcastle the B6318 road swings off left and then recrosses the line of the A1(T) to lead into the suburb of Wide Open, and this provides an alternative route into the Gosforth Park area and the hotel. At the 6-mile mark on the A1(T) the lake that feeds the **Seaton Burn** appears on the left by Brunswick Village, and within ½ mile the junction is made with the A108 Tyne Tunnel circuit road. Also from this point the A1068 leads off northwards to the Plessey Woods Country Park area on the river Blyth. Immediately after this junction the A1(T) road enters Northumberland close to Seven Mile House Farm.

5) Jesmond, Heaton, West Chirton and Cullercoats

The A1058 road eastwards from the city leaves by the line of the Jesmond Road, which has its exit from the central motorway east on the north-east side of the city or can be reached via Sandyford Road from the Civic Centre. Both routes out straddle the railway line by Jesmond Station. In Jesmond Road is **Jesmond Church**, designed by Dobson in 1858 in the Early English style with a large tower. Jesmond itself is a densely packed residential suburb in its early stages but opens out into something far more attractive at the park of **Jesmond Dene**, which follows the deep valley of the Ouse Burn and separates it from the adjacent suburb of Heaton. It was given to the city in 1883 by the 1st Lord Armstrong who had his home here. Adjacent to the Dene in **Reid Park Road** are the remains of the 12th-century **St Mary's Chapel**, sometimes known as **Our Lady of Jesmond**, a place of pilgrimage in the Middle Ages.

After crossing the *Ouse Burn* the A1058 enters **Heaton**, where there is a church (**St George's**), built in 1888 by T. R. Spence at the expense of Charles Mitchell, a partner of Lord Armstrong's. At Heaton also the A188 road, running north from Byker, crosses the A1058 and continues towards Bedlington with a link through to Blyth. Just north of Longbenton it is joined by the A189 emerging from the Jesmond area and passes close to the 'new town' of **Killingworth**, where there is an artificial lake used as a sailing centre. Killingworth also has an old village where George Stephenson lived while employed as engine-man at nearby Killingworth Colliery. His cottage is preserved as a private residence (Dial Cottage) in **Great Lime Road** and set into the wall is a sundial, designed by the father and carved by the son, Robert.

The A1058 from Heaton now becomes a fast transit road eastwards towards the coast. It is crossed by the A186 emerging from Wallsend and then the Tyne Tunnel road, the A108, as it skirts the riverside suburbs, through **West Chirton** and Preston to link up with the A193 coastal road close to **Cullercoats**.

6) Byker, Walker, Wallsend to North Shields and Tynemouth

There are three main highways eastwards from Newcastle along the northern river line and out towards the coastline. The A186 follows the line of City Road through the suburbs of St Anthonys and Walker and circles back north again to join up with the A187 at Wallsend. This latter road follows more or less the line of Hadrian's Wall which was later extended from Newcastle to Wallsend. It heads out along New Bridge Street and into the suburb of Byker, where it crosses the valley of the Byker Burn by Byker Bridge. **Byker** is a densely packed residential and industrial area with an important shopping centre. Great efforts are being made to replace some of the 19th-century housing, notably with such developments as the mile-long Byker Wall which has attracted much attention. At Byker the A187 splits into two, more or less parallel roads – the A187 and the A193 – by the Charles Dickens pub, where the street name of the Fossway (the Saxon name for a ditch) recalls the line of Hadrian's Wall. Here also the A188 runs northwards towards Heaton and Longbenton.

Both roads now run eastwards the 2 miles to Wallsend, where they almost converge north and south of Wallsend Station and are linked by Station Road which continues northwards as the A186 towards Earsdon. **Wallsend** was the original settlement that grew up around the Roman fort of Segedunum and later became one of the more important ship-building centres along the river Tyne. Grim streets of tightly packed houses, each with a 'netty' (an outside lavatory) at the back, are now being replaced by more modern estates. The main High Street has almost been completely redesigned and is now an important and busy shopping centre. At the main junction a pub, the Penny Wet, recalls the local nickname for the former Station Hotel, where the shipyard workers would slip out for a half-pint of beer for a penny. Southwards on Station Road are the shipbuilding yards of Swan Hunter, and close by, straddling what was Buddle Street, lay the site of the Roman fort. A local appeal launched in 1868 failed to raise enough money to preserve the site, but for many years it was marked out on the streets. Now, with the latest redevelopment schemes, it is a deserted area, but some of the relics are preserved in Wallsend Park, including a stretch of the Wall.

From Wallsend both the A193 and the A187 continue eastwards as parallel roads and link up with the Tyne Tunnel road (A108) at Howdon

Panns. Here, the A187 runs closer to the river line and serves to make the link with the dock area, including the Tyne Commission Quay from where the services to Denmark and Norway embark. It then runs through the suburb of Percy Main to link up with the A193 again at North Shields.

Considerably larger than its close neighbour Tynemouth, **North Shields** also has its roots in land originally owned by the Tynemouth Priory. Nowadays it is a lively town, almost wholly given over to commerce and industry. Its importance is fish, and the most interesting area is around the bustling Fish Quay. North Shields is also the birthplace of the steam-trawler. The town has some fine streets of both Georgian and Victorian houses, but there is much redevelopment going on at the present time. In Northumberland Square is **St Columba's Church**, designed by Dobson, and the figure of the **Wooden Dolly**, representing a Cullercoats fishwife, the original of which stood in a passageway leading to the quay.

From North Shields the A192 road runs northwards to **Earsdon**, a pleasant village with Georgian houses about its green and the 13th-century **St Alban's Church** which was reconstructed in 1836.

A mile to the east the A193 road runs from North Shields into Tynemouth. Along the left-hand side of the road just before entering the town are a series of Master Mariners' Homes, while on the opposite side is the way down to the Fish Quay.

---

7) Tynemouth

Bowls Northumberland Park, Smith's Park, Tynemouth Park, West End Park.
Early closing Wednesday.
Golf *Tynemouth Golf-Club*, King Edward Road.
Hotels *Grand*, *Park*.
Information office Grand Parade.
Population 67,090.

Sailing At Prior's Haven.
Sea-fishing At Prior's Haven. A sea-angling contest is usually held in the autumn.
Swimming-pools Tynemouth Indoor Pool, Preston Village. Open-air pool at the south end of Long Sands. Excellent bathing also available from the beaches of both Long and Short Sands.

Situated at the very mouth of the river Tyne, **Tynemouth**, together with its close neighbours Cullercoats and Whitley Bay, forms one continuous resort with over 3 miles of safe golden sands with plenty of pools and small rocky coves ideal for children.

Tynemouth marks a division between the long line of industry along the river and the coastline northwards. As a coastal resort it is less popular than its neighbours owing to the lack of amusements which it provides but is preferred by some for this reason and still has much to offer. It has a wider stretch of beach as well as three pleasant little coves at Cullercoats Bay, Short Sands and Prior's Haven, plus a long pier guarding the broad estuary of the river.

From the station a left turn leads to **Front Street**, with its 18th-century brick houses, and through to the **Clock Tower**, built in 1861, which faces the castle and priory where most of the incoming roads meet. **Tynemouth Castle and Priory** (*open DoE standard hours*) is the best place to start any tour. Inside the main entrance gateway in the middle of the green stand the priory ruins, the whole edifice on a promontory bounded by cliffs 30m (100ft) high which forms a natural division between river and sea. Originally, a timber chapel stood on this headland, built by King Edwin in 627 and rebuilt in stone by King Oswald some ten years later. It was repeatedly attacked by the Danes, who finally destroyed it completely in 875, and for two centuries it lay in ruins. Of these buildings not a trace remains.

The credit for rebuilding the monastery lies with the Benedictines of Durham. In 1075 the **Church of St Mary**, or what remained of it, was given by Earl Waltheof to the Jarrow monks, but they were removed to Durham in 1083. The second monastery did not last for long either, for the Benedictines quarrelled with Robert de Mowbray, then the Earl of Northumberland, who ejected them and asked the St Albans chapter for monks to found a third monastery on the site. With the arrivals from St Albans, the priory continued as a cell of the powerful Hertfordshire monastery until the dissolution in 1539, much to the annoyance of the Durham hierarchy, who naturally regarded Tynemouth as their rightful property.

Apart from the foundations of the **Chapter House**, the **Prior's Hall** and several minor appendages the existing remains of the priory consist solely of the magnificent **Church** which stood here and which, in size and beauty, must have ranked very close to Hexham. The building began in 1085, and in 1110 the remains of St Oswin were brought here. The unusual building plan followed that of St Augustine's old Norman Church in Canterbury and also the one at Fécamp, and although the east end was demolished in the 12th century, excavation has revealed the ground-plan.

After the dissolution the nave was used as a parish church up to 1688, by which time it was falling into decay. The original nave was lengthened westwards by two bays in the 13th century, and a considerable portion of

Tynemouth Castle

the west front built at that time still exists. The **Lady Chapel**, however, added in the 14th century, has only its foundations remaining.

Of the 12th-century chancel only the east end and south side of the **Presbytery** remain, one of the most imposing parts still to be seen. At the extreme east end is the small **Percy Chapel**, added in 1450, and the only part of the church to be completely preserved. Its single, small chamber is lit by a beautiful traceried rose-window and by six side windows. The intricate rib design of the vaulted roof combines a series of sculptured keystones.

The castle remains consist of a fortified **Gatehouse** and wall dating from the 14th century, although a castle stood on this site from the 11th century. Edward I granted permission for the priory to be fortified in 1296, and a century later, in 1390, the prior completed it. Both the priory and the castle were occupied by the monks, and a close relationship existed between the two for it was built primarily as their outer defence work. In the Civil War it was stormed by the Parliamentarians, and by 1681 was reported to be in a state of ruin.

Within the castle grounds now are some coastguard houses built in 1835 and a modern coastguard look-out station as well. The view from the walls is impressive: on a clear day the eye ranges southwards to Lizard Point with its lighthouse, four miles away as the crow flies, past Marsden Bay's Nature Reserve and Grotto and then turns to the Bay of South Shields, with the caravan park at the river entrance, the South Pier and light, the river Tyne with its masses of cranes and shipyards. Below on the green is the dominating statue to Admiral Lord Collingwood, who took over at the Battle of Trafalgar after Nelson's death. Northwards, the eye can just make out the towers of the aluminium plant at Lynemouth and the lighthouse on St Mary's Island beyond Whitley Bay.

On either side of the promontory are small sandy bays, the one to the north – **Short Sands** – with steep approaches, guarded by railings. On the south side the road winds down to the green, the left fork leading out to the **North Pier**, built in 1909 and nearly ¾ mile long. **South Pier** is about 1 mile long, and the two lighthouses on the ends close the river mouth to a gap of less than ¼ mile.

The right fork leads down to **Prior's Haven**, a small, sheltered and sandy bay, where the calm water is a favourite spot for fishing and sailing. The path continues around the low southern headland, passing an old fort-house known as the 'Spanish Battery' and on to the **Collingwood Monument**. Close by are the headquarters of the **Volunteer Life Brigade**. Offshore at this point are the dangerous **Black Middens**, a group of rocks that have brought disaster to many ships. Northwards along the coast road leads on to **Grand Parade**, past the Grand Hotel and the Plaza entertainment centre which has its own night-club. Beyond Sharpness Point **Long Sands** opens up with its firm beach and steps leading down to the fine tidal bathing-pool at the southern end. Opposite is **Tynemouth Park**, with tennis-courts, bowling-greens and a boating lake. Parts of the low grassy cliffs have been laid out as flower gardens.

At the northern end of Long Sands is **Cullercoats**. This was a fishing village once famous for its traditional fleet of 'cobles' (inshore fishing boats) which have now largely disappeared. Coast erosion seems to be something of a problem here. In miniscule **Cullercoats Bay** two jetties enclose a harbour almost dry at low tide, and both here and on the point to the south are some shallow caves. At the northern end of the village is the **Lifeboat House** and the red-bricked **Dove Marine Laboratory**.

Immediately around the point and less than 2 miles from Tynemouth is the major resort of the area, Whitley Bay, with a 2-mile spread of sand running up towards St Mary's Island.

---

8) Whitley Bay

Bowls Crawford Park, Rockliffe Park, Souter Park.
Buses To Newcastle, Tynemouth, North Shields and Blyth.
Camping and caravanning On the Links at the northern end of the bay.
Early closing Wednesday.
Golf *Whitley Bay Golf-Club*, Claremont Road.
Hotels *Holmedale*, *Newquay*, *Station*.
Ice-skating *Whitley Bay Ice-Rink*, Hillheads Road.

Information office Central Promenade (summer only).
Population 37,010.
Sailing From the beach.
Sea-fishing Excellent sea-fishing from several beaches and St Mary's Island, with contests usually held in the autumn.
Swimming-pools Safe bathing from the beach; *Whitley Bay Leisure Pool*, the Links.

Whitley Bay is not only Tyneside's leading resort, linked to Newcastle by a quick and frequent train service, but attracts visitors from all over the north of England, the Midlands and also Scotland. It offers every facility for a family holiday: on safe and extensive beaches sea bathing is regulated by beach patrols; fishing is possible both from boats and on the foreshore; there are paddling-pools for children, boating and ample facilities for bowls and tennis, with annual tournaments for both sports. There is also a golf-club, an ice-skating rink and a brand-new leisure pool which not only creates its own waves but is decorated with a mass of tropical plants and creepers down to the water's edge. It has a solarium, Turkish baths and a restaurant.

It is a place of some antiquity, reputedly founded by some Anglian settlers in the 6th century. Its first recorded mention was in 1100 when Henry I conferred it on the priory of Tynemouth. Later on it was mentioned in the charters of Henry II and King John who reconfirmed this appointment, but after the suppression of the monastery it reverted to the Crown. In 1551 Edward VI granted it to Dudley, Earl of Warwick and later the Duke of Northumberland. From that time onwards it was largely concerned with coalmining, which was carried on from about 1656 and exported from the staithes at Cullercoats. By 1882, however, the best of the surface coal had been worked out, and little has been mined since. It gradually became a residential area for commuters from Tyneside and Newcastle, as it still is, but it is now also a growing holiday resort.

From the station the road leads into **Whitley Road**, the main shopping centre, and the Esplanade continues then directly onto the broad Promenade. Below the Promenade is the **Central Lower Promenade**, with a cafeteria, and close to this, at the **Lifeboat House**, is one of the patrolled bathing stations. At **Table Rocks**, near the southern or Rockcliffe end of the Promenade, is an open-air swimming pool, carved out of natural rock, which is filled twice a day by the tide. At the foot of the cliffs on the **Southern Promenade** is a paddling-pool for children.

Northwards, the Promenade leads towards the **Spanish City** amusement centre, which includes an open-air market and an antiques fair. Here, the A193 main road northwards, emerging from the town, becomes the front with solid double yellow lines on both sides all the way. On the inland side are pleasant residential areas. The Promenade continues towards an area known as the **Links**, a common ideal for walking and picnics, where the **Panama sunken gardens** are, and below, **Panama Beach**. Here, another bathing station is regularly patrolled. At this northern end of the town also are the **Brierdene Golf-Club** and the new leisure pool, claimed to be the most modern in Britain. Northwards from the A193 the hilltop village of Hartley appears, and to the right St Mary's Island with its lighthouse. There is a caravan site close to this point.

St Mary's Island provides a short excursion from Whitley Bay. It is only an island at high tide, when the causeway is covered for four to five hours, so it is important to note the state of the tide. The best walking route lies along the seaward side of the Links, continuing along the low cliff line to join the track that leads out to Curry's Point and the start of the causeway. The island was once known as Bait Island after an Elizabethan gentleman who owned it known as Thomas Bates. There are a few cottages on it and a conspicuous white lighthouse, built in 1897 and 36m (120ft) high.

Beyond the northern extremity of Whitley Bay, following the A193 towards Blyth, there is a ½-mile patch of no-man's land up to the edge of Hartley village, where the Northumberland boundary is crossed, and the

road leads on into Seaton Sluice. (For a round-trip excursion from
Newcastle a return can be made via Seaton Sluice and Seaton Delaval
Hall following the A190 back to Newcastle.)

South of the Tyne

1) Gateshead

Bus station Wellington Street.
Early closing Wednesday.
Golf *Birtley Golf-Club*, Birtley; *Garsfield
and District Golf-Club*, Chopwell; *Heworth
Golf-Club*, Heworth; *Ravensworth
Golf-Club*, Wrekenton; *Ryton Golf-Club*,
Ryton; *Tyneside Golf-Club*, Ryton;
Whickham Golf-Club, Whickham.
Hotels *Five Bridges*, *Springfield*.
Information office Central Library, Prince
Consort Road.

Museums and art galleries Shipley Art
Gallery, Prince Consort Road.
Population 91,230.
Swimming-pools Birtley Baths, Durham
Road, Birtley; Blaydon Baths; Dunston
Baths; Leam Lane Baths, Felling; Mulgrave
Terrace Baths, Gateshead; Shipcote Baths,
Gateshead.

The proximity of **Gateshead** to Newcastle leads inevitably to their being
treated by all, except those who live there, as one environment. Five
bridges link the two huge urban areas and they are less than 1 mile apart,
but prior to 1974 they represented not only two sides of one river but also
two different counties. Now, with the changed county boundaries, their
unity is more close within the area of Tyne and Wear, and Gateshead now
finds itself responsible for a district ranging 10 miles west and 6 miles
south before the new county boundary is reached.

South over the Tyne Bridge, the A1 leads along East Street to the
roundabout, where a right turn leads into the High Street. In the northbound direction there is still much congestion by traffic through the
town, and this problem remains to be solved. The town has a large
industrial and shopping area that ranges from Low Fell to the Tyne, and
with the innumerable pedestrian crossings traffic is forced to crawl. Some
widening of the road over Low Fell has taken place in recent years, and
there are large numbers of new housing estates and high-rise flats to be
seen. In the **Saltwell Park** area in the centre of Gateshead there is a lake,
and close by is the **Library** and the **Shipley Art Gallery**, presented to the
town by Joseph Shipley, which houses a fine set of English and Continental paintings by a wide variety of artists.

Gateshead was the scene of the launching of the first river steamboat in

England in 1814, and amongst its other creative geniuses was Sir Joseph Swan, inventor of the incandescent lamp in 1878, after whom Swan House in Newcastle is named.

During the intense depressions of the industrial scene during the 30s the first ever government-financed industrial estate – the Team Valley Trading Estate – was initiated 2 miles south-west of the town in 1936. Over 1 mile square, it is the largest in England and provides employment for 20,000 people.

2) To Blaydon, Ryton, Prudhoe, the Derwent Valley and Rowlands Gill

From the south side of the Tyne Bridge the A6083 leads westwards towards the Team Valley Trading Estate and Swalwell. It is joined by the new bypass road around the western side of the metropolis, the A613, which runs from the A1 at the Birtley turn-off and on through Blaydon to cross the Scotswood Bridge and provides a good through route around the city.

Blaydon, with its residential area of Winlaton, has had a face-lift since the days of the famous Blaydon Races. The last meeting was held in 1916. From Blaydon westwards the A695 continues to **Ryton**, felt by many to be the prettiest village along the Tyne. There is a bridge across the Tyne here from Newburn. Ryton's 13th-century church is a fine example of the Early English style. Outstanding is the woodwork of the chancel screen and the oak stalls, both in the Cosin style and dating from the 17th century. Along the riverside is a stretch known as **Ryton Willows**, and Ryton's golf-club is at **Clara Vale**. The A695 continues west from Ryton through Crawcook and 2½ miles beyond Ryton crosses the Northumberland boundary at the Stanley Burn and leads into Prudhoe.

From Blaydon, turning south along the Derwent Valley, the A694 passes Axwell Park and the country park area created along this stretch of the river. On the opposite side of the river is the **Derwent Walk**, which follows the old railway line from Swalwell to Consett, now disused. This 10-mile stretch, formally opened in 1972, leads past **Hollinside Manor** at Wickham and **Winlaton Mill** and offers a pedestrian way through to the Gibside Chapel at Rowland's Gill and the woods at Chopwell.

Three miles south of Blaydon lies the village of **Rowland's Gill**, technically just inside Tyne and Wear, for here the river Derwent marks the boundary with Durham. Most people come here to see the **Gibside**

Chapel, owned by the National Trust, which has been restored and was formally opened by the Queen Mother in 1966. To reach it turn off left on to the B6314 towards Burnopfield where there is an entrance. The chapel, a fine example of Georgian elegance, was designed by James Paine in 1760 and completed much later as a mausoleum for the Bowes family. There is also a 42m (140ft) column, topped by a statue of Liberty, which graces the end of an avenue of oaks. The grounds were originally landscaped by 'Capability' Brown. (*Open April to September, daily except Tuesdays 2–6; March and October, Wednesdays, Saturdays and Sundays 2–6; November to February, Sunday only 2–6.*) Technically, the chapel is in Durham now, but returning to the village, the A694 runs south for another 1½ miles before it crosses the Durham boundary leading on to Ebchester and Consett.

From Rowland's Gill the B6315 road turns west and then north past Chopwell Wood and High Spen circling back to Ryton. A side-road leads into **Chopwell**, an industrial village, just north of the Milkwell Burn, here marking the Durham boundary, before it flows into the Derwent. **High Spen** and the 2,000 acres of **Chopwell Wood** provide some fine scenery and viewpoints.

Also leading south-west from Gateshead, the A692 climbs up past the Street Gate past Sunniside, where it splits into two. The right-hand fork continues as the A692 over Marley Hill to Byermoor and Sheep Hill where it links up with the B6314 from Rowland's Gill and crosses the Durham boundary by Burnopfield before continuing to Consett. The left fork becomes the A6076, skirting Marley Hill and heading for Causey, where the Durham boundary is crossed by Hedley West Farm House before the road continues directly to Stanley.

---

3) The Great North Road

South from Gateshead the A1(T) crosses over Low Fell to Birtley, where the A613 western bypass road from Scotswood and Blaydon now joins it. Directly south from this point the A6127 follows the line of the old Roman road to Ouston, where it crosses the Durham boundary and on to Chester-le-Street. In another mile the A1(T) becomes a motorway, and as the A1(M) is joined by the A194(M) from the Tyne Tunnel and South Shields. A mile beyond this point it reaches the large service area of the Washington–Birtley complex. From here the A1231 leads eastwards into Washington and on to Sunderland, while the A1(M) continues south towards Scotch Corner, crossing the Durham boundary just south of this junction, close to the grounds of Lambton Castle which are on the left.

4) Felling, Boldon and Sunderland

South-east from Gateshead the A184/5 road swings off left at the first roundabout and runs through the heavily built-up area of industrial **Felling**. In 2 miles the A185 turns off left to the Tyne Tunnel, Jarrow and South Shields. The A184 continues through solid housing estates for another 1½ miles to the interchange with the A194, leading north-eastwards to the Tyne Tunnel, Jarrow and South Shields and southwards as the A194(M) to the interchange with the A1(M). Here, the countryside begins to open up as the A184 heads for the **Boldons**. After crossing the A108(T) Tyne Tunnel road which links up with the A19 southwards to Seaham, **Boldon Colliery** is passed on the left and then **West** and **East Boldon**, twin villages 4 miles south of South Shields. At West Boldon is **St Nicholas's Church**, founded in the 13th century, which has some interesting mosaics. Another 'new town' has been built to the north of the original villages, while to the south lies the **Boldon Golf-Club**. The **Cleadon Hills** lie to the north-east, on the north side of which is the figure of a white horse.

After the Boldons the A184 swings southwards and in 2 miles joins up with the A19 running south from South Shields. Past the large restored **Mill** at **Fulwell**, it enters the northern outskirts of Sunderland, and in another mile the road enters the one-way system around three sides of a square, through the suburb of Monkwearmouth and crosses the Wearmouth Bridge over the river Wear.

5) Sunderland

Arts centre Sunderland Arts Centre, Grange Terrace.

Bus station Park Lane.

Distances Durham, 13 miles; Newcastle-upon-Tyne, 12 miles; Hartlepool, 21 miles; South Shields, 7 miles.

Early closing Wednesday.

Football Currently 2nd division.

Golf *Houghton-le-Spring Golf-Club*; *Wearside Golf-Club*, Coxgreen.

Hotels *Mowbray Park*, *Seaburn*, *Roker*.

Information office At Monkwearmouth Church and the various museums.

Museums and art galleries Grindon Close Museum, Grindon Lane; Monkwearmouth Museum of Land Transport, North Bridge Street; Ryhope Engines Trust, Pumping Station, Ryhope; Sunderland Museum and Art Gallery, Borough Road.

Population 214,820.

Post Office In new shopping centre.

Sports centre A new 2½-acre sports centre is now open in the centre of the town, with a large sports hall, a swimming-pool, badminton, netball, squash- and tennis-courts, plus a discotheque, restaurant and shops.

Swimming-pools High Street West Baths; Newcastle Road Baths.

Theatres *Empire Theatre*, High Street West.

Sunderland once claimed to be the largest shipbuilding town in the world, and its commercial growth has been closely tied to this industry. From the original two villages of Monkwearmouth and Bishopwearmouth, respectively on the north and south banks of the river Wear, Sunderland was added and gradually absorbed the other two. In AD 674 a monastery was founded at **Monkwearmouth**, and from land given by King Athelstan in AD 903 to the Bishop of Durham **Bishopwearmouth** emerged. It was only much later, in the 18th century, that a portion of land owned by the Monkwearmouth community towards the east and on the far side of the river was 'sundered' or separated off to form the new parish.

Coal shipments have formed the principal trade of the port since the 16th century, rising considerably at the time of the Civil War, when Newcastle became a Royalist town. From coal exports the natural turn led to shipbuilding, and by the 19th century both banks of the Wear were heavily engaged in such construction. Marine-engineering equipment and marine engines are also made along the riverside industrial area, and some evidence of this can best be seen from the main Wearmouth Bridge, opened in 1929. Further upstream the Queen Alexandra Bridge, built in 1909 and with its top railway track no longer in use, gives a viewpoint on to the recently constructed covered shipyards at Pallion and Southwick.

The dock area, between the river and the sea, was opened in the 19th century to cater for a rapidly expanding and mechanized coal trade. Nowadays, the docks mainly cater for incoming oil and general cargoes. From the northern end a pier projects across the southern arm of the estuary, and there is a lifeboat station here as well. On the northern side a similar pier extends out from the suburb of Roker.

The town itself has been thoroughly modernized in recent years, with a large, new shopping centre and just south of it, opposite Mowbray Park, a new civic centre. The latter, designed by Sir Basil Spence, Bonnington and Collins, is based on hexagonal blocks surrounding open courts and was opened in November 1970. In High Street West the 13th-century **St Michael's Church**, standing adjacent to the green, has been brought up-to-date with its 19th- and 20th-century restorations. Opposite is the **Empire Theatre**, opened in 1907 and now run as a civic theatre by the Empire Theatre Trust.

Sunderland has a wealth of museums. The **Sunderland Museum and Art Gallery** in Borough Road (*open weekdays 9.30–6, Saturdays 9.30–4, Sundays 2–5, Easter, Spring and Summer Bank Holidays 10–5*) has local collections of botany, geology, zoology, local history, models of locally built ships, pottery, silver and 19th- and 20th-century paintings. The **Grindon Close Museum** in Grindon Lane (*open weekdays 10–6, Sundays 2–5*) has also much local history in its Edwardian period rooms and shop interiors, including a chemist's shop and a dentist's surgery. This passion for collecting the evidence of the past extends also to railways, for the other famous museum in Sunderland is the **Monkwearmouth Station Museum** (*open weekdays 10–6, Sundays 2–5; Easter, Spring and Summer Bank Holidays 10–5*) just on the north side of the Wearmouth Bridge in North Bridge Street. The former station at Monkwearmouth was closed in 1967 and three years later reopened as the **Museum of Land Transport**. The station exterior remains exactly as it was when built to John Dobson's designs in 1845 and opened in 1848. There are many people who claim it was built by Thomas Moore, one of the architects of Victorian Sunderland. Either way, it was the 'Railway King' George Hudson, M.P. for Sunderland at that time, who extended the Newcastle railway here to serve the town. The interior has been restored faithfully to its Edwardian heyday, with a booking-office and many personal exhibits and mementoes from the former staff. There are also displays relating to St Peter's Church, and ambitious plans have already begun to expand the museum to take in rolling-stock as well. The museum was formally opened by the Duke of Edinburgh in 1973.

Also at Monkwearmouth is St Peter's Church, which is still the main reason why some several thousand visitors come to Sunderland each year. On the north side of the river Wear close to the shipbuilding yards, it takes a little finding with the new one-way traffic system. From the north, coming in by the A184/A19 road, follow the one-way system round with a left and then a right turn making for the city centre. At the far end of the second side of the square the left-hand lane leads to Roker and Whitburn (A183), the right towards the Wearmouth Bridge and city centre (A19). St Peter's Church is straight ahead. On the right turn immediately swing over to the left-hand lane in Dame Dorothy Street and take the first left, where there is room to park. The church stands in isolated glory on a preserved piece of green, next to the building of the Sunderland Boilermaker's Social Club. Coming in from the south, cross the Wearmouth Bridge and take the right-hand slip-road, signposted A183 (Roker and Whitburn), and follow on as before with two more right turns.

St Peter's Church was founded in AD 674 as a monastery by Benedict

Biscop (who later founded Jarrow as part of the combined monastery of St Peter and St Paul) when King Ecgfrith made him a grant of land on the north side of the river. All the Saxon work at St Peter's now to be seen is at the west end of the church. The chancel is mainly 14th century, while the north aisle was added in the 19th century. The west wall of the long, narrow nave may well have been erected in Benedict Biscop's time. The lower part of the tower probably dates from the 8th century, and its tunnel vault is the earliest in England. Above the doorway is a roundhead window over which are traces of a carving of the Crucifixion. The upper part of the tower is 10th- or 11th-century work. In the north transept is a collection of carved stonework of great beauty including two splendid lions.

A new chapter house was built in 1974 to commemorate the church's 1,300th anniversary, now the venue for an exhibition and film-show made by the vicar (*charge*) to which all visitors seem to be directed first. If you just want to see the church, turn right on entering and avoid it.

Saxon Church, St Peters, Sunderland

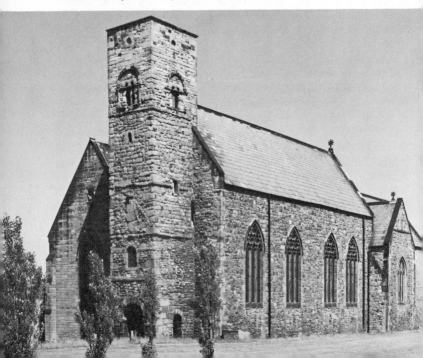

At the southern end of the Sunderland metropolis, 3 miles south of the Wearmouth Bridge following the A19 road, is the small village of **Ryhope** within ½ mile of the Durham boundary. The former **Ryhope Pumping Station**, a mid-Victorian water-pumping establishment that ceased providing for the public some ten years ago, has been turned into one of the best industrial monuments in the north-east. The Ryhope Engines Trust has turned the whole place into a museum where the public can watch the 1868 monsters working away. The maintenance and operation of the station is all done by voluntary labour and it is normally open at weekends from Easter to September. The museum has illustrations of water-pumping operations and traces the development of water-supply generally.

South-westwards from Sunderland, reached by the A690 road to Durham, lies **Houghton le Spring**, whose name, like that of its close neighbour Hetton-le-Hole, mixes Saxon and Norman French. Midway between Sunderland and Durham, Houghton le Spring has a number of old houses and a large and impressive-looking church – **St Michael and All Saints**. It was the home of the 'Apostle of the North', Bernard Gilpin, who was rector here from 1557 until his death in 1583 and who was celebrated for his love of the poor and various preaching tours well away from his parish. He inaugurated the annual Houghton Feast at which he gave a whole ox to be roasted and distributed throughout the parish. The custom is still celebrated today, usually on the first Friday in October.

The church, dating from the 13th century, has a south wall notable for its row of eight lancet windows. A passage leads into the two-storeyed and battlemented chapel of the Guild of the Holy Trinity, which dates from the late 15th century. In addition to two early monuments to knights the church contains the tomb chest of its famous rector as well.

Houghton le Spring is mainly a residential area nowadays and like many other former colliery areas, it has its 'new town' as well. To the south Hetton-le-Hole, and Easington Lane lie within the Tyne and Wear boundary, strung out along the A182 which runs north-westwards to join the A1(M) at Birtley. Just to the north is a large colliery area and the prominent landmark of **Penshaw Hill**, visible from many directions over several miles. It lies off the A183 road from Sunderland to Chester-le-Street, 4 miles from Sunderland and 2½ miles from Houghton le Spring. High above the Wear Valley, some 120m (400ft), the Greek Doric **Temple**, said to be a copy of the Temple of Thesis in Athens, is often regarded locally as part folly, part joke and part tribute. Erected in

1844 by local gentry in honour of John George Lambton, the 1st Earl of Durham, it was donated to the National Trust in 1939 by the 5th Earl of Durham. Although not listed as open in the National Trust's 1977 handbook, it can still be viewed outside the chain fence. Also lying to the west of Sunderland and reached by the A1231 road linking the port with the A1(M) motorway, are Hylton Castle and, what is probably the greatest draw for Americans visiting this country, the small but historically important village of Washington. Indeed, the area abounds with pre-1776 names, such as Philadelphia and Columbia both close by, and New York further north.

From Sunderland, across the Queen Alexandra Bridge, the A1231 follows the north side of the river Wear westwards. In less than 2 miles a right-hand turn leads to **Hylton Castle**, or it can also be reached via the A1290 from Southwick after crossing the Wear bridge. Surrounded by modern housing estates, this tower house castle was built about 1400 by William de Hylton to guard the deep dene approach to the river Wear against intrusions by the Scots. It was much altered in the 18th and 19th centuries. The house has a fine display of medieval heraldry, and on the front is a reproduction in stone of the Washington crest. Standing near to the castle is a 15th- to 16th-century chapel with half-octagonal transepts. The site is in the care of the Department of the Environment (*open DoE standard hours*), but only the exterior can be viewed.

From Hylton Castle the A1231 westwards quickly crosses the fast-moving dual carriageway road of the A108(T), the Tyne Tunnel–Teeside road, just north of the new Hylton Bridge which was opened in 1974 to cater for it. **Sunderland Airport** is just to the north of this junction, and 2 miles further west the outskirts of Washington's 'new town' are reached. The A1231 approaches the town along the Eastern Highway to Pattinson, and by approaching from the Sunderland side the entrance to the **Washington Waterfowl Park** is reached before the town on the left-hand side. It was founded by Sir Peter Scott in 1946, and the relatively new developments at Washington are still in the process of creation in conjunction with the Washington Development Corporation. The public is admitted to most of the area which lies between the river and the Sunderland expressway and covers about 40ha (100 acres) in all. The present collection is centred on about 12ha (30 acres) of pond area which are overlooked from the entrance building and where visitors can photograph birds at close quarters. Some of the more tame species can be fed by hand. The outer areas, where a series of nature trails are being laid out, provide the wilder refuges with a series of 'hides'. *The Waterfowl Park is open daily from 9.30 to 6.30 (or ¼ hour after sunset) with Sunday opening from 12.00 (Sunday mornings are reserved for Trust members).*

A mile further west along the expressway leads to the entrance road into the **Washington New Town** area. Consisting of a series of separate villages linked by footpaths and expressways with new industrial estates on the periphery, Washington nowadays is an expanding new town where some real attempt has been made for better living conditions. From the lead-in road, and just over ½ mile south of the turn-off, is a roundabout, where a left turn leads into the old village of **Washington** by the church, with the home of five generations of the ancestors of America's first President, George Washington, next-door.

Washington Old Hall was originally built in 1183 but largely rebuilt in 1610. In 1936 a preservation committee was set up which, aided by donations from both sides of the Atlantic, carried out a complete restoration. The house is now in the care of the National Trust, to whom it was transferred in 1956, and it contains a number of items connected with George Washington and the district in general. (*Open March to October, daily except Tuesdays 1–6, or sunset if earlier; November to February, Wednesdays, Saturdays and Sundays 1–6, or sunset if earlier.*)

The original owner of the house was a certain William de Hertburn, who came to Washington in 1183 and acquired the manor-house from the Bishop of Durham in return for services to the latter and, accordingly, changed his name to William de Wessyngton, which later became Washington. George Washington's grandfather was the man who emigrated to America in 1656, taking with him his coat-of-arms, containing the stars and stripes, which probably inspired the later American flag. There is a striking portrait of the President by John Trumbull of Salem painted on drum parchment.

South of Washington, seen from the road between North Biddick and Penshaw as well as the Washington expressway (A182), is the oldest bridge over the river Wear, the **Victoria Railway Bridge**, opened in 1838 and based on a Roman design. A mile away is the new bridge opened in 1975 to carry the Washington expressway (A182) across the river. Both now lie close to the Tyne and Wear boundary with Durham at this point.

North of Washington is an interesting industrial museum, the **Washington 'F' Pit Industrial Museum**, reached by returning to the A1231 Sunderland expressway and proceeding straight on at the roundabout into the Albany district. It lies along Windlass Lane, turning into

Albany Way. A decision was made in 1968 between the National Coal Board and the Washington Development Corporation to preserve the winding gear house and steam-engine of the Washington 'F' pit as a museum devoted to mining. In the museum a film-show records some of the former colliery activities: dug to a depth of almost 300m (1,000ft), it was one of the earliest pits in the country and was sunk in 1777. In its heyday it employed over 1,500 men and produced almost half a million tons of coal a year. (*Open weekdays 10–12 and Saturdays and Sundays 2–4, free.*)

Washington is less than 2 miles from the A1(M) motorway with excellent communications in all directions. A direct return to Gateshead and Newcastle can be made by following the A1231 westwards, joining the A182 Washington expressway northwards to the Birtley link with the A1(M) and the A194(M). From Sunderland another return to Newcastle can be made either by following the A19 northwards through the small residential village of Cleadon, at the foot of the Cleadon Hills, and into South Shields or by following the coast road (A183) northwards through Roker and Whitburn. Both routes can include a visit to the Roman fort of Arbeia at South Shields and St Paul's Church at Jarrow *en route*. On the Seaburn beach, just north of here, Lewis Carroll is said to have composed some of the lines of the 'Walrus and the Carpenter', while Roker's impressive church, built in 1906, is shaped in the form of an upturned keel.

Whitburn Bay follows, an attractive village with a 13th-century church which was drastically restored in 1865. There are a number of older houses around the green, but with 2½ miles of double yellow lines right along the front stopping is not encouraged. At the northern end of Whitburn Bay, where the road climbs across the isthmus of Souter Point, it is possible, but by that time the view has gone. Here, on the left is the now defunct **Whitburn Colliery**. The view begins to open out towards the north. Lizard Point with its red-striped lighthouse comes next, and both Tynemouth and the industrial towers at Lynemouth, far to the north, stand out on a clear day. So does the lighthouse on St Mary's Island, 7 sea miles away. Nearer at hand the South Pier runs out from South Shields, and topping the escarpment on the other side of the river is a foreboding range of modern buildings on the skyline called Knott's Flats.

Close by now is **Marsden Bay**, a nature reserve, where, at **Marsden Rock**, there is one of the principal bird sanctuaries between the Tyne and

Marsden Rock

Tees. Nearby is Marsden's famous **Grotto,** a fascinating one-man effort now turned into a public house and restaurant and reached nowadays by the convenience of a lift. Originally it was the work of a miner known affectionately as Jack the Blaster, who cut out a home for himself and his family among the caves in the limestone cliffs in 1782. It was later taken over and turned into a fifteen-room house. Marsden is close to the southern extremity of South Shields and it is but a short run into the centre of the town with a pleasant road along the front.

6) Hebburn, Jarrow and South Shields

From Gateshead the A184 road leads into **Felling**, where about the time of the Battle of Waterloo a terrible mine disaster took the lives of ninety-two people, who were buried in a mass grave just south at Heworth. Here, a left turn is made on to the A185 which runs along the south bank of the Tyne into **Hebburn**, where there are shipbuilding yards of Swan Hunter. This is an intense industrial area, but great efforts are being made at the present time to reclaim some of the riverside frontage and turn it back into promenades. Just south of Hebburn, at Monkton, is the site of **Bede's Well**, where it is said the monks from Jarrow came for their water.

Five and a half miles from Gateshead the A185 reaches the intersection of the A108 Tyne Tunnel road, with the tunnel entrance close by. The modern centre of **Jarrow** lies to the north of this junction, and much renovation has been carried out in recent years, with a new shopping centre, pedestrian precincts and a statue commemorating the Viking raids of AD 793–6. This is the town that became world-famous in the 30s when, in the intense depression of unemployment, hundreds of shipyard workers marched to London in the renowned 'Jarrow March' of 1936. It is a town that has seen much local sadness in the coal pits, for the Alfred Pit, the largest in the area which finally closed in 1845, claimed more than a hundred lives in its nineteen years of operation.

Half a mile to the east of modern Jarrow, continuing on the dual carriageway A185 towards South Shields, is the almost hidden site of **St Paul's Church** of Jarrow, the home of the Venerable Bede and, like its partner at Monkwearmouth, one of the most revered churches in the country. The A185 is conveniently sub-signed as the Bede Industrial Estate, and within ½ mile a left-hand turn is signposted to the church. After crossing the bridge over the trickling remains of the river Don, the Church is on the right by an open green.

Founded by Benedict Biscop in AD 681, the great monastery of St Paul was really part of the combined effort with Monkwearmouth and known better as the monastery of St Peter and St Paul. It was the home of the Venerable Bede, who lived and worked here for most of the next fifty-four years, writing some fifty ecclesiastical works on theology and many other subjects, including the most famous, his *History of the English Church and People* which tells us so much about the early Saxon developments in Northumbria. Undoubtedly, Bede was an exceptional scholar and was made both a deacon and a priest well ahead of the normal elapsed period of time.

Over the next three centuries the monastery was twice sacked by the Danes and later on destroyed by William the Conqueror in 1069, after the Bishop of Durham had fled there to escape the wrath of the Normans following the northern revolt. It was largely due to Bede's written work that Aldwin, the prior of Winchcombe in Gloucestershire, came north with two companions and started to rebuild the community. In 1083 both Jarrow and Monkwearmouth became cells of Durham and they maintained a monastic life until the dissolution. Since it had acted as a parish church, after 1536 it carried on in this capacity, and the rectors lived in the monastic foundation until 1715. Within fifty years of that time the church was in a very unsafe condition, and a new nave was built in 1782 which was replaced in 1866 by the present one, designed by Sir Gilbert Scott.

The best starting-point for a tour of the church is at the southern exterior, where the outlines of the second monastery of Prior Aldwin are visible. Inside, at the east end the original Saxon chapel, dedicated to St Mary and probably built in AD 681 with Roman stones, has survived as the chancel of the present church. Along the south wall is a Saxon aumbry and an ancient chair known as **Bede's Chair**. Some experts date it to the 14th century, but other tests suggest it may have survived from Saxon times. The four-stage tower dates from about 1075 and is a curious mixture of styles, for the third stage has a late Saxon double belfry window and then slopes inwards to form the square with Normal belfry windows. Above the tower arch is the original dedication stone of the church, still clearly bearing its Latin inscription, which marks the date as St George's Day, 23 April AD 681.

Opposite on the green stands the fine 18th-century house known as **Jarrow Hall**, now restored to provide exhibition room for some of the finds made by Professor Rosemary Cramp of Durham University – notably some Saxon glass and carved stones. There is an art centre here with varying exhibitions and a refreshment room. The annual Jarrow Lecture, which has been given every year since 1958, on a subject connected with the life of Bede, now takes place here.

From Jarrow to South Shields the A185 road winds its way around the Tyne Dock area eastwards, where it is joined by the A194 before running into the town. This latter road, branching off from the A1(M) at Birtley as the A194(M), still partly follows the line of the old Roman road of the Wrekendyke, which originally led from Wrekenton, close to Birtley, and headed straight for the Roman supply base at South Shields.

South Shields has fronts on both the river and North Sea coastline and grew into being from a very early settlement on the headland overlooking the estuary of the river Tyne. To the west are large shipbuilding and repair yards, while the eastern side offers a fine and long stretch of sandy beach. At its northern end is the long arm of the South Pier running out to meet its companion from Tynemouth. It is very much a seaside resort and caters extensively for visitors and, away from the main shopping area, it has a pleasant garden-suburb air about it, a wide open front with ample room to park, modern houses, green areas and trees. There seem to be plenty of local amusements, including the centre by **Gypsies Green**, and caravan parks at both extremes of the beach. The new leisure pool is situated in John Reid Road. There is also a metal art precinct.

Near the Pier Head is one of the earliest lifeboats, the *Tyne*, placed there as a monument to Willie Wouldhave, the parish clerk of St Hilda's Church, who dabbled in lifeboat design in his spare time. He received a prize of one guinea for his first design, the *Original*, but although it was the first one ever made with cork buoyancy and flotation tanks, no one seems to have been impressed at first. The **Lighthouse** at the end of the pier also attracts a number of visitors, for when it was being constructed in 1895 someone pressed a doll into the cement.

In the centre of the town, close to the Ferry Point across to North Shields, is the rebuilt market square. Here, the **Old Town Hall**, dating from 1768, faces **St Hilda's Church**, mainly of 19th-century design with a font created by Robert Trollope, who designed the Guildhall in Newcastle. The Town Hall was built on the site of the former medieval market-place where a market cross stood, and the shaft of this was incorporated into the building centre. Nowadays, on Saturdays and Sundays a lively open-air market takes place here.

One of the main attractions of South Shields is the well-preserved Roman fort of **Arbeia**, standing on a slope known as the Lawe at the north end of the town, signposted from the centre of the town. Although originally built as an extension of the line of Hadrian's Wall and linked to the fort at Wallsend by a series of signal stations, it very quickly changed its role to that of a major supply base, like Corbridge, backing up over a very short period of time the Roman invasion of Scotland. Built about AD 128, it guarded the Tyne entrance as well so that the Roman navy could bring up supplies from further south. The remains of some twenty-two granaries have been uncovered here, and they were certainly used in Severus' campaign against the Scots in AD 208.

By AD 220 South Shields reverted to living quarters with a slightly larger garrison being installed, and on the large site there are the well-preserved foundations of many buildings, including a strong room, barrack blocks, workshops and the headquarters building. The museum has reproductions of Roman steelyards and hanging balances and some interesting posters relating to the original discovery of the site. One of the most interesting finds is the superb tombstone, known as the **Regina Stone**, on which is depicted a woman in her armchair with her sewing basket and jewel box beside her. A freed Briton from the Catuvellauni tribe (mainly Hertfordshire), her husband and master was a Syrian from Palmyra, and the dual Latin and Palmyrene text, the Aramaic script reading from right to left, is the only example found in western Europe. Another stone, the **Victor Stone**, shows a Moorish freedman banqueting in paradise. His master, Numerianus, was a horseman in the 1st Ala of Asturians and erected the monument to him. Another notable item is a sword, with inlays depicting Mars in full armour, and its wooden scabbard.

The fort is set close to an impressive-looking Victorian school, and there is talk of further exploration after it has gone, which seems a pity as its façade seems worth preserving.

At the present time visible from the fort is **St Stephen's Church**, known locally as the 'fisherman's' or 'pilot's' church. Anyone not born close to the river bank was derisively known as a 'skate-ender'. Some opening up of the river frontage has occurred near here, and a road circles round the promontory back into South Shields.

Close to South Shields and really forming a part of it is the attractive village of **Westoe**, 1 mile south and now part of a conservation area. **Westoe Colliery** is one of the National Coal Board's high-production pits, extending under the North Sea and the subject of much reconstruction. It produces over a million tons of coal a year.

From South Shields a return to Newcastle can be made via the Tyne Tunnel road across to the north bank or a continuation made to Sunderland, 7 miles south.

21 The Roman Wall from Wallsend to Heddon-on-the-Wall

(For a historical introduction to the Roman Wall see page 191.)

In the new county of Tyne and Wear there are obviously far fewer Roman Wall remains than in Northumberland. The intensity of industrial and urban development has long since covered up most of the prime sites, and many of the original stones, based in this sector on a flag foundation course, have been removed for subsequent building operations. Yet, conversely, the finds made in the Newcastle area have been more than interesting, and great attempts are still being made to preserve them. Added to this is the fact that many worthwhile finds from the long stretch of Hadrian's Wall westwards have naturally gravitated into the local museums.

Originally, the Roman plan foresaw a wall stretching westwards from Newcastle, and it was only in the second phase of these building operations, when a sudden decision was made to cut the width of the broad Wall by (60cm) 2ft, that it was also decided to extend the Wall eastwards to Wallsend not only to survey the long reaches of the river Tyne from this point but to prevent infiltration from the north along the valleys of the Ouse Burn and Byker Burn in a way that would outflank the fort at Newcastle. To this extension must be added the fort of Arbeia, at South Shields, with a probable communication between the two by signal stations, thus not only guarding the river approaches from the sea but setting up a future supply base for later invasions of Scotland.

At **Wallsend**, a fort, shaped in the traditional playing-card shape with rounded corners, was erected with the name of Segedunum, and it had an extension wall to the south-east which went right down into the river. When the Swan, Hunter shipyards were enlarged in 1903, part of this wall was found and re-erected in **Wallsend Park**. The site of the fort was discovered in the 19th century, but a local appeal at that time failed to raise enough money to preserve it, and after some investigation the outline was marked in the streets between Wallsend Station and the river. Now, even this has gone, for the whole area is being redeveloped. Excavations are taking place during the summer months, but the visible remains are not extensive. The fort straddled Buddle Street, close to its junction with Station Road. It is thought to have had four double gates and a ditch around it, and some of the antiquities discovered here are now in **Wallsend Town Hall**. An associated *vicus*, or civilian settlement, grew up alongside along the river bank.

From Wallsend the line of the Wall went westwards, parallel to the main A187 road from Wallsend to Newcastle but slightly south of it where the suburb of Walker now lies. The line converges more or less with the A187 at Byker, where the A193 and the A187 meet by the Charles Dickens pub and the Roman Ditch gave rise to the name Fossway now found here. It aimed in the direction of Byker Hill and from there crossed the Ouse Burn by the point now known as Byker Bridge. From here it crossed the pattern of the many small streets between New Bridge Street and City Road, passing close to the junction of Buxton Street and Gibson Street and the Keelsmen's Hospital making directly for the now deconsecrated All Saint's Church. A milecastle site is thought to have been at the bottom end of Pilgrim Street, just where the modern A1 road enters the city from the Tyne Bridge, and although there is much conjecture on this point, the line of the Wall is presumed to have turned here towards the Roman fort of Pons Aelii, now represented by the Castle remains, and climbed the slope towards it, joining it at its north-east angle.

The Roman fort of **Pons Aelii**, named after the bridge across the Tyne, was discovered in 1929 when excavations revealed Roman buildings and a hypocaust heating system to the south and west of the Castle keep. It was a small fort, with its north frontage lying close to the Black Gate. Its main function was to cover the Tyne river crossing, and the Roman bridge erected there seems to have been so well built that it lasted right up to the 13th century. Even the new medieval bridge continued to use the original Roman foundations, which lay on the line of the present Swing Bridge. When the medieval bridge was replaced in 1775, the wooden piles and foundations of a Roman pier were still intact. A number of Roman coins were dredged up here, and when the Swing Bridge was built between 1866 and 1875, two altars were dredged up which were parts of the original bridge shrine.

From Newcastle westwards the line of Hadrian's Wall can be traced more easily, for it was the forerunner of the line of the Westgate Road, the main A69(T) road out of the city towards Benwell. The modern road traces the line of the Ditch on the north side of the Wall. Sometimes the modern road line crosses the northern Ditch, but few, if any, stones have been recovered in this sector. A milecastle site (No. 5) is indicated by the Westgate Cemetery at the junction of Corporation Street almost exactly 1 Roman mile from the bridge. At this point for the first time traces of the *Vallum* begin to be recorded, and evidence of both the northern Ditch and the *Vallum* on the south side of the road, close to the General Hospital, was noted in Victorian times.

The next main point of interest lies at **Benwell**, where the Roman fort of Condercum lay, and the site has been identified on top of a hill where a reservoir now lies, with the northern third of the fort's outline under this. The remainder is now part of the **Denhill Park** housing estate but was excavated to some degree both in 1926 and again in 1937, with the two most important parts being preserved. A dedication stone has been found, and the fort can be dated to a construction between AD 122 and 124 in the time of Aulus Platorius Nepos. The latter was the Governor of Britain at that time, charged by the Emperor Hadrian to build the Wall. The fort contained the usual headquarters' building, an underground strong-room cut out of solid rock, granaries and workshops and some evidence that local coal was used for heating. At the rear of the fort ran the *Vallum*, and at the foot of **Denhill Park Avenue** a section of this is preserved under the control of the Department of the Environment and is open at any reasonable time without charge. It is one of the best-preserved examples anywhere along the Wall of the *Vallum* together with its associated causeway that led into every fort. Here, too, the *Vallum* bent southwards to avoid the fort. Nearby, in **Broomridge Avenue** and indicated by a signpost from the main road opposite to the school, is a Roman temple dedicated to Antenocitius. The site is cared for by the Department of the Environment and is open at any reasonable time without charge.

The Wall continues along the line of the main road out of the city, and some 300m west of the fort a turret site (No. 6b) was discovered in the 18th century, just before the junction northwards along Two Ball Lonen. Further along, descending Denton Bank, is the first real fragment of the Wall itself, excavated in 1927. It lies close to **Denton Burn** on the south side of the road just past the junction of the A69(T) and the A191. Further along, and 100m short of Denton Hall, is **Turret 7B**, known as the **Denton Hall Turret**, which is recessed into the Wall, some adjacent lengths of which are also preserved. It is bonded on to the broad Wall width of 3m (10ft) and is the only visible example of a turret of this size bonded with the same width foundation. Just to the south of Denton Hall the line of the *Vallum* has also been traced. The site is in the care of the Department of the Environment and is open at any reasonable time without charge.

At **West Denton** another portion of the Wall is also in the care of the Department of the Environment (open at any reasonable time without charge), and parts of the *Vallum* are visible close to the West Denton roundabout, where the A69(T) swings off to bypass Throckley. Here, the B6528 road continues more or less straight on, following the line of the Wall. Up to this point the *Vallum* has been about 200m to the south of the Wall but now it converges to a distance of about 50m and remains there for several miles.

Ascending the hill from West Denton, still following the B6528, some signs of the Ditch are visible on the north side of the road, but the *Vallum* has been largely ploughed over. Some crossings, however, are identifiable close to Walbottle School. In 1928 **Milecastle 10** was excavated with its wall matching the broad Wall close to **Warbottle Dean House**. A slight turn in alignment occurs here as the Wall aims for Bank Top by Throckley, where Milecastle 11 stood, and on for the hill by Heddon-on-the-Wall. At the site of **Milecastle 11** a hoard of over 5,000 silver coins dating from AD 244–75 was found in 1879. The Wall also appears to have been broken through and destroyed here at some time, then rebuilt to a narrower width between the two known gauges. Entering **Heddon-on-the-Wall**, the B6528 road diverges from the line of the Wall, but the B6318 takes over. Here a section of Wall about 100m long is in the care of the Department of the Environment and is open at any reasonable time without charge. A medieval limekiln has intruded on the remains, and just to the east of this point, on the summit of the hill, the rock-cut *Vallum* can be seen, very close to the meeting-point of the boundaries of Tyne and Wear with Northumberland. (*For the continuation of route and the section of the Roman Wall from Heddon-on-the-Wall to Gilsland see page 191.*)

Part III: County Durham
by Hilda and Noel Turnbull

County Durham, which today has been overshadowed by its neighbour-ing giants Tyne and Wear and Cleveland, is one of Britain's secretive counties, a much maligned area which has been the victim of grave errors of imagery particularly at the hands of the media. It is the only county in England to retain in an Irish fashion the prefix County, and this is only one of Durham's unique characteristics.

Though Durham's prosperity was founded on the rich coal-seams beneath its fertile lands, the county has a history almost as old as man. Compared to other northern counties evidence of prehistoric man is scant, though important finds, such as the Bronze Age treasures disco-vered in Heathery Burn Cave near Stanhope and now in the British Museum, are proof enough that the dense forests and bleak moorland and valleys of prehistoric County Durham were inhabited.

The Roman occupation of the county is better documented owing largely to the presence of Dere Street, the Roman road which linked York with Hadrian's Wall, running through the heart of County Durham where there is still evidence of important forts at Piercebridge, Binches-ter, Lanchester and Ebchester.

The county of Durham played a major role in Northumbria's 'Golden Age' when Christianity was cradled at such centres as Chester-le-Street, the resting place for 113 years of St Cuthbert's coffin during the monks' flight from the marauding Danes, and St Peter's at Monkwearmouth, Sunderland and St Paul's at Jarrow, work places of the Venerable Bede now, sadly for County Durham, engulfed by the new county of Tyne and Wear.

Durham is rightly proud of her churches – the Saxon church at Escomb, one of the best preserved in the country, St Hilda's at Hartlepool and the lovely ruins of Finchale Priory. But Durham's most noteworthy claim to ecclesiastical fame undoubtedly lies on a loop in the meandering

Prebends Bridge and Mill house, on the Wear

river in the city of Durham where the majestic Norman cathedral has had heaped upon it throughout the centuries every superlative description worthy of such a masterpiece. Popularly regarded by layman and scholar as one of the finest examples of Norman architecture in Europe, Durham Cathedral has received saints and monks, royalty and bishops, refugees from the law, pilgrims and nowadays tourists by the thousand without losing its dignity and reverence.

Though some 75 miles from today's border with Scotland, County Durham and the city, in particular, were fully embroiled in the wars of the Debatable Lands. Durham Castle and other magnificent bastions in the county at Lumley, Brancepeth and Raby were all strategic strongholds which still stand today as witness of those bloodthirsty times. Even Durham's mighty cathedral fell victim of Border raids, being described by Sir Walter Scott as 'half church of God, half Castle 'gainst the Scot'.

History of a very different nature was born in County Durham in the 18th century. Prospectors were aware of Durham's reserves of coal as early as the 14th century, but it was not until the early 1700s that the black gold began to be exploited. The coalmining industry grew slowly at first largely because of the seemingly insurmountable problem of transporting coal from the bleak rugged lands in the west of the county to the coast. In 1825 Stephenson's *Locomotion* was to change all that. The success of the railways meant that most of County Durham could be disembowelled in search of the priceless fuel. By and large this development was the undoing of County Durham's image. The ravages and despoliation brought about by the mining industry and the subsequent development of other heavy industries dependent upon nearby sources of fuel have remained as the most popular image of County Durham. Yet in spite of this grim picture, the county possesses physical beauty unsurpassed anywhere in Britain.

The coastline and eastern border, following local government reorganisation, have come under 'attack' from the north by Tyne and Wear County and from the south by Cleveland County, so much so that such towns as Sunderland in the north and Hartlepool in the south are now no longer part of County Durham, though the majority of the inhabitants of both towns still seem to regard themselves as such. And in spite of the coastal ravages of the coal industry, there are stretches of coastline of firm clean sands as bracing as anywhere on the east coast of Britain. Radiating from the coastline of Durham are several unique denes, the most notable being Castle Eden Dene which today is almost lost in the modern development of Peterlee New Town. It is, nevertheless, County Durham's own paradise, a haven of wildlife and beauty.

In the 19th-century 'coal rush' the lands of mid and west Durham were littered with the 'props' of coalmining. Nowadays, as mechanization has meant the large-scale closure of small pits and the shift to ultra-modern workings on the coastal plain, mid and west Durham have reverted to their rural splendour which in fact has always been there. The county's two major rivers, though no longer exclusive to County Durham, the Wear and the Tees, meander through rich valleys bestowing a different face upon the county with almost every mile. Like County Durham's neighbours the county's industries have relied, and still do, on the rivers, and, consequently, urban development with one or two exceptions is still clustered around river mouths. Today, most of that urbanization is in the new counties of Tyne and Wear and Cleveland leaving County Durham almost exclusively rural.

County Durham is a land full of surprises. Where else in the world could you be on the outskirts of a dales market town and stumble upon a magnificent French château? Such is the surprise in store at Barnard Castle where the Bowes Museum is a veritable treasure-house which would be more at home in one of the great capitals of Europe. In complete contrast a stroll in Castle Eden Dene might lead you to catch a glimpse of the beautiful delicate argus butterfly found nowhere else in the world. And if you are driving in the vicinity of Ireshopeburn in Weardale almost any night of the week, don't be surprised to see a group of spur-clad cowboys. They will more than likely be a group of Wearsiders out for a night at the Rancho del Rio, an authentic Wild West evening set amid the hills of County Durham and just another example of the unique character of Britain's least known county.

22 The Derwent Valley:
Shotley Bridge – Derwent Reservoir – Blanchland – Consett – Lanchester – Beamish

From industrial Tyneside the A694 follows the meandering river Derwent south-westwards through Rowlands Gill, past Gibside Chapel and on to Ebchester. Upstream from the bridge the Roman road from York – Dere Street – crosses the River Derwent on its way northwards to Hadrian's Wall. The vulnerable river crossing was guarded in Roman times by Vindomora fort which covered 1·7ha (4 acres). At the southern edge of the site of the Roman fort stands Ebchester's Norman church built largely with Roman stone. On an interior tower wall can be seen a Roman carving of a fish and an eagle.

East of the village lies the hamlet of **Hamsterley**, home of the famous 19th-century literary figure Robert Smith Surtees, who created the celebrated hunting grocer, Jorrocks. Hamsterley Hall was also the childhood home of Field-Marshall Viscount Gort, V.C. At Ebchester the banks of the Derwent are at their loveliest, and some 4·5ha (10 acres) are owned by the National Trust. One of the newest amenities in the area is the **Derwent Walk** which follows the disused Derwent Valley Railway line for some 10½ miles from Swalwell to Blackhill in Consett. The 100-year-old line provides footpath, bridleway and cycle-track through wooded countryside abounding in animal and bird life. Two viaducts spanning the river Derwent and two others crossing steep ravines have been retained. Some of the station yards are being laid out as picnic areas. Ebchester Station, on the B6309 south of the village, is such a picnic area, and a signal cabin has been converted into an information centre. Several interesting buildings lie along the Derwent Walk, including Old Hollinside Manor, above Haugh Bank Wood comprising the remains of a late 13th-century pele tower and manor-house; Gibside Chapel; Friarside Chapel, founded in 1150 near a ruin situated in a field west of the walk and ¼ mile south of Rowland's Gill viaduct; Derwentcote, between Hamsterley and Hamsterley Mill on the west side of the A694 comprising a cementation furnace, the hub of the area's early steel-making industry, in use until 1880.

The Derwent Walk is an integral part of a 117ha (290-acre) country park which encompasses Thornley and Paddock Hill Woods between Rowland's Gill and Winlaton Mill together with Derwent Park at Rowland's Gill, where there is a caravan site, and Haugh Bank Wood.

The A694 continues to **Shotley Bridge** where the fast-rushing river Derwent provided power for the famous Shotley Swordmakers who made the town their home after fleeing from Solingen, in Germany, in 1687, victims of religious persecution. Cutlers Hall was built by William Oley, one of the most famous swordmakers in 1787, and today there remains the Crown and Crossed Swords Inn as a reminder of Shotley Bridge's former industry.

The area occupied by the cricket ground was once known as Shotley Spa, popular in the 18th and 19th centuries with such notables as Charles Dickens. From Shotley Bridge the A691 crosses the river Derwent and climbs steeply before crossing the A68 main through route north–south with fine views of the North Pennines and **Derwent Reservoir**. From **Edmondbyers**, a typical Durham moorland village with an interesting church founded in 1150 and a youth hostel, the B6306 road skirts the reservoir which provides excellent amenities for the visitor.

The B6306 road descends sharply 1½ miles west of Carrick's picnic site to cross into Northumberland by an old stone bridge and enter **Blanchland**, Northumbria's most famous 'model village', where despite a growing popularity the grey-stone buildings retain their timeless beauty (see under Hexham). From Blanchland an unclassified road leads over some of the most spectacular moorland scenery in Britain linking with the B6278 from Edmondbyers over **Stanhope Common**. Here and there the heathery moorland is broken by the scars of an industry which took a tremendous toll on the dales people of the 18th and 19th centuries – leadmining. Dale-hopping over Stanhope Common, the road descends steeply to join the A689 at Stanhope in Weardale.

From Shotley Bridge an alternative route (A691) leads to a completely contrasting face of Northumbria – industrial Northumbria. **Consett**'s skyline is dominated by the lofty chimneys of one of the most famous ironworks in the world. Consett Steelworks were founded in 1837, and within two years the Derwent Iron Company was born to capitalize upon the discovery of ironstone by John Nicholson. In those humble times the town's population was little more than 200. Today more than

10,000 people are employed in the iron, steel and ancillary industries.

With such a short existence there is consequently a dearth of historic interest in Consett's buildings. Of the modern architecture the Roman Catholic **Church of St Patrick**, built in 1959, has many admirers. Though the air in Consett is heavily laden with the grime of industry, the town boasts attractive parks and other modern amenities, and the moorland fresh Pennine slopes are close at hand. It is also famous as the home of the world's first Salvation Army Band, founded in 1879.

At the meeting of the A692, A691 and the B6309 a mile or so to the east of the centre of Consett stands the village of **Leadgate** where the most notable building is the 19th-century church dedicated to St Ives, who is also commemorated in the village of Iveston 1 mile to the south. The hamlet was founded on the coal industry, a mine being sunk as early as 1728.

Bypassing Iveston, the A691 continues east to **Lanchester**, a village whose history dates back to Roman times. The origins of the village lie on a hill to the west where a Roman fort was built at a strategic point on the main north–south Roman road – Dere Street – running from York to Hadrian's Wall. **Longovicium**, as the fort was named, was built in AD 122, at the same time as construction of Hadrian's Wall began. The fort housed infantry and cavalry until it was destroyed in AD 197. It was subsequently restored in AD 240 and was in use until the end of the Roman occupation in the 4th century.

Remains of the fort were visible as recently as the 18th century when stone from walls, temples, bath-houses and barracks were plundered for the construction of farm buildings and dwelling-houses. Several Roman altars were saved and can be seen in Durham Cathedral, and a further altar stone is preserved in the porch of Lanchester church which also benefited from Roman stonework during its construction. The **Church of All Saints** dominates the spacious village green and dates from the Norman and early English periods. Of particular architectural interest are the beautiful Norman chancel arch, the 13th-century chancel and three excellent pieces of stained glass, dating from the same century, which can be seen in the south window of the chancel. Among the notables buried in Lanchester is Dr William Greenwell, the eminent historian and archaeologist, a canon of Durham Cathedral whose avid pursuit of the art of angling resulted in his name being given to one of the most famous of all fishing flies – Greenwell's Glory. He was buried in Lanchester churchyard in 1919 at the age of ninety-seven. From Lanchester the A6076 and the A693 lead northwards to **Stanley** on the outskirts of which can be found the new Harperley Country Park and caravan site and the internationally important North of England Open Air Museum at Beamish.

Today Stanley gives an impression of a typically bustling and modern north-west Durham town, but its history stretches back to Roman times. Archaeologists have discovered remains of a 2nd- and 3rd-century cattle camp, though nothing can be seen today. It is also known that a Roman causeway ran from Stanley to South Shields, a supply base on the south side of the Tyne estuary. Today modern roads follow this route, which was known as Wrekendyke. Stanley's rise to importance was due entirely to the rich coal-seams first discovered in the early 18th century. On 16 February 1909 one of the Durham coalfield's worst disasters occurred at West Stanley Colliery when an explosion claimed the lives of 168 men and boys. A monument to the tragic loss can be seen at the entrance to East Stanley cemetery.

There are few ancient buildings in the town, the churches being typically 19th and 20th century. Most recent acquisitions are the award-winning swimming-pool and remedial baths and pleasant pedestrian shopping centre. The town is also well served by parks and playing fields, two nearby golf-courses and a greyhound-racing stadium.

Following the A693 eastwards through Stanley, signs divert the visitor to the **North of England Open Air Museum** at **Beamish** (*open Easter to end September daily, except Mondays, but open Bank Holidays; October to Easter reduced opening hours*). Since its birth in 1970 the Beamish Museum has become a major international attraction, a living record of a past way of life. Old buildings from all parts of the region have been carefully demolished brick by brick, painstakingly rebuilt on site and finally equipped with furnishings and machinery to recreate the original scene authentically. The site, measuring $\frac{3}{4}$ mile by $\frac{1}{2}$ mile, is set in undulating woodland and meadow. The area has been divided into various sections, each devoted to a particular industry or aspect of Northumbria's heritage. At Home Farm the early days of agriculture are recreated; a small colliery and winding engine are permanent reminders of County Durham's debt to coal. A row of pitmen's cottages, dating from the 19th century, paint a perfect picture of life in those hard times. The region's transport history too is highlighted. In Northumbria railways as a form of freight and passenger transport were born. At Beamish Museum a full-size, in-steam replica of *Locomotion*, the engine built by pioneer George Stephenson, can often be seen, sometimes in steam. The

The kitchen range, Miner's cottage, Beamish Open Air Museum

original engine has recently found a permanent home at the North Road Station Museum, Darlington.

The transport collection is varied indeed. Other exhibits range from a hearse from Weardale and a gypsy caravan to several old engines from the Durham County fire brigade and a Gateshead No. 10 tram on which visitors can usually enjoy a nostalgic ride around the site during the summer. Several unique exhibits are worthy of note. Particularly striking is an enormous steam navvy, the largest single item in the collection. This gigantic 'shovel' was built in 1931 and is the only one in existence today capable of being steamed. The navvy is steamed back to life regularly throughout the year.

That Beamish Museum is 'living' is obvious. That it will continue to grow for many years to come is equally clear. Latest developments include the complete reconstruction of Rowley Railway Station which was originally built near Consett in 1867. The station forms the nucleus of what will eventually be a complete railway centre. Plans are already laid to recreate a complete town at Beamish with the nostalgic sights, sounds and even smells, like home-made bread, that are sure to bring back memories of yesteryear.

Though the Open Air Museum is reason enough to visit Beamish, the predominantly 19th-century **Beamish Hall** is an added attraction. Today a large portion of the hall is devoted to a popular introductory exhibition – an A to Z of objects which the museum has acquired and which eventually will be housed in the reconstructed buildings. The exhibition comprises a bewildering array of everyday objects from a beautiful Durham quilt to a very early vacuum cleaner. The building itself is architecturally and historically interesting. It is recorded that a house has occupied the site since 1268 when Guiscard de Charron, a Norman Knight, lived here. His granddaughter married Bartram Monboucher, and five successive Monbouchers owned the manor of Beamish. Through intermarriages the estate passed to various families, the most notable being the Edens, well known in County Durham, and subsequently the Shaftos. Bobby Shafto, of sea-shanty fame, is remembered in the recreated pub within the hall named after him which is Victorian in every way except for prices. Other reconstructions in the hall include a Victorian schoolroom, a chemist shop and tea-room.

Because Beamish will never be complete it is possible to visit the site over and over again. New developments are continually being opened to the public providing a source of wonder for the young and a taste of pure nostalgia for the not so young.

From Beamish it is a short drive eastwards on the A693 to Chester-le-Street and the A1(M). Steps can be retraced south west on the A693 and A6076 to Lanchester and then on the B6296 to Wolsingham and Weardale.

23 The Wear Valley:
Alston – Stanhope – Wolsingham – Bishop Auckland – Witton le Wear

Few dales in England are as secretive as Weardale. County Durham's greatest river wends its way, first as a young burn, cradled by the high Pennines, then gaining strength and meandering south-eastwards beyond Wolsingham. On reaching Durham City the Wear takes on a majesty befitting its presence in the shadows of the Norman architecture of Durham Cathedral. The final miles of its course take it through clanking shipyards and so to the sea at Sunderland.

From Alston in Cumbria, England's highest market town, the A689 crosses the border into County Durham. Peaty burns – the Burnhope and the Killhope – collect the waters of innumerable hillside streams, and the Wear is born not unnaturally at Wearhead. The A689 accompanies the Wear through such villages as Ireshopeburn, St John's Chapel and Daddry Shield. On through the popular holiday centres of Westgate and Eastgate, as the river grows in size so hamlet becomes village: grey-stoned Stanhope ('Stannup') and Frosterley, famous for its unique marble, and ancient Wolsingham. From Wolsingham the A689 continues south-east along the river bank to cross the A68 through route which continues south to Witton le Wear, a popular playground for young and old.

Wolsingham, as gateway to Weardale, is serviced with several other roads from the east. The A689, having crossed the A68, continues east through Crook, Willington and Brancepeth and on to Durham City. The B6296 travels northwards from Wolsingham to link with the A691 Durham City road at Lanchester.

Alston

Bowls At Fairhill.
Buses Nenthead, Haydon Bridge, Hexham, Newcastle, Keswick.
Distances Newcastle, 45 miles; Hexham, 24 miles; Penrith, 19 miles; Scotch Corner, 45 miles; Carlisle, 29 miles.
Early closing Tuesday.
Fishing Licences from D. & B. Middleton, Front Street.
Golf *Alston Golf-Club.*

Hotels *George and Dragon*, Garrigill, *Hillcrest, Cumberland, Lowbyer Manor, Victoria.*
Information Office Railway Station, tel. 696.
Library County Library, Town Hall, Alston.
Population 2,000.
Post Office Alston, tel. 216.
Tennis At Fairhill.

Renowned as the highest market town in England, **Alston** stands proud on windswept moors, almost 300m (1,000ft) above sea-level. An extremely popular centre for walkers and hikers, the town is situated on the Pennine Way which a few miles further south crosses the highest peak in the Pennine chain at Cross Fell (879m, 2,930ft). The Way descends to Garrigill to pick up the B6277 which leads to Alston.

The history of Alston dates back to prehistoric times, gaining in importance during the Roman occupation when the town was established as a mining centre. Mining of several metals continued until the 19th century, during which time a harvest of lead, iron, copper, silver and other ores was reaped from the virtually barren hillsides. Today, the pace is slow, and the wide-spaced, cobbled market-place has changed little with the passing of centuries. In contrast to the spacious market square narrow, secretive streets radiate in all directions, accommodating several antique shops and traditional food stores. Of particular interest is '**Ye Olde Bottle Shop**', an Aladdin's cave specializing in the buying, selling and exchanging of old bottles. The market square is dominated by a market house with stone pillars which shelter an ancient cross. Nearby is the Friends' Meeting House which dates from 1732.

From Alston the A689 climbs steeply into the peat-clad hillside crossing the river Nent and in 5 miles reaches **Nenthead**. Picturesque in its remoteness, the village was built in the 19th century to accommodate the region's leadminers. Today the village's only claim to fame relates to its lofty site. Perched 600m (2,000ft) high in The Pennines, the village claims to have the highest church in England. It is believed there is an underground canal linking the village with Alston. The A689 continues east over deserted moorland which is excellent walking country, but beware of bogs hidden among the heather.

Three-quarters of a mile east of Nenthead the A689 reaches a height of 617m (2,056ft), the highest point of any major road in England. In a further mile the road descends in the shadows of one of the most striking reminders of Weardale's leadmining history – the **Killhope Wheel**. The mine remains, which dominate the picnic area, date from the 1860s. The wheel measures almost 12m (40ft) in diameter and provided power for the machines which crushed and washed the ore before it was transported by horse to be smelted at Allenheads.

During the late 18th and early 19th centuries Weardale was booming thanks to the presence of iron ore. Today, the valley is still littered with the hardware of leadmining. Derelict mines and miners' cottages are dotted along the entire length of the valley. The lead ore consisted of galena (lead and sulphur) mixed with other materials and impurities. Because of the unpredictable nature of the veins many shafts had to be worked on different levels. The initial process was to wash the ore to separate it from the impurities. This was carried out at the mine to reduce transportation costs, but smelting to remove the sulphur from the pure lead had to be done further afield. The pure lead in turn was taken to market at Newcastle upon Tyne or Stockton-on-Tees. The rise and fall of Weardale's leadmining industry was relatively brief. Soon after the construction of the workings at Killhope cheaper lead began to be introduced from abroad, and many leadmining families deserted the area to work in the ironworks and collieries further down the dale. Some families emigrated to North America. The Killhope Wheel complex has recently been restored by Durham County Council and in addition to the relics there is a sheltered picnic site and toilets.

Continuing east, the A689 is joined by the B6295 from Allenheads at **Lanehead**. The village is typically stone built and is the centre of an area of intensely productive farming land. From Lanehead several excellent moorland walks of varying degrees of difficulty radiate. To the west of the village a programme of afforestation is being carried out which will add yet another dimension to the stark, severe landscape.

On the eastern outskirts of Lanehead at Burtree Ford an unclassified road south leads in a mile or so to the Burnhope Reservoir, opened in 1937. The road then links up again with the A689 further east at Wearhead. As the name suggests, the village marks the spot where the river Wear is born. To the south-west towers the mighty **Burnhope Seat** which rises to a height of 736m (2,452ft), the highest point in County Durham. Less than 1 mile from Wearhead lies **Ireshopeburn** where a thorn tree, next to High House Chapel, commemorates the spot where John Wesley preached in 1749. The village's former school house has been imaginatively converted into a Wild-West centre – The Rancho del Rio – an entertainment and dining complex giving a taste of the American Wild West. From Ireshopeburn there is a walk to Burnhope Reservoir with panoramic views of the valley below.

Continuing east, a further reminder of the dale's intense occupation with religion can be found in the name of the village of **St John's Chapel** whose parish church is dedicated to St John the Baptist. The original chapel was founded in 1465 and rebuilt in 1752. The old building was replaced between 1881 and 1883 by the church which stands today. Of the many walks in the vicinity treks to **Chapel Dene** or the waterfalls at **Currah's Wood** are well-worth taking. Southwards from the village a moorland road climbs high over **Harthope Fell** (617m, 2,056ft) before descending again into Teesdale. Continuing east, the A689 passes several villages within a few miles. **Daddry Shield**, with its adjacent hamlets of Sidefoot and Sidehead, was once the centre of the sport of cock-fighting.

Westgate and **Eastgate** are interesting villages, the former being the site of the Bishop of Durham's castle and the latter named after the eastern entrance to the Old Park which was a popular hunting-course for a succession of bishops. At **High Westgate** foundations of the bishop's castle can be seen. Remains of an old mill and water-wheel are still visible, and there are several waterfalls at **Slitwood**. The village church is dedicated to St Andrew, the parish having been founded in 1867. In 1870 a hoard of Roman coins was dug up which may have some connection with a Roman altar found near Low Linn Falls on the Rookhope Burn, which is crossed by the A689 at Eastgate where it flows into the Wear. The altar was dedicated to Silvanus by the Prefect Aurelius Quirinus, who commanded the first cohort of Ligones at nearby Lanchester.

Prior to the 16th century some 200 deer were kept in Weardale Park which was bordered by today's Eastgate and Westgate. In Weardale Park in 1327 Edward III's army camped for almost a month while in conflict with the Scots. While the English attempted unsuccessfully to engage the Scots in battle, the latter apparently enjoyed themselves stealing and plundering, particularly the prime cattle of Weardale. They spent the time using the excellent hides to manufacture shoes, and when they retreated they left behind them more than 10,000 worn-out pairs of footwear.

Both Eastgate and Westgate are excellent centres for touring Weardale, and there is varied accommodation including caravan sites, camp sites, farmhouse and bed-and-breakfast accommodation. The scenery is rugged and varied, and the only blot on the spectacular landscape is the ugly and controversial cement plant, situated at the side of the A689, which can be seen for miles around.

From Eastgate the river Wear begins to grow in stature as civilization becomes more abundant. **Stanhope** is a market town regarded as the capital of Weardale and the gateway to Upper Weardale. The town's name is derived from the Celtic meaning 'stony valley'. Here in the shelter of the rolling hills the Stanhope Burn flows into the Wear. Another tributary, the Heathery Burn, leads to the site of one of the most important Bronze Age discoveries of all time. In Heathery Burn Cave the almost entire possessions of a Bronze Age family were discovered during the 19th century. The collection is now in the British Museum.

The hub of Stanhope is the market-place complete with stone cross, a reminder of the town's market held from 1421 until the turn of the 19th century. On the south side the battlements of **Stanhope Castle**, built in 1798 on the site of an earlier fortress, can be seen. The castle is now a school. Tall lime trees line the main street, and the **Church of St Thomas** dates from the 13th century. The church contains many interesting relics including some medieval glass. In the vestry is a Roman altar, and there are several medieval grave covers. Much older is the extremely detailed fossilized tree stump which is believed to be 250 million years old and was unearthed near Edmondbyers. It stands at the gateway to the church.

At Stanhope the Wear Valley maintains its reputation as a walkers' paradise. From the new swimming-pool a riverside walk leads to stepping-stones across the river to Unthank Hall, an Elizabethan farmhouse. Upstream is an early 15th-century bridge.

From Stanhope the A689 continues to skirt the river Wear with Weardale's radio and television masts dominating the skyline to the north. In three miles the road enters the village of **Frosterley** which is famous for its marble. The town is believed to have derived its name from the Bishop's forest which formerly covered the area with the Forresters' Arms adding further weight to this derivation. Frosterley was mentioned in Durham's own 'Domesday Book', the *Boldon Beuk* of 1183. At the nearby hamlet of **White Kirkley** there are remains of the arches of a Saxon church. St Michael's Church is of much more recent design having been built in 1866. Frosterley's real claim to fame is the 'marble' still to be found near the Bollihope Burn which flows into the Wear, east of the village. The marble is a unique black limestone impregnated with myriads of fossils. The stone has found its way into churches throughout the world, including Durham Cathedral. From Frosterley an old stone bridge carries an unclassified road over the river to link with the B6278 from Stanhope over Middleton Common to Teesdale.

From Frosterley eastwards the river Wear gains in strength and spreads its banks at **Wolsingham** which stands at the eastern entrance to Weardale. The town is steeped in antiquity, having been established in Saxon times. Wolsingham was one of the original eight market towns in County Durham, a weekly market being established as early as 1506.

Although almost completely rebuilt in the 19th century, the parish church was founded before 1200. Norman remains include a remarkable arch and the lower section of the tower. Close to the church are the Chapel Walls, high grassy mounds reputed to have been moated, complete with drawbridge. Their history is obscure, although it is believed that the area was the site of a Bishop's hunting-lodge destroyed by Scots in 1316. Wolsingham boasts many interesting buildings. The grammar school dates from 1614, while the town hall was built in the 19th century.

The dale hereabouts continues to provide excellent walking country. Two miles upstream of Waskerley Beck lies **Tunstall Reservoir**, below which stands **Bail Hill**, a former pele tower inhabited by the bishop's bailiff. The Wolsingham and Wear Valley Agricultural Show, known locally as 'Ye Olde Showe', still takes place usually during the first week-end in September. It is reputed to be the oldest agricultural show in the country. In contrast modern amenities include two picnic areas, varied accommodation and catering facilities.

From Wolsingham the B6296 runs north to Lanchester, while the A689 continues to follow the Wear for a further 2 miles before leaving the river's course as it turns south. The road then crosses the main A68, leaving the dale's rural splendour behind as it enters the town of **Crook**. The town has little of historic interest but has an air of spaciousness. Its name is derived either from the bend or crook in the Beechburn Beck, which flows through the town before joining the Wear, or from the name Crok or Croke, a well-known local family name.

The wide market square is dominated by the **Church of St Catherine**, built in early English style as recently as 1842. The Roman Catholic Church, built a year later in Perpendicular style, stands on Church Hill. The market-place is locally known as the green, having been common grazing land. In the market-place stands the **Devil's Stone**, also known as the 'Blue Stone', which is a stranger to the geology of the area and is believed to have been brought from the Lake District, though the reason is obscure. On the northern outskirts of Crook the land rises to over 300m (1,000ft) on Dowfield Hill and Mount Pleasant with panoramic views of the town centre and beyond.

From Crook the A690 continues eastwards through Willington before veering north through Brandon and Byshottles and into Durham City. **Willington** is a typical County Durham town whose fortunes were founded on coal mined at nearby Brancepeth Colliery. Today, the dereliction left when the colliery closed has been cleared for the benefit of both resident and visitor.

There are several excellent walks within easy distance of Willington. The road to the hamlet of **Hunwick** is particularly picturesque. Three miles east of Willington stands the magnificent **Brancepeth Castle**, whose future at the time of writing is uncertain. Currently in private ownership, the castle is the ancestral home of the Boyne family and has a

Escomb Church

history dating from Saxon times. Other residents in the castle's long history were the Bulmers and the Nevilles who lived here in preference to Raby Castle near Staindrop. The castle was rebuilt after coming into the possession of William Russell and his son in 1796. Russell, who came from Sunderland, was a banker whose fortunes were founded on Durham coal. In 1828, following a marriage, Viscount Boyne came into possession of the castle, and almost 100 years later in 1927 it became the headquarters of the Durham Light Infantry. **Brancepeth Church** is equally fascinating. With a tower dating from 1240 and a 13th-century nave, the church is most noted for its 17th-century woodwork. From Brancepeth the A690 runs north-east through a predominantly built-up area before the lofty towers of Durham Cathedral come into view on the city's outskirts.

The A689 from Crook to **Bishop Auckland**, home of the Bishop of Durham since the 12th century, skirts Pixley Hill following the line of the Beechburn Beck as it flows south on its way to join the Wear just west of Bishop Auckland. The town stands high above the river Wear which is spanned to the west by a 15th-century bridge and a 19th-century railway viaduct. The market-place is wide, spacious and bustling, particularly on market days when modern shops contrast with traditional market stalls.

The history of Bishop Auckland goes back to Roman times. Today's Newgate Street follows the line of the Roman road Dere Street, which ran from York to Hadrian's Wall. At nearby **Binchester** the remains of the Roman fort of **Vinovia** ('Pleasant Spot') have been excavated. Regrettably (but understandably) **Auckland Palace**, the Bishop of Durham's residence, is private, though it is possible to visit the Palace Park and deer shelter situated 300m north-east of the castle. It was built in 1760 and is a fine example of the Gothic architecture of the period. The 324ha (800-acre) demesne in which the castle is situated contains parkland which is well endowed with trees and is breached by the river Gaunless, yet another water which gives strength to the Wear. Bishop Auckland's **Church of St Andrew** is said to be the largest parish church in County Durham. Saxon and Norman remains are to be found in the fabric.

The villages surrounding Bishop Auckland all have their own story to tell. Most notable is **Escomb**, situated 2 miles west along the A6073. The Saxon church at Escomb, which today is surrounded by modern housing, is regarded by many historians as the oldest church in England and exists almost in its original construction. In regular use and dating from the 7th century, the church was largely built with Roman stone from the fort at Binchester. Roman carvings can be seen on several of the stones. The chancel arch is entirely Roman with traces of 12th-century painting on the underside. The church also has an Anglo-Saxon sundial on the south wall, said to be the oldest dial in England still in its original position. Architects regard the Saxon Church at Escomb as one of the most complete examples of Anglo-Saxon ecclesiastic architecture in western Europe.

Continuing westwards from Bishop Auckland, following the meandering river Wear, the road leads to **Witton Castle** (*grounds open daily, castle also open – public bar, caravan park open April to October*) and **Hamsterley Forest**, forming one of County Durham's most important leisure and recreation areas. Witton Castle dates from 1410 but was extensively altered in the 18th and 19th centuries. It is picturesquely situated by the river Wear opposite the village of Witton le Wear. The castle grounds provide many modern amenities including camping and caravan parks, swimming- and paddling-pools, games and recreation areas and catering facilities.

Two miles west of the A68 at Witton le Wear is **Hamsterley Village**, and 1 mile west of the village lies the entrance to Hamsterley Forest where the Forestry Commission have set aside for recreation 445ha (1,100 acres) in the heart of the 2,204ha (5,500-acre) forest between Teesdale and Weardale. Amenities include a 4½-mile forest drive with several picnic areas, nature trails and forest walks. Toilet facilities are available, and an information centre operates at weekends during the summer months.

The area around Bishop Auckland undoubtedly owes its industrial prosperity to coal. The problem of getting the coal from the western sector of the Durham coalfield to the coast for shipment to London and the Continent taxed the minds of engineers and colliery owners. After much debate it was decided that a railway was preferable to a proposed canal. Railway pioneer George Stephenson was entrusted with the work of building a railway from Witton Park via Shildon and Darlington to Stockton-on-Tees. Local interest in the new form of transport was so great that on 27 September 1825 the inaugural journey of the world's first public fare-paying passenger railway was able to run along the line intended originally to carry only coal. A form of passenger transport destined to revolutionize the world was born. Today, much remains of those early days of the birth of railways. A rail trail has been specially devised to cover much of the original route of the first railway and is well signposted.

From Bishop Auckland the A6072 leads to Shildon where the cottage of Timothy Hackworth, a contemporary railway pioneer of George Stephenson, has been restored and converted into a museum (*open April to September, Wednesday to Sunday*). Hackworth is regarded by many railway historians to be the forgotten man of railways. Several pubs in Shildon maintain a railway theme, and Hackworth is buried in the churchyard of the 19th-century parish church at the head of the town's main street. In the spacious public park a bronze statue is raised to his memory.

An unclassified road westwards from Shildon leading to the A68 passes the Brusselton Incline, a noteworthy section of the original route where stone sleepers can be seen, together with the winding house used to haul wagons up the incline. Though now incorporated into private housing, original Stockton and Darlington Railway plaques can be seen on the walls, and the stretch of line is incorporated into the on-foot Rail Trail.

Two miles south of Shildon on the A6072 lies the village of **Heighington** where Stephenson's engine *Locomotion* was first placed on the rails on the eve of its eventful inaugural run. The engine was brought by road from Newcastle upon Tyne. Sections of the original low platform can still be seen, and Heighington is today an unmanned halt on the Darlington to Bishop Auckland diesel line which runs along much of the original route. Today's journey takes the traveller through North Road Station, Darlington, which in addition to being an unmanned halt is a museum devoted to the history of the world's first passenger railway and northeast railways in general. Stephenson's original engine *Locomotion* is preserved in the museum (*open daily*).

Other centres of railway history in Northumbria include Berwick-upon-Tweed (see page 23) with its famous Royal Border Bridge; Wylam (see page 132) where Stephenson's birthplace still stands; Newcastle Museum of Science and Engineering (see page 256); Killingworth's Dial Cottage (see page 260) where Stephenson lived; Sunderland's Monkwearmouth Station Museum (see page 273); Beamish North of England Open Air Museum (see page 295); Stockton Ticket-Office and Preston Park (see page 366); and Yarm (see page 367), where the inaugural meeting of the Stockton and Darlington Railway Company took place.

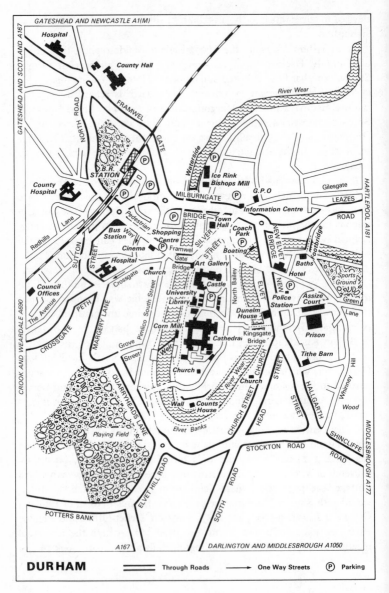

Hospital

County Hall

River Wear

GATESHEAD AND SCOTLAND A167

NORTH ROAD

FRAMWEL GATE

Park

B.R. STATION

County Hospital

Waterside

Ice Rink
Bishops Mill

G.P.O

Gilesgate

HARTLEPOOL A181

LEAZES

MILBURNGATE

ROAD

Information Centre

Redhills Lane

SUTTON STREET

Bus Way Station

Pedestrian Way

Shopping Centre

BRIDGE

Town Hall

Coach Park

NEW ELVET BRIDGE

Footbridge

Baths

Hotel

Sports Ground

Cinema

Framwel Gate Bridge

SILVER STREET

Boating

Hospital

Art Gallery

Crossgate

Church

Castle

North Bailey

ELVET

NEW

Police Station

Green

Assize Court

Council Offices

The Avenue

CROSSGATE

PETH

MARGERY LANE

Grove

Pimlico South Street

University Library

Corn Mill

Weir

Dunelm House

Cathedral

Kingsgate Bridge

River Wear

CHURCH STREET

HEAD STREET

Prison

Tithe Barn

HALLGARTH STREET

Whinney Hill Wood

CROOK AND WEARDALE A690

Street

Church

Church

MIDDLESBROUGH A177

QUARRYHEADS LANE

Wall

Counts House

Elvet Banks

Playing Field

STOCKTON ROAD

SHINCLIFFE ROAD

ELVET HILL ROAD

SOUTH ROAD

POTTERS BANK

A167

DURHAM Through Roads One Way Streets P Parking

24 Durham City

Angling Stretches of the river Wear.
Boating Brown's Boats for hire, Elvet Riverside.
Bowls Lowes Barn Playing Field, Riverside.
Buses Hartlepool, Sunderland, Bishop Auckland, Darlington, Middlesbrough, Newcastle upon Tyne, Stockton-on-Tees.
Camping and caravanning Finchale Priory.
Cinemas *Classic*, North Road.
Cricket Durham City Cricket Club at Elvet Waterside.
Distances Darlington, 22 miles; Middlesbrough, 23 miles; Newcastle upon Tyne, 16 miles; Sunderland, 13 miles.
Early closing Wednesday.
Football Durham City AFC at Ferens Park.
Golf *Brancepeth Castle Golf-Club*; *Durham City Golf-Club*, Littleburn.

Hotels *Neville's Cross Hotel*, *Ramside Hall Hotel*, *Redhills*, *Royal County*, *The Three Tuns*.
Ice-skating Durham Ice Rink, Freeman's Place.
Information centre Claypath, tel. 3720.
Market day Saturday.
Museums and art galleries The Dormitory Museum and new Treasury Museum, Durham Cathedral; Durham Light Infantry Museum; Gulbenkian Museum of Oriental Art and Archaeology.
Population 24,744.
Post Office The GPO is at 33 Claypath.
Rugby football Hollow Drift, Old Elvet.
Swimming-pools Elvet Waterside.
Tennis Durham and Wharton Park; Lowes Barn Playing Field; Archery Club Ground off Margery Lane.
Theatres None, but plays, concerts, etc., performed in association with Durham University.

Throughout the centuries there have been many superlative compliments bestowed upon the ancient City of Durham. Yet even today its timeless beauty and unique history fail to gain the recognition of other centres of Christianity in Britain. Too often the only impression of Durham is a towering cathedral obscured by the evening mists and fleetingly viewed from the London to Edinburgh train as it passes over the viaduct high above the city.

Durham is uniquely situated on a horseshoe peninsula formed by the meandering river Wear. The physical advantages of the site from a strategic point of view were recognized in prehistoric times though early records are scant. So too are reminders of the city's role during the Roman occupation, in spite of its close proximity to Dere Street, the Roman road from York, which passed through Lanchester and Binches-

Durham Cathedral

ter just a few miles to the west. Recently, some Roman remains have been found in the city which have lead some historians to think that there was a minor Roman road into the peninsula on which Durham is situated. Durham's rise to fame is centred upon Northumbria's role as the 'Cradle of Christianity'. In AD 634 at Heavenfield near to Hadrian's Wall King Oswald defeated the pagan troops of Cadwallader and sent to the Island of Iona for missionaries to attempt to tame his wild Northumbrian subjects. After several failures St Aidan arrived and successfully founded a monastery on the Holy Island – Lindisfarne, a semi-isle off the Northumberland coast. From these humble beginnings the importance of Lindisfarne grew as missionaries spread the Christian word far and wide.

At the time of the Battle of Heavenfield a son was born to a shepherd in the Border hills who was to play a major role not only in the spread of Christianity from Lindisfarne but also in the founding of Durham City. Cuthbert was his name. Eleven years after his death his body was found to be incorrupt. His monastic brothers placed his remains in a wooden coffin which was to become the symbol of the foundation of Durham City centuries later.

By AD 875 fierce Danes were powering across the North Sea in their sturdy longships intent on plundering the riches of Northumbria's monasteries. Reluctantly, the monks fled from Lindisfarne carrying with them the coffin of St Cuthbert. Their wanderings took them to Chester-le-Street where they rested for 113 years, then on to Ripon before returning northwards again. The see of Lindisfarne had followed Cuthbert's body to Chester-le-Street and was subsequently transferred to Durham. In 1093 Bishop William of St Calais began the building of the present-day Durham Cathedral, a feat which was miraculously completed in only forty years.

Almost thirty years earlier in 1069 William the Conqueror had visited the rocky peninsula and was so impressed with its almost impregnable physical features and its growing ecclesiastical reputation that he decided to make the site a powerful bastion against the threatening Scots. Thus the Palatinate of Durham, ruled over by a non-hereditary bishop, assumed tremendous importance and power. The Prince Bishop enjoyed the privileges of royalty within the Palatinate. He had his own parliament and mint, subjects carried out their military duties under the bishop and not the king, and the bishop presided over his own court. The King of England even found it necessary to seek the Prince Bishop's permission before entering the palatinate or bishopric. On a more mundane level the bishop also enjoyed the spoils of wrecks along the Durham coast together with any whales or sturgeon fish that were captured.

By 1081 the Norman invaders led by Duke William had caused almost total devastation in northern England. In this year however Bishop William de St Carileph was given authority over the Christian settlement at Dunholme. After several years' exile in France as a result of being wrongly accused of plotting against the monarch, the bishop returned to Durham and ordered the construction of the mighty Norman cathedral to begin. Sadly, he did not see the completion of his architectural masterpiece. He died before the building was completed in 1132.

Throughout succeeding centuries bishops have added their own individual contributions to the cathedral – not all meeting with general approval. Bishop Pudsey (Puiset) made several major alterations and additions in the 12th century including the construction of the Galilee Chapel at the west end. Though regarded as the finest Norman cathedral in western Europe, Durham also contains magnificent architecture of other periods. Geometrical and Perpendicular styles are both represented.

The Benedictine monks remained at Durham for several hundred years until the dissolution of the monasteries. Through the Middle Ages the cathedral was a shrine to which pilgrims journeyed from far and near to worship at the Shrine of St Cuthbert. Sir Walter Scott described Durham Cathedral as 'half Church of God, half castle 'gainst the Scot', and this description was no more apt than in 1650 when the cathedral was used as a prison to house 4,000 Scottish soldiers captured by Oliver Cromwell. Regrettably, the prisoners burnt the beautiful choir stalls and other unique woodwork in order to keep warm.

The City of Durham was an important strategic stronghold during the Scottish Wars. As early as 1139 a peace treaty was signed in Durham between King Stephen and David I of Scotland. On the western outskirts of the City stands **Neville's Cross**, named after one of the north's most celebrated families and a name which commemorates one of the most decisive Border battles fought here in 1346. At the time Edward III was in France, and in an attempt to revert the king's interest homewards Philip VI implored his Scottish ally David II to attack England. Edward's queen, Philippa of Hainault, bravely amassed an army on her travels north. She was supported by the Archbishop of York, the Nevilles and the Percies, Northumberland's most famous warriors.

Guidebooks to **Durham Cathedral** are readily available, and often vergers are at hand to give guidance. In 1978 the famous grotesquely shaped head fashioned in bronze which for centuries acted as a sanctuary knocker giving fugitives protection was removed for restoration. It will be replaced by a replica but the original will still be displayed in the Cathedral's new Treasury Musuem. Particular attention should be paid to the majestic Romanesque pillars of the nave with their characteristic chevron pattern. The roof of the nave is vaulted, and Durham was the first cathedral to incorporate such a novel architectural design. At the west end of the cathedral by the font is a distinct line of Frosterley marble incorporated into the floor. The line demarcates the point beyond which women were not permitted to pass into the main body of the church.

To accommodate female worshippers Bishop Pudsey built the **Galilee Chapel** at the west end of the cathedral in 1175. Today the chapel is the resting-place of another ecclesiastical master, the Venerable Bede.

Both transepts were begun before the death of Bishop de St Carileph in 1096 and thus contain some excellent examples of early Norman architecture. The south transept contains a remarkable astronomical clock recently restored, though originally dating from 1500. Curiously, the clock displays only forty-eight minutes. In the north transept is a stained-glass window depicting Jesus in his suffering which is more than 600 years old.

At the entrance to the choir Frosterley marble is visible in the huge pillars. The choir stalls were carved some 300 years ago and replaced those burnt by the Scottish warriors imprisoned in the cathedral by Oliver Cromwell. Within the chancel and beyond the choir stalls is the tomb of Bishop Hatfield. Above it is the bishop's throne or *cathedra*. The throne is regarded as the highest in Christendom, an indication of the status of the Bishop of Durham.

Behind the high altar is the beautiful **Neville Screen**, an ecclesiastical embellishment unequalled in the world. Dating from 1375, it is carved from Caen stone and has 107 spaces for statues. The screen was made in London and brought by sea to the north-east. Much of the cost was borne by Lord John Neville whose father triumphed at the Battle of Neville's Cross. Behind the screen is the tomb of St Cuthbert whose remains have rested here since 1104. In 1827 the tomb was opened, and in addition to Cuthbert's relics an additional skull was discovered which some historians believe was that of St Oswald. These and other relics are now on display in the new **Treasury Museum** (open Monday to Saturday 10–4, Sunday 2–4). The collection includes Cuthbert's coffin, maniple and cross, together with manuscripts and other treasures of the cathedral. There is also a display of plate silver. The Monks' Dormitory will continue to serve as the cathedral library and will house various exhibitions.

The eastern transept of Durham Cathedral is dominated by the **Chapel of the Nine Altars** which dates from 1242. Constructed in Early English style, its delicate structure makes an ideal contrast to the rugged Norman architecture. The chapel was built to accommodate the vast numbers of pilgrims who came from far and wide to worship at the shrine of St Cuthbert.

Proceeding westwards along the nave, a door is reached in the south aisle which leads to the cloisters. Immediately on the right a huge door leads into the **Monks' Dormitory**, dating from 1400, which now houses the cathedral library (*entrance fee*).

One of the latest developments within the cloisters is the provision of a tasteful restaurant and bookshop in the undercroft. Beyond the refectory on the south side of the cloister are various private residential buildings and an 18th-century water-tower. Gardens, including one in memory of the City regiment the 7th Durham Light Infantry, lend colour to the peace and quiet, little changed from centuries gone by. Narrow alleys, known locally as vennels, snake their way towards the wooded river bank below.

From Durham Cathedral it is just a short step across the Palace Green, past the grotesquely worn sandstone of ancient buildings now largely taken over by the University, to Durham Castle, home of succeeding bishops from 1072.

As befits such an important seat of power, **Durham Castle** is as architecturally splendid as its mightier ecclesiastical neighbour. The castle's history is no less absorbing. It is believed that some form of fortification was raised on the peninsula almost immediately after the arrival of Cuthbert's coffin in 995. Historians believe that the great mound of the keep and ramparts of earth on the northern face of the castle are remains of early attempts at fortification. It is also recorded that as early as 1006 Scottish attacks were being repelled. It was in 1072 that William I ordered the rebuilding of the castle, and each bishop seems to have made his own individual additions to the building. It was never taken by the Scots and remained the main seat of the bishops until 1837 when it became the home of University College, five years after the founding of Durham University.

The castle is entered at the north-west corner of the Green through a gateway which was originally Norman but largely reconstructed in the 18th century. On entering the courtyard, one can see architecture from several periods. The high keep, originally built by Bishop Hatfield in the 14th century, was reconstructed in 1840. Through the elevated door to the left is the Great Hall built by Bishop Bek in 1300. Subsequent enlargement took place in 1350 by Bishop Hatfield, but the Hall was reduced in 1500 by Bishop Fox. To the left is the kitchen which is still in use today. Originally the Norman guardroom, conversion work was carried out by Bishop Fox nearly 500 years ago.

Durham Castle achieved a much more residential aspect at the hands of Bishop Tunstall (1530–59) who added a gallery to the exterior wall of the central block to give access to his chapel. The gallery covered the lower part of Constable's Hall built in the 12th century by Pudsey. As a result of the protection afforded by the 'new' gallery, the original Norman doorway of Constable's Hall has been retained in almost pristine condition. Indeed, it was not until the 19th century that it was rediscovered, after being hidden under subsequent layers of plaster. The ornate carving is regarded as one of the finest examples of Norman architecture in Britain. Tunstall's Chapel was extended by Lord Crewe in 1700 and is still in use today. Particularly appealing are the richly carved misericords humorously depicting a witch being carried in a wheelbarrow, a pig playing the bagpipes and several other unusual scenes.

In 1640 the Scots held possession of Durham Castle during the Civil Wars, creating serious damage to the structure and the interior. In 1649 the castle was bought for the princely sum of £1,267 0 10d by Thomas Andrews, Lord Mayor of London, but little is known of his occupation.

Bishop John Cosin (1660–72) restored the castle to its former glory, and further restoration, improvements and sometimes irrational alterations were carried out by succeeding bishops until 1837 when the building came into the possession of Durham University, founded five years earlier. From Bishop Tunstall's gallery a dramatic black oak staircase leads to the Pudsey Norman gallery above. The staircase, originally 'flying', was built on the instruction of Bishop Cosin in 1663.

Though not normally included in the public tour, the Senate Room and associated apartments are full of interest. Tapestries from the 16th century adorn the walls, and the fireplace is exquisitely carved with coats of arms. Below the Senate Room is the oldest part of the castle – the Norman chapel, built in the late 11th century although the north wall may be even earlier. The chapel was badly damaged when the keep was restored in 1840, but in 1952 considerable restoration work was carried out, and like the Tunstall Chapel the Norman chapel is used regularly by University students. (*Durham Castle is open to the public, except during University functions, weekdays first weeks of April, July to end September. At other times Mondays, Wednesdays and Saturdays 2.00 p.m. to 4.00 p.m.*)

Around the city

Though castle and cathedral dominate the City of Durham, there are many other interesting buildings, intriguing streets, ancient bridges and churches.

The hub of the city is the **Market-Place** which has recently undergone a transformation. Gone are the traffic jams, the fumes and the noise which were the order of the day before a pedestrianization plan incorporating new bridges across the Wear came into operation. Today, cobble-stones echo centuries past as some streets have become totally traffic free, while others have had their traffic considerably reduced. Sadly, however, the freeing of the market-place from traffic has meant the demise of one of Durham's unique features. The control box from which traffic was controlled by close-circuit television was made redundant.

The market-place is dominated by several architecturally interesting buildings including the **Town Hall**. Originally a Guildhall dating from 1356, it was rebuilt 200 years later by Bishop Tunstall. Subsequent restoration work was carried out in 1665 by Bishop Cosin, and the building was almost completely rebuilt again in 1752–4. A completely new town hall was built in the mid-19th century, its design being a copy of Westminster Hall in London. In the corridor by the entrance are several remarkable exhibits belonging to one of Durham City's most eccentric inhabitants. Count Boruwlaski was a Polish dwarf who lived in the city from 1820 until his death in 1837 at the age of ninety-eight. A fascinating character measuring just short of 100cm (39in), he was a very talented musician and thrilled court circles with his mastery of the violin and his ready wit. The Count made such a great impression in Durham that he was given a final resting-place in Durham Cathedral. In the Town Hall his suit, slippers, violin and other relics are displayed.

The tall elegant spire of **St Nicholas's Church** dominates the eastern entrance to the market square. One of several interesting churches in the city, St Nicholas has been described as 'the most beautiful modern specimen of church architecture in the North of England'. It was built in 1857–8 on the site of an original Norman church of which no traces remain. To the west is the site of the palace of the great Neville family, Earls of Westmorland, but modern development has removed all trace.

The centre of the market-place is dominated by a huge greenish-hued equine statue of the third Lord Londonderry who found fame and fortune as militarian and politician. He also founded the town of Seaham Harbour, a leading coal port on the Durham coast. The statue by Raffaelle Monti is in plaster, electroplated with copper, a revolutionary method of sculpture at the time. The legend that the sculptor committed suicide after realizing he had forgotten to fashion the tongue in the horse is unsubstantiated.

From the market-place several streets lead towards the river. Flesher-gate, as the name suggests the butchers' quarter, leads to **Saddler Street**, a street ripe with the scent of history. Here was Durham's thriving theatre land where Stephen Kemble and his famous sister Mrs Siddons appeared from time to time. Kemble who is buried alongside his good friend Count Boruwlaski in Durham Cathedral managed a theatre which stood behind No. 61. A plaque on a narrow vennel aptly called Drury Lane reminds the visitor of the city's fame as a theatrical centre. History of another kind can be related to the rear of No. 73 Saddler Street where Durham's famous mustard factory was situated.

At the head of Saddler Street where Nos. 49 and 50 now stand and where Saddler Street is joined by Owengate stands **Northgate** which as the name implies is the site of the North Gate built by Bishop Langley in the 15th century. The origins of the name Owengate are not known. The street's most impressive building is a Tudor-style house with a timbered façade. Several almshouses opposite were built in 1838 to replace original almshouses which still stand on Palace Green but are now used by the University.

The eastern flank of Palace Green is notable on account of the 17th-century **Bishop Cosin's Hall** and the original almshouses which were founded in 1668 by Bishop Cosin for the city's poor and distressed. In the south-east corner of Palace Green stands **Abbey House**, a Queen Anne building also now under the jurisdiction of the University. The western flank of the Green houses in the south-west corner the ancient **Grammar School**, built in 1661. Other buildings include the University Library, built by Bishop Neville in 1450 on the site of the Bishops' stables, and Bishop Cosin's library, dating from 1669.

Retracing one's steps to the bottom of Owengate and continuing south leads along North Bailey where most of the buildings have been taken over by Durham University's Hatfield College. The period is predominantly 18th century. The city's War Memorial stands below the great rose window of the cathedral. Here Dun Cow Lane runs down to North Bailey from Palace Green. On the opposite side Bow Lane continues down to the modern, award-winning **Kingsgate Foot-bridge** spanning the river Wear.

At the corner of North Bailey and Bow Lane stands the **Church of St Mary-le-Bow** which reopened in 1978 not as a church but as the **Durham Heritage Centre** (*open daily free*). The 'bow' suffix relates to the original building which incorporated an arch from the city's walls. The present building dates from 1683 and the tower was added in 1702. Some historians believe the site of St Mary-le-Bow is the exact location where the coffin of St Cuthbert rested on arrival in the city.

Bow Lane was formerly known as Kingsgate around which an amusing anecdote rests. Legend relates that William the Conqueror visited Durham to determine for himself whether St Cuthbert's body was incorrupt. As soon as he entered the cathedral he became overwhelmed with an unaccountable panic. Ignoring the crowds amassed on Palace Green, the king mounted his horse, fled down to the river ford and never stopped until he had left the Palatinate. His route was henceforth known as Kingsgate.

On the corner opposite St Mary-le-Bow Church stands the modern St Chad's College founded in 1903. Together with the contemporary college of St John's, the University has taken over most of the elegant buildings along the Bailey where once the defensive forces of the castle and monastery lived.

North Bailey gives way to South Bailey as it runs towards the river. Set back from the narrow cobbled road is the church of **St Mary the Less**. The first church on the site was Norman, and a carving over the vestry door is believed to be of the period. The original church was founded by the Nevilles in the 12th century. The present building dates from 1846. Durham's musical dwarf is commemorated here too. A plaque to his memory can be seen on the west wall. St Mary the Less is today the chapel of St John's College.

Continuing south towards the steeply wooded banks of the Wear, the narrow Bailey ends abruptly at **Watergate**, an archway built in 1778. At the gate is one of the best preserved sections of the ancient city walls. A pathway descends steeply through a sylvan setting to another of the city's bridges – **Prebends Bridge**, named not after any contours of the river but in honour of the canons, or prebends, who financed it. Looking towards the cathedral from across the bridge gives the most famous view of the Norman splendour towering above the Wear and the **Fulling Mill** below (*open Wednesdays and Fridays 10–1 and 2–5. May be extended at a later date, check at Tourist Information Centre*) which houses archaeological finds in Durham dating from the Stone Age period to the Anglo-Saxon period.

From Prebends Bridge the tree-lined riverside path stretches in both directions to take in the complete horseshoe of the Wear. Tracing the river upstream, the path passes a small building constructed in the Doric style of a Greek temple. This building has been mistakenly called the Count's House although Boruwlaski never lived there. The building was simply a summer cottage and dates from the early 19th century. The riverside path continues under the new Kingsgate Bridge and on towards one of the city's ancient bridges, **Elvet Bridge**, originally built by Bishop Pudsey in 1160. Repairs were carried out by Bishop Fox in 1495, but during the Great Flood of 1771, which devastated most river bridges in northern England, three arches were washed away. The bridge was widened to twice its original size in 1804–5, but the original construction of Pudsey is still clearly visible. From beneath the bridge various types of river craft including punts and rowing-boats are available for hire during the summer months. At the eastern end of the bridge lies **Old Elvet** and the **Royal County Hotel**. Predominantly 18th century, the hotel has recently been enlarged but has retained many of its original features including the balcony from which dignitaries still greet the Durham miners when they march into the city for the annual Miners' Gala, or 'Big Meeting'. Here the new Elvet Bridge spans the river diverting traffic from the market-place on a through route south.

From Elvet Bridge in the opposite direction Saddler Street leads back into the market square. **Silver Street** is another intriguing road leading from the square to yet another historic crossing of the Wear at **Framwell-gate Bridge**, built several years prior to Elvet Bridge in 1128 by Bishop Flambard. The north side still bears some of the original stonework, though the bridge was almost completely rebuilt in the 15th century by Bishop Langley. The most notable house in Silver Street is No. 39 which was inhabited in the 17th century by John Duck, a former Mayor and a merchant, whose wealth was founded on the odd combination of meat

Old Elvet Bridge, Durham

and Durham coal. He was knighted for his services to the community, died in 1691 and is buried in St Margaret's Church. From Framwellgate Bridge the riverside path skirts the towering castle and cathedral to link with Prebends Bridge upstream.

Though the heart of Durham's ancient city beats in and around the rocky promontory on which castle, cathedral and market-place are sited, the outskirts of the city are, nevertheless, full of interest. Not surprisingly, the outlying districts are rich in ecclesiastical history. Several churches are worth visiting. **St Oswald's Church** in Church Street on Durham's eastern flank is dedicated to King Oswald of Northumbria who fought the decisive battle at Heavenfield which subsequently led to all Northumbria being evangelized. The building standing today is basically 12th century, though much altered throughout subsequent centuries. Originally, the site was occupied in Saxon times, and the parish covered some 30 square miles. **St Margaret's Church**, situated on the corner of South Street and Crossgate, is medieval with some Norman traces. Sir John Duck, merchant and Mayor of the City, is buried in the nave. Yet another ancient church is found in Gilesgate where **St Giles's Church** was founded in 1112 by Bishop Flambard. Only the north wall of the nave of the original building survives.

Durham City has two museums which are unique, and both are situated away from the city centre but within reasonable walking distance.

The Gulbenkian Museum of Oriental Art and Archaeology (*open daily; Sundays – afternoons only; no weekends Christmas to Easter*) is reached from New Elvet via Church Street across the A177 at the New Inn and into South Road which is flanked by the modern complex of colleges – St Mary's, Grey, Trevelyan and St Aidan's. At the head of the ascent of South Road a sign directs the visitor right into the University complex where the Gulbenkian Museum is situated. The ultra-modern building houses an internationally important collection of Oriental art, including a comprehensive collection of Egyptian antiquities many of which are unique and universally recognized. The 4th Duke of Northumberland was responsible for the major part of the collection which he amassed during his travels in Egypt in the 19th century.

The museum also contains a collection of Chinese jade and hardstone carvings, a large gallery of Chinese paintings, ivories, printed books and bronzes. India and Tibet are featured in the collection of paintings and sculpture, and there are also important works from the Near East. There is also a growing collection of intriguing Japanese art, but the largest collection in the museum consists of Chinese pottery and porcelain, the basis of which is the private collection of the Right Honourable Malcolm MacDonald.

The split-level displays in the museum are first class and allow general appraisal as well as close detailed study. Though the museum is essentially part of the University complex, visitors are made most welcome. A comprehensive guidebook is available and parking is convenient.

The Durham Light Infantry Museum and Arts Centre (*open daily except Mondays*) is the second of Durham's museums and is situated just a short distance from the city centre. It is reached by crossing the new Milburngate Bridge and turning right at the first roundabout to ascend Framwellgate Peth. The road leads under a bridge carrying the main Edinburgh to London railway line, and a short distance further on before you reach County Hall the ultra-modern building which houses the museum can be seen, set back in a landscaped area to the right.

The museum, which incorporates an arts centre, traces the complete history of the famous regiment from its inception in 1758 to its disbanding in 1968. During such a long and distinguished career the brave fighting 'faithfulls', as they became known, saw action in the four corners of the world, including the West Indies in 1764–73, the Peninsular War, the Indian Mutiny and the Crimean War. The Boer War and the Great War witnessed the Regiment's finest hours. During the latter the Regiment comprised no less than thirty-seven battalions, more than any other regiment in the British Army. The honour roll includes every major battle on the Western Front and further afield in Italy, Macedonia, Salonika and Russia. In five years no less than 12,006 men lost their lives. In the Second World War too the DLI played its part, and the museum displays a vast range of reminders of these troubled times, including uniforms, weapons of all nations and captured enemy possessions. The prize exhibit is the 2-pounder anti-tank gun on which one Private Wakenshaw won a posthumous VC in 1942. The DLI continued in active service long after World War II serving the United Nations in Korea (1952–3) and in Cyprus (1958) during the EOKA uprising.

Sadly for County Durham the Regiment's individual identity disappeared in 1968 when the fighting 68th – the 1st Battalion of Durham Light Infantry – was merged with three other light infantry regiments to become simply the Light Infantry. Memories die hard in Northumbria, and the new regiment is maintaining the traditions of the 'fighting Durhams'. Fortunately too the DLI Museum will ensure that future generations are made aware of the distinguished history of the Regiment.

In addition to the permanent displays the museum's Arts Centre presents a varied and inspired programme of special events throughout the year. There is ample parking and a cafeteria.

25 Environs of Durham

From Durham City there are several circular routes ideal for day tours incorporating many interesting new attractions and historic relics. Leaving Durham City by Milburngate Bridge and Framwellgate Peth, the DLI Museum and Arts Centre and County Hall, the administration headquarters of Durham County Council, are passed. Continuing ahead on an unclassified road signposted Aykley Heads, the village of **Pity Me** is reached in a mile or so. The derivation of the unusual name is believed to come from the French 'Petit Mer', though the reasoning is obscure. From Pity Me an unclassified road signposted Newton Grange crosses the main north–south railway line, passes through Low Newton and descends to the banks of the river Wear and the sylvan setting of the ruin of **Finchale Priory** (pronounced Finkle), which is open daily at DoE standard hours.

The romantic ruins are idyllically set in a loop in the meandering river Wear. The priory's foundations centre on St Godric who was born in 1065 and devoted his life to spreading the Christian gospel. Like so many saints and monks before him, including St Cuthbert, Godric secretly yearned for solitude. While living as a hermit in Wolsingham, he learnt in a vision of a place called Finchale and by divine guidance he found a paradise by the tranquil waters of the Wear. On his death in 1170 his retreat at Finchale passed into the hands of the Prior of Durham and subsequently became a cell for the city's monastic order. In the 14th century Finchale became a holiday retreat for monks from Durham. A group of four monks in turn were outposted for three weeks to enjoy the peace and seclusion by the river amid natural beauty which has changed little down the centuries.

Today the extensive remains of the priory at Finchale give an insight into the monastic life. The earlier buildings include the **Chapel of St John the Baptist**, where a crude stone tomb can be seen which is believed

323

to be that of St Godric. The walls of the chancel of the church remain almost to their original height. The four giant piers of the central tower are a monument to the architectural skills of the priory's builders. Finchale has other attractions besides the priory. Riverside walks give an opportunity to study the Wear's wildlife at close quarters, and there is also a shop and cafeteria, caravan site and picnic areas. A foot-bridge crosses the Wear enabling the visitor to explore both banks of the river.

From Finchale Priory it is necessary to return to Newton Grange, turn right at the 'T' junction and continue to join the old A1 road now renumbered the A167 at Chester Moor. Continuing north in 1 mile, the A167 gives way to the A6137 which enters the bustling town of **Chester-le-Street**.

The town is situated where the Con Burn flows into the river Wear some 6 miles from Durham City. As the town's name suggests, the Romans occupied the site where the Roman road from Binchester ran northwards towards Pons Aelii – Newcastle upon Tyne.

Chester-le-Street came to prominence in the 9th century when the monks from Lindisfarne fleeing from the marauding Danes with the coffin of their beloved St Cuthbert found a resting-place here in AD 882. The coffin remained near the site of the Roman fort for 113 years until the year 995 when further fears of attack from across the North Sea forced the monks to flee once more. They journeyed south to Ripon before finding a final resting-place for the remains of Cuthbert in Durham City.

For more than a century, while the body of Cuthbert rested in a crude shrine at Chester-le-Street, the town became the centre of Christianity for a vast area of northern England. The see was ruled over by no fewer than nine Saxon bishops, and it was only when the monks, with the body of Cuthbert, were guided by a vision to Durham that the see transferred there and Chester-le-Street's golden age was over.

Early in the 11th century Bishop Egelric decided that the town was worthy of a new stone church which turned out to be a fortunate decision for the bishop. During excavation work a hoard of Roman coins and treasure was discovered which the Bishop claimed, and he subsequently disappeared back to his native Peterborough. In spite of putting much of his new found wealth to good use, he was imprisoned in the Tower of London by William the Conqueror for his deeds. Egelric's church was almost completely rebuilt in the 13th century and again a century later. Further restoration work has been carried out during more recent times.

The tower is a sturdy 13th-century construction, and the cell built on to the tower's north wall is regarded as one of the best preserved anchorages in England.

The interior of the **Church of St Mary and St Cuthbert** is architecturally and historically well worth visiting. Particularly noteworthy are a group of fourteen effigies of the Lumley family, most of which date from Elizabethan times. They can be seen in the north aisle.

Modern-day Chester-le-Street is typical of the larger Durham County towns, busy, bustling with varied shops, a good selection of inns and eating-places and an open-air market held every Friday in the shadows of the railway viaduct which carries the main east-coast line between Durham City and Newcastle. On the outskirts of the town between the A1 and the Wear are landscaped recreation areas in a riverside setting.

From Chester-le-Street the A693 leads to Stanley and the North of England Open Air Museum. The A1(M) through route bypasses the town. The B1284 eastwards crosses the river Wear and skirts one of Durham County's most impressive castles, **Lumley Castle**, now a four-star hotel and venue for Elizabethan banquets held most nights (prior booking necessary). Lumley Castle is set in elevated parkland which also accommodates a first-class golf-course. The castle dates from the latter half of the 14th century, although the Lumley family descend from the time of Edward the Confessor. The castle was built after the Bishop of Durham and the King of England gave Sir Ralph Lumley a 'licence to crenellate' in 1389. Apart from extensive alterations in 1580 and some fine interior work by the celebrated architect Sir John Vanbrugh in 1721 the four-square battlemented castle retains its original appearance. Not surprisingly, the conversion of Lumley to modern-day use has meant the inclusion of 20th-century amenities, but the building has retained its historic features including the ghost of a white lady, one Lily of Lumley.

Continuing on the B1284, in just over 1 mile from Lumley Castle by a signpost right to Great Lumley an unclassified road left leads by virtue of a notorious hairpin bend situated under the towering span of the A1(M) to the A183 at Houghton Gate. After turning right, signposted Sunderland, and passing Burnmoor (or Bournemoor) Church and cricket ground, the lion-topped columns on the left mark the entrance to one of County Durham's newest attractions, the **Lambton Pleasure Park** (*open daily, March to October*) accommodated in the vast Lambton Estate and providing a bewildering array of pastimes and diversions for young and old. The Lambton Pleasure Park was opened originally as a safari park, and the thrill of driving through natural parkland where exotic wild animals freely roam is still one of the park's greatest attractions. There are many other facilities, including the conversion of Lambton Castle into a fairy castle complete with moving tableaux from the world's most famous fables and nursery rhymes. The drive through the safari park enables the visitor to see at close quarters lions, elephants, eland, giraffes and a host of other exotic beasts. There are safe areas where you can leave your car and meet the elephants or watch the hysterical antics of the ostrich. Open spaces abound in the non-animal sections of the Pleasure Park where there are picnic areas, a small fairground and catering facilities. The Park also has a touring caravan site.

In 1½ miles the A183 reaches Shiney Row where the new highway left leads to Washington. The A183 continues through Penshaw by Penshaw Monument and on to Sunderland. From Shiney Row the A182 leads through the oddly named villages of Philadelphia and Newbottle to Houghton le Spring, a pleasant town whose prosperity was founded on Durham coal and which is now incorporated into the new conurbation

Washington, village church

of Sunderland Borough Council. Houghton le Spring is situated on the A690 which links Durham City with Sunderland.

From Houghton le Spring the A182 leads in 1 mile to Hetton and continues through Easington, a largely urban area founded on Durham coal, and links with the A19 north–south artery at Easington Lane. At Easington the **Church of St Mary** dates from Norman times, though the original church was rebuilt in the 13th century with the exception of the tower. Restoration work was carried out in the mid-19th century. From Hetton an unclassified road to the right returns to Durham City passing through the village of **Pittington**, noted for its Saxon-Norman **Church of St Lawrence**. The tower and font, once used as a cattle trough before being returned to the church, are Norman. On the south wall is a Saxon sundial.

A more scenic route eastwards leaves Houghton le Spring on the B1404, crossing **Warden Law** which rises to 195m (650ft) and is one of the highest points in the eastern half of the county. At **Copt Hill** is the earliest prehistoric barrow in the county. Six miles from Houghton le Spring the B1404 crosses the new A19 through Seaton and reaches the sea at Seaham Hall on the northern outskirts of the town of Seaham. On the cliff top Durham County Council has provided a car park and picnic area, and steps give access to a fine stretch of beach and promenade which leads to the harbour at Seaham.

Seaham Harbour was founded in the first decades of the 19th century out of the need to provide a port for shipping Durham coal to London and the Continent. Hitherto there had been little or no development on this stretch of coast, notorious as a graveyard of ships. The foundation stone of the harbour was laid in 1828, and three years later the first collier brig *The Lord Seaham* sailed with the first cargo of coal. Railways replaced horse-drawn wagon ways and the town grew in size and prosperity. The quest for coal has continued to play a major role in the life of the town's 23,000 inhabitants, as pits have become more modernized (although fewer in number) as they shift towards the coast to exploit coal reserves under the North Sea. There was an appalling tragedy in 1880 when 164 miners and 181 pit ponies were killed. In more recent times the town suffered a second tragedy in 1962 when the lifeboat capsized with the loss of its entire crew. Since 1972 the town has been incorporated into the new Sunderland Borough.

Amid the town's bustling shops stands the **Church of St John the Evangelist**, built in 1835. The original village **Church of St Mary** is much more interesting, dating from Saxon and Norman times. It lies near the cliffs near **Seaham Hall**, now a hospital but once the residence of the Millbanke Family and Lord Londonderry, the coal magnate. The hall was the scene of Lord Byron's ill-fated wedding in 1815 to Ann Isabella Millbanke, and their signatures are recorded in the register of the church. The eastern extremity of the B1404 where it meets the B1287 at Seaham Hall is known as Byron's Walk.

The beaches to the north of Seaham deserve much more attention. Long, firm sands provide plenty of space, and the coastline is totally uncommercialized. Excellent sea-fishing is available, and open competitions are held from time to time. The Autumn All Comers' Angling Championship at Seaham attracts record entries. The town is well endowed with public parks and playgrounds.

Leaving Seaham the A19 south links with the A182 at Easington, and in 2 miles bypasses **Peterlee New Town**, situated some 10 miles east of Durham City. The New Town was founded in 1950 and is a massive, sprawling conurbation of industrial development and private housing. Some of the architecture, however, is not without appeal: the town's three churches – the Roman Catholic Church, St Cuthbert's Anglican Church and the Peter Lee Memorial Methodist Church – are all fine examples of modern ecclesiastical architecture.

The town was named after one of County Durham's most famous sons, Peter Lee, a self-made man who is one of the most respected figures in the history of the Durham coalfield. He was born at nearby Trimdon Grange and began working in the mines at the age of ten. After years of disciplined study, he obtained work abroad travelling extensively in Africa and the United States. In 1909 he was elected Chairman of Durham's first Labour County Council. A great champion of the miners' cause, he was appointed secretary of the Durham Miners' Association, and in 1933, two years before his death, he was elected President of the Miners' Federation. He is buried at nearby Wheatley Hill.

One of the finest features of Peterlee New Town is the spaciousness and greenery to be found amid private housing and industrial premises. The town also enjoys its own 'Garden of Eden', as the heavily wooded **Castle Eden Dene**, which wends its way seawards on the southern extremities of the town, is known. The Dene, covering 1,417ha (3,500 acres), is the result of the death throes of the Great Ice Age when great torrents of water were hurled seawards gouging massive ravines out of the County Durham rock. The Dene is 4 miles long and is accessible at a number of points along its route, including several entrances in Peterlee Town Centre. Gently sloping footpaths wend their way along the entire length of the Dene past places with strange names, such as Ivy Rock, Devils Lap Stone and Dungy Bridge. Castle Eden Dene is renowned as a haven of wildlife. More than seventy species of bird have been recorded, and the botanist will also find much of interest. The Blomers Rivulet, a rare species of moth, and the Eden Argus Butterfly were first discovered in the Dene. The latter gives its name to one of Peterlee's public houses.

There are ample spaces for picnics in the Dene as it travels eastwards crossing the A1086 coast road and broadens to reach the sea at Horden. It is fair to say that this stretch of coastline is not the most picturesque in County Durham, having been despoiled in the past as a result of the dumping of colliery waste. Conservation plans now under way should go a long way to restoring this coastline to its former glory.

The A1086 coast road continues south to Blackhall Colliery where the B1281 leads inland to **Castle Eden** where the **Church of St James** dates from 1764.

Three or four miles south of Blackhall the A1086 crosses the Crimdon Beck, where **Crimdon Dene** provides a popular seaside resort served by a fine stretch of sheltered beach. Sponsored by the local council, Crimdon Lido provides an excellent playground for local inhabitants with additional amenities for the visitor including a camping and touring caravan site. As well as the natural attractions of the coastline, Crimdon also provides car park, picnic areas, paddling-pools, amusement park and catering facilities. To the south there is an eighteen-hole golf-course.

The area to the south-east of Durham City between the A1(M) and the A19 is typical of the landscape of the east Durham coalfield. The B1283 and the A181 link Durham City with the A19. The B1283 passes through Sherburn and Sherburn Hill, the land rising to the village of Haswell Plough. Further south the A181 traverses the east Durham coalfield through such colliery villages as Thornley, Wingate and Trimdon.

Kelloe, lying just south of the A181 and north of Trimdon, is a village which enjoys interesting links with the poetess Elizabeth Barrett Browning. **Kelloe Church**, dating from the 13th and 14th centuries, still has in use the 18th-century font in which she was baptized. She was born in 1806 at Coxhoe Hall which stood nearby but was demolished some years ago. A monument, erected by public subscription in 1897, stands on the south side of the church to commemorate Kelloe's famous daughter. Another monument in the churchyard commemorates the mining disaster of 1882 at nearby Trimdon Grange when seventy-four miners, many of them still children, lost their lives. Bronze Age remains are unearthed from time to time in the surrounding hills. Trimdon is said to be the legendary spot from which King Canute began his barefoot pilgrimage to the shrine of St Cuthbert in Durham between 1017 and 1036.

One of the main routes from Durham City to Teesside, in addition to the A1(M), is the A177 which on the outskirts of Durham passes through the village of **Shincliffe**, another successful competitor in the National Britain in Bloom Competition. The road out of the city passes university complexes and the internationally recognized Houghall Agricultural College. Shincliffe parish church has a curious stone spire dating from 1870. On the outskirts of the village Roman remains have been unearthed.

The A177 crosses the A1(M) Durham motorway in 3½ miles and continues south towards Teesside. In a further 5 miles an unclassified road right leads to **Bishop Middleham**, where on grass-covered mounds to the south of the parish church bishops of Durham had their castles prior to moving to Bishop Auckland. Two bishops ended their days here in 1283 and 1316. The **Church of St Michael** dates from the 13th century. There are several monuments in the church relating to the Surtees family of whom Robert (1779–1834) is best remembered for his *History and Antiquities of the County Palatinate of Durham*. The Surtees family lived at nearby Mainsforth Hall demolished in 1962.

Three miles further south is the town of Sedgefield, to the west of which by the A177 is the new **Hardwick Hall Country Park**, covering some 16ha (40 acres). A 60ha (150-acre) landscaped park was constructed here from a design by the celebrated architect James Paine between 1754 and 1758. The gardens enjoyed all the features of the classical English garden of the period incorporating serpentine, waterfall, tree-lined avenues and numerous follies, including a temple to Minerva. Hardwick was the seat of the Burdon Family, but the ambitious plans for a sumptuous dwelling worthy of the landscaped park never came to fruition. The unprepossessing Hardwick Hall, incorporating the remains of a medieval manor-house, was rebuilt in 1750 and last occupied by Lord Boyne in 1923. Regrettably, the ruins of garden adornments, including the magnificent Banqueting Hall, are in a dangerous state and must be given a wide berth, but some 16ha (40 acres) of the estate have been recently acquired by Durham County Council and, with assistance from Sedgefield District Council, the area has been imaginatively developed into a country park. A nature trail along raised railway sleepers runs through a 2ha (5-acre) fen-carr, and the serpentine is a haven of wildlife. There is ample space for car-parking within the park. Picnic sites and other usual amenities are provided.

The town of **Sedgefield** itself is dominated by the 13th-century **Church of St Edmund** to which the well-known Northumbrian philanthropist Robert Rodes added a fine tower in the 15th century. Rodes also bestowed upon Newcastle upon Tyne its cathedral church of St Nicholas. Sedgefield has a race-course and is one of a handful of towns and villages in Britain which still retains the traditional Shrove Tuesday football match.

Continuing south-east through Thorpe Thewles, in 9 miles, the A177 enters Stockton-on-Tees. A mile or so west of the road *en route* lie the villages of Great Stainton, Bishopton and Redmarshall. **Great Stainton** is a hamlet situated on the Roman road from York to Hadrian's Wall. **All Saints Church**, though rebuilt in 1876, retains a Norman font. **Bishopton** is situated on high ground above the beck of the same name. To the south of the village lies Castle Hill, believed to have been man-made. A medieval fortress was built under the auspices of the Bishop of Durham, hence the name of the village. The **Church of St Peter**, though largely 19th century, contains some 13th-century walls. The Blue Bell is one of the most respected inns in County Durham. **Redmarshall**, just a mile from Stockton, is believed to derive its name from the medieval description of the village 'hill by a reedy lake'. The secluded church contains some Norman work and a fine 15th-century transept.

26 Teesdale:
Alston – High Force – Middleton in Teesdale – Barnard Castle – Raby Castle – Gainford – Darlington

It is very noticeable to the visitor that each Northumbrian dale has a character all its very own, and within each individual dale are many physical contrasts. For instance, few people who survey the industrial ravaged waters of Teesmouth would ever believe that the same river just an hour or so's drive west could be the life-blood of such remote and beautiful countryside teeming with wildlife. Like its sister river the Wear, the Tees is born high in the barren, remote Pennines on the Cumbria–Durham border by the lofty ridges of Cross Fell which rise to almost 900m (3,000ft). Here the Pennine Way wends its way northwards to the highest point along the backbone of England before descending towards Garrigill and Alston.

Teesdale has an air of timelessness. The remote, rugged hills have changed little since the time they were inhabited by prehistoric tribes possibly as early as 5000 BC. The Romans knew the dale existed, and so too did the Vikings. Today the valley is largely farm land and lonely moorland with villages and a few large towns scattered here and there. In addition to the main dale there are several smaller dales fed by the Lune, Balder and Greta, and there are several important reservoirs. Wildlife is varied and sometimes unique, so much so that thousands of hectares of the upper dale are a protected nature reserve. Communications are sparse in Teesdale, but those roads that are available are good. The main artery – the B6277 – runs from Alston to follow for a time the South Tyne river as it flows in the opposite direction, northwards.

In just over 2 miles from Alston at Sillyhall an unclassified road right leads in 2 miles to the delightful village of **Garrigill** situated on the Pennine Way. The village is an ideal centre for fell-walking, though inexperienced walkers should take great care. From Garrigill the walker can trace the origins of the South Tyne and Tees to the summit of Cross Fell, Little Dun Fell and Great Dun Fell. Ruined leadmines live to tell the tales of hardship suffered by the 19th-century inhabitants of this bleak and inhospitable area where, today, moorland birds are likely to be the only company.

Returning to the B6277, the road climbs to its highest point over the aptly named Windy Brow and the Cumbria – Durham border before crossing the Crookham Burn and descending over Grasshill Common to the village of Langdon Beck. From here a fine walk leads to **Cow Green Reservoir**, one of six reservoirs in Teesdale. It was completed in 1971 amid great concern by conservationists. Botanists, in particular, expressed fears that the reservoir would mean the destruction of alpine plants which had grown undisturbed since the glaciers retreated from the landscape. Some species are found nowhere else in the world. The developers won the battle, but, thankfully, there are still areas of Teesdale where rare plants still flourish. Visitors should obey the golden rule of all Teesdale and never pick any plant even though it may look like a common buttercup or daisy. The reservoir serves the iron and steel industries of Cleveland at the mouth of the Tees.

The south-eastern shore of Cow Green Reservoir marks the boundary of the **Upper Teesdale National Nature Reserve** which incorporates the area of Widdybank Fell to the east and the banks of the river Tees between Cauldron Snout waterfall and High Force waterfall. On the south bank the nature reserve extends over Cronkley Fell and Mickle Fell. The scenic beauty of the reserve is wild and rugged. Below Cow Green the Tees tumbles through a rocky chasm in a series of cataracts. If the descent from first cataract to last is measured, **Cauldron Snout** constitutes the highest waterfall in England. From here the river powers its way past Falcon Clints, a cliff of basalt rock. From Falcon Clints the Tees bends northwards to Widdybank Fell back towards the B6277 road. A right of way follows the route of the Tees, and just south of where the Harwood Beck flows into the river the footpath runs north-east to rejoin the road. In 2 miles the B6277 reaches the High Force Hotel where there is parking to visit via a wooded walk (*toll*) the cascading torrents of **High Force waterfall** which cascade in a foam of peaty brown water some 20m (70ft). The waterfall is incorporated into the vast Raby Estate, the extent of which can be determined by noting that every white-painted farmstead and dwelling in the entire area belongs to the estate.

Continuing the descent of the dale from High Force, the B6277 skirts Holwick Fell where the Tees is crossed by the Winch Bridge, a suspension foot-bridge. In 2 miles from High Force the village of Newbiggin is

High Force Falls

reached. Winch Bridge, which can be reached from here, is said to be the successor to the first suspension bridge in Europe, built originally for leadminers, which collapsed in 1820. Low Force Falls are situated just above the bridge.

The B6277 continues to follow the river Tees for a further 3 miles or so into **Middleton in Teesdale**, the capital of the upper dale. A rugged grey-stone town, Middleton's rural setting and tranquil air belies its reliance on ancient heavy industries. Throughout the 19th century the town bustled as the centre of the leadmining industry. The London Lead Company have left their mark in the town in the form of several sturdy rows of dwellings and public buildings. The bridge over the river Tees at Middleton was built in 1811 replacing an earlier one which collapsed. Middleton's parish church was also rebuilt in 1876 but retains some earlier relics including a series of medieval gravestones in the north wall of the nave. The belfry, situated a short distance away from the church, is believed to be the only detached belfry in the county. Middleton offers varied accommodation and is ideally situated as a base to tour the dales of Northumbria. Walks, both easy and strenuous, branch out in almost all directions.

With Middleton as a focal point several roads other than the B6277 radiate from the town. Northwards, an unclassified circular road runs up the valley of Hudeshope Beck to merge into the heather-clad hills by Coldberry Mine before doubling back to Middleton by way of Monks Moor, High Skears and Snaisgill. Eastwards, the B6282 follows the Tees on its journey to the sea to Eggleston and beyond, while from the south bank of the river the B6276 travels south-westwards by Selset Reservoir through a number of hamlets, including Nettlepot, to leave County Durham and reach the moorland town of Brough.

The B6277 continues to accompany the river Tees eastwards, though now on the river's south bank. In 3 miles the road passes through the one-street hamlet of **Mickleton** where remains of prehistoric man have been discovered. On the western outskirts of **Laithkirk** stands the parish church, which was formerly a tithe barn. Two miles or so further on lies the village of **Romaldkirk**, one of Teesdale's prettiest villages. The parish church dates from Norman times but has been greatly restored. The village was the proud owner of a brewery in the 17th century. Along the B6277 at this point several minor roads run south to peter out in the hills over Mickleton Moor and by Balderhead Reservoir.

Two miles from Romaldkirk the next in the series of the dale's villages is reached – **Cotherstone** – famous as the only village in Northumbria to boast its own cheese. History relates of a castle at Cotherstone built in 1200, of which only a tiny section of wall remains at 'The Hagg'. Baldersdale to the south was once a famous deer park. In just over 1 mile the village of **Lartington** is reached, where the most imposing building is Lartington Hall (*private*) which dates from the 17th century.

In 2 miles Barnard Castle, the capital of Teesdale and one of Northumbria's most intriguing towns, is reached.

Barnard Castle

Buses Bishop Auckland, Darlington, High Force, Middleton in Teesdale, Richmond.
Camping and caravanning Thorpe Hall Caravan Site, Whorlton.

Cricket Cricket Club at Baliol Street.
Distances Darlington, 16 miles; Durham, 25 miles; Richmond, 11 miles.
Early closing Thursday.

Golf To the north of Barnard Castle.
Guided tours Walkabout leaflet available
from information bureau.
Hotels *Blagraves, Golden Lion, Montalbo,
Morritt Arms,* Whorlton, *George and Dragon
Inn.*
Information bureau Galgate. Weekdays
only, tel. 3481.

Market Day Wednesday.
Museums and Art Galleries The Bowes
Museum.
Post Office The GPO is in Horsemarket.
Population 5,000.

Barnard Castle derives its name from the Norman castle, the ruins of
which still perch precariously above the river Tees. The Romans were
aware of the site, as evidence has been unearthed that the Roman road
from Bowes Moor to Binchester crossed the river Tees where the gas-
works now stand. The origins of the fortress date back to the 11th
century, when a castle was built on the site by Guy de Balliol, Lord of
Bailleul in France. The castle was rebuilt in 1150 by Bernard who gave
his name to the town which grew in importance from that time. Bernard's successor was John Balliol who founded Balliol College, Oxford.
Future owners of the castle included Richard Neville, better known as
'Warwick, the Kingmaker'. Richard died at the Battle of Bosworth Field
in 1485, and the castle came into the possession of Henry VII. In 1625 the
castle was dismantled by Sir Henry Vane.

Barnard Castle was at one time one of the largest castles in all England,
and the ruins still cover some 2·6ha (6·5 acres) today. The great circular
keep dating from the 14th century is the castle's most striking feature.
The castle is in the care of the Department of Environment, and a
detailed guidebook is available.

To reach the castle by the B6277 it is necessary to cross the Tees by the
bridge which dates from 1569. Major rebuilding took place after damage
was caused by the disastrous floods of 1771. Prior to then the bridge
accommodated a tiny chapel at which illegal marriages took place. Over
the bridge a path leads left to the castle and right along the A67 towards
the market-place and town centre. The road ascends The Bank which at
its base is known as **Thorngate**, the town's centre of Georgian elegance.
Thorngate House bears witness to this period, and nearer the river
Thorngate Mill and the weavers' cottages give a clue to the town's
flourishing 19th-century industry.

Half-way up The Bank on the right-hand side is **Blagraves House**, one
of the most interesting and probably the oldest house in Barnard Castle.
Now housing a cosy family restaurant offering the best in traditional
English cooking, Blagraves, or Blagroves as it is sometimes called, has an

interesting history. It exhibits the emblem of Richard III, as the house was supposedly given to Miles Forrest who was one of the gaolers of the Princes in the Tower. From 1672 the house was occupied by the Blagrave family. It achieved fame as an inn, and Oliver Cromwell is said to have been entertained with 'cakes and ale' when he visited the town on 24 October 1648. The exterior of Blagraves is decorated with 17th-century figures depicting musicians, and the house is the only one in the town of the Tudor period which retains a medieval interior.

At the head of The Bank stands the **Market Cross**, not simply a cross but a former Town Hall, an octagonal building which was built in 1747 and financed by a Barnard Castle notable, Thomas Breaks. The building has had a variety of uses. The town council met here and the courts held session in the top storey. Market stalls were set up in the arcades of the ground floor. At one time the building served as the local gaol.

The spacious market-place is dominated by the **King's Head Hotel** where on 2 February 1838 Charles Dickens is said to have stayed while researching his masterpiece *Nicholas Nickleby*. His most famous quotation during his stay has lived with the establishment ever since – 'Say you know me and they will give you ale free', but this is not guaranteed to work today. Dickens's stay at Barnard Castle resulted in a further literary work. Opposite the King's Head Hotel a clockmaker's shop stood which held a particular appeal for Dickens. *Master Humphrey's Clock* was inspired by the shop which was regrettably demolished some years ago.

Continuing north, the market-place gives way to the **Horse Market** with several interesting buildings. **Witham Hall** was built in 1850 in memory of H. M. T. Witham who founded the town's Mechanics' Institute. Further along the curving thoroughfare with its jigsaw puzzle of façades the half-timbered **Golden Lion Inn**, dating from 1770, is particularly appealing. A plaque on the wall of the Horse Market close to the pedestrian crossing marks the site of the Hospital of the Durham Militia built in 1759. On the corner where the Horse Market joins Galgate stands **Holy Trinity Methodist Church**, built as recently as 1894 and designed by Morley of Leeds.

Galgate, which carries the A67 out of the town towards Darlington, follows the line of the Roman Road to Binchester. It gets its name as a result of being the site of the town's gallows in more bloodthirsty times. At the extreme end is a group of houses called **The Grove**, dating from the 18th century. Visitors can easily pass through Barnard Castle by the A67 oblivious of several of the town's unique treasures. At the corner of the market-place and Newgate at the top of The Bank stands the **Church of St Mary** which is largely Norman and Transitional in period. The tower dates from the 19th century and is evidence of a considerable restoration programme. The churchyard contains several intriguing and poignant epitaphs including a simple stone cross commemorating Barnard Castle's saddest year – 1849 – when 143 inhabitants died of Asiatic cholera.

A mile eastwards along **Newgate** leads to one of the biggest surprises not only in Northumbria but indeed in all Britain. Like a mirage the **Bowes Museum** (*open daily*) peeps through the mists as though it were a giant decoration on an enormous cake. Founded by John Bowes, son of the 10th Earl of Strathmore, and his French wife Josephine in the second half of the 19th century, the museum is one of the treasure-houses of Europe. It was designed by Jules Pellechet as a museum to house and exhibit to the public the great collection of paintings and works of art which the Bowes family had spent a lifetime collecting. Construction of the 'château' started in 1869, because, it is said, the Bowes could not find suitable premises in their beloved France. Sadly, they both died before their life's work was opened to the public in 1892. In a corner of the estate stands **St Mary's Church** which is Roman Catholic. The Bowes's gravestones can be seen outside the east wall.

Today, the museum is under the control of Durham County Council, and displays have been widely extended in scope. The collection includes paintings by El Greco, Goya, Sassetta, Tiepolo, Boucher, Gainsborough and others. There are also vast collections of British and Continental porcelain and pottery, silver (including a unique animated silver swan), glassware, tapestries and sculpture. English and French period rooms have been realistically restored to their former glories and exquisitely furnished. A children's gallery and a music room contrast with the museum's latest acquisition, a costume gallery opened in 1976 by the Queen Mother who, as a Bowes-Lyon, is related to John and Josephine Bowes. More humble but, nonetheless, intriguing galleries have been constructed in the vaults where displays are devoted to regional archaeology, local history and natural history. Temporary exhibitions are also held, and there are catering facilities.

Continuing east along Newgate away from the town centre, in almost 1 mile the road right descends to the battlemented arch of Abbey Bridge which crosses the Tees and right to the gaunt ruins of **Egglestone Abbey** nestling on the river bank amid pasture and woodland. The monastery was founded in 1190 by the White Canons of the Premonstratensian Order who gave Blanchland, further north, its name. The abbey was enlarged during the ensuing three centuries, and remains of all periods can still be seen. The finale of Sir Walter Scott's work *Rokeby* is set among the weather-beaten stones of Egglestone Abbey. The beauty of Teesdale hereabouts was Scott's inspiration. A few miles downstream stands Rokeby itself where the rivers Greta and Tees meet. On the banks of the Greta stands Mortham Tower, another of Scott's romantic locations.

The route back to the market-place can be retraced via Newgate, or, alternatively, the unclassified road by which Egglestone Abbey stands continues to follow the Tees to Barnard Castle Bridge.

Several major roads radiate from Barnard Castle. The A66 runs via Abbey Bridge and Rokeby along the route of the Roman Road from Carlisle to join the A1 at Scotch Corner. In the opposite direction the B6278 'dale-hops' northwards via Eggleston into Weardale. The A67 travels east through Gainford and Piercebridge to Darlington. The A688 runs more north-east to Staindrop, Raby Castle and on through Bishop Auckland to Durham City.

Staindrop is situated some 7 miles from Barnard Castle and is one of County Durham's most interesting villages. Built largely around the spacious green, the village enjoys close associations with Raby Castle. The outskirts of the castle's vast estate border the village along the banks of the Langley Beck. The grey-stone dwellings which line the main street of Staindrop are predominantly 18th century, but the town's history goes back much further. In 1378 Lord John Neville was granted a licence to crenellate at Raby, and, coincidentally, a charter was proclaimed that a weekly market and an annual fair should be held at Staindrop.

Even earlier history can be found in the **Church of St Mary**, one of the most interesting in the county. Much larger than most village churches, it stands sturdy and squat by the bridge which takes the A688 out of Staindrop towards the public entrance to Raby. A church was established on the site in Saxon times, remains of which can still be seen in the form of two windows and a sundial to the left of the chancel arch. The tower is Norman except for the summit. St Mary's Church was enlarged in the 12th, 13th and 14th centuries and is the burial-place of successive generations of nobility who have resided at nearby Raby Castle. The collection of alabaster figures is remarkable, the oldest dating from 1260. Both the Neville family and their successors, the Vanes, are represented. In the churchyard can be seen a huge neo-Gothic mausoleum, also a tribute to the Vane family and, in particular, the Duchess of Cleveland.

Staindrop boasts several other interesting buildings. The **Manor Office** stands on the south side of the village green in Office Square and dates from the 16th century. Adjacent is a typically Georgian building which serves as the **Raby Estate Office**. Remnants of the stone posts and chains which penned in the sheep and cattle brought to market every week until 1858 can still be seen around the village green. By the deanery at the western end of the village an arch of a former coach-house is clearly visible, though the entrance has been blocked. Directly opposite the single-storey building with leaded criss-cross windows is the former blacksmith's shop. Since 1971 the centre of Staindrop has been officially designated as a conservation area.

Within 1 mile of Staindrop church on the A688 towards Bishop Auckland the road skirts the **Raby Estate** with the magnificent castle in the distance. The public entrance to the grounds and castle is clearly signposted (*open Easter Saturday, Sunday and Monday; all Sundays in April; Wednesdays and Sundays in May; Wednesdays, Saturdays and Sundays in June, July and September; daily except Friday in August, or by appointment on other days*). Raby Castle is one of County Durham's most imposing fortresses, set in a landscaped park where herds of deer freely roam. Its origins go back to the time of King Canute (Cnut) 1017–1035, who took a great interest in Northumbria's role as the 'cradle of Christianity' and made many pilgrimages to the north's centres of Christian learning. It is known that a crude fortress stood at Raby at this time, but it was in the 12th century that Raby began to make an impact on the history of England. The estate came into the possession of the great Neville family, Geoffrey being the very first Neville Lord of Raby. He was the son of Isabella de Neville, a rich and powerful Norman heiress. Neville upon Neville succeeded Geoffrey as the family's power and the castle grew. Major improvements were made during the 14th century after Bishop Hatfield of Durham gave licence to crenellate in 1378. The Lord of Raby at the time was John Neville, whose father Ralph was the hero of the battle of Neville's Cross fought near Durham City in 1346.

The Nevilles held Raby until the 16th century, when on 13 November 1569 the ill-fated 'Rising of the North', aimed at replacing Queen Elizabeth by Mary Queen of Scots, was plotted at Raby. As a result of the disastrous failure of the plan Raby was lost to the Nevilles and fell into the hands of the Crown where it remained until 1626 when it was

The Bowes Museum, Barnard Castle

purchased by Sir Henry Vane, a member of another great Northumbrian family. Sir Henry's family roots can be traced back to 11th-century Wales, and the present Lord Barnard's ancestors can be linked with both illustrious Raby families – the Nevilles and the Vanes.

Raby Castle is undoubtedly one of the finest historic houses open to the public in England. Public access is available to several of the castle's major rooms where helpful guides are usually available. In the coach-house near to the castle horse-drawn vehicles are on display, including the state coach and the estate fire-engines. The gardens nearby are also open to the public, and there is a tea-room in the stables.

From Raby Castle the A688 continues north-east through West Auckland, crossing the route of the original Stockton and Darlington Railway and the associated rail trail west of Brusselton Incline, and continues to Bishop Auckland.

A mile or so from Raby an unclassified road left leads to the village of **Cockfield**, noted as the birthplace of Jeremiah Dixon, a self-taught genius who was responsible with a fellow surveyor Charles Mason for founding the Mason and Dixon line (the boundary between Maryland and Pennsylvania) in the United States of America. Though Cockfield's church dates from the 13th century, little remains of that period. The building was almost completely rebuilt and enlarged in 1911.

From Staindrop two roads run eastwards to the A1(M) and Darlington. The B6279 runs amid fertile farm land and through the hamlets of Ingleton and Summerhouse. Shortly after Summerhouse a detour for 1 mile left on an unclassified road leads to the hamlet of **Denton**, a tranquil retreat where the Norman church, rebuilt in the 19th century, has an interesting 12th-century gravestone in blue marble incorporated into the wall of the vestry.

Leaving Staindrop southwards, the B6274 links with the most picturesque and interesting route to Darlington via the A67 which follows the course of the meandering river Tees. The B6274 joins the A67 at **Winston**, where the most notable feature is the stone bridge dating from 1764 and believed to have the largest single-span arch, measuring 33m (111ft), in western Europe. The parish **Church of St Andrew** stands above the rushing river Tees. Though dating from the 13th century (the font dates from that period), there were major alterations in the 19th century. From Winston westwards the A67 climbs over Westwick Moor to Barnard Castle.

Eastwards, the A67 continues to one of the prettiest of south Durham's villages, **Gainford**. The main village is centred on the spacious village green to the south of the A67, and though some new housing development has taken place, the austere Georgian houses and church dating from Saxon times retain the village's ancient character. The first church was built in Gainford in the 9th century by Bishop Eadred of Lindisfarne. The present building, dedicated to St Mary, is almost wholly late 13th century. It is believed to have been constructed, according to the custom prevalent for centuries in Northumbria, by using stone plundered from the Roman settlement at nearby Piercebridge. Several Roman remains, including altars, and a number of Saxon crosses have come to light in the environs of the church in recent times. Some are incorporated into the church's structure; others have been put on display in Durham Cathedral's museum.

Between the village green and the A67 one of Gainford's prettiest crescents, **High Row**, runs parallel with the main road. From the Cross Keys Inn the terrace of gaily painted, flower-decked houses reflect the prosperity of the village in the 18th century when Gainford was a popular residential area for the rich merchants commuting to and from Darlington. Every house is different. In High Row and on the opposite side of the road well-tended gardens complement the window-boxes and flower tubs which adorn every dwelling.

At the end of High Row stands the austere Jacobean **Gainford Hall**. It was built in 1605 and recently restored, though it retains its rather ghostly appearance. Regrettably, the hall is not open to the public. In the grounds of the hall, visible from the road, stands a 17th-century dovecote. By the church a footpath leads in a short distance down to the banks of the river Tees. In 1771 disastrous floods created havoc in Gainford, so much so that the course of the river was changed. Part of the land which belonged to Gainford and was therefore in County Durham was transferred overnight on to the other bank of the river as it changed its course and thus moved into Yorkshire.

The banks of the river upstream provide a pleasant walk, though the going is rough in places. The walk is well-worth while, however, for in just over 1 mile **Gainford Spa** can be found, which in the early 19th century was regarded as one of the most beneficial sulphur springs in the north and attracted visitors from all over England. Water still gushes from a huge stone font on the river bank, and the acrid smell of sulphur can be located at some distance. Since 1971 the historic parts of Gainford have been designated a conservation area which will assure the preservation of the character of the village.

From Gainford the A67 continues to follow the river Tees eastwards on its way to the sea and in a further 3 miles reaches **Piercebridge**, a village with a history stretching back to Roman times. The neat houses around the village green stand near one of the most strategic points on the Roman Dere Street which ran from York to Hadrian's Wall and crosses the river Tees at this point. Local inhabitants say that the oak remains of the Roman bridge abutments can still be seen when the river is very low about 400m below the present bridge. A fort begun in AD 125, three years after the commencement of Hadrian's Wall, eventually covered some 4ha (10 acres). Excavation of the fort is being carried out, though at present excavations are in no way as extensive as at Roman sites further north. Nevertheless, interesting and important finds have been unearthed which are on display in museums throughout Northumbria and also in the British Museum.

The Tees is crossed by a bridge which was rebuilt in the 16th century and again in 1789. In 1642, during the Civil War, Lord Fairfax was attacked and routed by the Earl of Newcastle leading the Royalists. Skeletons of horses and soldiers are still unearthed in the vicinity from time to time.

The **George Hotel** at Piercebridge houses a grandfather clock around which revolves a legend of particular interest to American visitors. The clock is reputed to have stopped at the very second its owner died and inspired an American composer, Henry C. Work, to write the immortal popular song *My Grandfather's Clock*. In contrast to Piercebridge's ancient Roman heritage the **Church of St Mary** is of relatively recent construction dating from 1873.

From Piercebridge the B6275 follows the route of Dere Street northwards to Royal Oak where it joins the main A68 artery. Southwards, the B6275 joins the A1(M) east of Melsonby. The road is arrow-straight in both directions, a distinguishing characteristic of Roman road-building.

After passing Piercebridge the river Tees embarks upon a meandering course as it wends its way south of Darlington. At the edge of the first of a series of great horseshoe bends 1 mile east of Piercebridge stands the village of **High Coniscliffe** whose history dates back to the 8th century. Its name dates from the Saxon period, being a derivation of Konig's Cliff or King's Cliff. The church is Early English with a Norman window and north doorway. There are also fragments of Saxon stonework in parts of the walls. The church is dedicated to Edwin, the saint, who was one of the best-known kings of Northumbria and who gave his name to Edwin's burgh – today's Edinburgh. Curiously, it is the only church in England dedicated to this saint.

High Coniscliffe is situated some 4 miles from the centre of Darlington. After crossing the A1(M) in just over 1 mile, the A67 continues into the town, while the river Tees veers south-east in a series of great arcs towards the village of Croft.

Darlington

Aero Club Middleton St George.
Autodrome Motor cycle and club motoring racing at Croft.
Bowls There are numerous greens in the parks.

Buses Barnard Castle, Bishop Auckland, Carlisle, Durham City, Hartlepool, Middlesbrough, Middleton in Teesdale, Newcastle upon Tyne, Redcar, Stockton-on-Tees, Sunderland, Tees-side Airport.

Cinemas *Odeon*, Bondgate; *ABC*, Northgate.
Cricket Railway Athletic Club, Brinkburn Road.
Distances Bishop Auckland, 12 miles; Durham City, 20 miles; Newcastle upon Tyne, 36 miles; Stockon-on-Tees, 11 miles.
Early closing Wednesday.
Football English League ground at Feethams.
Golf *Darlington Golf-Club*, Haughton Grange; *Dinsdale Spa Golf Club*, Dinsdale; *Blackwell Grange Golf-Course*, Blackwell; *Stressholme Golf-Course* (municipal).
Guided tours Walkabout leaflet available from information office.

Hotels *Europa Lodge, Hallgarth, The King's Head, St George Hotel* at Tees-side Airport.
Information office Public Library, Crown Street, tel. 62034.
Market day Mondays and Saturdays.
Museums Darlington Museum, Tubwell Row; North Road Station Railway Museum.
Population 98,000.
Post Office The GPO is in Northgate.
Rugby Darlington RFC, McMullen Road; Darlington Railway Athletic RFC, Brinkburn Road; Mowden Park RFC.
Swimming-pools Kendrew swimming-pool, Gladstone swimming-pool.
Tennis There are numerous public courts.
Theatre Darlington Civic Theatre, Parkgate.

Darlington is a town synonymous with the development of railways and is situated on the route of the original Stockton and Darlington Railway, the world's first public, fare-paying, steam passenger railway. The town lies on the river Skerne, a tributary of the Tees. Though there is little of great antiquity in the town itself, recorded evidence proves that Darlington and its environs have a long history. Its origins lie in a small Saxon settlement which grew up on the banks of the Skerne. By Norman times Darlington had expanded into a thriving market town described in a contemporary survey as the best market town in the bishopric after Durham.

It was undoubtedly the development of the railways which made the greatest impact on Darlington in the late 18th century. The town's other claim to fame is as a Quaker stronghold, and it was one of the fraternity, Edward Pease (1767–1858), who was the champion of the railway-engine as a means of transportation of Durham coal from the coalfields in the west of the county to the coast for shipping to London and the Continent. He supported George Stephenson both morally and financially and ensured that the railway triumphed over a counter-proposal to build a canal to transport the 'black diamonds'.

Darlington soon became established as the railway centre of the world. Skilled craftsmen built locomotive after locomotive for almost 150 years until 1966 when the great railway workshops were sadly silenced. The town refused to die, and new industries sprang up to employ the innate skills of Darlingtonians, including the manufacture of such diverse products as knitting-wool, a throwback to the 18th century when the town

345

was a leading woollen-spinning centre, structural steel, chemicals, furniture and electronic equipment. Bridges produced in Darlington are in use today spanning such rivers as the Amazon, the Nile, the Bosphorus, and nearer home the Tyne.

The new Borough of Darlington is an attractive mixture of old and new, and there are several historically interesting buildings in the town centre and its environs including an important new attraction, **the North Road Station Railway Museum** (*open Easter to end October daily, November to Easter weekdays only.*) It is a tribute to the town's railway history that Darlington has two stations in use today. The main East Coast line passes through the town, and **Bank Top Station** is an important halt on this route. The station was rebuilt in 1887 by William Bell, the well-known North Eastern Railway architect. Until recently passengers travelling through Darlington's main line station caught a glimpse of George Stephenson's original *Locomotion*, the engine which made the historic first journey between Shildon, Darlington and Stockton. The engine has now found a permanent and much more fitting home in Darlington's new North Road Station Museum.

North Road Station is situated in Station Road off Northgate on the northern outskirts of the town. The building is still used as an unmanned halt on the branch line between Bank Top main line station and Bishop Auckland. The line which is today served by modern diesels travels along much of the original route of Stephenson's railway. Though the station is still in daily use, a large part of it has been given over with separate access to housing the new museum devoted to the history of north-east railways in general and the Stockton and Darlington line in particular. The building dates from 1842 and replaced the original station which served as a halt on the inaugural line. It is architecturally appealing and incorporates some cast-iron work. The new museum presents a storehouse of railwayana from full-size engines, including the original *Locomotion* and *Derwent* (also used on the Stockton and Darlington Railway and dating from 1845), down to tickets, timetables, publicity posters, lamps, signals and station name plates recalling lines now long since axed. The museum was opened by HRH Prince Philip, Duke of Edinburgh, in 1975 to mark the 150th anniversary of the Stockton and Darlington Railway and is administered by an active trust.

The centre of Darlington is almost encompassed by streets still known today as 'gates', just as they were in medieval times. Skinnergate, Houndgate, Bondgate and Northgate each have their own particular appeal. A short distance from Bank Top Station stands Darlington's **Civic Theatre** in Park Gate. Originally the New Hippodrome, the building dates from 1907 and is one of the best examples of a civic theatre in the country today.

At the base of Park Gate the eastern outskirts of the town centre are ringed by the Skerne and St Cuthbert's Way. Close by the Skerne stands **St Cuthbert's Church** which can be reached by a foot-bridge across the river. The church dates from 1192, having replaced an important Saxon church on the site. Nikolaus Pevsner in *The Buildings of England* describes St Cuthbert's as 'one of the most important churches in the County and one of the important Early English Churches in Northern England'. Building was ordered in the 12th century by the Bishop of Durham, Hugh Pudsey, and alterations and additions were made in more recent times. In 1864 the chancel was rebuilt, and in 1752 the spire had to be rebuilt after it was struck by lightning.

Opposite St Cuthbert's and in complete contrast stands the ultra-modern **Town Hall**, or Civic Centre, opened by HRH Princess Anne in 1970. The Town Hall is built on the site of a manor-house owned by the Bishop of Durham, which was believed to be haunted. The manor was demolished in 1870 and to date there is no evidence that the building's supernatural inhabitants have progressed into the new building. The Town Hall and churchyard lead directly into the market-place where there are several interesting buildings. In Horse Market stands **Bennet House**, a fine three-storey Georgian edifice by the side of which Bull Wynd links the market-place with Houndgate. The **Wynd** is one of the town's oldest thoroughfares, and its name is a throw back to the time when bull-baiting was practised. On the corner of Bull Wynd and Houndgate (on the right-hand side facing Houndgate) stands the house where Edward Pease (1767–1858), champion of the railways, was born, and directly opposite in Houndgate stands a row of fine Georgian residences.

At the western end of Houndgate the road joins Skinnergate, where immediately on the left the **Friends' Meeting House** is evidence of Darlington's importance as a Quaker stronghold. The building dates from 1839, though there was a Quaker place of worship on the site much earlier. At the rear is a Quaker burial-ground. The Mechanics' Institute, built in 1853, stands directly opposite.

Post House Wynd links Skinnergate with High Row, at the north end of which stands a statue of Edward Pease's famous son Joseph Pease, MP

(1799–1872). Both Skinnergate and High Row lead to Bondgate where, in addition to the sturdy Methodist chapel dating from 1812, there are several examples of Darlington's 'yards', some named according to the workers who lived there. A century ago there were more than 100 'yards' in Darlington.

The centre of the market-place is dominated by the Clock Tower, Market Hall and Old Town Hall. The latter was built in 1853, and the clock was installed in 1864. Tubwell Row, on the northern side of the market-place, houses Darlington's town museum (*open daily except Sundays*) which contains local history displays relating to the town and surrounding district. Across the road in Crown Street is the **Library** (*open daily except Sundays*), incorporating a tourist information centre and art gallery. The building, which was opened in 1855, was built from money donated by Edward Pease's grandson, also called Edward (1834–80), the son of Joseph Pease.

Within the Darlington Borough boundary there are no fewer than six major parks with a further eighteen recreation areas and public open spaces. South Park, bordered by Parkside, Grange Road and Victoria Embankment, covers 40ha (100 acres), and nature trails are usually organized during the summer months. All the usual recreational amenities, both active and passive, are provided, and there is also an aviary. The park is the venue for the annual Darlington Show, usually held in August, as well as other special events throughout the year. From Blackwell to Broken Scar the banks of the river Tees provide peaceful walks and picnic areas.

Several main roads, in addition to the A67 west, radiate from the centre of Darlington. Northwards, the A167 links with the A1(M) in 6 miles just after passing through the hamlet of Coatham Mundeville where there are records of a chapel as early as 1264. From Coatham Mundeville an unclassified road running north-east leads in ½ mile to the hamlet of **Brafferton**, noted as the birthplace of Britain's most famous bull, 'Comet', bred by the Collings Brothers at Ketton Farm. The legendary bull was sold in 1810 for the sum of 1,000 guineas and became the progenitor of the Shorthorn breed of cattle. **Orchard House**, a private dwelling to the west of the village, is a former coach-house on the ancient road out of Darlington which at Newton Ketton to the east of Brafferton crossed the old Pack Horse Bridge, still standing today.

The unclassified road bears east through Great Stainton, situated on the Roman road, and the village of Bishopton where evidence of a motte-and-bailey castle can be seen on the eastern outskirts of the village. From Bishopton several minor roads run eastwards to the northern boundary of County Durham and Cleveland.

The main route between Darlington and Stockton-on-Tees to the east is the A66. On the outskirts of Darlington, this road runs through the villages of **Houghton-le-Skerne** and **Sadberge**. The church of the former is mainly late Norman. The latter was the medieval capital, or wapentake, of the area of Northumbria between Middleton in Teesdale and Seaton Carew on the northern estuary of the Tees. The earldom of Sadberge was originally held by the Bishop of Durham and subsequently by the Crown. A stone on the village green commemorates Queen Victoria's jubilee and describes her as Queen of the United Kingdom, Empress of India and Countess of Sadberge. A few stones from an early church are incorporated into the parish **Church of St Andrew** which dates from 1831.

From Sadberge the road continues east through **Long Newton** where the Vane family of Raby Castle once had their manor-house. The **Church of St Mary** dates from 1856 and contains a Vane mausoleum and other reminders of the village's association with the family. A mile further east away from the new section of road stands the hamlet of **Elton** whose tiny **Church of St John** measures only 15·6m (52ft) in length. Though constructed in 1841, it retains a Norman doorway and chancel arch.

Within 2 miles from Elton the urban conurbation of Stockton-on-Tees is reached. To the south of the A66 another road runs parallel linking Darlington with Yarm. The road, newly classified A67, is notable since for much of its length it follows the original railway line from Darlington to Stockton passing such well-known landmarks on Stephenson's route as Fighting Cocks, Oak Tree, Goosepool and Urlay Nook. The road also skirts Tees-side Airport at Middleton St George. Near the village of **Middleton One Row** the river Tees, which until this point has run several miles to the south, makes a northerly diversion before looping away again south-east and on to Yarm. Middleton One Row and its neighbour **Low Dinsdale** were popular spa centres in the late 18th and 19th centuries. Here the old Roman road Pounteys Lane crossed the Tees on its way through Sadberge to Durham. Before the construction of Croft Bridge this was the main route across the Tees. To the west of the village on **Tower Hill** there is an earthwork, now fir clad, which is believed to be a relic of a castle built to guard this strategic crossing of the river. Middleton's **Church of St Lawrence** dates from 1871.

The A167 serves as the main route south from Darlington to the east of the A1(M) artery. On the outskirts of the town it passes **Blackwell Grange**, a fine 18th-century residence set in parkland which includes a golf-course. Blackwell Grange, built in 1736, is now a luxury hotel. It was the birthplace of George Allan, who devoted his life to the study of natural history. His collection of specimens and the fruits of his research were left to the Hancock Museum, Newcastle upon Tyne, on his death in 1800.

Blackwell, a village now serving as a suburb of Darlington, is noted for its phenomena known as the **Hell Kettles**, a macabre collection of ponds situated 1 mile to the south of the village on the main road. Care must be taken when parking as no official facilities exist. The Hell Kettles are believed to be bottomless ponds which were the result of an earthquake on Christmas Eve, 1179. Their waters have a permanent green translucent hue and are associated with many tales of weird and mysterious happenings. Humans and animals, compelled by unknown forces to wander across the fields to the ponds, have been drowned here. It is said that no living creature can exist in the turbid waters.

In a further mile the Skerne joins the Tees at **Croft**, where formerly the old Great North Road crossed the river on the Yorkshire–Durham border. Croft is notable on several accounts. It has strong literary connections, being the village to which Byron travelled to spend part of his honeymoon with Isabella Milbanke. The village was also the place where Charles L. Dodgson grew up. His father was rector, and there is no doubt that the gardens of the rectory, which dated from Elizabethan times, set the scene for such epics as *Alice in Wonderland*. Croft's other claim to fame is as a spa. It was regarded as superior to other spas in the area, including Gainford, and attracted visitors from far and wide. The **Church of St Peter** is pleasantly situated by the Tees near the bridge. Like many other churches in the district it includes visible fragments of Norman architecture, though most of the building is 14th century. The tower dates from the 15th century. One of the church's most outstanding features is the Milbanke Pew which stands high above the rest of the congregation and is reached by a magnificent staircase. Byron and his new bride are said to have worshipped here, and the pew was also regularly occupied by the notorious George Hudson, railway king and MP. He is said to have refused to face the congregation during the service, while his wife sat with her umbrella opened during the sermon.

Near to the church the **Croft Spa Hotel** accommodated 18th-century visitors. It was at Croft Bridge that newly appointed bishops of Durham were presented with the Conyers Falchion given by the Lord of Sockburn, a village situated a few miles downstream on the Tees. Legend relates that the falchion was used to slay the Sockburn Worm, a monster which terrorized the district. The tale compares with that of the Lambton Worm, Northumbria's version of the George and Dragon fable. The latest sporting attraction is Croft Autodrome motor-racing circuit.

From Croft the A167 continues south into Yorkshire, while an unclassified road east reaches in 1 mile the village of Hurworth and continues in a further mile to Neasham. **Hurworth** is a spacious, attractive village with fine Georgian houses surrounding the village green. **All Saints Church** was rebuilt in 1831, except for the tower which dates from the 15th century. It was extensively restored in 1870. **Neasham** was a bustling village in medieval times. A Benedictine abbey occupied a site near the ford which crossed the Tees. It was dissolved in the 16th century.

From Neasham the road travels northwards to join the Darlington to Yarm road at Middleton One Row. A detour from Neasham leads back to the banks of the Tees to the hamlet of Low Dinsdale where there are pleasant riverside walks beloved of William Wordsworth who visited the area with his sister in 1799. The hamlet is noted as a spa, the medieval waters having been discovered by coalminers in 1789. The **Church of St John the Baptist** was founded in 1196 on the site of an earlier Saxon church. It was largely reconstructed in 1875.

27 Through route:
Scotch Corner – Darlington – Durham – Chester-le-Street – Gateshead – Newcastle upon Tyne (42 miles) or Tyne Tunnel (45 miles)

N.B: All mileages shown in brackets are from Scotch Corner

Scotch Corner has been a landmark on the A1 east-coast route between London and Edinburgh since the old coaching days. At this important junction two roads join the A1 from the west, the A66 which runs due west over Bowes Moor to Brough and on to Penrith, and the A6108 which runs south-west to Richmond. Eastwards from Scotch Corner an unclassified road leads via Middleton Tyas to Croft.

Two miles north of Scotch Corner the A1 becomes the motorway A1(M). At this junction the B6275 runs due north on the line of the old Roman road to Piercebridge. The A1(M) continues north and in 3 miles is joined from the east by the A66(M) which runs to Darlington town centre (9 miles). The A1(M) crosses the river Tees and intersects the A67 which follows the river Tees westwards through High Coniscliffe to Piercebridge, Gainford, and Barnard Castle. Eastwards, the A67 leads into Darlington town centre (9 miles).

Continuing north on the A1(M), in a further mile the B6279 also enters Darlington to the east. Westwards, the B6279 reaches Staindrop in 9 miles. In a further 2 miles the A1(M) crosses the A68 main through route via Corbridge, Carter Bar and into Scotland. South-east, the A68 enters Darlington town centre in 3 miles. In a further 2½ miles at Coatham Mundeville the A1(M) crosses the A167, formerly the A1 Great North Road. The A167 runs almost parallel to the A1(M) northwards through Newton Aycliffe (13 miles) to Durham City (25 miles). South-wards, the A167 also enters Darlington. The A1(M) immediately crosses the river Skerne and continues north through open countryside for a further 5 miles. At the Bradbury Interchange (16 miles) the A1(M) crosses the A689 which runs westwards for 7 miles to Bishop Auckland.

Barnard Castle and bridge

In 2½ miles eastwards the A689 passes through Sedgefield and in a further 7 miles reaches Wolviston before reaching the coast in a further 6 miles at Hartlepool.

The A1(M) continues north intersected by several minor roads leading to Bishop Middleham, Ferryhill and Cornforth. In 4½ miles from Bradbury the A1(M) is intersected by the B6291 which westwards leads in 3½ miles to Spennymoor and eastwards in 1 mile to Coxhoe. In a further mile at Bowburn (22 miles) the A177 running north-west to Durham City via Shincliffe and south-east to Stockton-on-Tees is crossed. Three miles north of Bowburn the A1 is intersected by the A181 Durham City road which runs eastwards to link in 8 miles with the A19 south of Peterlee.

The A1(M) continues through predominantly open countryside to Carrville Interchange (27 miles) where the A690 Durham City to Sunderland road crosses the motorway. Three miles south-west from the intersection the A690 enters Durham City. North-eastwards, the A690 reaches Houghton le Spring in 5 miles and in a further 5 miles enters the western outskirts of Sunderland. Six miles from Carrville the A1(M) descends through open countryside to cross the river Wear and bypass Chester-le-Street. On the descent towards Chester-le-Street a glimpse of Lumley Castle can be seen among the trees to the left.

Immediately after crossing the Wear several roads link with the A1(M) (33 miles). The A183 east skirts the boundary of Lambton Pleasure Park to pass through Shiney Row and enter the outskirts of Sunderland via Penshaw in 8 miles. Westwards the A693 climbs through Pelton to Beamish and the North of England Open Air Museum. The A167 which has run northwards from Coatham Mundeville parallel with the A1(M) passes through the western outskirts of Durham City and Chester-le-Street before rejoining the A1(M) at this point.

The A1(M) continues northwards with the outskirts of Washington New Town visible to the east and the industry of Birtley to the west. In $1\frac{1}{2}$ miles from Chester-le-Street before the Washington/Birtley Services the A1231 east leads to Washington New Town with signs leading to Washington Old Hall, Washington Waterfowl Park and Washington 'F' Pit Museum. A mile north of the Washington/Birtley Services (35 miles) new designations have come into effect at the time of writing. The A1(M) – formerly the A194(M) – veers right to link with the A194 and in 10 miles reaches the Tyne Tunnel (45 miles).

Continuing north on the former A1(M), now signposted A69 Hexham, in a further mile this new road veers left to provide a fast link with the A69 Newcastle to Carlisle road, completely bypassing the city of Newcastle. Continuing northwards, the old A1 (A6127) leads through Low Fell and Gateshead to Newcastle (42 miles).

N.B: All mileages shown in brackets are from Scotch Corner

Two miles north of Scotch Corner two routes continue north. The B6275 follows the route of the Roman Road and in 5 miles crosses the Tees at Piercebridge continuing north to join the A68 in a further 5½ miles. Alternatively, the A1(M) can be taken. In 8½ miles from Scotch Corner the road is joined directly by the A68. From this junction the A68 travels north-west through open countryside to pass through the hamlet of Bildershaw in 6 miles. In a further 2 miles the road runs through the urban development of West Auckland and the outskirts of Bishop Auckland. At West Auckland the A68 is joined by the A688 which runs south-west via Raby Castle to reach Staindrop in 5 miles and Barnard Castle in a further 6 miles. From West Auckland the A68 climbs steeply to High Etherley and Toft Hill (18 miles). Two miles from Toft Hill in rural scenic surroundings the A68 crosses the river Wear, where an unclassified road west leads to Hamsterley Forest. A mile to the east stands Witton Castle. In a further 3 miles the A68 passes through the hamlet of Fir Tree and crosses the A689 which leads east in 2 miles to the colliery areas of Crook and on to Willington. The A689 continues north-east to Durham City, westwards to Wolsingham and in 10 miles to Stanhope – gateway to Weardale.

The A68 continues north-west climbing over Tow Law (26 miles) with Tunstall Reservoir to the west with expansive views of moorland and fell. Eight miles from Tow Law the scenery changes as the A68 reaches Castleside and the junction with the A692 from Tyneside. Though the industrial deprivation of Consett and its ironworks is but a stone's throw away to the east, the despoliation is thankfully contained in a surprisingly restricted area.

A mile or so from Castleside the A68 crosses the Derwent river and passes from County Durham into Northumberland. In a further 3 miles the A68 crosses the B6278 at Carterway Heads which descends westwards to Edmondbyers and eastwards to Shotley Bridge. To the west the moorland and north Pennine hills roll away into the distance and the valley is dominated by the shimmering blue waters of Derwent Reservoir.

The A68 continues northwards across delightful moorland outcropped by evergreen forest. The undulating road is rarely busy and affords an opportunity to enjoy the scenery. Six miles from Carterway Heads the road passes through the hamlet of Broomhaugh and almost immediately enters Riding Mill (44 miles), one of south Northumberland's best-known villages. From Riding Mill the road follows the fertile Tyne Valley to link with the A69 Newcastle to Carlisle road at Corbridge where the river Tyne is crossed.

29 Through route:
Scotch Corner – Greta Bridge – Bowes – Brough – Appleby – Penrith (50 miles)

N.B: All mileages shown in brackets are from Scotch Corner

From Scotch Corner the A66 is the main east–west through route which runs north-west and then west across some of the most inhospitable but scenically spectacular country in Britain.

For 10 miles from Scotch Corner to Greta Bridge the road runs straight as a die following the route of the Roman road through fertile pastureland. One mile from Greta Bridge the river Greta is crossed and on the boundary of the wooded Rokeby Park an unclassified road leads ahead for 2 miles to Egglestone Abbey and on in a further $1\frac{1}{2}$ miles to Barnard Castle.

Immediately after crossing the river Greta the A66 bears sharply left and begins the ascent to Bowes Moor. In 2 miles from Greta Bridge at Cross Lanes the B6277 runs north and in 2 miles also enters Barnard Castle. Four miles from Cross Lanes the A66 reaches Bowes village, a remote, grey-stone village situated high on the wind-swept moors. At Bowes the A67 runs north-east for 4 miles to Barnard Castle.

On the left of the A66 just after the junction with the A67 stands the desolate ruin of **Bowes Castle**. Bowes was the Roman settlement of Lavatrae, and the castle, which was no more than a keep, was completed in 1187 and was originally built for Henry II. It contains Roman stones from the nearby fort. The fort was plundered for stone to construct the **Church of St Giles**, which has traces of Norman architecture though the exterior was extensively restored in 1865. The interior is largely late medieval. In the church is a memorial to a 19th-century villager, George Ashton Taylor, who died in 1822 at the age of nineteen years. He is believed to have been one of many victims of the barbarously cruel William Shaw's Academy which so moved Charles Dickens during a visit to Bowes. It is widely thought that the academy became Dotheboys Hall and George Ashton Taylor was the archetype of Smike in the novel *Nicholas Nickleby*.

From Bowes the A66 continues to climb to 390m (1,300ft) above sea-level by the friendly, if isolated, **Bowes Moor Hotel** (20 miles), one of the few buildings to be seen across the bleak terrain of Bowes Moor to the north and Stanmore Forest across the river Greta to the south. On the opposite side of the road by Vale House 1¼ miles before reaching the Bowes Moor Hotel is the site of the **Roper Castle** signal station. A further Roman signal station lies 250m east-north-east of the hotel. In approximately 2 miles the A66 leaves County Durham and enters Cumbria, and the road reaches its highest point almost 450m (1,500ft) above sea-level. In 1½ miles an unclassified road left, then first left, skirts **Moudy Mea** 510m (1,700ft) and ascends south-westwards turning back into County Durham for 6 miles to the **Tan Hill Inn**, reputed to be the highest public house in England standing 527m (1,758ft) above sea-level. The A66 begins its descent and reaches Brough (29 miles) and then continues to Appleby (37 miles) and Penrith (50 miles).

30 Through route:
Thirsk – Stockton-on-Tees – Billingham – Wolviston – Peterlee – Sunderland – South Shields (57 miles)

N.B: All mileages shown in brackets are from Thirsk At the time of writing extensive reclassification of Cleveland's main roads is taking place in several areas. Please check for changes.

The A19 runs northwards from York bypassing Thirsk. In 17 miles the new A19 bypass is reached and the former A19 has been reclassified A67 which veers left and enters Cleveland passing through Kirkleavington and Yarm. The new A19 continues north to Middlesbrough and across the Tees. In a further 4 miles (21 miles) the A174 east leads to Teesport, Thornaby and Redcar. The B1130 (23 miles) leads to Stockton-on-Tees and Acklam. The A66 (24 miles) leads to Middlesbrough and Stockton-on-Tees. North of Yarm the A67 veers west to Darlington, while the A135 continues north to Stockton-on-Tees.

North of the Tees the A19 passes through Wolviston where the A689 intersects from the coast to the east at Hartlepool and continues west to the A1(M) at Bradbury Interchange. North of Wolviston the A19 continues through arable farm land to leave Cleveland and enter County Durham just north of Elwick (36 miles) at the junction of the A179 eastwards to Hartlepool.

In a further 2½ miles the A181 joins the A19 from Durham City. The A19 continues north skirting Peterlee to the east and Easington before leaving County Durham and entering Tyne and Wear 1 mile from Dalton-le-Dale (45 miles) to the west of Seaham Harbour. At this point new road designations have been brought into force at the time of writing. The A19 runs north-west forming the Sunderland bypass (formerly the A108) which crosses the river Wear east of Washington and continues to link with the Tyne Tunnel (57 miles). Northwards, the A19 becomes the A1018 and continues through Ryhope to Sunderland. Continuing northwards, the A1018 finally reaches the river Tyne at South Shields (57 miles).

Roseberry Topping, Cleveland Hills

Part IV: Cleveland
by Hilda and Noel Turnbull

Cleveland is a county born of County Durham and North Yorkshire parents in 1974 when local government boundaries were reorganized. Spreading out from the estuary of the river Tees, which was formerly the boundary between County Durham and Yorkshire, it is a county which is perhaps best known as an intense industrial centre. The county comprises one of Britain's great ports, a giant industrial complex producing iron, steel and chemicals, and is also playing its part in the great oil boom. In contrast Cleveland is an area of great physical beauty. Almost in the shadow of towering chimneys and belching furnaces. Cleveland hill and dale, countryside and coast paint a very different landscape.

Today, Cleveland is still in its cradle, but the areas which make up the new county are as ancient as man. The moors and hills which sweep towards the sea are rich in prehistoric remains, particularly of the Bronze Age. The Romans guarded the towering cliffs particularly at Huntcliffe near Saltburn – indeed, Cleveland is believed to mean 'cliff land'. The Vikings too knew the coastline of Cleveland well. Their influence remains today in place names such as Lazenby, Yearby and Lackenby. Medieval remains are scattered throughout the county. At Hartlepool and at Guisborough the ruins of a Norman Augustinian priory and subsequent remains remind us of Cleveland's association with the de Brus family, progenitors of Robert the Bruce, King of Scotland.

However, it is the Industrial Revolution which made the greatest impact on Cleveland. The Stockton and Darlington Railway opened up the Tees as a coal-shipping river. Navigation of the river as far as Stockton was possible fifteen years before the track was laid, and further improvements were made immediately after the railway's inaugural run on 27 September 1825. The Tees Navigation Company had been established earlier still in 1808. The great thinkers behind the Stockton and Darlington railway did not rest on their laurels. They continuously worked towards improving their services, and by 1830 Middlesbrough, on the then Yorkshire side of the Tees, had emerged as a coal-shipping town. By 1840 the first ironworks had been established in the town and they very soon began exploiting the natural iron ore resources of the nearby Cleveland Hills.

The 19th century also saw the birth of Thornaby on the south side of the river from Stockton. A bridge was built as early as 1771. By 1840 Thornaby – the name is derived from a manor-house which served Guisborough Priory – had thriving potteries, glassworks and iron foundries. The first iron-built ship built on the Tees was launched at Thornaby in 1854. Eleven years earlier the river's first steam-powered vessel was also launched.

Hartlepool too played a major part in the industrial development of Teesside. Prior to 1974 Hartlepool was firmly situated in County Durham, being situated to the north of the river Tees. Developing parallel to its counterparts further south, the first coal was shipped from Hartlepool in 1835, and in 1840 the Victoria Dock was opened. Seven years later the West Hartlepool Docks and Harbour opened.

Billingham, also formerly in County Durham, is synonymous today with the manufacture of the varied products of ICI (Imperial Chemical Industries Ltd). Though the history of the area goes back to the 9th century, the industrial development of the town is essentially 20th century, the first chemicals being produced in 1918.

Not all of Cleveland's pioneer industries were on a gigantic scale. Developments were as diverse as the countryside. Stockton's most famous son was John Walker, inventor of the humble, though none the less important, friction match. Stockton-on-Tees was also the birthplace of furniture-maker Thomas Sheraton.

Perhaps Cleveland's most famous pioneer found fame thousands of miles from his birthplace at Marton. Captain James Cook, intrepid explorer, experienced the first tangy salt-laden scent of the North Sea on the Cleveland coast. His resultant voyages of discovery to the four corners of the world made him one of the most celebrated explorers of all time.

Contrast is everywhere in Cleveland. Fourteen miles of first-class beach provide seaside pleasures for residents and visitors. Recreational facilities in the larger towns include theatres, restaurants, night-clubs, casinos, sports halls and leisure centres. The escape from urban civilization is simple. The vast North York Moors National Park still retains many of its natural secrets – undiscovered history, secluded villages and some of the finest walking country on the east coast amid unsurpassed scenic splendour. And perhaps most important of all the local population, in spite of the influx of 'foreigners' seeking a living from Cleveland's industry, still provides a warm and friendly welcome.

31 Stockton-on-Tees and environs

Bowls Ropner Park.
Buses Billingham, Bishop Auckland, Darlington, Durham, Edinburgh, Glasgow, Hartlepool, Middlesbrough, Newcastle upon Tyne, Redcar, Sunderland, Yarm.
Cinemas *Classic*, Dovecot Street; *Odeon*, High Street.
Distances Sunderland, 25 miles; Middlesbrough, 4 miles; Darlington, 11 miles.
Early closing Thursday.
Golf There are courses at Eaglescliffe, Thornaby and Billingham.

Hotels *Swallow*, *Stork*, *Teesside Post House*.
Information centre Dovecot Street.
Market day Wednesdays and Saturdays.
Museums and art galleries Preston Park Museum.
Population 164,000.
Post Office The GPO is in High Street.
Racing Teesside Park.
Swimming-pools Stockton Baths.
Tennis Ropner Park.
Theatre *Forum Theatre*, Billingham.

Following local government reorganization, the county boundaries have forsaken their natural physical boundaries. The boundary between County Durham and Yorkshire, for example, was formerly the river Tees, but since 1974 the dividing lines have become much less obvious and the new county of Cleveland has been born out of parts of County Durham and parts of North Yorkshire. **Stockton-on-Tees** is one of several towns which have moved counties and is now firmly in Cleveland having been previously in County Durham. Travelling east from Darlington on the A66, the county boundary lies midway between Sadberge and Long Newton some 4 miles from Stockton town centre. The town also lies on the main A19 through route which links with the Tyne Tunnel and York.

The origins of Stockton-on-Tees are obscure. The name is said to derive from 'town of the monastery' (*stoc*), and it is known that the oldest part lies where the suburb of **Norton** is today. In the last decade of the 10th century Norton was given to the Bishop of Durham by the son of the Earl of Northumberland, and within 100 years Norton was established as the regional see. It was to remain as the headquarters of the church for nearly 700 years.

The name Stockton is first recorded in the *Boldon Beuk*, Durham's version of the 'Domesday Book'. **Stockton Castle** was established originally as a manor-house in the 12th century and was regularly frequented by the Bishops of Durham until the 16th century. The castle was captured by the Scots who held it from 1644 to 1647, and within five years the building was razed to the ground.

Stockton's reputation as a port and commercial centre goes back to the middle of the 13th century when the bishop conferred borough status on the town. Stockton market was given a charter by Bishop Bek in 1310, and the market is still held each Wednesday and Saturday in Stockton's High Street, believed to be the widest street in England.

In 1713 the roles of Norton and Stockton were reversed. Until then Stockton was part of the parish of Norton, but in that year Stockton was granted parish status, and today Norton is part of Stockton. In the same year the parish **Church of St Thomas** was completed. It is believed that Sir Christopher Wren was an advisor to the builders. Prior to the construction of St Thomas's Church the only ecclesiastical building had been the chapel at Norton. Other churches quickly followed, the second oldest parish being Holy Trinity dating from 1857. St James in Portrack Lane (1867–8), St John in Alma Street (1873–4) and St Peter (1880) are all typical of the period. St Mary's Roman Catholic Church in Norton Road dates from 1841, and the Congregational Church in the same road dates from 1845. Stockton's Methodist churches are earlier. The building in Dovecot Street dates from 1823, the church in Norton Road a year earlier. In addition to the town's numerous churches most other buildings date from the 18th and 19th centuries. The **Town Hall**, in the middle of the High Street, dates from 1736 and is built on the site of the Old Tollbooth.

Undoubtedly, the greatest influence on the development of Stockton-on-Tees came in 1825 when the Stockton and Darlington Railway was inaugurated. Until then the area had remained predominantly agricultural, but the industrial revolution quickly made its mark. Industry was not completely new to the town, but there is no doubt that the coming of the railways was the single major factor influencing the prosperity of the town.

On a much more humble though, nonetheless, universal level another invention which first saw light of day in Stockton was the friction match. John Walker, a chemist at 59 High Street, concocted a mixture of potassium chlorate, antimony sulphide and gum which he sold as friction lights. The first matches went on sale on 7 April 1827. Walker died in 1859 without taking out a patent and therefore made little profit from his invention. He is buried in Norton churchyard and a square in the new town centre is named in his honour. The luxury **Swallow Hotel** devotes the 'Matchmaker Room' to his memory.

Thomas Sheraton, furniture designer and maker, was also born in Stockton in 1751. Little is known of his life in the town, although it is recorded that he was employed there as a 'journeyman cabinet maker'. In 1790 he moved to London where he made his name. He died in 1806 and is buried in St James's Church, Piccadilly, London.

Though Stockton retains its traditional markets, the town also has modern shopping developments at the Castle Centre adjacent to the High Street. Stockton's Sports Centre provides all the usual amenities expected of such an ultra-modern building. The town is also well-endowed with open spaces. Ropner Park was given to the town by Sir Robert Ropner, one of the town's shipping magnates. To the south of the town on the Yarm Road stands Preston Park which was purchased by the council in 1947. **Preston Hall**, a graceful building situated in the Park's 47ha (117 acres), has been restored and is put to good use as a museum of social history (*open daily; closed Mondays October to March*). Within the grounds are recreational areas, wooded walks and pastimes for young and old alike. The original route of the Stockton and Darlington Railway ran along the boundary of the park adjacent to the Stockton to Yarm road. At the time of writing Preston Park Museum, including the transport section, is undergoing further redevelopment.

Another of Stockton's historic buildings, the use of which is currently being reassessed, is the original booking-office which stands where the first Darlington to Stockton line crosses the main road to Yarm a short distance south of the Swallow Hotel. Arguably the oldest railway booking-office in the world, the building at one time housed a small railway history museum, but at the time of writing the museum is closed.

Environs

The main route south from Stockton A66 (A135) Yarm Road follows the route of the river Tees and also the line of the original Stockton and Darlington Railway to reach **Egglescliffe** in 4 miles. The village is situated high on the left bank of the Tees which is tidal up to this point. A medieval bridge (built in 1400 on the instructions of Bishop Skirlaw) spans the river, and the railway line is carried over the Tees by a great railway viaduct (built in 1849) comprising forty-three arches. The **Church of St Mary** has traces of Norman architecture – notably the south doorway. The chancel and tower date from the 15th century.

Leaving Egglescliffe, the road immediately enters the historic market town of **Yarm** on the A67. The rise of Stockton and Middlesbrough proved to be the demise of Yarm, a town with a history spanning at least thirteen centuries. In 1207 Peter de Brus was granted a charter by King John to hold a weekly market and two annual fairs at Yarm. Until 1700 the town was the main port on the Tees and a thriving market town trading farm produce and lead.

In the 18th and 19th centuries Yarm was associated with an amazing variety of industries, including shipbuilding, brewing, clockmaking, tanning, papermaking, ropeworks and the manufacture of barrels and nails. Yarm is almost surrounded by a loop in the river Tees on which the town's prosperity was formerly based. Like its neighbour Stockton, Yarm is dominated by a wide cobbled High Street where there are several interesting buildings. The **Town Hall** is situated in the centre of High Street and dates from 1710. The weighbridge, formerly used by horse-drawn vehicles, dates from the 19th century, the weighing office comprising the two south-east arches of the Town Hall. Through the windows it is possible to see a bushel measure which was in use as early as 1686. The alarm bell originally located in the tollbooth dates from 1690 and has been used as a flood warning for centuries. Indeed, because of its location on a loop in the Tees Yarm has been liable to frequent flooding, and there are flood marks on several buildings in the town including two on the Town Hall.

North of the Town Hall on the right of High Street stands an inn which was the scene of one of the most historic meetings which ever took place in Northumbria. On 12 February 1820 the **George and Dragon** was the venue for a meeting between Thomas Meynell, Benjamin Flounders, Jeremiah Cairns, Richard Mills and Thomas Miles which was to revolutionize world transport. At this meeting the seed of the Stockton and Darlington Railway was sown. A plaque on the wall records the event.

Continuing north past Carlton Terrace on the corner of Silver Street, from which the Tees used to be crossed by a ford, stands Yarm's oldest building, another historic inn, the **Ketton Ox**, commemorating the famous beast reared at Brafferton. A few metres further north stands **Tom Brown's House**, formerly an inn where Tom Brown, the hero of the Battle of Dettingen, lived. He is buried in Yarm churchyard. By the river near the end of Carlton Terrace stands Yarm's **Methodist Chapel** which dates from 1763 and was beloved of John Wesley who visited the town many times staying with friends at 17 High Street.

The southern end of High Street is still dominated by elegant Georgian merchants' houses. On the boundary of the Snaiths Field recreation area can be seen some remains of the wall of Yarm's **Dominican Friary** which was founded in 1260. A further fragment of wall can be seen on the eastern side of High Street just north of the town's Roman Catholic **Church of St Mary and St Romuald** which dates from 1860.

Yarm's **Church of St Mary Magdalene** is tranquilly situated on the western edge of the river Tees and dates from 1730, though it is known that a church has existed on the site for 1,300 years. The riverside walk by the church is known locally as 'True Lovers' Walk'.

On the outskirts of Yarm the B1264 veers to the south-west following the course of the Tees to link with the A167. A mile south of the town centre the B1264 becomes the A1044 as it runs north-east towards the southern outskirts of Middlesbrough.

The A67 continues south and in 2 miles reaches **Kirk Leavington**, a village which dates from Saxon times. The family of de Brus, progenitors of Robert the Bruce, King of Scotland, held Castle Hill at Castle Leavington 1½ miles east-north-east. Here a medieval fortress stood, and the moat and a crescent-shaped earthwork are still visible. Henry Percy took possession of Kirk Leavington in 1700. It was a gift from one Ada de Brus as thanks for taking her to chapel from Skelton Castle each Christmas. **St Martin's Church** dates mainly from 1883, but there are several Saxon fragments built into the structure. The chancel dates from the 13th century. A chancel arch and south doorway are Norman.

On leaving Kirk Leavington the A67 continues south crossing the border between Cleveland and North Yorkshire. East of the A19 at Stockton-on-Tees the A67 gives way to the A1045 and the A174 which both pass Thornaby-on-Tees before joining with the A1044 linking Yarm with the coast.

Thornaby, situated on the south side of the Tees opposite Stockton, has enjoyed long associations with the latter. The town was first recorded in the 9th century when land was owned by a Danish nobleman, Thormod, who perhaps gave his name to the town. Thornaby found a permanent place on the map as an industrial town following the birth of the railways. Prior to that the hamlet was linked to County Durham across the river by a ferry belonging to the Bishop of Durham and then in 1769 by a stone bridge.

The coming of the railways and improvement in river communications led to rapid development, and Thornaby gained a reputation as a pioneer shipbuilding centre. In 1897 the original stone bridge was replaced by the present Victorian bridge. The town was locally known as South Stockton but was a part of Stainton parish until 1844. The old village of Thornaby is now officially designated as a conservation area, though there is new development around the spacious village green. Near the green is the **Church of St Peter ad Vincula** which dates from the 11th century and retains a Norman chancel arch. **St Paul's Church** in Thornaby Road dates from 1857, and **St Luke's** in Acklam Road was built between 1901 and 1904. Modern amenities include Thornaby Pavilion which was opened in 1968 and is situated in an ultra-modern shopping complex. The Pavilion provides all the usual sporting and leisure-time facilities. Another recent acquisition at Thornaby is the Harold Wilson Playing Field which covers 5ha (12 acres).

Stainton, under whose control Thornaby remained until 1844, is situated 3 miles south of Thornaby just off the A1044. It is a peaceful retreat which for several centuries was owned by the Pennyman family, better known for their associations with Ormesby Hall. The village and surrounding area contain some fine woods and its rural character belies Stainton's close proximity to industrial Teesside. The **Church of St Peter and St Paul** dates from the 13th century but contains Saxon fragments. The tower dates from the 15th century. Stainton church was bestowed upon Guisborough Priory by Robert de Brus. An unclassified road south from Stainton leads to Stokesley in North Yorkshire.

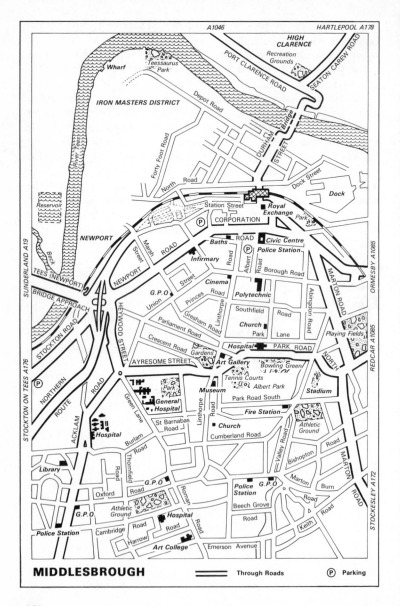

MIDDLESBROUGH   ═══ Through Roads   Ⓟ Parking

Bowls There are numerous greens in the parks.

Buses Loftus, Whitby, Scarborough, Redcar, Stokesley, Newcastle upon Tyne, Northallerton.

Camping and caravanning Coatham Caravan Site, Redcar, tel. 71096.

Cinemas *ABC 1–3*, corner of Linthorpe Road and Borough Road; *Odeon 1–3*, Corporation Road.

Cricket Middlesbrough Cricket Club, Acklam Park.

Distances Newcastle upon Tyne, 40 miles; Durham City, 25 miles; Darlington, 15 miles; Whitby, 31 miles; York, 53 miles.

Early closing Wednesday.

Football Football League, Ayresome Park.

Golf *Middlesbrough Golf Club*, Brass Castle Lane, Nunthorpe; *Municipal Course*, Netherby Farm, off Ladgate Lane.

Greyhound racing Cleveland Park Stadium, Stockton Road.

Horse racing Teesside and Redcar.

Hotels *Ladbroke Dragonara*, *Wolsingham*, *Blue Bell Motor Inn*, *Crest*, Highfield.

Information centre Albert Road, tel. 45432.

Museums and art galleries Dorman Museum, Linthorpe Road; Stewart Park, Marton.

Population 153,900.

Post Office The GPO is in Marton Road.

Roller skating Albert Park Rink.

Rugby Union Middlesbrough Rugby Club, Acklam Park, Green Lane.

Speedway Cleveland Park, Stockton Road.

Swimming-pools Central Baths in Gilkes Street, Berwick Hills baths in Crossfell Road.

Tennis There are numerous courts in parks and recreation grounds.

Theatres Middlesbrough Little Theatre, concerts in Town Hall.

Turkish suite and slipper baths Gilkes Street.

When Mr Gladstone visited **Middlesbrough** in 1862 he said, 'This remarkable place, the youngest child of England's enterprise is an infant – but it is an infant Hercules.' This astute statement provides an admirable description of a town which was born as recently as 1830 and which has grown with amazing rapidity. Though Middlesbrough as we know it today is still in its youth, the area which envelops recent urban development is rich with the scent of history. Almost 1,300 years ago the banks of the Tees hereabouts were the site of a cell built in honour of St Cuthbert on the instruction of St Hilda, Abbess of Whitby. The name 'Middleborg' and its various derivations are said to be Norse in origin and are believed to refer to the area's geographical location midway between Whitby and Cuthbert's Shrine at Durham City. A Church of St

Hilda was consecrated on the instruction of Robert de Brus in 1119 and was administered by Benedictine monks until the dissolution of the monasteries.

It was the advent of railways which, as with Stockton and Thornaby, sparked off the development of Middlesbrough. In 1830 the Stockton and Darlington Railway was extended to Middlesbrough to provide improved shipping facilities further downstream on the river Tees. Twelve years later Middlesbrough's new docks and coal depots were opened, and the town experienced a boom in trade and commerce which surprised even those early pioneers, including Joseph Pease. The coal-shipping boom, however, was short-lived, and by 1851 shipments were on the decline. Coincidentally, prospectors were beginning to discover the rich iron ore deposits in the Cleveland Hills to the south of the river, and within months iron replaced coal as Middlesbrough's lifeline. The turn of the century saw other industries thriving. Salt was exported in great quantities, and Linthorpe Pottery was winning national and international acclaim.

In 1911 the unique Transporter Bridge, which today still stands out as a monument to Teesside engineering, was opened linking Middlesbrough with Port Clarence on the north side of the river. The bridge is also a reminder of Middlesbrough's pioneer reputation for bridge construction. The Sydney Harbour Bridge, the Lambeth Bridge, the crossing of the White Nile and the Volta are all the results of Cleveland enterprise.

As a result of the industrial problems besetting Britain in the 20th century Middlesbrough suffered particularly badly during the depression between the two World Wars, and subsequently efforts have been made to attract new light industry to the area to lessen the need to rely on the more traditional industries.

The centre of Middlesbrough has undergone a complete redevelopment in recent years, and further major plans are on the drawing-board. The ambitious development plan has meant that Middlesbrough has every claim to be the regional capital, though city fathers in Newcastle upon Tyne probably disagree. Ultra-modern buildings include the Law Courts overlooking Victoria Square built at a cost of £1,500,000 and opened in 1973. On the Albert Road side of the square stands the new Cleveland Centre covering 2ha (6 acres) and comprising covered shopping precincts, car park and public services. Built at a cost of £5 million, the centre provides some of the best shopping facilities in the north-east.

The Transporter Bridge, Middlesbrough

Linthorpe Road, Middlesbrough's main shopping 'street', has undergone a scheme of pedestrianization designed to increase the comfort of shoppers. Other buildings in the square, including Council Offices and Middlesbrough's Central Library, have been given a very beneficial face-lift. The town centre also boasts a new four-star hotel, night-club and casino.

Compared with the ancient cities and towns of Northumberland there is little of great antiquity in Middlesbrough. The Transporter Bridge which crosses the Tees from Ferry Road is without doubt the town's most intriguing monument. It is 255m (850ft) long and stands more than 60m (200ft) high. The massive transporter which is hauled back and forth across the river can accommodate some nine cars and 600 people. A further reminder of Middlesbrough's bridge-building prowess can be seen further upstream on the western edge of the town where the Newport Bridge has a lifting span 80m (270ft) in length. It was the first vertical lift bridge in England. Today, even this bridge has been superseded with a new construction just to the west which carries the new bypass.

Middlesbrough's ecclesiastical buildings are perhaps less interesting than their ancient counterparts in Northumbria. Nevertheless, the town does have an outstanding **Roman Catholic Cathedral of St Mary** in Sussex Street dating from 1872. There are several churches dating from the 19th century.

Middlesbrough is justly proud of her industrial pioneers. In **Victoria Square** stands the statue of John Vaughan who with an enterprising German, Henry Bolckow, not only set up the first iron-smelting works but also pioneered most of the town's other industries. Bolckow is remembered at the entrance to **Albert Park** where his statue stands proud. He gave the park to the town which owing to such philanthropic gestures is well endowed with open spaces and parkland, so much so that notable achievements have been made in the national Britain in Bloom Competition in spite of Middlesbrough's dominant heavy industry.

At the entrance to Albert Park stands the **Dorman Museum** (*open daily, except Sundays, 10–5.30*), given to the town by Sir Arthur Dorman in memory of his son and comrades who fell in the Boer War. The museum contains a wealth of information on the regional history of Cleveland from prehistoric times to the present day. A small art gallery can also be found. New galleries in both museum and art gallery are being planned.

Albert Park covers some 29ha (72 acres) and provides varied leisure facilities including a boating lake. The town's other major park, **Stewart Park**, lies to the south of the town at **Marton** and enjoys close association with Captain James Cook. There are smaller parks in Middlesbrough at Pallister, Westbourne and Thorntree.

Middlesbrough's recreational facilities designed for resident and visitor alike are second to none. Sporting activities, both active and passive, and cultural pastimes are varied indeed. National and international sporting events take place at Clairville Stadium, and Middlesbrough FC currently enjoy first division status. The Bewick Hills swimming-pool was completed in 1968. Middlesbrough is the venue for the biennial Teesside International Eisteddfod (Inter TIE) which attracts performers from all corners of the world. A comprehensive programme of entertainment takes place throughout the year at the 1,300-seat Middlesbrough Town Hall, while Middlesbrough Little Theatre presents an equally varied programme.

Environs

Several major roads span out from Middlesbrough. Northwards, the A178 runs across the Transporter Bridge to Seaton Carew and Hartlepool. The A1130 over the Newport Bridge joins with the new A19 to continue north to Billingham and on to Sunderland and the Tyne Tunnel.

Eastwards, several roads link Middlesbrough and its environs with the coastal playground which stretches southwards from the Tyne estuary. The A175 and the A1085 pass North Ormesby and South Bank through Cleveland's most industrialized area. The B1380 and newly constructed A174 run parallel east–west a few miles further south linking the A19 with the coast. Off the new A174 the A1032 leads north to Acklam and Middlesbrough centre. South the B1365 leads to Hemlington and **Coulby Newham** where one of Middlesbrough's newest attractions is situated. The **Newham Grange Leisure Farm** (*open daily 10–6.30*) is a conventional working farm which offers a perpetual open day for visitors who can wander at leisure through cow byers and sheep-pens, among crops and through farmyard. The Leisure Farm incorporates an agricultural museum, an agricultural merchant's shop, and a 19th-century veterinary surgery and saddlers' shop.

The Visitors' Centre tells the story of Newham Grange Farm from the 17th century through to the present day. It is possible to trace the families who have occupied the farm and the major farming developments which affected their lives. There is an audio-visual and projects room for schools and organizations, shop and craft-demonstration rooms where special events are held from time to time. For younger children the farm incorporates a pets' corner and chicken incubation house. There are spacious picnic areas and nature and farm trails.

The A172 runs south from Middlesbrough to cross the B1380 just to the north of Marton, the birthplace of explorer Captain James Cook, before crossing the new A174 and continuing into North Yorkshire to Stokesley. Continuing east, the A174 is joined by the A171 also from Middlesbrough on the outskirts of the village of **Ormesby**. The tree-clad village is dominated by the beautiful estate in which **Ormesby Hall** (*open May to end September, Wednesdays, Sundays, Bank Holidays*) is situated. The hall is now in the care of the National Trust. The building dates from the middle of the 18th century and is constructed on the site of a

Highland cattle at Newham Grange Open Farm

medieval dwelling. The estate has been in the ownership of the Penny-man family whose progenitor, James Pennyman, was knighted by Charles I in 1600. Dorothy Pennyman (*née* Wake), a daughter of the Archbishop of Canterbury, married James Pennyman and was responsible for the construction of the present house. She died in 1754. The three-storey mansion, which was given to the National Trust by the late Colonel J. B. W. Pennyman in 1961, is opulently decorated and includes some fine plasterwork. The features of the Jacobean House have, unfortunately, been lost in its conversion into the kitchen wing of the Georgian Hall, but one remarkable doorway remains on which can be seen an exquisitely carved family crest. Nothing is known of the architect employed by Dorothy Pennyman. The stables are believed to have been designed by Carr of York.

The nearby **Church of St Cuthbert** is situated in a rural setting. Records show that a Saxon church occupied the site, and there are fragments built into the walls. The building dates largely from 1871 to 1875. A mile east of Ormesby, the A174 is joined from the north by the

A175 before reaching in a further ½ mile the suburb of **Eston**, which is overlooked from the south by the Eston Hills. **Eston Moor** is the most northerly outcrop of the Cleveland Hills rising to 240m (800ft) on **Eston Nab** where Iron and Bronze Age settlements have been discovered. From the summit magnificent views of Teesmouth can be enjoyed. The monument which can be seen for miles around is modern having been erected by ICI in 1956 from the remains of a Napoleonic signalling tower. The village grew as a result of the discovery of iron ore in the Cleveland Hills in the 19th century. It is known that a Norman church existed thereabouts, but Christ Church dates from 1883.

A mile east of Eston the A174 passes through Lackenby and Lazenby, once a Quaker stronghold. The scene is now dominated by the great ICI Wilton industrial complex. An unclassified road south climbs a mile or so into the foothills of Eston Nab to one of Cleveland's several castles – **Wilton Castle** – which, regrettably, is not open to the public having been taken over by ICI for use as offices. The nearby **Church of St Cuthbert** is Norman but was almost completely rebuilt in 1907. The view from Wilton over the vast industrial complex to the north is remarkable, particularly at night when belching furnaces and chimneys light the night sky in a blaze of synthetic colour.

One and a half miles east from Wilton on the A174 lies the village of **Kirkleatham** one of the most architecturally interesting villages in all Cleveland. Formerly surrounded by a deer park, the parish church of West Lidum, as the village was known, was mentioned in the 'Domesday Book'. William de Percy owned the manor in the 11th century and subsequently the estate belonged to the Lumley family. In 1623 the estate came into the hands of John Turner of Guisborough whose family fortunes were founded on the mining of alum. The Turner family held the estate until 1949, but the 17th-century mansion, extensively altered by John Carr of York, was demolished five years later. The stable block now stands adjacent to a modern school. The **Church of St Cuthbert** was largely rebuilt in 1763 having been designed by Robert Coney, a local architect. Several years earlier a huge mausoleum was constructed in memory of Marwood Turner, and this dominates the chancel. The vicarage by the church dates from 1750.

By far the most striking aspect of Kirkleatham is the Sir William Turner Hospital (*open daily*). The almshouses, founded by William Turner in 1662 and constructed in 1676, were rebuilt in 1742. They range around three sides of a courtyard. In the centre section a chapel dating from 1742 is incorporated. It boasts the finest early Georgian interior decoration in Cleveland. It is designed after the style of Christopher Wren having been masterminded by Nicholas Hawksmoor one of Wren's protégés. In its heyday the 'hospital' accommodated in twenty cottages twenty aged men and women of the Church of England faith and incorporated a free school for a similar number of poor boys and girls. Opposite the hospital stands an interesting Queen Anne building which was originally used as the Free School.

33 Hartlepool and the Cleveland coastline

The coast of Cleveland County runs north and south of the river Tees estuary. To the north lie Seal Sands and Hartlepool's seaside playground of Seaton Carew. To the south of Teesmouth, where the South Gare Lighthouse guides giant tankers in and out of Tees Bay, a coastline of firm sandy beaches, rocky outcrops and towering cliffs stretches towards Yorkshire.

Hartlepool

Boating Yacht and Sailing Club, Middleton Docks.

Bowls Greens in public parks, also Indoor Bowling Centre, Raby Road.

Buses Billingham, Bishop Auckland, Darlington, Durham, Middlesbrough, Newcastle upon Tyne, Redcar, Stockton-on-Tees, Sunderland, Thirsk.

Camping and caravanning Burntree Caravan Site, Queen Street, Seaton Carew; Happy Valley Leisure Park, Dene Mouth Caravan Park, Crimdon.

Cinemas *Odeon*, Raby Road; *Fairworld*, Raby Road.

Cricket At Park Drive.

Distances Middlesbrough, 9 miles; Newcastle upon Tyne, 31 miles; Stockton-on-Tees, 11 miles; Sunderland, 21 miles.

Early closing Wednesdays.

Football Hartlepool Football Club, Clarence Road.

Golf *Seaton Carew Golf-Club*, *Hartlepool Golf-Club*.

Greyhound stadium Clarence Road.

Hotels *The Grand*; *Staincliffe*, Seaton Carew.

Information centres Summer months only: kiosk in Victory Square and at Seaton Carew; winter months: Leisure and Amenities Department, Civic Centre, Victoria Road, tel. 66522.

Market day Thursday.

Museums and art galleries Gray Museum and Art Gallery, Clarence Road; Maritime Museum, Northgate.

Population 100,000.

Post Office The GPO is in Middleton Grange Shopping Centre.

Rugby Hartlepool Rovers RFC, Hartlepool (West) RFC.

Stock Car Stadium Clarence Road.

Swimming Mill House Swimming-Pool, Raby Road.

Tennis Courts in public parks.

The headland at **Hartlepool** is reached on the A1049 2 miles from Crimdon Dene. The A689 passes through the town centre. Hartlepool is one of the towns which was subject to a change of county during local government reorganization in 1974 moving from County Durham to the new county of Cleveland.

The old town dates from the 7th century, and the 19th-century development of industry on the river Tees saw the rapid growth of the industrial conurbation of West Hartlepool. Today, the whole area is known simply as Hartlepool. The town's earliest records relate to the founding of a monastery in AD 640 on the site where St Hilda's Church now stands. The Heugh, as the headland is known today, is reputed to be named after Hein, an Irish princess, who was the monastery's first abbess. In AD 649 Hein was succeeded by St Hilda, who subsequently found fame as Abbess of Whitby. In AD 790 the monastery was completely destroyed by marauding Danes. The area also came in for attack from William the Conqueror in 1068. Following the Norman Conquest the town came into the possession of the great Norman family of de Brus, progenitors of Robert the Bruce. The family also owned the nearby village of Hart and Guisborough Priory.

Hartlepool was walled as protection against the Scots, and the harbour grew in importance as trade increased. In the early 17th-century Hartlepool was described as the only port on the County Durham coastline. The port suffered a decline in the 18th century following its capture by the Scots and its destruction during the Civil War. But with the onset of industrial development during the 19th century and in particular the coming of the railways prosperity returned to the port. The Hartlepool Dock and Railway Company was formed in 1832 to transport coal from nearby Haswell and Thornley, and three years later the first exports were shipped from the port. In 1840 the great Victoria Dock was opened, and a year later the Stockton and Hartlepool Railway came into being.

Today, Hartlepool is experiencing yet further change. A decline in industry, particularly shipbuilding, has led to the need for diversification. By 1965 the port had become the main north-east coast base for North Sea gas and oil exploration, but in spite of this unemployment is still the town's biggest problem. The Hartlepool Order of 1966 was instrumental in amalgamating the 'Hartlepools', and in spite of the decline of traditional industries the town has prospered and has successfully embarked on ambitious redevelopment plans though retaining the town's historic links.

The **Heugh** headland is still the focal point of the town's history. Adjacent to the harbour a fine stretch of medieval town wall can still be seen rising some 5·4m (18ft) and being up to 2·7m (9ft) thick in places. The wall incorporates Sandwell Gate which leads to the town's spa. On the wall of the swimming-pool by the breakwater in the south-eastern corner of the Heugh is a bronze plaque marking the site of a Saxon burial ground discovered in the 19th century.

St Hilda's Church is regarded by architects and historians as one of the finest and most interesting in the county. Dedicated to St Hilda, it was founded in 1185 by Robert de Brus IV. Though the church has been restored, its architectural features are largely original and of a contemporary period, with the exception of the Norman south portal which belonged to a church which formerly occupied the site. The church incorporates a Bruce Chapel in which a great tomb of Frosterley marble is said to be that of the founder of the church.

Several other churches in Hartlepool are well-worth visiting. **All Saints** at **Stratton** dates from the 13th century. In the churchyard lies the grave of William Humphrey, the clockmaker from Barnard Castle, who found his way into the works of Charles Dickens. Sir Compton Mackenzie is another literary figure born in West Hartlepool in 1883. St Mary's Roman Catholic Church, Brougham Street, St Paul's, Grange Road and Holy Trinity, Vane Street, all date from the 1850s.

With such an intriguing history of industrial development and a great reliance on the sea it is not surprising to discover two museums devoted to the town's industrial and maritime heritage. The **Gray Museum and Art Gallery** in Clarence Road (*open daily*) is named after the famous shipbuilder Sir William Gray, who gave the fine building to the town. Displays concentrate mainly on the town's history and local industries. The Art Gallery has an excellent collection of local scenes. Hartlepool's **Maritime Museum** in Northgate (*open daily, not Sundays*) concentrates on the town's fishing, shipbuilding and marine-engineering history. Displays include a reconstructed fisherman's cottage and a ship's bridge.

Though Hartlepool's prosperity has been founded on heavy industry, the town's fathers have not neglected to provide recreational amenities. **Ward Jackson Park** on the eastern outskirts is always a blaze of colour. The park commemorates Ralph Ward Jackson, the founder of the West Hartlepool Harbour and Railway Company. His statue stands in Church Square. Floral decoration has figured largely in Hartlepool's amenity plans in recent years, so much so that the town has the distinction of being joint national winners together with the historic city of Bath in the annual Britain in Bloom competition.

From the centre of the town the A179 leads west to the peaceful village of **Hart**, noted for its Saxon church which preceded St Hilda's. The Manor came under the control of the Bruce family, and the most important relic in the church is the ornate 15th-century font which is fashioned out of local limestone. From the centre of Hartlepool the A178 skirts the coast by Long Scar rocks and in a mile or so reaches **Seaton Carew**, Hartlepool's traditional seaside playground. **Holy Trinity Church** dates from 1831, and the houses surrounding the trim green date from the same period. On the sea front south of the green some attractive Georgian residences face the sea.

The A178 continues south towards the industrial sprawl of Teesmouth past **Seal Sands** where the giant steel construction of great rigs, platforms and other apparatus usually dominates the skyline – witness to the mammoth scale of North Sea oil exploration. In complete contrast to industrial development Seal Sands cover 607ha (1,500 acres) and have the distinction of being an ornithological paradise, frequented at certain times of the year by thousands of migrant waders. Regrettably, industrial development is proving the death-knell of Seal Sands as a sanctuary. Skirting Seal Sands the A178 finally crosses the Tees by the Transporter Bridge.

The A1085 from Middlesbrough enters the new borough of **Langbaurgh** on its journey eastwards towards the sea just 2 miles west of the residential area of Grangetown. The borough of Langbaurgh covers some 24,000ha (60,000 acres), including the main industrial development of Tees Port which incorporates one of the world's largest chemical manufacturing works and one of Britain's largest steel plants. Yet amidst this throbbing industry the Borough's 150,000 inhabitants can enjoy the exhilarating freedom of countryside and coast right on their doorstep. The name Langbaurgh is derived from the Saxon 'long hill'.

In 3½ miles from Grangetown the A1085 enters the seaside resort of Redcar via its northern suburb Coatham. Between Coatham and the South Gare breakwater at Teesmouth lies Coatham Common on which is situated a first-class golf-links.

Redcar was formerly a fishing village which in the early 19th century became established as a highly respected seaside resort attracting the rich merchants of Cleveland. Today, however, the resort has much more popular appeal. The town's greatest natural asset is its long beach of clean firm sand backed by a promenade lined with gaily coloured fishing cobles. All the usual amenities of a family seaside playground can be found in Redcar. The **Coatham Amusement Park** is the largest indoor fun-fair in the north-east, and along the promenade are other amusements, donkey rides, dancing, discotheques and night-clubs. Regular concerts catering for all musical tastes are held at the Coatham Bowl. Sporting enthusiasts can enjoy the 'sport of kings' at the town's racecourse, one of the finest in the north of England, which was established in 1875. Summer attractions at Redcar include a week-long annual carnival usually held in late July and preceded by a week-end folk festival.

With such a close affinity to the sea it is not surprising to discover that Redcar has an intriguing maritime museum, the **Zetland Museum** (*open daily, except Sundays 10–5.30*). It is named after the *Zetland*, believed to be the oldest surviving lifeboat in the world, which is the museum's proudest exhibit. The *Zetland* was built in about 1800 and was originally stationed at Spurn Head in Yorkshire. In 1802 she was bought by the fishermen of Redcar for £100 and has remained in the town ever since. The Zetland Museum, on the promenade facing the North Sea, has displays relating to the history of the lifeboat on the north-east coast and paints a vivid picture of the hazards facing shipping throughout the centuries. Galleries are also devoted to the history of the river Tees and the development of the fishing industry.

The **Saltscar** and **Redcar Rocks** are full of interest at low tide for young and old explorers alike, and the town has three major parks. **Locke Parke** features a large lake with boating and angling facilities. Among **Zetland Park**'s features is a novelty eighteen-hole golf-course, while **Borough Park** provides facilities for all the usual activity pursuits and games.

Redcar is an ideal centre for touring. It provides varied accommodation from large caravan park to comfortable guest-house. Architecturally, the town is unimportant. **St Peter's Church** in Redcar Lane was built in 1829.

From Redcar the A1085 follows the coastline south skirting the firm sands which run along the entire shoreline between Redcar and the resort of **Marske-by-the-Sea**. The old village of Marske nestling between hills and sea is today almost enveloped by the spread of Cleveland's urban development. A reminder of Marske's distinguished past remains in the shape of **Marske Hall**, one of the finest buildings in the county dating from the 17th century. The hall was built in 1625 by Sir William Pennyman whose family also built Ormesby Hall. Dominating the cliff top is the tower of **St Germain's Church**, formerly the parish church of Redcar. Only the tower remains, the rest of the building having been demolished in 1960. The father of explorer Captain James Cook is buried just a few metres west of the tower. **St Mark's Church** dates from 1867 and has a Norman font. At Errington Park Woods, New Marske, amenities have recently been provided for picnics and woodland walks, and magnificent views of Tees Bay can be enjoyed.

From Marske the A1085 gives way to the A174 continuing southwards to **Saltburn-by-the-Sea**, a popular seaside resort catering especially for day trippers. The town is dominated by the 90m (300ft) high **Huntcliff** which towers over the resort's southern boundary and is in complete contrast to the flat seascape to the north. The town is known to have been inhabited by a hermit in the 13th century, and the area was also a centre for alum-mining and smuggling. Today, the resort offers amusements, a boating lake, swimming-baths, a miniature railway and golf-course. The Skelton Beck flows into the sea at Saltburn, and upstream from the coast are fine walks through steep-sided glens and the town's Italian gardens which were designed in the 1860s. Sadly, two of the resort's most distinguished features are no more: the pier has almost finally succumbed to the ravages of the North Sea and not a few marine collisions, and the Halfpenny Bridge has been literally blown up.

Saltburn is the most northerly coastal point on the Cleveland Way long-distance footpath which was opened in 1969. The route travels the coastline from Saltburn to Filey and inland runs over the Cleveland Hills and south through the Hambleton Hills before ascending the famous Sutton Bank and terminating at Helmsley.

Saltburn was a popular bathing town in Victorian times, and many buildings date from that period, including several hotels and guest-houses which continue to provide first-class accommodation. Those not wishing to descend or, more probably, ascend the steep roadway to and from the beach can make use of the 19th century hydraulic-powered cliff tramway.

From Saltburn-by-the-Sea the A174 continues south, though turning a mile or so inland, to journey through the former mining village of **Brotton** where in the latter half of the 19th century ironstone mining reached its zenith. The road crosses the Kilton Beck which runs to

Skinningrove, where the scene is still dominated by gigantic, drab steel-works, and on to **Loftus** which was the centre of the alum industry in the 17th and 18th centuries. Ironstone mining also flourished in the 19th century, but both industries are now dead. Remains of the alum works can still be seen above **Hummersea Scar** on the coast immediately south of Skinningrove. **St Leonard's Church** dates from 1901, but a tower dating from 1811 is incorporated.

South of Loftus the A174 passes through the village of **Easington** which lies atop a hill midway between Loftus and Staithes. The **Church of All Saints** was rebuilt in 1888–9 but contains several medieval fragments from its predecessor. Opposite the church is the site of a moat believed to be that of a manor-house.

From Easington the A174 turns eastwards towards the sea descending to **Boulby**, where the skyline is dominated by the works of one of Cleveland's current mining industries – the search for potash. At **Boulby Head** the cliffs rise to the highest point on the east coast of England at 204m (679ft) and they are a treasure-ground for fossil hunters.

A mile and a half from Boulby a left turn on to a minor road leads to the car park above **Staithes**, one of the prettiest fishing villages on the east coast. The Roxby Beck which flows into the sea at Staithes forms the county boundary between Cleveland and North Yorkshire. In high season the popularity of the narrow streets and alleyways of Staithes is such that only essential vehicles are permitted to descend the steep hill into the heart of the village, but car-parking is ample at the top of the hill.

Staithes (derived from the dialect word 'steers', meaning landing-place) owes its foundation to its sheltered location which has proved to be eminently suitable for successive generations of sturdy inshore fishermen to land their catches. Today, the village has changed little from centuries gone by. Tiny red-roofed cottages seem to perch almost on top of each other in a maze of narrow streets. At the harbour itself the tang of ozone is almost overpowering, and when heavy seas run the harbour-side dwellings, including the Cod and Lobster tavern, are almost engulfed in foaming spray.

Fresh, locally caught crab, lobster and fish are usually available, and the visitor may be fortunate to catch a glimpse of fishermen's wives in their traditional Staithes bonnets. The natural charm of Staithes has been recognized by the celebrated painter Dame Laura Knight who set up a painting school in the village, which was also the residence of Captain

385

Staithes Harbour

Cook during his apprenticeship as a grocer boy before the tang of the sea got the better of him and he ran off to Whitby.

From Staithes the A174 and the Cleveland Way footpath continue south through Yorkshire. Several interesting routes emanate from the A174 between Saltburn and Staithes. From Easington an unclassified road runs inland passing in 4 miles on the left **Grinkle Park**, now a hotel but since 1865 the estate of the famous Tyneside shipping family of Palmer. The family's interest in the estate arose out of the rich deposits of ironstone in the area which were shipped from the Tyne. The mansion was built in 1883 by Sir Mark Palmer, and the Grinkle ironstone mine was worked until as recently as 1934. The hotel is situated in the heavily wooded estate.

Three miles from Grinkle Park the unclassified road from Easington joins the main A171 Guisborough to Whitby road. Turning left at the T junction leads in 1½ miles to **Scaling Reservoir** which is crossed by the Cleveland–North Yorkshire boundary. The modern reservoir provides access for all the usual sporting and recreational activities associated with this type of water.

Another road, the B1366, links the A174 coast road at Loftus with the A171 moorland road. The B1366 passes through only one village of note – the ancient hamlet of **Liverton** with an imposing church incongruously situated in such a small outpost. The **Church of St Michael** dates from the 12th century, though it was considerably restored in the 19th and 20th centuries. Its most remarkable asset is the magnificent Norman chancel arch. Liverton Mines were opened in 1866 and gave rise to a quaint row of miners' cottages. The Waterwheel Inn on the outskirts is aptly named, displaying a huge wheel by the entrance. South-west of the A171 several roads undulate over vast expanses of moorland which stride across the Cleveland border into North Yorkshire.

Cleveland County is obviously not as famous as its Northumberland and Durham neighbours when it comes to castles. But Cleveland does contain several interesting bastions, though most are private or relatively inaccessible. Brotton, on the A174, is the starting-point for the trail to Kilton Castle, one of the least known of Northumbria's castles. From the centre of Brotton opposite the Green Tree Inn Kilton Lane should be taken, bearing left at the first fork and then right into Kilton village. After passing a row of cottages on the left, the road veers to the right. A track continues left towards a gamekeeper's cottage where permission must be obtained before visiting the ruin.

Kilton Castle is one of the most remarkable sites of any castle in Northumbria, being precariously situated on the edge of a deep tree-clad ravine. Because of the nature of the location the castle was constructed to an extremely narrow design. It was believed to have been founded in 1140 by Pagan Fitz Walter and was in ruins some 200 years later. Another school of thought puts forward the theory that Kilton Castle was built by Robert de Brus in the early 13th century. In the early days of the castle's life it is recorded that the estate was owned by the de Thweng family who subsequently married into the famous Lumleys of County Durham.

Few ruinous castles possess so much atmosphere as Kilton. Still largely overgrown, it is reputed to be haunted. Because of the nature of the terrain great care must be taken when visiting the site. Visitors must sign an indemnity against accident at the gamekeeper's cottage, and it is not recommended that the infirm visit the castle. Children should be accompanied.

From Brotton the A173 runs inland to Guisborough passing through **Skelton** where one of Cleveland's finest 'castles' stands in a landscaped estate, which is private property open only on special occasions. Skelton has been an important stop on wagonways between the Cleveland Hills and the coast for centuries. In about 1100 the manor was given to Robert de Brus, and no doubt the first Skelton Castle soon followed. The building which occupies the site today was constructed as recently as 1794. **All Saints' Church** dates from 1884, and an old, now defunct, church (a contemporary of the castle) stands near the entrance to the estate. The remains of an old market cross still stand on the village green.

From Skelton the B1267 runs north-east to Marske-by-the-Sea. A mile and a half from Skelton at the crossroads with the B1268 a left turn leads in 1 mile to the tiny church of **Upleatham**, reputed to be the smallest church in England. Robert de Brus' influence can be found here too. He gave the pre-Conquest church formerly occupying the site to nearby Guisborough Priory. The building which is visible today dates from 1684, and though it claims the distinction of being the smallest church in England, it is something of a misnomer since it is only a part of the original building. The village itself comprises stone-built houses clinging to the hillside above the church. Even higher stands the 19th-century **Church of St Andrew** whose most prized possession is a 12th-century font.

The B1268 through Upleatham joins the A173 Skelton to Guisborough

388

Road 1 mile through the village. In a further 3 miles the A173 enters historic **Guisborough,** one of the most interesting and ancient towns in all Cleveland. Nestling in the shadows of the Cleveland Hills, Guisborough is a market town of many contrasts. The ancient ruined priory contrasts with modern housing development and a new art gallery. Quiet cobbled streets come alive on market day when gaily coloured stalls attract bargain hunters from far and wide. The hills around Guisborough are littered with the hardware of pre-history, and the place was mentioned in the 'Domesday Book'. But it was the upsurge in religious interest in the early 12th century which brought the town to prominence. The **Priory of St Mary of 'Gisborough'** was founded for Augustinian canons by Robert de Brus some time between 1119 and 1129. As the result of a disastrous fire in 1289 no remains, with the exception of the Norman gatehouse, are earlier than this date. The priory soon became one of the most impressive treasure-houses in the north of England. Though little remains of the vast monastic buildings, the great towering east end of the church and the Norman gateway are well worth visiting. The warm rose-tinted stone of the east end of the church rises almost 30m (100ft), balancing precariously above the Department of the Environment's manicured lawns. The architecture resembles that of Ripon Cathedral to the south. At the opposite end of the walled area, facing the road, stands the remarkable Norman gatehouse which had two entrances, one for pedestrians, the other for carts. Immediately to the north of the priory ruins stands the **Church of St Nicholas** which dates from 1500, though the building was extensively restored in 1794. The most important treasure to be found in the church is the Brus cenotaph which was rescued from the priory on the dissolution of the monasteries. The tomb-like structure is ornately carved and depicts both the Cleveland and the Scottish Bruce families.

Though priory and church dominate Guisborough, there are several other buildings of interest. **Guisborough Hall,** ½ mile east of the priory, was built in 1857 and enlarged in 1902 and is now a hotel. Guisborough's **Market Cross** is Georgian, and the **Town Hall** dates from 1821. The town boasts several intriguing inns and taverns where a warm welcome is assured. Guisborough's newest attraction is the **Chapelbeck Gallery** in Fountain Street which presents a regularly changing series of events, displays and exhibitions, including art and design and rural crafts. The centre incorporates a **Tourist Information Centre** (*open daily, except Sundays, 10–5.30*).

Guisborough is also an excellent centre for walkers. Leisurely strolls can be enjoyed around the environs of the town and into the Cleveland foothills or along the ancient railway line on the southern edge of the town. Other recommended walks include Guisborough to Ayton and to Commondale through countryside unsurpassed in beauty. The town offers varied accommodation including a camping and caravan site at **Tockett's Mill** nearby.

From Guisborough the A171 runs westwards, then north to Middlesbrough. The B1269 runs due north from the town to link with the A174 Marske to Thornaby road at Kirkleatham.

34 Captain Cook country

Undoubtedly, Cleveland's greatest son, Captain James Cook, RN (1728–79), has found greater fame thousands of miles from his homeland than he has in Cleveland where he was born and spent his early life. 1978 saw the celebration of the 250th anniversary of the birth of the world's most famous explorer which has hopefully created much greater awareness of his achievements.

Cook's story is one of the greatest adventure yarns of all time more suitable to fiction than to fact. He was born on 27 October 1728 in Marton in Cleveland, just a few miles south of Middlesbrough, the son of a farm labourer from Ednam in the Scottish Borders who moved south to take a Yorkshire wife.

Marton is the starting-point of Cleveland's Captain Cook tour and is reached by taking the A172 from Middlesbrough centre. In approximately 2 miles where the A172 crosses the B1380 stands the entrance to **Stewart Park**. Cook was born in a two-roomed thatched cottage on the south lawn of **Marton Hall**. The first hall was built in 1796 by a prominent Teessider, Bartholomew Rudd, who demolished Cook's birthplace in 1768. A new hall was built by H. F. W. Bolckow in 1853. The hall was purchased by a well-known councillor, the late M. T. D. Stewart, in 1923. Councillor Stewart, whose name is perpetuated by the name of the park, gave the estate to the council for the enjoyment of Middlesbrough's residents. The site of Cook's birthplace is marked by a granite vase. The small museum at the entrance to Stewart Park has been superseded by a magnificent new **Captain Cook Birthplace Museum** (*open Monday to Saturday 10–6, winter 10–dusk*). The museum situated in Stewart Park will have three galleries devoted to Cook's discoveries in Australasia and Canada. The museum will also concentrate on Cook's early life of which little is currently known. Four galleries will be devoted to his youth in Cleveland and North Yorkshire. The 'Cook Pavilion' will also incorporate an interpretation centre, lecture theatre and reconstructions of Cook's ships *Resolution, Adventure* and *Endeavour (open daily)*.

St Cuthbert's Church, Marton, saw the baptism of the infant James Cook on 3 November 1728. The original register still on view claims '1728 Nobr 3 James ye son of James Cook day labourer baptized'. The church contains other reminders of the explorer including a memorial stained-glass window. The church dates from Norman times but was rebuilt, largely to the original design, in 1840. Some ten years later the James Cook Memorial School was built, and yet another reminder of the village's hero can be found on the spacious green where a memorial plaque carved in stone was brought from Point Hicks Hill in Victoria, Australia, the first land in Australasia sighted from the *Endeavour* in April 1770.

When James was eight, his father was appointed foreman labourer to Mr Scottowe at Airy Holme farm near **Great Ayton**. The family lived in the village, now just across the border in North Yorkshire, but the cottage in which they resided was allowed to be demolished in 1934 and shipped to Australia where it has been authentically re-erected. In exchange Great Ayton received another piece of Point Hicks granite which marks the site. Scottowe was obviously impressed with young Cook and agreed to finance his schooling in Great Ayton. The school was built in 1704, rebuilt in 1785 and considerably altered since. Today it is a second museum in Cook's honour.

Great Ayton is a village with immense charm. The river Leven flows beside the main street and radiating from the spacious village green are narrow streets of stone-built buildings. A sturdy stone bridge crosses the river near to which stand Great Ayton's two churches. **All Saints**, situated behind the modern **Christ Church**, boasts pre-Norman origins, and several remains of the earlier church are incorporated into later designs including fragments of Saxon crosses. Christ Church dates from 1876. In the churchyard of All Saints lie the remains of Mr Scottowe beside the grave of Cook's mother and five of his brothers and sisters. One and a half miles north east of Great Ayton an important collection of prehistoric cairns can be found.

Towering above Great Ayton lies **Easby Moor** which can be reached by footpath from the village. Its crowning glory is an obelisk in memory of James Cook which is visible for miles around. The monument, erected in 1827, stands more than 300m (1,000ft) above sea level.

The A173 leaves Great Ayton *en route* to Guisborough to the east.

Midway lies the hamlet of **Newton** under the towering **Roseberry Topping**, one of the most spectacular climbs in Cleveland. The summit shares the pure moorland air with nearby Easby Moor at a height of 300m (1,000ft). The hill is steeped in folklore and legend and is easily climbed from Newton. The view from the summit in all directions, but particularly towards industrial Teeside, is well worth the strenuous climb.

Cook left Great Ayton in his thirteenth year to taste the salty tang of the sea for the first time at Staithes where he was apprenticed as a grocer's boy. The love of the sea proved too strong, however, and in a few years he made his way down the coast to Whitby where he became apprenticed on Whitby colliers and learnt most of his seamanship. In 1755 he joined the merchant navy as an able seaman, and a year later the Seven Years' War broke out. Cook soon made his mark, and promotion was swift. During the war he surveyed the St Lawrence river, and his work on the eastern seaboard of Canada in subsequent years was one of his greatest achievements. In 1768, by Government edict Cook was despatched to discover the mysterious continent in the southern hemisphere which the Dutch had already made known and christened New Holland. His first expedition in the *Endeavour* was followed by a second voyage in 1772 this time in the vessels *Resolution* and *Endeavour*. The journey lasted three years and encompassed a distance equal to three journeys around the world. In 1776 he was able to demonstrate other of his scientific disciplines by observing the eclipse of the sun. In this year after only a few months rest Cook set sail again on the third of his famous voyages in the *Resolution* accompanied by the *Discovery*. The purpose of the journey was to chart a shorter route to the East Indies. It was to be Cook's last voyage. While held up by bad weather in Hawaii, his crew became involved in a skirmish with some natives, and during his peace-keeping efforts the great explorer was killed on 14 February 1779.

35 Roman roads of Northumbria

With such a long and distinguished occupation of Britain it is not surprising to discover that the Romans were not only extremely expert builders of fortifications but were also talented road engineers. Much modern-day road construction throughout Britain is based on original Roman routes which traversed the length and breadth of Britain reaching further north than even the Antonine Wall. The Romans were highly dependent upon their road system, and Roman roads are characteristically straight, an indication of the builders' all-conquering power. They had no need to meander around private land or property.

Roman roads in Britain were constructed differently from those in Italy. In Britain roads were built in three parts, a raised mound or *agger* with drainage ditches on both sides. Kerbstones were used to hold the raised centre, and main roads were between 6·3m (21ft) and 7·2m (24ft) wide. Minor roads were usually some 3·5–5·4m (15–18ft) in width. Materials used in Roman road construction were always those that were close at hand.

Watling Street (Dere Street)

One of the most important Roman roads in Northumbria and indeed throughout England is Watling Street, the route of which begins in Dover and stretches north beyond the river Tweed. Between the Tees and the Tweed it is still known as Dere Street, though the original Roman name for the road is unknown. It is remarkable to note that until as comparatively recently as 1751 Watling Street was the only 'made-up' road in the areas it traversed. It was begun by Petilius Cerealis and completed by Agricola between AD 78 and AD 85.

From York (Eboracum) to Newstead the road passes through, or near to, twelve major Roman forts – Aldborough, Catterick, Piercebridge, Binchester, Lanchester, Ebchester, Corbridge, Risingham, High Rochester, Chew Green, Cappuck and Newstead. These forts were built on high ground and enjoy varying degrees of excavation and accessibility. The total length of Dere Street from York to the Tweed is approximately 142 miles. Between York and Scotch Corner the Roman road is still followed almost without deviation by the old Great North Road (A1) which in turn is now superseded by a motorway.

Watling Street enters Northumbria north of Catterick and assumes the name Dere Street. The road runs along the eastern boundary of Piercebridge Roman station. The reasons behind the relatively close proximity of Aldborough, Catterick and Piercebridge is believed to relate to the constant threat from nearby Stanwick, a great Brigantian stronghold.

From Piercebridge the Roman road coincides with the 20th-century road almost as far as Auckland, crossing the main Darlington road west of Denton. Along the first stage from Piercebridge to Legs Cross the road rises to 180m (600ft) over Whin Sill, a rocky outcrop geologically identical to the physical feature along which much of the central sector of Hadrian's Wall is constructed. Eight miles or so from Piercebridge Dere Street reaches Brusselton, better known, perhaps, as a feature of another form of communication, railways. The Roman road continues on its own course until it rejoins the modern road as the main street of Bishop Auckland. Hummerbeck Lane is believed to be on the route of a little-known Roman way to Chester-le-Street, an important Roman town in east Durham. Near Bishop Auckland the road crosses the river Gaunless 120m east of Fieldon (or Fielding) Bridge and then crosses the main river Wear 180m west of the Roman fort of Vinovia (Binchester), though it is known that the course of the river here is not as it was in Roman times. From Binchester it is known that a branch road ran to Pons Aelii (Newcastle upon Tyne).

Between Binchester and the next Roman fort of any importance at Lanchester the exact route of Dere Street is rather obscure. It is known that the road passed through Hunwick where older residents still recall that an old track, long since gone, followed the original route of the Roman road. From Hunwick Dere Street continued to the colliery town of Willington where the burn of the same name is crossed. The route continues north through Oakenshaw and Brandon Down, where historians believe there was a Roman camp. On through Hill House, Flass

Wood and Heugh, across the river Browney and on via the Bar Gate to Longovicium (Lanchester). From Lanchester the route of Dere Street continues its journey north climbing through New Houses, Woodside and Leadgate in the shadows of the giant Consett complex, a scene far removed from that gazed upon by Roman soldiers during their journeys north.

From Leadgate it is a short journey to Ebchester, a route along which the physical aspect changes from urban to rural. The Romans built a small fort at Ebchester which they called Vindomora. Here the route crosses the river Derwent.

The scenic beauty of Northumbria continues to improve as Dere Street runs through Whittonstall where woods line the route just as they probably did in Roman times. At Apperley Dene, where there was believed to be a small Roman stronghold, the route leaves the modern road which is rejoined at Broomhaugh. Here the route veers west following the course of the river Tyne to Riding Mill. From Riding Mill the road makes a major river crossing over the river Tyne to the important Roman town and fortifications of Corstopitum (Corbridge). Here Dere Street becomes better known as Watling Street, a name still seen today in the town. Upstream from the modern bridge the Roman bridge abutments can still be seen when the water is really low.

Watling Street continues north over the undulating Northumberland countryside with Hadrian's Wall just a few miles away. The road does, of course, have a modern day equivalent in the A68, which is one of the most popular and scenically spectacular routes from Scotch Corner to Scotland.

For 7 miles from Corbridge the route of the Roman road does not deviate from the modern A68. Then after deviating for 1 mile to cross a stream Dere Street crosses Hadrian's Wall at Portgate by today's Stagshawbank bisecting the Military Way (B6318) which runs parallel to Hadrian's Wall. North of the Wall the Roman Road builders had to traverse a wild and barbarous region. There is no doubt that Agricola chose this route during his first foray north in AD 80 and that Dere Street was constructed immediately following his advance in AD 81. A feature of the stretch between Hadrian's Wall and the northerly terminus of the road is evidence of several temporary camps used by marching infantrymen.

North of Stagshawbank the road veers north-north-west at Bewclay where there was an important camp and follows the A68 passing several

Corbridge

reservoirs including West Hallington, Little Swinburne and Colt Crag. North of Colt Crag the route passes an area to the east known as the Waterfalls which was the scene of a dramatic gathering of Jacobites in 1715 where a plot against the House of Hanover was hatched.

Less than 1 mile north of the crossroads at the Waterfalls lies the site of an important Roman camp to the left of the road. Here the course of Dere Street leaves the route of the A68, which veers right to Ridsdale, then sharp left to West Woodburn where the route of Dere Street is taken up again as it crosses the river Rede. On the south bank of the river lay the strategic Roman camp of Risingham (Habitancum), also known as Dike Head. Risingham was one of the permanent forts on Dere Street built later than most by Lollius Urbicus in the second century. There are traces of subsequent building in the third century, though access is through farm land. The fort was manned firstly by a cohort of Gauls and subsequently by the 1st Cohort of Vangiones. There was further reconstruction at Risingham in the fourth century.

Once across the river Rede both Dere Street and the A68 conjoin except for minor deviations all the way to the site of the next major Roman settlement at The Dargues some 6 miles north of Risingham. The site of this temporary fort is reached about 1 mile after the A68 crosses the B6320 which leads to Otterburn, more famous of course for later military activities during the Border Wars when the famous battle of Chevy Chase was fought in the moonlight of 19 August 1388. A minor road left to High Green is passed, and immediately after the A68 crosses the Dargues Burn, the site is situated to the left. The eastern rampart of Dargues is clearly visible.

Half a mile north of Dargues the A68 once again deviates from the route of Dere Street as it swings sharply to the right. At the deviation Blakehope Fort was situated, though little is visible. Half a mile further on the A696 from Newcastle upon Tyne joins the A68. Continuing along the A68 in a further mile, just past the road leading right to the modern army camp at Otterburn is the site of another temporary camp at Bagraw where the west rampart is visible.

One and a half miles from Bagraw is situated one of the most important sites on Dere Street, High Rochester (Bremenium). Dere Street runs to the east of Bremenium, and along a 700m stretch south of the fort were situated several huge monuments believed to be tombs. One of the most remarkable is known as the Roman Well. Visitors should also keep a continuous look-out for stones with Roman inscriptions built into several of the local farm buildings and dwellings.

From the A68 at the northern end of Rochester village a track leads right to another temporary camp called Birdhope which is also extremely well preserved. From here northwards along Dere Street a word of caution is essential. The route lies within the confines of Redesdale Army firing ranges, and great care should be exercised. Red flags fly when firing is in progress but it is safer to check first by telephoning Otterburn 6581.

While the A68 runs north-west to cross into Scotland over Carter Bar, two minor roads run north from the Army Camp following the line of Dere Street passing through several Roman camps including Bellshiel, Sill Burn South and Sill Burn North, Silloans and Featherwood East and West camps. Most of these are difficult to locate, and a good Ordnance Survey map is essential.

Continuing northwards, the fort at Chew Green is reached. The first camp dating from AD 80 has been superseded, enlarged and reconstructed. Around Chew Green evidence has been unearthed throughout the centuries of several other forts and camps. The area is excellent walking country, and keen historians can trace Dere Street on foot into Scotland passing, 3 miles north of Chew Green, Woden Law and Brownhart Law where there was an important signal post. It is possible to reach Brownhart Law by car by taking the A68 into Scotland passing the A6088 left and taking the next turning right in 3 miles signposted Edgerston Tofts and Hownam. In a further 4 miles take the road to Hownham. In a further mile the temporary camp of Pennymuir is reached. Here the modern road rejoins Dere Street and after fording Kale Water a path leads to Woden Law.

The route of Dere Street as it crosses into Scotland enters the county of Roxburghshire where from Shibden Hill the route clearly runs north for 6 miles. From here to the 'end of the road' the route is obscure but it is believed to run parallel to the main road to Newton St Boswells, thence along the road to Melrose and on to Newstead where Agricola founded the camp known as Trimontium – the fortification by three hills – the name alluding to the brooding Eildons. Further north there is evidence that the Roman road continued to the Antonine Wall which was, of course, the very northern limit of the Roman Empire albeit a temporary boundary. The permanent northern limit was the better-known Hadrian's Wall.

It is natural that such an important road as Dere Street should have a network of other roads branching from it. One of the most spectacular of these was the route which travelled west from Scotch Corner and which is largely followed today by the A66. Along the route there is evidence of much Roman activity, though excavations and access are by no means as extensive as further north. For 11 miles from its junction with the modern A1 the A66 follows the Roman way until it reaches Greta Bridge where rampart and ditches of the fort of Maglona are visible. In a further $5\frac{1}{2}$ miles at Bowes was the Roman fort of Lavatrae, which provided a

Vindolanda on Hadrians Wall

control point for the eastern access to the pass over Stainmore. The ruins of a Norman castle occupy the site today. Continuing west across the bleak and inhospitable Stainmore for 13 miles, the road leads to the fort which guarded the western access to the pass. The route across the fells is littered with remains of signalling posts, the most obvious of which is the Bowes Moor near the Bowes Moor Hotel. Two miles west of the hotel the Moor rises to its summit almost 450m (1,500ft) at Rey Cross which is regarded as one of the best preserved of temporary camps.

One mile west of Rey Cross the A66 leaves the route of the Roman road. They rejoin later to pass several other important remains in Cumbria including Maiden Castle, Brough, Brougham Temple, Sowerby near Kirkby Thore from which the Maiden Way Roman road ran straight to Hadrian's Wall.

Wrekendike

The road-building activities of the Romans seem to be one of the aspects least documented by historians. Whereas Dere Street, or Watling Street, is well known, there are several other important Roman roads, and there must be dozens of minor roads which have long since been forgotten.

Wrekendike runs at an angle across County Durham and Tyne and Wear and links with Dere Street at Lanchester. The Northumbrian section is believed to be the northern counterpart of Rikenild Street which runs from West Wales through Worcester and modern-day Birmingham to enter Northumbria and ultimately link with the river Tyne at South Shields.

The word Wrekendike is believed to mean 'old ridge way', and the exact route through Northumbria bisects industrial Tyneside. The Tyne estuary was an extremely important area both from a strategic and supply-base point of view. Consequently, good communications to and from the river mouth were vital. It is known that one of the road's main purposes was to facilitate the transport of Northumbrian corn to waiting vessels which shipped the valuable commodity to the Roman armies occupying the Rhinelands. Obviously, there would be considerable imports carried along the road too.

The route of Wrekendike begins at South Shields where a Roman signal station was built on the law above the estuary. The route traverses modern-day Biddick Lane running from East Boldon to Jarrow Slake and on along Boldon Lane to Heworth Fell Gate. Wrekendike continues to Monkton, Mill Lane, Upper Heworth and Usworth and into Leam Lane where the old ridgeway is still visible. Here, the name Wrekendike still appears on maps as the route traverses Eighton Banks to High Eighton. From here to Stanley the straight line of the ridgeway is visible. *En route* the way passes on the south side of Lamesley and Kibblesworth north of Urpeth and then south of Causey. From Stanley Wrekendike climbs to Maiden Law, an important Roman statation, and on to Lanchester where it links with Dere Street.

Stanegate

Linking north-east with north-west, Stanegate was built by Agricola at the same time as Dere Street and subsequently became an important supply route for Hadrian's Wall. Ease of access and communication was essential for the successful defence of Hadrian's Wall, and the Stanegate was ideally suited for this purpose.

Originally, Stanegate ran from Corbridge where it linked with Dere Street running north–south. From Corbridge the Stanegate ran to the North Tyne, then via Newborough and Vindolanda (Chesterholm) to Carvoran, one of the greatest Roman forts on the Wall yet to be excavated. From Carvoran Stanegate follows the course of the Wall to Nether Denton after which the exact route is obscure until Irthington is reached. The course runs to High Crosby east of Stanwix.

As a result of excavations at such places as Vindolanda, Corbridge, Nether Denton and Carlisle, where first century camps have been unearthed, it is confirmed that Stanegate's origins are contemporary with Dere Street, having been founded by Agricola.

Although Stanegate preceded the construction of Hadrian's Wall, there is no doubt that it was lengthed in both directions behind the Wall. The Military Way linking the forts on Hadrian's Wall also provided an important means of communication. The exact date of building of the Military Way is not certain, but it is believed to have been built by Severus, since the earliest milestones are dated AD 213. The Military Way linked fort with fort, milecastle with milecastle, while every turret was served with a path from the main road. The road sometimes travelled a surprising distance away from the Wall to ensure the easiest gradients for servicing ox wagons and other vehicles. It was constructed to the usual design, being about 6m (20ft) wide, and was successfully cambered and kerbstoned.

The Devil's Causeway

Immediately north of the Portgate on Hadrian's Wall near Halton Chesters Dere Street divides, and the eastern branch, known as the Devil's Causeway, strikes north-east across the rich fertile farm land of Northumberland. The route is characteristically straight, passing east of the village of Ryal before crossing the A696 Newcastle upon Tyne road at Edgehouse. The road seems shrouded in mystery, and particularly along the southern stretch there is no documentary evidence of any visible remains.

West of Morpeth at Hartburn, where the B6343 and the Hart Burn are crossed, it is known that a Roman station existed. In the north wall of the parish church are several Roman stones said to come from the fortification. The route of the Devil's Causeway continues straight across country and crosses the river Font east of Netherwitton before turning away in a more northern direction at Whinney Hill. The road then crosses the river Coquet a little way below Brinkburn Priory where ancient historians relate that the piers of the Roman bridge abutment can be seen, though this fact has not been authenticated in recent times. Records of the early 19th century tell of traces of a Roman villa on a hill above the priory, but the exact location is obscure.

North of Brinkburn the route passes west of Longframlington to join the modern A697 for several miles before deviating to cross the B6341 road between Alnwick and Rothbury, passing west of Edlington to Low Learchild in the vicinity of which is believed to have been situated the Roman fort of Alauna. From Alauna a Roman road joined Dere Street at Rochester. The route continues along to the west of the A697 skirting Glanton to Powburn. At Powburn the A697 runs along the Causeway for $1\frac{1}{2}$ miles to Percy's Cross. Here, the A697 strikes north-west as the Devil's Causeway continues straight ahead crossing the B6348 west of Chatton and then the river Till. The route then runs along a modern unclassified road between East Horton and Lewick continuing due north to reach the river Tweed at Springhill where the most northerly fort is known to have been situated.

Though there is documented evidence of the existence of the main Roman roads in Northumbria, many minor roads appear only on ancient maps, and the exact routes are obscure. Even the better-known routes are a matter of conjecture along certain sections.

Visitors intent upon walking the Roman routes should be well equipped with suitable maps. Care should always be taken to ensure public access.

Acknowledgments

The black and white photographs were kindly supplied by the following: A. F. Kersting (pp. 103, 144, 194, 217, 304, 341, 353); R. A. Smith (pp. 149, 234, 274, 279, 296, 320, 397); The British Tourist Authority (pp. 19, 23, 26, 30, 33, 34, 37, 45, 48, 53, 58, 61, 62, 69, 88, 90, 95, 107, 120, 130, 138, 151, 162, 168, 177, 181, 190, 208, 221, 227, 245, 251, 264, 289, 310, 326, 334, 360, 373, 376, 386, 400).

Index